PLAUSIBLE PREJUDICES

ESSAYS ON AMERICAN WRITING

JOSEPH EPSTEIN

W. W. NORTON & COMPANY
NEW YORK
LONDON

Published simultaneously in Canada by Penguin
Books Canada Ltd, 2801 John Street, Markham,
Ontario L3R 1B4.
Printed in the United States of America

The text of this book is composed in Galliard, with display type set in
Michelangelo and Old Style Garamond.
Composition and manufacturing by the Maple-Vail Book
Manufacturing Group
Book design by Holly McNeely

The essays in this volume originally appeared in the following
publications: *The New Criterion, Commentary, The Times Literary
Supplement,* and *Book World.* They are reprinted with the kind
permission of the editors.

First Edition

Library of Congress Cataloging in Publication Data
Epstein, Joseph, 1937–
    Plausible prejudices.
    1. American literature—20th century—History and criticism—
Essays. I. Title.
PS221.E6 1985   810′ .9′005   84-10119

ISBN 0-393-01918-7

W. W. Norton & Company, Inc.
500 Fifth Avenue, New York, N.Y. 10110
W. W. Norton & Company Ltd.
37 Great Russell Street, London WC1B 3NU

1 2 3 4 5 6 7 8 9 0

FOR MARK AND BURT EPSTEIN,
SONS WHO MAKE ME
VERY PROUD

Plausible
Prejudices

Contents

Acknowledgments

I WISH TO ACKNOWLEDGE the valuable help of a number of superior editors in the composition of this book: Neal Kozodoy of *Commentary;* Erich Eichman and Hilton Kramer of *The New Criterion;* John Gross, formerly of the *Times Literary Supplement,* and Carol Houck Smith, of W. W. Norton. Without their aid and encouragement, this book would not exist.

Introduction

SOME FIVE OR SIX YEARS AGO I met with a young man, the son of friends, who was an undergraduate at the University of Chicago. He had come there to study literature but had begun to feel he had made a mistake. "You know, Mr. Epstein," he said, "I don't think I want to spend the better part of four years looking for symbols and investigating metaphors." I didn't attempt to dissuade him. Instead I suggested that, being a habitual reader, which I knew him to be, he would probably eventually get around to reading the key books in the English curriculum, and so perhaps he would do better while at the university to study history or philosophy. Apparently my small nudge was the one that pushed him into a decision, for not long afterward I received a letter from his mother, a woman of some intellectual power, who thanked me for talking with her son and added that she "didn't raise the boy to be an English major."

The remark reminded me of the mother of the late heavyweight champion Rocky Marciano, who, upon learning that her son was abandoning a career in baseball for one in boxing, is supposed to have said, "Thank God! I didn't raise the boy to be a catcher." Here I must add that my mother didn't raise me to be a literary critic. ("If you can't say something nice," mothers of my generation used to say, "don't say anything at all.") Nor did I raise myself to be one. If literary critic I am, I seem to have fallen into the job, in a largely unplanned way, the way most people fall in love. What I do think of myself as being is a reader; not someone who merely takes pleasure in reading—though I do take passionate pleasure in it—but someone for whom reading has been one of the main experiences in his life. Still, without ever intending to, I seem nonetheless to have become a literary critic; or so I have to feel upon contemplating the rather hefty volume that follows this introduction. To paraphrase the punchline of an Alka-Seltzer commercial of several years back, "I can't believe I wrote the whole thing."

And yet I still do not quite see myself as a literary critic. I was educated in the middle and late 1950s—the height of the age of criticism, as Randall Jarrell called it. Through those years and the decade following, I read a great deal of literary criticism. The literary critics then at work seemed to me imposing figures; many of them still seem so. Three literary critics in particular contributed greatly to my education: F. R. Leavis, who taught me why literature was so central a subject, or at least ought to be; Lionel Trilling, who taught me all sorts of interesting connections between literature and the wider culture of which it is a significant part; and Edmund Wilson, who taught me about the vastness of literature and through whose essays I caught something of Wilson's own passion for books and writers. Part of my difficulty in viewing myself as a literary critic is that, in such literary criticism as I have written, I do very little of any of the things that Leavis, Trilling, and Wilson did.

Perhaps, too, my unwillingness to see myself as a literary critic has to do with the (to me) fact that the literary critics who came after Leavis, Trilling, and Wilson do not seem anywhere near as serious, intelligent, and—to use a very plain word—good. Matthew Arnold once noted that "first-rate criticism has a permanent value greater than that of any but first-rate works of poetry and art." Yet so little of the literary criticism being written today seems to me first-rate. Much of it has become academic exercise, written by English professors to be read by other English professors. Some of this criticism is ingenious in its complication, but if its complicatedness is not what is most appealing to you about literature, then this criticism is not likely to be for you. I know it isn't for me. Being unable to read the vast majority of academic literary criticism, I felt no strong inclination, by writing such stuff myself, to add to the already ample Gross National Ennui.

Although the exact relation between the quality of literary criticism and the quality of primary literary works (novels, poems, essays) is difficult to demonstrate, that there is such a relation cannot, I think, be seriously doubted. But the relation between literary criticism and literary production is different at different times. In his brief but majestic essay "Criticism," Henry James remarked that the part criticism "plays may be the supremely beneficent one when it proceeds from deep sources, from the efficient combination of experience and perception. In this light one sees the critic as the real helper of the artist, a torch-bearing outrider, the interpreter, the brother." But there is help and there is help, brothers and brothers. There are periods—the great age of modernism, which saw the introduction of the writings of Joyce and Proust, T. S. Eliot and Yeats, was such a period—when the critic's main task is explaining what new writers are about, smoothing the way for them, elaborating upon their virtues and importance. Such periods are fine times for criticism; in such periods critics can function as James says: as helpers, torchbearers, interpreters, and brothers.

But there are other periods when critics function best not as outriders but as part of a posse to head writers off at the pass. I believe that we are going through such a period currently. We have among us no shortage of interpreters, critics ready to compare the works of Thomas Pynchon to the greatest landmark works in world literature, to announce such novelists as John Updike and Philip Roth as masters, to make the case that John Ashbery is our John Keats, to run through the streets screaming about the arrival of yet another literary genius. Do we need more such critics? May I be allowed to doubt it? I think we could do instead just now with more critics who function rather more like sheriffs, who stand ready to apprehend delinquent writers. Without consciously setting out to do so, I seem, as someone who writes literary criticism, to have become such a sheriff. I'll say this for the job—the pay may be low but you're never out of work.

Who, you might ask, appointed me sheriff? It is, I have to report, a self-appointed office. Among the equipment needed for the job is a certain amount of learning, curiosity, knowledge of the traditions of literature, an unshakable belief in the importance of writing to both private lives and the public world, and a passionate love of literature. About such items I think most people would agree. But I would add one further item: anger at what one deems literary injustice. To see a mediocre writer lavishly praised, to find a good writer put down for extra-literary (which usually means political) reasons, to discover inchoate ideas that no one really believes in nonetheless vaunted in literary works—these things stir anger in a critic of the sheriff type. Such a sheriff critic believes that good books can sustain us and make life better, while bad books wrongly praised can cause real harm in life. I do not think that the essays in *Plausible Prejudices* are conspicuously angry, though some among them have stirred anger in others. But many of them have had their origin in anger—specifically, in their author's anger at ignorant praise, wrongful neglect, hypocritical belief. Yet to the extent that these essays succeed, to that extent will the anger behind them be submerged in the general argument that each essay sets out to make.

Argument is a key word. Suave, gentle, polite though many critics may seem, concerned with elucidation, definition, and theorizing though many critics may appear, in fact the critic is inevitably conducting an argument. He is arguing, always and forever arguing. It could scarcely be otherwise. Literary criticism operates wholly through persuasion. Randall Jarrell—correctly, I think—once wrote: "The best critic who ever lived could not *prove* that the *Iliad* is better than *Trees;* the critic can only state his belief persuasively, and hope that the reader of the poem will agree—but *persuasively* covers everything from a sneer to statistics." H. L. Mencken made much the same point, only more tersely. "Criticism," he wrote, "is prejudice made plausible." The critic makes his case, he makes his prejudices plausible, through his authority. As for whence his authority derives, the most authoritative statement on critical authority comes from Edmund Wilson: "The implied position of the people who know about literature (as is also the case in every other art) is simply that they know what they know, and that they are determined to impose their opinions by main force of eloquence or assertion on the people who do not know."

What, I ask myself as I consider the essays that comprise *Plausible Prejudices,* is my case? My case is that literature is going through a very bad patch at present—that there is something second-rate about it, especially in America, though not here alone. I find the case I have to make extremely sad because I believe that literature, considered as an institution, is in important respects a barometer that measures the quality of the culture as a whole. I also believe that literature can be a joyous thing in and of itself and that of late, in this regard, it has been failing its audience badly.

Mine is not an easy case to make—either through statistics or through sneers—yet I think I know some of the factors that have contributed to making contemporary literature less good than it ought to be. The entry into university studies of contemporary writing has, I believe, played an important role. By teaching living writers in the university, teachers have implicitly elevated them to the status of classics. Here, too, it must be added that those contemporary writers who tend to be taught are—I hope this doesn't seem too obvious—those who are most teachable. By most teachable I mean those writers whose books most readily lend themselves to the solution of difficulties in the text. The puzzling, the knotty, the self-reflexive books, through the very nature of the activity of teaching, tend to take precedence—this for the reason that these books give teachers the most to do.

Politics enters into the equation, and has done so increasingly in recent years, particularly in the university study of literature. Universities wish to do what they construe to be the right thing politically. Thus, in university curricula, women writers are featured, so are black writers where possible, and if it has not already happened so soon will homosexual writers. The point is not that there haven't been considerable women, black, and homosexual writers; the point is that they are included specifically because they are women, black, or homosexual. The effect of this has been further to elevate contemporary writers. This might make for what appears to be enlightened politics, but it doesn't make for a stronger sense of standards in literary judgment. What might seem benign politics can be positively inimical to literature. And I believe that literature that calls for dealing with writers largely from the standpoint of how their writing deals with the question of "women" or "blacks" or "homosexuals" is inherently insulting to the writers so dealt with and also helps to diminish the importance of writing itself.

The invasion of politics into culture, in my view to an improper extent, has also helped to make literature in our day seem second-rate. Perhaps I am blinded by my own politics, but as I look about me I find that culture today in the United States is very much in thrall to political liberalism. The point is a bit complicated, but, as I view it, I find that, while the country is not particularly liberal, the culture has become increasingly so. If proof is wanted, I would point to the books that win prizes in the United States, to the politics of the men and women who constitute the overwhelming majority of the membership of the American Institute of Arts and Letters, to the critical and literary assumptions upon which so many contemporary American writers base their work. Politics is part of the business of literature—it is, that is to say, an altogether proper subject for writers—but literature ought not to be part of the business of politics. "It is the business of literature," wrote Desmond MacCarthy, "to turn facts into ideas." Yet today so many critics and writers work instead the other way round—by turning their ideas into facts. So at any rate I have found in reading such (in my view) over-praised writers as E. L. Doctorow, Norman Mailer, and Robert Coover and reading such (again in my view) wrongly neglected writers as James Gould Cozzens and John Dos Passos. In *The Liberal Imagination,* Lionel Trilling warned about the incursion of politics into literature; but the issue, far from having disappeared, has grown more insistent with the passing years. It, too, has made American writing seem less than it ought to be.

Another factor that has diminished the importance of literature today is the strength of the tradition of modernism in writing. As understood by writers and critics who take sustenance from this tradition, the tradition itself has been very selectively understood. From the famous modernist writers—Joyce, Proust, Kafka, Eliot, Nabokov, Beckett—contemporary writers have chosen to select out their difficulty and their bleakness. I say "select out" because I believe that the modernist tradition is wider and much more various than these contemporary writers and their critics seem to be aware. Kafka and Proust, for example, are, when carefully read, very funny writers, or at least they are often funnier than anyone would know from reading criticism about them. Nabokov and Joyce, in many of their works, are filled with love of life, with exuberance for the details of everyday existence. But to take modernism as implying that stories can no longer be told, that cause and effect no longer have any serious relation with each other, that life was dreadful yesterday, wretched today, and figures to be worse tomorrow—to accept these as one's working assumptions is to guarantee that one's writing will be shriveled and dreary at the outset. If literature is to regain its significance, battle must be done with these assumptions.

While it is not a factor of the same magnitude as the others I have mentioned, I think that the uses that writers have made of the new freedom to write about sex has also contributed to the diminishment of contemporary literature. As someone who has read a great many contemporary novels over the past few years, I have noticed over and over again the way that sexual description has bailed out, or at least seemed to bail out, so many novelists who, without sex to write about, do not seem to have much in the way of a story to tell. Sex, like politics, is part of life, but among so many of our contemporary novelists it comes to loom as easily the major part. The main activity in ancient Egypt, to hear Norman Mailer tell it, was fancy fornication. Without sex I do believe John Updike's man Rabbit would have to cease running, Portnoy would be without complaint, and a great many other, less commercially successful novelists would simply be out of business. Sexual interest is also at the center of a great many contemporary literary biographies. I once wrote that the novels of the future would feature a group of genitals sitting around discussing fashionable ideas. I can now say, to wring a change on Lincoln Steffens, that I have seen the future and it doesn't work.

Well, here by and large is my case, and it is the case argued, sometimes directly, sometimes indirectly, in the essays in *Plausible Prejudices*. Given this case, I think it will be evident that this is not going to be a book filled with enthusiastic praise for contemporary writing. I have in fact been accused by one young critic of being "penurious with praise," which isn't a bad phrase. Yet, as I read over the essays in this book, I see that I seem to have been —as I remark in my essay about Van Wyck Brooks's own *modus operandi*—kind to the dead and hard on the living. Being hard on one's contemporaries when one feels that they have let down the side is not always the most comfortable position to take. Just as I did not set out to be a critic, neither did I expect, in my criticism, to be a nay-sayer. Yet many—though far from all—of the essays in this book do, in one way or another, say nay. I have come greatly to distrust people who arrogate virtue to themselves, but in spite of this I am about to do so on my own behalf. I think that the reason I have so often come to say no when presented with the work of a particular novelist or tendency in contemporary literature is love for literature itself.

My education was literary; I was one of those English majors I helped talk my friend's son out of being. A great deal of what I know I have learned from literary works. Novelists, especially, have been among my most important teachers. If I can be said to have a point of view in life—and, heading toward fifty, I had better have such a point of view—it is that of a literary man. What it means to have the point of view of a literary man, I believe, is that one is above all impressed with the immense variety of life, its multi-facetedness, its unpredictability, its extraordinary richness. What literature teaches, what it has taught me, is that life is more various than any intellectual or political system can ever hope to comprehend. Life, one learns from literature, is filled with sadness and joy, tragedy and splendor, despair and dignity in despair, hatred and laughter, and more doublets of this kind than any single sentence can hope to contain. Literature is about life, which is a commonplace; yet literature is also on the

Saroyan

side of life, which, if it too is a commonplace, is frequently forgotten.

As someone writing criticism, I know that, when I come to judge a particular writer, one of the questions in the back of my mind is, Is he or she on the side of life? That is not always an easy question to answer, but if you read with attentiveness, I think you can tell. In certain writers joy in life is evident from the outset: Dickens, Tolstoy, H. L. Mencken. In certain other, seemingly gloomy writers—Kafka and Orwell come to mind—their gloom is about those things that interfere with their love of life. But for me love of life—no simple Rotarian optimism but love of life in all its vast complexity—is the ultimate test of a writer's worth. What is more, I invariably find that those writers who love life are the writers I most love.

So while a certain amount of no is being said in these pages, behind every no I believe there is a larger yes: a yes to life, a yes to literature, a yes to the necessity of holding writers up to the highest standard, a yes to the act of writing itself. Writing these essays has given me a great deal of pleasure, and I hope that something of my own pleasure in writing them is passed along to the book's readers. If it is, that will constitute yet another lovely yes.

Criticism is prejudice made plausible.
—H. L. MENCKEN

ONE | THE SCENE

The Literary Life Today

ASSUMING FOR THE MOMENT that something called literary culture exists in the United States, where, exactly, might it be found today? From sea to shining sea, I suppose the answer is, but before putting one's hat over one's heart and finishing the song perhaps one would do well to ponder the significance of having to ask the question in the first place. Thirty, fifty, a hundred, a hundred and twenty years ago the question of where literary culture could be found would not need to have been raised, for the answer, though it might differ from time to time, was always evident.

The whereabouts of literary culture in August 1860 was certainly not a serious question for William Dean Howells. Then still a young newspaperman from Columbus, Ohio, Howells checked in at the Tremont Hotel in Boston. Howells had had four poems published in the *Atlantic Monthly,* and now had set himself up to see literary culture firsthand. Literary culture in 1860 meant Boston, where, as Edward Weeks put it in his memoirs, "most of the best writers in America lived within thirty miles of the Massachusetts State House."

In *Literary Friends and Acquaintances,* Howells recalled what the literary culture of Boston looked and felt like. His first call was on James Russell Lowell, then the editor of the *Atlantic Monthly,* who treated him with great kindness and gave him a note recommending him to Nathaniel Hawthorne. Lowell also set up a dinner for Howells at the Parker House, at which the young Midwesterner met the publisher James T. Fields (of the firm of Ticknor & Fields) and Oliver Wendell Holmes, Sr. At one point during the dinner Holmes, looking from Lowell to Howells, remarked, "Well, James, this is something like the apostolic succession; this is the laying on of hands."

Later, using his letter from Lowell, Howells paid a call on Hawthorne, who treated him most agreeably, then passed him along to Emerson with a card on which he had scribbled, "I find this young man worthy." Howells met Emerson, then Thoreau, then Longfellow, and eventually nearly every other figure of importance in the burgeoning American literary culture. In time, of course, Howells himself became the editor of the *Atlantic Monthly*, where, notable for the catholicity of his taste, he published and promoted the careers of Mark Twain and Henry James, respectively the ultimate Redskin and Paleface of American literature. When, in 1885, Howells left the *Atlantic Monthly* to become editor of *Harper's* in New York, it was said that the center of literary culture in this country moved too, from Boston to New York, where it has since remained.

But has it? For a long stretch it seems to have done, with occasional lapses. Early in this century Chicago set out claims to be the literary capital of the United States—Theodore Dreiser, Sherwood Anderson, and Carl Sandburg were working there at the time—and H. L. Mencken said that nearly everything of interest in American writing originated in Chicago. Mencken himself never lived in New York, but commuted from Baltimore while editing first *The Smart Set,* then the *American Mercury*. In the early 1920s American literary culture kept a home office in Greenwich Village and a fourishing European branch in Paris (send mail c/o Gertrude Stein, 27 rue de Fleurus). In some rough sense, New York remained the scene and center of literary life in this country through World War II and beyond. Sometimes this literary culture seemed rather thin, as in the instance of the characters who gathered round the Algonquin Hotel dining room and who were in any case not strictly literary but part of the New York worlds of theater and smart journalism. Later, in the persons of the *Partisan Review* crowd, literary life would become scruffier and more political and intellectual than strictly literary, but a magazine such as *Partisan Review* seems impossible outside New York.

Still, New York was never absolutely indispensable to the national literature in the way that London and Paris have been indispensable to the literature of England and France over the past two centuries. But New York until very recently exerted a powerful attraction upon provincial young Americans aflame with literary ambitions. In his essay "My Lost City," F. Scott Fitzgerald, himself precisely such a provincial, recalled sighting from the back seat of his taxi the young Edmund Wilson, "nourished," as Fitzgerald put it, by "the Metropolitan spirit." Manhattan was the name of Fitzgerald's desire, and even today its expense, cumbrousness, and sheer weight in aggravations do not deter a great many young literary men and women whose notions of a literary life are inseparable from life in New York.

Yet one is hard pressed to think of the names of New York writers. After one has named Norman Mailer, added after thinking a bit about it Donald Barthelme, one descends to journalists and critics. Part of the reason is that New York is not always the best place for a writer to get work done. It remains a nice place for writers to visit their editors and publishers, in the hope of having their wallets fattened and vanities fed. But the great names in New York literary life today are those not of writers but of cultural middlemen—agents, publishers, editors, people with such names as Scott Meredith, Robert Gottlieb, Tom Congdon. Literarily, New York seems increasingly to belong to them.

If I have dwelt so long on Boston and New York, it is only because when one thinks of literary culture, as of culture generally, one thinks (as anthropologists have taught us to think) of a network of institutions, roles, traditions, rituals, and not least of settings. But writers today, more so than ever before, do not live in a single setting or even in two or three primary settings. Major and minor, younger and older, American writers are strewn across the land. Publishing houses, most of them, are still in New York, with a few in Boston and a few others in Chicago and northern California. The majority of magazines that writers care most about appearing in are still in New York, and all the powerful literary agents are there. New York is where writing is most intensely talked about; it is where reputations are pumped up, also deflated. It is, beyond dispute, the mecca of literary publicity. Yet the attractions of New York to the young are no longer what they once were. All that the very young may nowadays think of in connection with the literary life is that it has to do with being photographed for *People* and appearing at some point on the "Today Show."

Economics has a great deal to do with the lessening attraction of New York, and with radical changes in literary culture generally. One of the great problems for a young writer is how he is to get from, say, age twenty-two to age thirty. Literary talent needs time to ripen. Although there are instances of writers doing splendid things in their early twenties—Turgenev wrote *A Sportsman's Notebook* at twenty-three, Rimbaud was even more famously precocious, and, closer to our time, Delmore Schwartz turned out his best poetry before he was thirty—most writers do not burst so brilliantly out of the starting gate. The question then becomes what can they do until they are ready to do their best.

Living through this incubation period was once much easier than it is currently. The novelist Albert Halper, now in his seventies, has recently recounted his early days as a writer come from Chicago to New York. He more than once refers to how cheaply he lived. "My total weekly living expenses," Halper recalls, "ran around eight dollars, including rent." That was in the 1930s, of course. But even as late as the 1960s a young writer could make do on fairly little. I not long ago talked about this with Frank Conroy, in whose past I had noted an eight-year gap, a time during which he was evidently preparing to write his autobiography, *Stop-Time*. It turns out that Conroy had a small inheritance, from his grandmother, of two hundred dollars a month: he was able to live in New York largely on that. Today in New York two hundred dollars might cover monthly cab and subway costs.

Without an inheritance, a working husband or wife, or the unusual good fortune of an early-blooming talent, getting from age twenty-two to age thirty has never been all that easy. But there were, formerly, more places to lay low while the years passed. Europe for one. Not only did living abroad offer a young writer the opportunity to widen his own culture, but he could until recently depend upon doing so on the cheap, thanks to the powerful position of the American dollar. And if Europe wasn't one's dish of tea, in more recent years there was always that four-to-six-year continuous summer camp known as graduate school. Graduate school was thought to be a good place to hide out for would-be writers with no place else to go. But no longer. The grant money is not there when one starts out, the jobs aren't there when one finishes, and the idea was probably a bad one in the first place. Many writers who hang around universities too long learn one skill above all—self-loathing.

Whether a writer is young or old, it remains difficult to earn a living writing, or, at any rate, writing what one wishes to write. In the summer of 1981 a largely statistical report was put together by the Center for Social Sciences at Columbia University. The most notable finding was that, on the average, American writers earned less than $5,000 a year. In publishing circles, there was a small flap about this report; a small flap, in publishing circles, usually means a not very readable article in *Publishers Weekly,* which in this instance contested the accuracy of the Columbia study. I would contest it, too. I think the figure is too high. (The *Publishers Weekly* article thought it was too low.) Surely it is too high if one includes poets, for the only serious American poet in this century said to have been able to live off his poetry was Robert Frost. Even so famous a poet as W. H. Auden had to depend on journalism and poetry readings for his livelihood— not poetry. The great majority of poets of reputation today— Anthony Hecht, Richard Wilbur, A. R. Ammons—have depended on regular teaching jobs for theirs.

Among serious writers generally—"I am speaking here of writers who treat of great subjects," Schopenhauer remarks in his essay "On Authorship," "not of writers on the art of making brandy"—I would guess that there are not many more than two hundred who are able to make their living primarily from their writing. This is not to say that there are not many more men and women justified in calling themselves writers; but these men and women will, I suspect, be found to be drawing the bulk of their incomes from activities auxiliary to literature: from teaching, from lecturing and reading, from editorial work of one kind or another. Despite news of great financial scores for writers—seven-figure paperback sales, movie deals, etc.—contemporary literature in the United States has an economic profile rather like that of a typical Latin American country: a few very rich people at the top, scarcely any middle class, and a vast peasantry.

That not many writers can make their living through writing alone is important, even crucial, because the economy of literature has sent many writers into university jobs—at least those writers who are fortunate enough to land such jobs. This, concomitantly, has thinned out New York as the literary capital of the United States. The center of literary life today is the university. Which university? No one university, or even no five or six universities, but merely "the university." Which is a roundabout way of saying that the center of literary life today does not exist except in an attenuated and abstract form. It is a center without a center.

Over roughly the past thirty years the greatest single change in literary life in this country has been the gradual usurpation of literature by the university. Not only are the majority of writers —novelists, poets, critics—today at work in universities, but contemporary writing is increasingly becoming part of the regular university literary curriculum. The consequences of this are mixed. On the one hand, the university has run a very effective employment service—a WPA program that goes by the name of creative-writing classes—for writers who might otherwise have had to go into the mail-order business. This much—and it is no small thing—the university has done for writers. Whether this has been good for writing is another question altogether.

Universities seem tolerable enough places for poets, so many of whom live, literarily, in their imaginations. Much less do universities seem so for novelists, who need to live more in the world if their work is to deal with anything beyond fornication and fashionable ideas, which seem to be the chief forms of experience and knowledge available at contemporary universities. But a great many contemporary novels do not deal with anything beyond fornication and fashionable ideas, of course; and one of the new phenomena in the literary culture of our day is what I think of as the English Department Novel. Written by such writers as Jonathan Baumbach and Ronald Sukenik, and at its higher reaches by John Barth, this is the kind of novel that no one outside an English department would for a moment consider reading.

Critics may at first glimpse seem more naturally a part of the university, yet it was not always so. As recently as the 1920s, critics —certainly critics of contemporary literature—were less than fully welcome in universities, whose members still thought of universities as communities of scholars. Van Wyck Brooks was never permanently attached to a university; nor was Edmund Wilson. Today one is hard pressed to think of an important literary critic who works outside the university. (On the other hand, one is hard pressed to think of an important literary critic.) Yet the university may not be a much better place for criticism than it is for the novel. In a university setting a critic may lose sight of what literature is supposed to be about—itself nowadays a great intramural literary-critical question—and confuse what is most teachable in literature with what is most important. Having critics resident in universities has also legitimized criticism itself as a scholarly function, which has had the effect of vastly increasing the glut of trashy criticism that is part of the current scene: hopeless journals such as *Diacritics* and *Wisconsin Fiction Studies* and useless series of books such as the Twayne series on contemporary authors and the University of Southern Illinois's Cross Current series. But these, as everyone in the racket knows, aren't actually to be read; they are only part of the apparatus of university publication that makes promotion possible.

One of the results of legitimizing criticism in the university has been to professionalize it. Much literary criticism today is written for colleagues, not for people interested in books. But then whole books are no longer written for people who are interested in books. There is, for example, much current debate in literary theory about the way people read texts and about the meaning of language, much demonstration of techniques for proving that reality doesn't exist. It is all very ingenious, this work of structuralists, semiologists, Foucaultists; it is also all very boring. Yet it dominates the current literary-critical scene in a way it could never do if literary criticism were not so securely centered in the university, where people seem to have endless time for such nonsense and where to oppose it—as such critics as Gerald Graff and Frederick Crews have done—is to condemn oneself to spending a good part of one's days rushing about screaming, "The world is round! The world is round!"

The larger point is that the usurpation of contemporary literature by the university continues to grow, so that today it sometimes seems as if there are two literary cultures: academic literary culture and non-academic literary culture. To be sure, there is some crossover. Saul Bellow teaches literature at the University of Chicago, and yet he does not seem a university writer. Thomas Pynchon, so far as anyone knows, does not teach in a university, and yet it is difficult to imagine many people outside universities reading his novels. Many writers seem to drop in on universities from time to time, spending a quarter or an academic year teaching. Some are happy to have the work, some curse the society that will not reward them sufficiently to allow them to work at their writing without interruption.

With its creative-writing courses (sometimes entire "programs"), its conferences and symposia on literary subjects, its poetry readings, the university might appear to be, from the outside at least, a true termite mound of literary activity. From the inside, though, it tends to look rather different. Take, for example, poetry readings. Sometimes it seems that the skies must be dark with poets aloft, flying to their various campus readings, so many have been the poetry readings on American campuses. I myself was not long ago at a university in Ohio, a small liberal-arts school, where conversation revealed that an almost endless chain of poets had read there: Ignatow, Levertov, Wakoski, et al. Do many people show up for these poetry readings? I asked. Usually eight or ten kids, I was told, or as many students as the teacher of the modern poetry course could roust out.

One poet who apparently draws unfailingly large crowds at universities is the feminist Adrienne Rich. I have never see Miss Rich in performance. Doubtless hers is a fine enough show. Yet it does say something about the present state of literature that the only poet who can consistently draw large crowds at a university is a thoroughly politicized one. Universities have political agendas; they seem to want to do what they construe to be the right thing by all groups within the university community. Thus universities are quick—or at least they were quick, when the money was at hand—to set up black studies programs, women's studies programs, you name it. Because universities are disposed to this general view, literature under their auspices has come to look a little like the Democratic Party under George McGovern.

Years before the intervention of contemporary writing in the university—or has it been the other way round: the intervention of the university in contemporary writing?—nothing was conceded to a writer because she was a woman or he a Jew or she was a black or he was a homosexual. There was something called the Republic of Letters, and this republic took no census. It included only people who were serious about writing. There was also a fairly simple division of writers, or at any rate only one division that mattered: good writers and bad. How different this is from today, when a great writer like Willa Cather is by and large excluded from the academic canon of American literature for having written stories and novels with insufficiently feminist views. The problem, clearly, is that what is judged the best in literature by the university is not always what people who passionately care about literature know to be the best. If what the university judges to be the best in writing—based on the books used in classrooms or the research done on particular authors— were indeed the best, then Virginia Woolf would be a greater writer than Tolstoy, which, as Virginia Woolf herself would have told you, is scarcely so.

No one knows how many writers work in universities and how many work outside them. There are, along with those writers permanently attached to universities, writers who have never been connected with universities: William Styron, John Updike, and

Norman Mailer, to name three novelists. Among writers in the baggy category known as non-fiction, Tom Wolfe, Edward Hoagland, and Gay Talese have pretty much steered clear of the university. The novelist Robert Stone and the critic Susan Sontag seem to duck in and out. Joan Didion is not a university writer, though she seems to fill her purse fairly regularly by writing screenplays. These are writers of established reputation. Well below them is a group of writers, literary gypsies as I think of them, who swing about the country, arranging a few months or weeks at one or another of the writers colonies (Yaddo, McDowell, Bread Loaf in the summer), teaching a stint where they can find it, doing a writing "workshop" one week, waiting for a check for a book review the next, living pretty much from hand to mouth. Sometimes impressive in what they have sacrificed for their writing, sometimes comically fraudulent in their pretensions, they are the Coxey's Army of contemporary American literature.

While the academic segment of literary culture has become more specialized, more professionalized, more sepulchered within university walls, the non-academic segment has become more public, more gaudy, more vulgar—and in a big way. Judging by media time and space, there appears to be a nearly endless if altogether superficial interest in the lives of writers, novelists chief among them. Writers in this connection have come to seem an arm of the entertainment industry. The financial details of Saul Bellow's difficult divorce were treated in the press as national news. Gore Vidal and the late Truman Capote have been established television personalities. Norman Mailer is permanently hot copy, which his actions do nothing to discourage; indeed, he seems to live his life in order for it to be framed in newsmagazine prose. Everywhere writers are dropped onto talk-show couches, where they are questioned about their private lives. Those who tend to stay away from such Venus's-flytraps of gossip, Philip Roth for instance, make up for this by revealing more than one wishes to know about them in their own fiction. And on the subject of gossip, why should I, who never met him, know that a dignified man such as the late John Cheever seems to have had a serious drinking problem? The reason is that John Cheever some-how felt he owed it to Dick Cavett to tell him so. We have among us today so many would-be Boswells, and no Dr. Johnsons what-soever.

Neither inside nor outside the university has contemporary literature been able to produce a towering literary figure. A figure of the kind I have in mind is usually not strictly an artist, but usually a man of letters. Voltaire was such a figure for the French Enlightenment. Dr. Johnson, holding entirely different views, fulfilled a similar function for his age in England. In the nine-teenth century in Russia the key literary figure was Vissarion Gregorevich Belinsky (1811–1848), a critic who expressed the pas-sion of his age—expressed it and embodied it. Of Belinsky, Isaiah Berlin has written:

> For him the man and the artist and the citizen are one; and whether you write a novel, or a poem, or a work of history or philosophy, or an article in a newspaper, or compose a symphony or picture, you are, or should be, expressing the whole of your nature . . . and you are responsible as a man for what you do as an artist.

It is not clear whether America has ever had such a figure, though some might argue that Emerson came close in the middle nineteenth century, others that H. L. Mencken, roughly between World War I and the beginning of the Depression, achieved something like this literary authority. I suppose that there are those who might put forth Edmund Wilson for this special as-signment, though I think that his rather commonplace political views disqualify him (and Wilson was a very political character). Be that as it may, there is no one even remotely in contention for the role today. And that there isn't speaks to the thinness of current literary culture.

In its intellectual life, ours has been preponderantly a political age. By age I mean roughly the past twenty-five years or so; by political age I do not mean to imply that no interesting literary work has been done in that time, only that the chief issues, questions, and preoccupations have been political, not literary. Communism, the Cold War, the Third World, the kind of society America is or ought to be, these are among the subjects that have used up so much of the intellectual oxygen of the past quarter-century. Nothing in literature has been able to hold a candle to them. Experimentalism in literature, a towering question to the modernist writers, towers no longer; it is of interest only to its few practitioners and to those few academics caught up in the notion that there has to be a perpetual literary avant-garde, the equivalent in literature of Trotsky's permanent revolution. Well, there will always be a literary avant-garde, as there will always be an England, but our avant-garde—producing concrete poetry, novels that come in boxes, books that can be shuffled like cards —is quite beside the point, not to say boring well past tedium.

Although I have never heard anyone speak of it, one of the reigning questions about the literature of our day is why so few American literary masterpieces have been produced in the past quarter-century. Cyril Connolly once said that "the true function of a writer is to produce a masterpiece and no other task is of any consequence." I myself do not quite believe that, though I do wonder why contemporary American writing has produced so few books that seem indispensable. There is no point in stopping to name particular works here, but I suspect the titles in contention for the status of literary masterpiece can be counted up without the need for removing both hands from one's pockets. During this period much graceful poetry has been produced, some extraordinary novels, and a number of interesting autobiographies, but few works about which one can confidently say, "If this had not been written, life would seem less rich," which is one definition of a masterpiece.

If it seems too hard on literature to ask it to produce masterpieces at regular intervals, consider yet another point: that ours has also been an age without great literary magazines. Sadly, no large-circulation magazine can today sustain itself by publishing chiefly literary fare. Indeed, it doesn't seem to have been possible for the past half-century or so. But the *Atlantic Monthly* under Edward Weeks was noted for its sympathy for fiction. Even the old, square *Saturday Evening Post* was fiction-minded, publishing, along with many sappy stories, works by William Faulkner and John O'Hara. When *Life* obtained the rights to Hemingway's *The Old Man and the Sea,* it advertised it as a great coup. One used to think of the *New Yorker* as a great magazine for short stories, the home of Cheever and Salinger and Updike and (later) I. B. Singer and Ann Beattie. Indeed, it remains hospitable to good fiction; but can anyone doubt that the heart of the magazine has changed from the literary to the political? Not only is this true of its "Talk of the Town" section, but easily the most discussed pieces to run in the *New Yorker* in our day have been pieces of political conse-quence: Rachel Carson's *Silent Spring,* Hannah Arendt's *Eich-mann in Jerusalem,* James Baldwin's *The Fire Next Time,* Charles Reich's *The Greening of America,* Jonathan Schell's *The Fate of the Earth.*

In intellectual journalism surely the two most interesting American magazines of the past few decades have been the *New York Review of Books* and *Commentary.* Each, it needs to be em-phasized, has derived its energy and élan from politics, although the *New York Review* has lost some of its luster since the Vietnam War. *Partisan Review,* the premier intellectual American magazine of the forties and the better part of the fifties, grew spavined trying to keep up with cultural trends in the 1960s: it ran essays on the Beatles, pornography, and other subjects unworthy of a magazine that had once published George Orwell, Albert Camus, Ignazio Silone, and André Malraux.

Mention of these four names—Orwell, Camus, Silone, and Malraux—is a sad reminder of two further changes in literary culture in our day. First, there are few figures in Europe today to compare with these men; with the possible exception of Günter Grass, I can think of none. Consequently, there no longer seems much reason to look to Europe for any sort of cultural guidance or literary example. Second, each of these men functioned, for the better part of his career, as an independent literary intellec-\
tual: in the United States today the independent literary intellec-tual, never a flourishing breed to begin with, is all but extinct.

Orwell, Camus, Silone, Malraux, each of them lived in a time

of great political passion, each was himself political in the most
serious way. But as literary intellectuals they wrote on political
subjects with the authority of literature behind them. In the
United States today things tend to run the other way round. Such
novelists as Robert Coover, E. L. Doctorow, and Robert Stone
create literature with the authority of politics behind them; for
them the novel is politics by other means. Great writers have
always had their politics. Think of Dostoyevsky and Tolstoy. Or
think of Joseph Conrad. Conrad obviously detested the revolutionary personality; and yet one doesn't have to agree with Conrad's political views in order to recognize that there is more at
stake in, say, *The Secret Agent* than politics alone. Reading E. L.
Doctorow, on the other hand, is a different experience entirely:
if one disagrees with Doctorow's politics, the pleasure is drained
from his novels; if, in other words, you do not believe that the
Rosenbergs were innocent or that Henry Ford was ridiculous,
you are excluded.

Traditionally, it has been the job of the literary intellectual to
blow the whistle when politics infringed upon literature or popular culture. Orwell is the example of the modern literary intellectual par excellence; like a finely tuned Geiger counter, he could
tick off unfailingly the political content in works of high and low
culture. He spoke for things above politics. One of the deplorable
features of the current scene is that, just as the literary intellectual
is disappearing, political purposes are increasingly infiltrating literature. Not that they haven't done so fairly steadily since at least
the 1930s. Nearly every one of the printed opinions of Malcolm
Cowley and Dwight Macdonald, to cite two examples, needs to
be fumigated for possible political motive. But so thoroughly
politicized has contemporary literary life become that most people assume that it is the literary man's duty to be on the side of
revolution, to find the United States racist and the members of
the middle class either desperate dogs or insensate swine.
Whether such notions are by now more literarily uninteresting
than untrue or more untrue than literarily uninteresting is difficult to say.

What isn't difficult to say is that political argument has badly torn up what was left of New York literary life. So many people who otherwise have so much in common no longer speak to one another because of political differences. Not to live in New York, to put a bit of distance between oneself and such a scene, in these circumstances seems sensible. "As you grow older as a writer," Saul Bellow recently told an interviewer in *Esquire,* "you become more and more accustomed to talking to yourself. In what the punks like to call the literary milieu you'd think you'd find some *milieudniks* to talk to. You'd think there were heaps of people to attach yourself to. But you have to pick yourself through heaps of *no goodniks,* casts of thousands in the literary world who don't know what the hell I'm talking about."

Writers have always grumbled, of course. Some of the chapter titles from Isaac D'Israeli's early nineteenth-century book *Calamities of Authors* name conditions that have not greatly changed in our own time: "The Sufferings of Authors," "The Pains of Fastidious Egotism," "The Despair of Young Poets," "Literary Hatred," and "Miseries of Successful Authors." When writers complain about their work—when I complain about my own— it is useful to recall Mencken's scoffing retort to authorly moaning: "If authors could work in large well-ventilated factories, like cigarmakers or garment workers, with plenty of their mates about and a flow of lively professional gossip to entertain them, their labor would be enormously lighter."

And yet, normal grumbling aside, that there is so little in the way of solid literary culture in the United States at the present time has serious consequences. When literary culture, like culture generally, becomes too attenuated, something snaps, rituals lose their significance, traditions wear away, life changes—and not necessarily for the better. To mention but a single ritual, consider the bestowal of literary prizes in America. Pulitzers, Guggenheims, American Academy of Arts & Letters awards—every publisher's or critics' prize has been drained of its importance; any value it might have had has been dribbled away by its having been given too many times to second- and third-rate writers. To win certain literary prizes is nearly enough to encourage self-doubt. In a world of less than perfect justice rewards have often gone to the richly undeserving. Yet the fact is that twenty-five years ago if a novel won a National Book Award there was a good chance that it was a fairly impressive piece of literary work. One can't, I think, say the same today; so dwindled in significance have such literary prizes become that scarcely anyone can remember who, over the past five years, has won them.

The only prize serious writers can now unequivocally esteem is good readers. Good readers are the unknown variable, the great mystery, in current American literary culture. Good readers are those readers who read not only intelligently—with mental acuity, an ardor for language, a sense of humor—but also in the hope of having their souls stirred by literature. How many such readers are there in the United States? Impossible to know, though it seems fairly safe to guess that their numbers are not legion. Apart from poets and people who aspire to write poetry, how many people read contemporary poetry? Again, impossible to know. Serious fiction sometimes sells in great numbers, but what do these numbers mean? Saul Bellow, some years ago, remarked that he thought himself a fortunate writer: "When I publish a novel," he said, "roughly fifty thousand people buy it in its cloth edition, five thousand or so actually read it through—and five hundred care." Those numbers sound fairly accurate to me. What's more, having five hundred readers who really care sounds very impressive.

This is, I believe, the place to insert the standard paragraph on the baleful effects of television. The reason people aren't reading good books, this paragraph usually runs, is that, slack-jawed, they are sitting in front of their television sets. Worse: their children sit there even longer, even slacker-jawed. No one reads anymore. Ours is becoming a visual culture . . . and so forth. The standard paragraph on the baleful effects of television tends to overlook the fact that before there was television there was bridge and bowling and the corner saloon—one's taste in these matters depending on one's social class. There was never a shortage of excuses for not spending time with books. Today, though, in the era of the crushing best seller and what sometimes seems like nearly universal higher education, writers feel all too often that readers disappoint them. Even so, much as one wishes it were otherwise and no matter how many B.A.s, M.A.s, and Ph.D.s roam the range, reading serious books has always been and will probably remain a minority taste. That serious books do break through from time to time—Santayana's *The Last Puritan,* I always remind myself when sending a manuscript off to a publisher, was a Book of the Month Club Main Selection—is nice but never to be expected.

What is not nice but now usually to be expected is that a book, the result usually of years of effort, will appear in bookstores for two or three months and then disappear without trace. Under current publishing arrangements, this happens fairly regularly, and to good books quite as frequently as to bad. In a strong literary culture if a book fails with the public a writer can at least hope for the appreciation of his literary peers. But now, unfortunately, it is not always there. Too often good books are stupidly read by their reviewers, half-heartedly supported by their publishers, ignored by the public, and too soon meet their pulper. When real talent goes unappreciated it is yet another sign of a weakened literary culture—and we live today in a greatly weakened literary culture, in which foolish books are frequently praised and subtle books are frequently dumped.

Over a local FM station not long ago I heard a jazz musician describe his musical education. "I don't know, man," he said, "I copied from cats like Charlie Parker, Ben Webster, Art Tatum. I guess they copied from cats like Louis Armstrong, Fats Waller, Earl Hines. I don't know who those cats copied from, but I'm sure it was somebody." Although he never mentioned the word, this particular cat was explaining the way tradition works in the arts—one generation borrowing from the one preceding it, each artist adding his own special touches, point of view, and vision to what has gone before. In literature, it is beginning to feel as if the tradition is breaking down. It could be that literary culture is merely going through a bad patch. But it feels as if more than a bad patch is involved: it feels as if circumstances are conspiring to make literature seem a second-rate activity.

Still, although a rich literary culture is a true boon to a writer, its absence can't kill off serious writing altogether. If evidence for this is wanted, the dissident Russian writers of our day, who have worked in circumstances in which everything possible has been done to demolish literary culture, provide it in excelsis. It is difficult to say just how many of our potential writers will decide, for want of reinforcement in literary culture, that the writing life is not for them. Certainly more than a few. Others will persist, largely for the reasons that Edward Gibbon gave for his own literary persistence: "some fame, some profit, and the assurance of daily amusement." Nevertheless, that something fundamental in the nature of the literary life has been altered, this cannot be doubted.

Imagine, in this connection, F. Scott Fitzgerald as a very young man today. Assume—what is today unlikely, since he was not a very good prep-school student—that he attends Princeton, and there takes creative-writing courses from such teachers on the staff as Joyce Carol Oates and Geoffrey Wolff. His teachers encourage the young Scott Fitzgerald, and so, before graduation, he applies to and is accepted by the University of Iowa Program in Creative Writing. At Iowa he is considered among the most promising of students, though during his first year there his teachers talk him out of writing a rather shapeless novel he plans to call *This Side of Paradise*. Concentrate, they tell him, on the short stories, for he shall need a full book of them to qualify for his doctorate in creative writing. (Around this time he meets and falls madly in love with a student in the English department, a Southern girl named Zelda Sayre, but when her fellowship is not renewed she is forced to leave Iowa City, and eventually they fall out of touch.) Scott's stories, meanwhile, are meeting with some success: one is published in *Salmagundi,* one in the *Virginia Quarterly Review,* and two are accepted by *TriQuarterly*. He is on his way, or so it seems. He is offered a job at the University of Michigan, teaching freshman composition and two courses in creative writing. It is a tenure-track job. At Michigan, between classes and grading papers and academic committee meetings, he begins a story about a young man who, through illicit means, has made a great deal of money, with which he sets out to recapture

the past, chiefly symbolized by a beautiful woman, a lo͟
who has since married. The story works out wonderfully,
did beyond his own expectations. But is is rather too lon͟ ͟ͅ ͟
short story and too brief for a novel, or so a number of editors
say. If he will agree to cut the story radically, one magazine editor
tells him, he, the editor, will be glad to look at it again. A publisher's editor has ideas for expanding the book: flesh out the
character Wolfsheim a bit, give Daisy two daughters, etc. He tries
cutting, he tries expanding, but either way it is no go. The story
seems just right to him as it is. He decides to put it away for now.
It is around this time that he begins to drink. At age forty-four,
exactly ten years after he has been awarded tenure at the University of Michigan, his heart, weakened by a steady consumption of
alcohol, gives out. But then, who ever said that the literary life
was easy?

The New Criterion 1982

Reviewing and
Being Reviewed

B OOK REVIEWS ARE among those things people who
write books despise but find it difficult to live without.
Edmund Wilson, in his essay "The Literary Worker's
Polonius," noted: "For an author, the reading of his reviews,
whether favorable or unfavorable, is one of the most disappointing experiences in life." Yet in *Upstate,* a collection of journal
entries from his last years, Wilson remarked that "getting older,
for a writer, did not necessarily give you self-confidence. . . . I
sometimes got up at four o'clock in the morning to read old
reviews of my books." The worst of writing, as more than one
writer has written, is that one depends so much on the opinions
of others.

Allow me to take up Wilson's first point, about reviews being
one of the most disappointing experiences of an author's life, by
way of personal example. One day, upon returning home from a
business lunch, I found an enticing package waiting. It was from
Jonathan Cape Ltd, the English publisher of a book I had recently
written; the package contained *all* the English reviews of my
book. There must have been twenty of them. Some were from
the English weeklies, some from the London, some from the
provincial press. I no longer have copies of these reviews, but
many, I seem to recall, were written by people named Ian or
Jeremy; the one from the *Manchester Guardian,* I do recall, was
written by someone with the lilting name of Monica Furlong.

Well, thought I, here's a splendid little snack for the ego; some twenty reviews of a book of mine, and written by men and women who, so far as I knew, brought no parti pris to their comments. So, like a fat gourmand who had traveled far for his meal, I sat down and began to plow into these reviews. "Let down" does not begin to describe my feelings as I read my way through the first six or seven of them. Some praised my book, some attacked it. But, in praise or in attack, there was a dreary sameness to the reviews that left me a little depressed. Reading the remaining thirteen or fourteen reviews suddenly seemed in the nature of a chore. They were so low-grade; they had no intellectual precision, no originality of thought or even of phrasing. And whether the reviewers liked my book or hated it they failed to convince me of anything, because they were merely tossing off opinions, and the thing about opinions is that, except for those that are meant to be scandalous, one really is as good as another. "Epstein is very sensitive in his treatment of women," one reviewer might write, only to be followed by another: "Epstein is quite insensitive to the condition of women." "Epstein is not your typical modern intellectual." "Your typical modern intellectual, Epstein . . ." "Wisely, Epstein does not crowd his pages with statistical matter." "His case would have been much more persuasive had Epstein provided more statistical evidence." And so it went. What, finally did it all prove? Nothing more than that, for reasons best known to themselves, Ian thought well of my book and Jeremy didn't.

I have never kept count, but my guess is that I have had roughly three hundred reviews bestowed on books I have written. From these three hundred or so reviews I have learned nothing, either about my books or about my quality as a writer. Of all these reviews, one pleased me, and for the following reasons: it understood the intention of my book exactly, it was elegantly phrased, and it was written by a writer whose work I myself admired and whose views I could not predict. For the rest, reviews of my books have been mostly muddle, politics by other means, and unintended comedy. I have seen my books used to work out personal problems, even scores, release resentments. Stendhal once said that to write a book was to risk standing up to be shot in public. But he never mentioned the embarrassing places where you might be hit.

Worst of all can be the praising reviews. To have your book praised for things you yourself despise, virtues you have no wish to claim, ideas that are as far as possible from your own—all this can induce real discomfort, like a letter citing you for strength of character from, say, Spiro Agnew or Ted Kennedy. Sometimes the praise, because of its ineptitude, only makes you all the more dubious. "Personally insightful," a review from *Newsweek* called one of my books: "Linguistically dopeful," I reply. "Joseph Epstein is an excellent companion on a thinking trip," someone in the *New York Times Book Review* noted of the same book, making me wonder what an unthinking trip might be. In the *Washington Post* I once had my prose compared to a fine Chinese meal. What, I wondered, could this mean? An hour after reading me you're looking for something else to read?

But the praising review that sticks in my mind—and in my craw—is that of a book of my essays that began by stating that the essay was a splendid and endlessly flexible form. Among its practitioners, the reviewer claimed, have been Montaigne and Pascal, Hazlitt and Lamb, Camus and Orwell, and yes, in our own time, the brilliant John Leonard. Joseph Epstein as an essayist, the reviewer continued, is of their company. Now of all contemporary writers I disesteem John Leonard easily heads the list. I do not want to be of his company. Indeed, at the very mention of the name John Leonard it seemed that Montaigne threw his mantel across his shoulders and left the room, followed by Pascal delicately lifting the skirt of his vestments; Hazlitt said he had a previous appointment at the fives courts, Lamb muttered something about his sister not being well, Orwell stubbed out his cigarette. Camus buckled the belt on his trenchcoat, and they were all gone, and so was any sense of pleasure I might have taken in the praise the rest of this review lavished on my book.

Being frequently reviewed might seem to some people to fall in the category of what are known as happy problems. To be ignorantly reviewed is, doubtless, better than being ignored altogether. Many a writer of lofty reputation has found neglect to be the last circle in literary hell. *"The Common Reader* came out 8 days ago and so far not a single review has appeared," Virginia Woolf wrote in her diary for May 1, 1925, "and nobody has written to me or spoken to me about it or in any way acknowledged the fact of its existence; save Maynard, Lydia, and Duncan. Clive is conspicuously dumb; Mortimer has flu and can't review it; Nancy saw him reading it, but reported no opinion; all signs which point to a dull chill depressing reception; and complete failure."

Some writers claim not to be in the least affected by bad or stupid reviews. Arnold Bennett said he never read his reviews— he only measured them. Not so John O'Hara. O'Hara cut his profitable connection with the *New Yorker* when a mean review of one of his books by Brendan Gill appeared in its pages. O'Hara arranged to have his books published on Thanksgiving Day be- cause he knew that that was a day on which Orville Prescott did not publish reviews in the *New York Times*. And it was always a point of pride to him, who had been attacked by so many writers in the intellectual quarterlies, to have had Lionel Trilling write admiringly about him.

I like to think myself above such petty passions. Unfortunately, I am not, and my guess is that few writers are, at any rate com- pletely. In an otherwise fast fading memory, I seem to retain the names of most of the men and women who have reviewed my books roughly. After I read a rough review, my first impulse is to write a sulphuric little note to the reviewer, reviewing his review: "Mon cher M. Le Twerp, Sorry you did not find my book to your taste, if taste be the correct word to apply to views as coarse as those you displayed in your review. Still, I wonder if, in your crude fury, you didn't forget something—such as telling your readers what my book was about. But then I suppose, even in the hands of a real craftsman like yourself, a book review cannot be expected to do everything." I soon calm down and decide to save the postage. During such times as these it helps to recall Menck- en's dictum: it is not injustice but justice that hurts.

Of course the best reviews are not reviews at all but the care- fully considered criticisms and, one hopes, appreciations of those men and women whose literary intelligence one truly respects—

one's peers, in the old and fine sense of the word. After that, the best criticism often comes through the mails, in letters from strangers who are not themselves writers but who read books in the passionate, heartfelt way of people who yearn to learn and are not weighed down by prepackaged opinions. You can sometimes learn a thing or two from these letters. One woman wrote to me to say, of a collection of familiar essays I had published, that they may have been familiar but they weren't very personal, which seems to me a subtle and useful criticism.

Yet the reviews that can control a book's fate are those that appear in print. And book reviews are today more important than ever before. Under the current dispensation, a trade book has a bookstore shelf life of roughly ninety days. As Sybille Bedford not long ago put it, publishing nowadays is all serve and volley, and an author has to get to net quickly. Fifteen years ago a book might have remained in a bookstore for eighteen months or two years; even an ignorantly reviewed good book had a chance to find its readership by word of mouth. No longer. Word of mouth does not travel as fast as word of computer. A few well-placed stupid reviews can go a long way toward killing an excellent book, even causing its early banishment from bookstores, preventing it from reincarnation in a paperback edition, snuffing out its existence—and its author's hopes—quickly and effectively.

The books of already well-known and commercially successful writers are less vulnerable to the vagaries of reviewing than are those of young writers and writers belonging to the category known as "middle authors": in the middle between trade and scholarly in their work, in the middle between selling well and selling poorly. For the well-known and commercially successful writer the big financial decisions about print-run, advertising budget, and paperback sale have generally been made before reviewers have had a go at his book. When his book is being reviewed only his ego is on the line. But reviews for the young or middle author can be decisive. It is not uncommon for a publisher to print a small pressrun of such a writer's book, awaiting the response—by which is meant the reviews or the interest shown in the book by various television and radio talk shows—before deciding to print the book in substantial numbers.

Perhaps I ought to make a distinction between good reviews and reviews that sell books. The best book reviews are only rarely what the publishers can call "sell reviews." Sell reviews tend to be blurby: "Don't exhale till you have read this." Good reviews can sell books, yet sell reviews are not usually good. Sell reviews are a part of advertising, and it is always a bit embarrassing witnessing a good writer setting out to write one. Even Edmund Wilson was not above this sort of thing. It is sad to read his review of Svetlana Alliluyeva's *Only One Year,* for instance, which will take its place, Wilson tells us, "among the great Russian autobiographical works: Herzen, Kropotkin, Tolstoy's *Confession.*" I don't know why Wilson wanted to give a push to the feeble literary effort of Stalin's daughter, but push, clearly, he did, for the line I have quoted is, along with not being true, sheer *blurbissimo.*

What is a good book review? A first-blush answer is, I suppose, the product of an interesting mind thinking about a book. But there is more to it than that. A reviewer has certain obligations to the book he's reviewing and to his own readers: he must report what the book is saying; he must make a judgment about how well the author gets it said; and he must determine if what has been said was worth saying in the first place. Not to be dull, not to be fearful, not to scamp the duties of clear summary—these are the minimum requirements that a good book reviewer must meet.

Yet another quality ought to be part of his tempermental equipment, and this is a controlled anger aroused by breaches in literary justice. When bad writers are praised or good writers neglected or ill-understood, he should feel personally offended. His pique, though, ought to be more than personal. Judging books correctly is of the utmost seriousness to him; misjudging a novel is of no less consequence than, say, misjudging a friendship.

Not all good reviewers have had this anger, of course, although most have. H. L. Mencken could scarcely function without it. V. S. Pritchett, on the other hand, seems scarcely to have had any anger at all in his long career, and even today he puts his best energies into making careful literary discriminations, not berating authors. Still, if it doesn't offend you that American literary academics are able to publish structuralist studies of John Irving, then you probably ought to be in another line of work.

Along with possessing at least a modicum of anger, a good book reviewer ought not to show too much generosity. While always hopeful of discovering real talent—both for the new and the different and for work of a traditional kind—and ready to encourage it with measured praise, the book reviewer must at the same time always be skeptical. Dubiety ought to be his normal condition. Books, unlike criminals, are best judged guilty until proven innocent—for innocent, in this context, read without falsity, fudging, or flagrant flaw. Most current-day reviewers err on the side of generosity—doubtless they want to seem friends to literature—and so literary masterpieces are announced more frequently than station breaks. Generosity, like humility, can be carried too far. Doris Grumbach, Robert Coles, and Robert Towers are three people who review too generously. Their liking a book carries no weight—they like so many.

Anyone of any literary maturity knows that, even in a population of roughly two hundred forty million people, rare is the year in which more than fifteen to twenty truly first-class books are published. Of course, there are interesting bad books, and interesting failed books, and books that have been wildly acclaimed and need to be shot down. There are older books that are usefully re-evaluated in the light of a later day and books that have been unfairly neglected. In sum, there is no shortage of reviewing work to be done.

Where the shortage exists is in the number of competent workers to do it. Has it ever been thus? Quite possibly it has. In 1914, in a brief essay entitled "Reviewing: An Unskilled Labour," Edward Thomas referred to the majority of reviewers as "a rabble of ridiculous and unlovely muddlers." In the same essay he divided book reviews into four kinds: "the interesting and good; the interesting but bad; the uninteresting but good; the uninteresting and bad." And, Thomas noted, "most are of the last kind." Raymond Chandler, writing to his English publisher Hamish Hamilton in 1949, is scarcely cheerier on the subject of reviewing: "There are far, far too many novelists reviewing other novelists. There is far too much consideration for books that are obviously going to get nowhere, and far too little understanding of what it is in books that makes people read them. And there is a tight group of critics or reviewers who are monotonously willing to say something nice about almost any book at all." Recall, please, that both Thomas and Chandler were writing not about America, where complaints about the thinness of culture have long been commonplace, but about England, where traditions of intellectual journalism have run deeper than they have run here.

Part of the reason for the paucity of able reviewers, now as in the past, has to do with the difficulties and disadvantages inherent in the form of the book review itself. To begin with, it has never been quite clear what the purposes of a book review are. Should a review grade the author, passing out complaints and criticism along the way? Should it chiefly perform a service for readers, informing them whether the book under review is or is not a waste of their time? Or should it combine both tasks, an aid to both writers and readers? And there is the question of whether a book reviewer can do these things while still being mildly entertaining. Book-review readers and book-review editors are not noted for desiring their edification straight.

Then, too, in the view of the world there is something slightly second-class about book reviewing, this despite the fact that many of the great essays of the nineteenth century, including those of Macaulay and Sainte-Beuve, began as book reviews. Cyril Connolly and Edmund Wilson were two of the best book reviewers to have written in English in our own century, yet neither of them, I suspect, would very much have liked to think himself a book reviewer chiefly, even though, if you laid out their writing by the yard, the amount of prose they expended on book reviews in their careers would be city blocks longer than that of any other form they worked in. But then reviewers one approves of are not known as reviewers but as critics. Something of the odor of Grub Street still clings to the activity of book reviewing; something of the foul reputation of hackwork, however undeserved it may be.

A critic is assumed to be deeper than a reviewer, but one of the significant differences in the working conditions of the two is that the critic usually has more space available to him to work out his ideas, and more time to think them through. Unlike the reviewer, he does not work under deadline pressure. Edmund Wilson cited H. L. Mencken and Van Wyck Brooks as "reviewer critics," noting: "These are extremely rare. Most people who are capable of first-rate criticism do not want to interrupt their other work for jobs as unremunerative as book reviews." And the critic who is able to write a competent review is rare as well. It is difficult to imagine, say, R. P. Blackmur writing well—or even intelligibly —at fifteen hundred words. Or Yvor Winters or F. R. Leavis.

Space is almost always a serious limitation. As someone who still does a certain amount of book reviewing, I know I have decided against taking on at least three assignments in recent months because the length at which I would be allowed to write seemed inhibiting. One request was to review, for the magazine *New York,* John Kenneth Galbraith's autobiography; nine hundred words were wanted. Another was to review the most recent edition of *The American Heritage Dictionary* for the *New York Times Book Review* at, roughly, fifteen hundred words. The third was to review *A Margin of Hope,* Irving Howe's autobiography, for the *Chicago Tribune* at nine hundred words. I chose not to do the Galbraith because I felt disposed to attack him, and thought that if I were to do so effectively I needed more space to lay out such artillery, armor, and troops as I possess. *The American Heritage Dictionary* I felt best written about at essay length. As for Irving Howe, about his career I have rather complicated feelings that I didn't think I could sort out in under a thousand words. (The *Chicago Tribune* was probably not the best place to sort them out in anyway. I could already see the *Tribune's* newspaper-like headline over the review—"Jewish Critic Sees Hope" —which was in itself a discouragement.)

If too little space is often discouraging to reviewers, too much space is quite as often discouraging to readers. And not merely to newspaper readers. Once the *New York Review of Books* got under way in earnest, one of the first complaints one heard from many of its readers was about its reviewers going on at what was felt to be monstrous length. John Gross, while editor of the London *Times Literary Supplement,* used to send me books to review without ever specifying any length. I was, apparently, to write about the book at the length I thought suitable, which in my case meant my turning a review into an essay of four or five thousand words. I was delighted, of course, but I'm not sure I can say the same for the readers of the *TLS*.

Who reviews? Apart from those professionals who review books full-time for weekly magazines and for the few American daily newspapers that are large enough to employ book reviewers regularly, the people who review books in the United States tend to be academics, novelists, and poets who need a bit of extra money, people with bookish interests who for one reason or another work at non-bookish jobs, and the young who wish somehow to break into the literary life and find doing so through reviewing easier than other ways. Professional reviewers are few in number, and Paul Theroux, writing in *Harper's,* thought this an unfortunate thing. Theroux wrote:

> Most of all, university patronage has spelled the decline of book reviewing in the United States. After the foundations delivered novelists into the arms of the universities, there was no need for anyone to engage in the habitual tasks associated with the profession of letters. A campus of creative writers does not mean that the local newspaper will be lively with literary journalism; it means its opposite. Book reviewing, the literary essay, the feuilleton—all of these went out the window when university patronage came in the door; and a sharp, and I think, unfair, distinction came to be drawn between the literary man and the literary journalist.

I rather doubt it. The decline of reviewing cannot, I think, be blamed on the university. It was not, after all, very good before.

Dwight Macdonald years ago used to call Charles Poore and Orville Prescott, the regular daily reviewers of the *New York Times,* "the lead-dust twins." Francis Brown, when editor of the *New York Times Book Review,* used to prefer what he called "up" reviews—"up" standing for "upbeat," for which read positive, pro, sell reviews. If anyone can remember a time when the *Saturday Review* ran good book reviews he must be in his eighties at least.

Good reviews do get written, but most book reviewing in this country is mediocre, and quite possibly always will be. The people who do reviewing do it as a bit of work peripheral to work that is more truly at the center of their lives. Reviewing doesn't pay very much, and most book reviewers tend to give dollar value— that is to say, also not very much. A review that is properly done —with the reviewer reading all the other books of the author under review, looking into connected works on the same subject, and taking serious pains in composing his prose—will probably earn a reviewer well under the minimum wage. As a motive for reviewing, money isn't a very good one.

But when one begins to talk about motives for reviewing one enters very tricky terrain indeed. In classifying book reviewers, Edmund Wilson mentioned "people who want to write about something else." As a subsection of this category, I would add people who want to write but don't otherwise have anything in particular to write about. When I think back to my own early days as a reviewer, my chief motive for reviewing was writing itself and—no small thing—appearing in print. I looked for books to review that I thought I might be able to say something interesting about. With a brashness that now rather impresses me, I accepted all books that were offered to me for review whether I knew anything about the subject or not. If I didn't know anything about a subject, I would read up on it before sitting down to write the review. One week I might find myself reviewing the memoirs of Alexander Herzen, another week the collected writings of Santayana, a month or so later the autobiography of Bertrand Russell or a biography of Frank Lloyd

Wright. This, I believe, is what is known as getting one's education in public, and this, through book reviewing, is what I did.

The advantage of book reviewing for the young is that it gives them something to write about. I know it did me. I would not go so far as to say that any of the reviews I wrote in my twenties were of intellectual interest, but I always took great care with their composition, and so at least produced highly burnished clichés. Thus I admired Bertrand Russell's idealism, Santayana's exquisiteness, Frank Lloyd Wright's radicalism. None of this was exactly front-page news; still, I got away with it, for the editors of the journals I reviewed for believed in these clichés, too. I was reminded of my own youthful performances only the other day when I rejected, for *The American Scholar,* a review that came in over the transom of Gershom Scholem's *Walter Benjamin, The Story of A Friendship,* written by a young man who had graduated from college in 1978. It was a crisply written review but observant of every pietistic cliché about Walter Benjamin, and the author of the review seemed not to consider the possibility that of the two men, Scholem and Benjamin, it was Scholem who was the towering figure. But then a person under thirty who could write well about this particular book would probably have to be at least as smart as Scholem himself.

One of the things that reviewing taught me was that certain kinds of books made for better reviews than do other kinds. Biographies, autobiographies, diaries, journals, and collections of letters I have always found pleasurable to write about. The reason for this is that, even in fifteen hundred words, such books permit me to do a portrait in miniature of the author under review. Novels are less easily reviewed, especially if they are shoddily made, though it is best to be able to review a novelist who has written a number of novels so that one's review can turn on his career. Although I have reviewed books about poets, I have never attempted to review a book of poetry, and I have yet to see this delicate job well done in book reviews of normal length. The sad thing is that, given the lack of interest in poetry in the great world, few book review editors feel justified in allowing reviews of poetry to run beyond the normal length; more often, they do not review poetry at all, except that written by established names —under the assumption, apparently, that what cannot be done well should not be done at all. Poets reviewing other poets is rarely a solution.

The ideal book reviewer ought to be someone whose passion for literature is evident in everything he writes. His own literary quality should be obvious in his prose. If he is an academic, he shouldn't allow this to show through. His point of view ought to be clear, recalling in this connection a remark made in a V. S. Naipaul novel that a collection of opinions does not necessarily add up to a point of view. Wit is helpful but not absolutely required. Courage is. If the reviewer cannot say what he thinks, he does best to keep silent and not try to fudge his true views. A conscience is called for, too; for while the reviewer ought to be skeptical about new books, he must also be fair in his account of them. Finally, if this does not seem a contradiction, the ideal book reviewer probably does best not to review books too often, lest he become what Edith Wharton once called "a magazine bore." Too much book reviewing dulls the mind.

I have rattled on at considerable length about the limitations of book reviews and of book reviewing, yet I myself continue to read book reviews and I continue to review books. On the latter front, though, I find myself more and more frequently turning down offers to review books, and not just because of insufficient space. For example, a late Friday afternoon call comes in from an editor of the *New York Times Review;* he informs me that he has in hand a book by a man who has written essayistically about the effects of women's liberation on men. It appears to be a serious book, he says, quite well written. He thinks I am the sort of person who has thought about such things, and could write interestingly on them. Unfortunately, he is wrong. I could not write well on such things; I could not write well on them because I have not much thought about them. And I do not much care to think about them. Women's liberation, midlife crisis, sexual identity, such items make up what I think of as the contemporary noise, and, thank you for asking, I would just as soon keep my voice out of it.

Yet I do find myself agreeing to review books I feel I ought to be reading. Novels, for instance. I have in recent years found it exceedingly easy not to read contemporary novels. A fat Styron, two Malamuds, three Robert Stones, four John Updikes, five John Irvings had passed through unread by me. Raymond Carver, Ann Beattie, Manuel Puig, a whole new generation of novelists had come into being without my having read them. I felt a certain bad conscience about this and have since partially remedied it by agreeing to review fiction fairly regularly for *Commentary* magazine. There is this, too: writing about these novelists gives me a chance to have my say, or, as T. S. Eliot put it in his essay "The Function of Criticism," "to correct taste," for I have strong views about the novel.

Along with the aesthetic pleasure of forming what I hope are interesting sentences, the soupçon of glory to be had from appearing in print, and the delight in being paid money to read and write books, the attraction of reviewing books for me has indeed been the chance it offers to correct taste—and I say chance because I am not aware of having specifically corrected any. Still, in reviewing a book one likes to think—I certainly began my own career by thinking—that one is in a serious conversation about the shape and fate of culture, itself a most serious thing. Ideally, the part of reviewing in this conversation is to place the books under review in their line or tradition and to judge their quality and importance. In reality I can think of no finer description of what this so-called conversation has become than Eliot's famous description of criticism generally as "no better than a Sunday park of contending and contentious orators." In this park everyone has his soapbox—feminists, Marxists, Poundians, Freudians, structuralists, deconstructionists. It sometimes seems as if only nudists and vegetarians are missing, and I am not too sure about the vegetarians.

The age of the lead-dust twins is long over; the rhinestone kids now hold sway. I continue to read book reviews but now chiefly to take a reading of the intellectual weather. Certainly reviews are not very much help in discovering what the good new books are. Reviewers like lots of books, but why they like them is often a mystery. Thus, to cite an example near at hand, the front page of the September 5, 1982, *New York Times Book Review* has a review of Joyce Carol Oates's novel *A Bloodsmoor Romance* by Diane Johnson. Miss Johnson is herself a novelist and a biographer, and a woman of some literary cultivation. She apparently thinks well of Miss Oates's novel. I say apparently because while she appears to be praising this six-hundred-odd-page work she never tells us what is good about it. The review is all plot summary, with a touch of explication (". . . Joyce Carol Oates has found a way to assuage our Puritanical guilt about escape by writing romance that is satirical, and thus about something, but which is still successful as romance") and a grain of criticism ("One seldom feels that from book to book one comes to know her better"). It ends on a fine note of ambiguous puffery: "Even those who find balloon abductions thin should be satisfied by this richness of detail."

The formula of Miss Johnson's review—limpid summary combined with limp criticism—has become increasingly common in the age of the rhinestone kids. Because of this abnegation of criticism in reviewing, writers who do not seem to grow better with age—Philip Roth, John Updike—nonetheless somehow become proclaimed masters, John Irving's novels receive praise of a kind that would have brought a blush to the cheek of Caesar, and the *New Republic* can run a piece of puffery by R. W. B. Lewis on the new editions of The Library of America next to the spewing flattery of which the normal television commercial sounds like Schopenhauer. In the rhinestone age, there is a great deal of glitter but very few gems.

The intrusion of politics into culture—one of the major motifs in the cultural history of the past quarter-century—has of course not been without its effect on reviewing. If you write a book of criticism or history today, or any other kind of nonfiction, you get a sense of how very politicized our cultural life has become. Reviewing, you quickly learn, turns into a game of friends and enemies, and the way to tell a friend is that he shares your opinions. Your book either gets into the hands of reviewers who agree with your opinion, and who will praise your book for having the good sense to agree with the reviewer, or into the hands of reviewers who disagree with your opinions and who will smash your book for your having the effrontery to think differently than they. Most journals are pretty much lined up beforehand, and you can predict, depending on the opinions expressed in the book, how, say, the *Nation* and *National Review* will treat the book. In some cases you can't always guess in advance whether the book will be sent out to someone who will agree or disagree with it, and so you wait, as in roulette, for the ball to fall. But in the end it usually comes to the same thing: agreeing or disagreeing, neither of which is quite the same as reviewing.

"Hidden agendas," as the fine new phrase for secret motives has it, frequently can be read in book reviews in all sorts of places. In the cowardliness of a reviewer's repressed views can be read a fear of upsetting such powers as are thought to be, a hope for an improved social life, a wish to be invited back to do another review. Praise for books the reviewer obviously did not take pleasure or instruction from—Miss Johnson, for example, on Miss Oates—can mask a subconscious desire not to make waves, to show that one can be counted on to go along with the game. (The game in this particular case is to build Joyce Carol Oates into a major novelist, which, but for one little drawback, seems to be working: the little drawback being Miss Oates's novels.) Other reviews are clearly a matter of friends passing puffs, as when, a year or so ago in the *New Republic,* Mark Harris wrote a throttle full-out praising review of a collection of short stories by Richard Stern, Mr. Stern—*ahem*—being the dedicatee of Mr. Harris's own previous book. Other crimes could be catalogued here.

Yet one of the differences between life and literature in the United States is that in literature, with the possible exceptions of fraud and plagiarism, crimes go unpunished. A shame, really. What is needed is a court that, in the spirit of the Lord High Executioner, metes out literary punishment to fit literary crimes.

Such a court might sentence Diane Johnson to read, and show proof that she had read, all thirty-odd of Joyce Carol Oates's books. It would require reviewers who have shown in their reviews distinct evidence of cowardice or obsequiousness to write ten reviews of Graham Greene's autobiography—five praising, five damning. Mark Harris and Richard Stern would be sentenced to slam, in conspicuous places, each other's next three books. As for first-time and minor offenders, they would be sentenced to read the collected reviews of John Leonard, and to discover in each review the exact point at which that particular rhinestone reviewer disappears up his own metaphors.

The New Criterion 1982

Literary Biography

W HEN I WAS A YOUNG MAN, at a time when publishers'
advances were even easier to procure than divorces are
now, I signed on to write a life of John Dos Passos.
Why, you ask, John Dos Passos? Dos Passos himself supplied as
good an answer as any when I wrote to him to ask his coopera-
tion. "Well," he replied, "I suppose somebody's got to do it."
This was my view, too, and who better than yours truly? I recall
even now the joys in setting up biographical shop: acquiring all
of John Dos Passos's many books, including a first edition of a
book of verse entitled *A Pushcart at the Curb;* marking a folder
for each year in his life, into which I planned to drop disparate,
discrete, and decisive facts; buying two thick notebooks, in one
of which I planned to straighten out, for my own mind and later
for my biography, the chronology of my man's life, and in the
other of which I planned to inscribe my own large and penetrating thoughts. I could scarcely wait to begin scribbling away.

  In John Dos Passos I had, I thought, a fairly juicy subject. He
was a man who had been born out of wedlock, to a sickly Southern mother and a highrolling lawyer father. This may not be a
fine start for a human being but is an excellent start for a biographer. I had my opening sentence: "John Dos Passos was born a
bastard but an upper-class bastard." His boyhood was spent
going to an English boarding school and living in hotels with his
mother. He went off the Harvard at a time when Harvard was
filled with interesting people. The First World War, expatriate

days in Europe, the romance with Communism, Harlan County
with Dreiser, interesting marriages, a complicated relationship
with Hemingway, a sharp political turn to the right (which
brought about a drop in his reputation)—well, why go on? As a
biographical subject Dos Passos offered everything a biographer
could possibly wish for: a fine fat chance to play shrink, cultural
historian, literary critic, and political pundit. I thought I could
bring this baby in at just under seven hundred pages.

There was a complication, though it was an interesting one,
and this was that John Dos Passos was still alive. On the one
hand, I believed that biographical subjects, like most varieties of
snake, were best dead, so that they couldn't charm and ultimately
bite you. On the other hand, Dos Passos seemed a literarily intelligent being and therefore possibly helpful. "Writing the life of a
novelist," he wrote to me, "is an impossible task. A novelist tends
to use everything that happens to him, often in distorted or re-
vamped form, so that there's nothing left for a biography." He
also seemed immensely likable. Responding to some pieces that I
had sent along to him with my request to do his biography, he
wrote: "I'll consent to your doing this life under two conditions:
(1) that you put the liberal ideology in mothballs for the duration;
(2) that you promise never to use the word 'explicate' again. I like
neologisms when they are useful, but doesn't 'explain' fill the
bill?" Then, in longhand, he added: "Don't take my teasing too
seriously, but honestly, it's a job I wouldn't care to take on," and
signed off "Cordially, John Dos Passos."

Well, for a complex of reasons too elaborate to go into here,
writing the biography of John Dos Passos turned out to be a job
I didn't care to take on either. What is more, I am glad I did not.
If I had I would have produced a volume of considerable bulk
but little weight. It's composition would probably have cost me
at least five and perhaps more years of my writing life. Oh, I
might have uncovered a dirty secret or two—an attempt by a
crazed Zelda Fitzgerald to seduce Dos Passos, a homosexual passion on his part for the young Ernest Hemingway—but the
world doesn't really need many more such secrets. I do not think
I would have written a very interesting book, and this would not

have been John Dos Passos's fault. Roughly two years ago a book appeared perhaps not so very different from the one I might have written: *John Dos Passos, A Twentieth Century Odyssey* by Townsend Ludington. A tome of 568 pages, it is in all respects a workmanlike performance—"Ideas for the new fiction Dos Passos wanted to write were growing"—yet it is also a work I never got very far in reading. In art, it is said, there are no rules, except that there are no rules. But here is one: Nobody should try to write what he himself doesn't truly wish to read.

"Funny ting, a man's life," says a character in Dos Passos's *Manhattan Transfer,* and the older one grows the funnier and funnier a ting it begins to seem. And few seem funnier—that is to say, odder—than the lives of literary men and women. In André Malraux's *The Walnut Trees of Altenberg,* the following bit of dialogue takes place:

> "Essentially a man is what he hides . . ."
> Walter shrugged his shoulders and brought his hands together like a child making a mud pie.
> "A miserable little pile of secrets . . ."
> "A man is what he does!" my father answered sharply.

The father in that snippet of dialogue spoke for Malraux, who was interested primarily in the world's doers, the shakers and movers of history. But does it apply to the literary man? Is a literary man what he does? Or does a literary man hide his miserable little pile of secrets in those mud pies otherwise known as novels and plays and poems?

That is a question for which no clear answer is available, nor is one soon likely to be. Yet it is a real question, and it is in the hope of finding answers to it that one continues to read literary biography. Not so long ago it was not considered a pertinent question at all. The use of biography in connection with the study of literature was thought to be bad form. The literary work, it was felt, ought to be allowed to speak to its readers directly, with as little mediating interference as possible, like a direct-dial long-distance call. The New Critics, who by and large felt this way, have been somewhat maligned when the claim is made against them that they believed that literature should be studied in isolation from history and biography; as the New Critics argued in their own defense, they expected, even assumed, that scholars and serious students knew something of the history of the time in which a literary work was created and the biography of the artist who created it. But it is fair to say, even if one allows for this defense, that the New Critics did not feature the biographical aspect of literary works. The devil take the dancer, they went for the dance.

During the reign of the New Criticism, in the forties and fifties, the one major critic who retained an unflagging interest in the connections between biography and literature was Edmund Wilson. In his own special literary-critical program, which involved trying to capture the drama of ideas by placing them in their historical context, Wilson could scarcely avoid biography. Not, one hastens to add, that he wished to. Although he never wrote a full-dress biography, almost all Wilson's longer literary essays are at bottom biographical, bounding back and forth between the literary work and the forces that shaped the man or woman who created it. Because of his biographical method, Wilson was written off for a long time as a mere journalist—and what journalist isn't "mere"?—or, worse, hopelessly old-fashioned. Yet he persisted and, in two ways, prevailed. First, his own critical works, written out of this biographical impetus, remain more readable than those of any other American critic of the past half-century; for it is biographical criticism that alone among all forms of literary criticism can lay claim to being a species of art. Second, though Wilson never really set out deliberately to fight it, he helped win the battle for biography, which is now, thanks to the books of a number of talented biographers, perfectly respectable once again.

This battle has been won to the extent that no one would argue today that you should not study both the artist and his work. Common sense calls for it; common decency is no longer able to prevent it. Ours is an age of exposure, in which it is difficult not to think with reference to biography, especially when so much contemporary literary art is itself heavily larded with autobiography. To resist exposure is one of the surest ways of having it thrust upon one. Among literary figures, both Auden and Orwell asked that no biographies be written of them; their wishes have been honored with at least four full biographies, and more are in the offing. T. S. Eliot, who also wished no biography, will be the next to fall. Attempting to cut off the literary-biographical hyenas already snuffling around the corpse, his widow is now searching for a jackal of her own—that is, an official biographer.

I make myself sound as if I am four-square on the side of decency here. Yet I am not so sure. Return to T. S. Eliot for a moment. While no good unofficial biography has been written about him, a lot has been written about Eliot in the form of memoirs and other people's now published journals, diaries, and autobiographies. From this material it begins to seem as if the crucial event in T. S. Eliot's adult life was his marriage to his first wife, Vivien, who, not long after she and Eliot were married, went mad. The humiliation, the sadness, the tragedy of this marriage cannot but have had the most chivvying effects on Eliot's life as well as on his work. In point of fact he wrote *The Waste Land* at a particularly low period in this marriage. The reigning view of *The Waste Land* is that it is an elegant condemnation of industrial society. But can one discount the fact that its author was living day-to-day with a woman who was out of her mind? People talk chattily about the wasteland, about the abyss of modern life, but Eliot lived with the most terrifying waste, the darkest abyss; she sat across the breakfast table from him on God knows how many mornings. The longer one thinks about this horrendous biographical fact, the less certain one becomes that *The Waste Land* is an attack on industrial society. In his criticism Eliot insisted on the impersonality of poetry, but in his own most important poetry he might well have been locked into personality with a blue vengeance.

It is no longer possible, then, to ignore the importance of biography to literary study. While this is true, it is also true that biography has not yet moved into the university and hence has not been, in the full pejorative sense of the word, "academicized."

Biography has not thus far been academicized, my guess is, because, even though it is central to literary study and unarguably an art in its own right, it is not very teachable. And in universities what is not very teachable—shocking to report—tends not to be taught. True, some biography makes its way into the current university curriculum: a bit of Izaak Walton, two or three of Johnson's *Lives of the Poets,* selections from Boswell's *Life of Johnson,* possibly one of the figures among Strachey's *Eminent Victorians.* But rarely are these studied as works of biographical art as such. More troublesome still, the contemporary works of biography that have been most praised—Leon Edel's five-volume *Henry James,* Richard Ellmann's nearly 900-page *James Joyce*—are too ample to render classroom service. Besides, even in that ideal university of the mind—where time expands endlessly, allowing a teacher to spend three hundred and eleven weeks on Proust— biography as a subject would present difficulties. Its history can be taught in a superficial way: selections again. But how study it for itself, as poetry and fiction are now studied?

Part of the difficulty is that there is nothing like a consensus about what makes for a good biography. Better than a consensus, though, is the actual appearance of good biographies. Since I intend to go on and say some fairly stringent things about what I take to be the larger trends in the writing of modern biography, allow me to mention here a number of what seem to be fine literary biographies of recent vintage: the John Wain and the W. Jackson Bate biographies of Samuel Johnson, the Frederick Brown biography of Jean Cocteau, the Henri Troyat biography of Tolstoy, the James Mellow biography of Gertrude Stein and her circle, and the first volumes of John Clive's biography of Macaulay and of Joseph Frank's biography of Dostoyevsky.

It will be seen from this rather odd lot, written as they were under quite different methodological assumptions, that, aside from the idea that the facts need to be got straight, there is very little agreement, even among the better biographers, on how biography ought to be written. Nor is there agreement on which are the canonical works of modern biography and what critical tools ought to be brought to bear in the judgment of biographical works. Take Edel's *Henry James* and Ellmann's *James Joyce*. They have been highly praised, but each has also been savagely condemned: the Edel for what some critics feel is its excessive psychologizing, the Ellmann for what its critics feel is its pedantic detail. Nor should anyone be shocked that there is vast, even passionate, disagreement on the subject of biography. In biography, after all, the very largest issues are at stake, some of which can be formulated thus: How is human nature formed? What are the mainsprings of men's and women's lives? What in life is most significant? On such questions agreement simply isn't available. Yet each of these is a question that no biographer can hope to avoid.

If the university has not been able to appropriate biography into its curriculum, to absorb it, as the radicals used to say, nonetheless a number of literary academics have become biographers, and these have included the more cultivated literary academics. I have already mentioned Leon Edel and Richard Ellmann. But there are also Walter Jackson Bate, Aileen Ward, and Ernest Samuels. From outside the university scholarly biographies in recent years have been written by Justin Kaplan, Jean Strouse, and James Mellow. I mention here writers whom I think of as professional biographers, men and women who upon completing one biography set to work on another. How did they happen to become biographers? Through a love of the study of character, through a penchant for psychologizing, through want of any better arena in which to work their literary talent? One would perhaps have to have a biography of each of them to know with certainty.

One factor that has undoubtedly aided the rise of biography, at least in recent years, has been the decline of criticism. I had better qualify that to read the decline in the quality of criticism, for in its quantity, its sheer tonnage and bulk, I am not certain that criticism has declined. But for quite a while criticism—the literary act of judgment, interpretation, and valuation—has been nowhere near so central to our cultural life as it once was. In part, this is so because it appears as if all the major interpretations and valuations have been done by now. Is there really anything fresh left to be said, for example, about Kafka, about whom thousands of articles and books have been written and from whose work everything possible has been made except chopped liver? The great cannon of criticism, though still smoking, has been firing blanks for years. Proof of this point can be found in the fact that the hot names in academic literary departments at present are those names associated with the subject of literary theory. Literary theory, though, provides marshy lands and not every literary-minded person can—or would wish to—build upon them.

If literary theory seems too drearily obscurantist, literary criticism too tautological, that leaves, for people of literary sensibility who are not themselves imaginative literary artists, literary biography. I do not have statistics to back this up, but my sense is that a great number of literary biographies are now being written, especially by academics. A gold rush—or perhaps more accurately a zinc rush—is on, sufficiently so to make pointed a bit of dialogue in Barbara Pym's novel *No Fond Return of Love,* in which a character informs another that she is lucky to have found an obscure eighteenth-century poet to do research upon. " 'You were lucky to find one so obscure that not even the Americans had "done" him. . . . It's quite serious, this shortage of obscure poets.' " And there is a whiff of prophecy, too, in Max Beerbohm's send-up of the Garnetts' discovery of Dostoyevsky, which he entitled "Kolniyatsch": "Their promised biography of the murdered grandmother is awaited eagerly by all who take—and which of us does not take?—a breathless interest in Kolniyatschiana."

While we have not yet had the promised biography of Kolniyatsch's murdered grandmother, we may one day have a biography of our own, unmurdered grandmother. In Portola Valley, California, there is an institution calling itself the American Lives Endowment, which helps ordinary people write biographies of their own family members, presumably for family as well as general historical purposes. In 1977, at the University of Hawaii, the Biographical Research Center was founded; its chief function has been the publication of a quarterly journal, *Biography,* and of monographs on biography. In Australia—at Griffith University in Brisbane—there is now something called the Institute for

Modern Biography. For so long the homely sister of history and the dull cousin of criticism, biography is setting up shop for itself as a separate discipline. New approaches, new methods, new directions, such is the prevailing chatter among the biographia literati. Mr. George Simson, the editor of *Biography,* has been quoted in the *Chronicle of Higher Education* as saying that he believes the rise in interest in biography can be explained by Max Weber's notion that individuals gain in prominence at times when the prestige of institutions is low, as they certainly seem to be at present. Walter Jackson Bate, in the same article, is quoted as saying that what we are witnessing is a "natural flowering, the result of the decline of the old Victorian novel as a big, panoramic portrayal of a slice of life. In most novels since Thomas Mann, story and hero have been lost. The novel is no longer the prevailing form. Biography is stepping into the breach, portraying particular people and times the way the great novels of the past did. It's as simple as that."

In partial defense of Professor Bate, it must be said that few compliments please a biographer more than being told that his work reads like a novel—or, rather, like novels used to read. Honor, shame, loyalty to ideals, the hunger for achievement— such items, although rapidly disappearing from contemporary novels, remain at the center of biography, even if the biographer postulates a morally indifferent universe. Around such items character is formed, and the formation of character is what biography is about. Whether biography ought to be a separate discipline seems to me, in every sense of the word, an academic question. The chief thing is that biography, whatever its academic standing, has the great subject—human character. "There is properly no history," wrote Emerson, "only Biography." That is of course quite wrong, but in the middle of reading a powerful biography one is almost ready to believe it.

Biography has its own history, and no better opening to it is available than Arnaldo Momigliano's *The Development of Greek Biography* (1968). In this elegant, slim volume Professor Momigliano sketches the origins and ironies of biography's early history. Not least among the ironies is that in the ancient world autobiography was often bound to factuality and biography was expected to be encomiastic, while today things tend to be quite the reverse. Professor Momigliano surmises that the first man to give biography its new shape—outside and beyond the encomium— was one Aristoxenus of Tarentum (born ca. 370 B.C.), a cosmopolite of Pythagorean training who also studied under Aristotle. Of Aristoxenus, Professor Momigliano writes:

> He must have picked up the loose threads of fifth-century biography, availed himself of the variety of biographical techniques displayed in the early fourth century, and appreciated the new trends of erudite research favoured by Aristotle. He was the man to produce a new blend: learned, yet worldly; attentive to ideas, yet gossipy. Perhaps he was also the first to make anecdotes an essential part of biography. . . . I suspect that we owe to Aristoxenus the notion that a good biography is full of good anecdotes.

One could, I suppose, draw a thread from Aristoxenus through Plutarch and Suetonius through the Church hagiographers through Vasari through Johnson and Boswell through Strachey through Freud—with many a side stitch along the way—and end up with an odd baggy garment that might be called the history of biography. But that history is perhaps better understood as being made up of the fortuitous, and sometimes ironic, couplings of hero and biographer. Every so often someone comes along to give the subject a sharp theoretical twist, as Samuel Johnson did by turning away from panegyric and toward serious literary criticism, or Lytton Strachey by turning prosecutor and putting many of his subjects on the stand as defendants, or Freud by turning the biographer's study into a psychoanalyst's office.

Yet, as inevitably with biography, rules refuse to remain intact. Thus Samuel Johnson, in his *Rambler* essay on biography, could lay it down that "if the biographer writes from personal knowledge, and makes haste to gratify the public curiosity, there is danger lest his interest, his fear, his gratitude, or his tenderness, overpower his fidelity, and tempt him to conceal, if not to invent." Enter Boswell, filled with personal knowledge, anxious to gratify public curiosity, loaded with interest, gratitude, and tenderness, only to produce one of the landmark biographies. Then there is Lytton Strachey in 1918 announcing: "The art of biography seems to have fallen on evil times in England. . . . Those two fat volumes, with which it is our custom to commemorate the dead—who does not know them, with their ill-digested masses of material, their slipshod style, their tone of tedious panegyric, their lamentable lack of selection, of detachment, of design?" That description, two volumes and all, fits nothing so well as Michael Holroyd's *Lytton Strachey,* which appeared fifty years later.

When did modernity begin for literary biography? We know that Virginia Woolf set the date for the change in human nature —by which she meant a change in the nature of human relationships—at "about 1910." For Willa Cather the date life changed was 1922. But when was human nature, when were lives, portrayed differently in works of biography? Perhaps the watershed year is 1918, the year of the publication of Strachey's *Eminent Victorians.* The critical success of Strachey's book implied, at least for the time, that intelligent people were no longer quite able to believe in the standard panegyrical biography that had dominated the genre before the First World War. (For a fine example of the type see G. Otto Trevelyan's biography of his uncle, *The Life and Letters of Lord Macaulay.*) With Strachey the biographer had ceased to be a man who performed an official function—that of placing a wreath of prose over the graves of great men and women—and had become an independent producer, an artist if he were good at his productions, and a writer with a point of view that did not always imply sympathy for his subject. And sometimes, as with Strachey, it implied quite the reverse, though here it must be recalled that Strachey, that menace of the Victorians, wrote a touching, really quite sentimental biography of Queen Victoria herself.

André Maurois, in *Aspects of Modern Biography* (1928), set forth three chief characteristics of modern biography. The first was the search for truth, by which Maurois meant exposing the whole story, letting the chips fall where they may. The second was the abandonment by the biographer of classical psychology, in which people were locked into strict psychological types, in favor of more fluid, diverse views that met the new insistence on "complexity of personality." The third was the element of doubt that had entered into the making and reading of biographies: "We ourselves live in an age of doubt and that is why we like to find in the lives of great men that they, too, have had their doubts and have nevertheless succeeded in achieving something." Maurois had put it this way earlier in his book: "the greatness of a character comes home the more closely in proportion as we feel the character to be human and akin to our own." To put it less kindly, a taste had begun to develop to cut biographical subjects down to size, the size being about a 42-short, leaving plenty of room in the back for an unresolved Oedipal complex.

Increasingly, the tendency of modern biography has been to make its subjects a little smaller. I am hard pressed to think of many literary biographies—aside from the interesting case of Edel's *Henry James*—that leave their subject with much in the way of grandeur. Partly this is because when seen close up—which is the way modern biography likes to view its subjects—everyone seems a bit odd, a bit shrunken. Certainly James Joyce does not emerge larger than one had imagined him from Richard Ellmann's biography, and there can be no question of Ellmann's goodwill, not to say admiration, toward Joyce. Partly it is because the effect of elaborate literary psychologizing—in Frederic Karl's book on Joseph Conrad, for example, or Rudolph Binion's book on Lou Andreas-Salomé—is to diminish its subjects, again quite apart from whatever admiration biographer may feel toward subject. And partly it is because modern biographers—like modern people generally—do not quite believe in grandeur, and feel duty bound to chip away at any pretense to it. "A man's biography," H. G. Wells observed, "should be written by a conscientious enemy." But in modern biography, serious enmity is not required; if a biographer is conscientious, he will soon be enemy enough.

There have been contemporary literary biographies motivated by admiration, even idolatry, and most have been written out of goodwill toward their subjects. But where they have been admiring—for example, Ian Hamilton's *Robert Lowell*—the admiration cannot cover over the squalor of the life. Where they have been idolatrous—for example, Elisabeth Young-Bruehl's biography of Hannah Arendt—they have not been very persuasive. Goodwill usually does not prove strong enough to make up for ill-led lives. The fact must be faced: the subjects of most modern literary biographies have not exactly led lives that provide, in the idiom of the day, "fine role models." Consider the roll call: Theodore Dreiser, the Fitzgeralds, Ernest Hemingway, Robert Frost, and now, the most recent victim of the modern biographer's guillotine, Katherine Anne Porter. But no matter how an author has led his life, he will eventually feel the blade. Approaching the stairs now is Willa Cather, about whom a "revelatory" biography charging her with lesbianism has recently appeared. Still waiting in the tumbrel below are Edmund Wilson, Allen Tate, and Marianne Moore.

The only two writers I can think of who seem to have held up under the hot magnifying lens of modern biography have been Henry James and Samuel Johnson. No matter how much biographical work is done on these men, they somehow refuse to be diminished. What it turns out they have in common—neither was exemplary, each *sui generis*—is that both were very good men. And a good man, in literary life as in the old pop tune, is hard to find. But then there is no strong evidence that modern biographers are looking very scrupulously. The category of goodness, as it relates to literary work, does not seem to weigh heavily in modern literary biography.

The scenario for the typical modern literary biography is moral in a different way. It is morality weighted in favor of art, so that the creation of art justifies almost anything. In this kind of biography such disorder and continual sorrow as the artist suffers is gone into as fully as the material allows. An account might be offered of how our hero, a poet, trashed his first marriage, began drinking in earnest, and entered into a hopeless love affair with a student while writer in residence at, say, Wesleyan University. Bad reviews of his third book put him on pills and helped break up his second marriage, although the year of his divorce he published his famous essay on Whitman in the old *Kenyon Review*. His son from his first marriage tried to kill himself the following year, the year his sonnet sequence won the Sophie Pritzker Prize at *Poetry* magazine. Well, anyone who has read recent biographies of contemporary poets—Delmore Schwartz, John Berryman, Robert Lowell—could finish the story himself. The poet dies at fifty-two, leaving general devastation behind, but there was that first wonderful book of poems, three or four essays as good as any that have appeared in our time, and the fragment from the only just begun critico-autobiographical book on Wallace Stevens and Robert Frost. Art wins again. Or does it?

Whenever there is a change in psychology, a change in morality follows; and whenever there is a change in morality, modes of judgment change. In the psychological revolution wrought by Freud, Jung, and the various Ottos, Annas, Brunos, and Wilhelms who make up the great Viennese chorus, biography, especially the biography of artists, has been shaken profoundly. It has been pushed in the direction of regarding men and women—to refer again to Malraux's phrase—as "a miserable little pile of secrets." It could scarcely have been otherwise. If you believe in the doctrines of Freud & Co. you are, whether you wish to think so or not, lashed to the belief that a man is likely to be hiding what is most important about himself. In psychoanalysis the patient is made aware of his painful secrets and taught how best to live with them. In biographical psychoanalysis, the reader is made aware of the biography's hero's secrets, but it is not clear that as a result anyone lives any better.

By no means do all modern biographers psychoanalyze, though they all, to a greater or lesser extent, psychologize. The temptation to do so upon writers and artists of any kind probably can no longer be foregone, so clearly is the making of art now felt to be a psychological transaction, chiefly handled by the firm of Sublimation, Inc. Because of the way in which modern psychology tends to regard the creation of art—as the work done by men and women who would really rather be doing something else: guess what?—the artist is viewed as a not quite healthy character and thus he is granted the moral equivalent of diplomatic immunity. In biography it is only the artist—and, at very high levels, the scientist and philosopher—who is permitted to be a person of deeply flawed or even bad character. An artist is to be judged, finally, on his art. From the standpoint of criticism, this makes good sense. From the standpoint of biography, however, it is often a disaster. It leaves the biographer without the means of judging character, and it largely narrows his task down to the search for those miserable little secrets.

This search has more than a little to do with the lengthening of modern literary biographies. The one indisputable point about modern literary biographies is their propensity to grow longer and longer. Henry James's fine story about the problem of finding the key to an author's work is entitled "The Figure in the Carpet." Modern biographers continue to look for that key, only now they lay the carpet of their subjects' lives wall to wall. Biographical studies of modest length—such as John Morley's *Edmund Burke,* in The English Men of Letters series, or F. W. Dupee's *Henry James,* in The American Men of Letters series—have departed the scene. No publisher is asking for them, no writers are writing them. The trend toward biographical elephantiasis seems to have begun with Mark Schorer's *Sinclair Lewis: An American Life* (1961), a book of 867 pages in which Schorer seemed to demonstrate less and less regard for his author as his biography sloughed its wooden way to its close. Today most literary biographies weigh in at more than 500 pages, quite apart from their subjects' intrinsic importance, or so at any rate do Paul Mariani's *William Carlos Williams,* Joan Givner's *Katherine Anne Porter,* Ian Hamilton's *Robert Lowell,* and Martin Seymour-Smith's *Robert Graves.* Hilary Mills's *Mailer: A Biography,* true enough, is a slender 477 pages, but then her subject has miles to go before he sleeps. The heart sinks a little, at least mine does, at the sight of such bricklike tomes, tomes weighty, one feels, only in the literal sense.

Length, per se, is not the problem. George D. Painter's two-volume *Marcel Proust* does not seem to me in the least excessive. Leon Edel's *Henry James,* though it runs to five volumes, seemed to be over too soon. Both Painter and Edel are men of considerable literary culture and both write extremely well. (A biographer, it occurs to me, cannot always hope to be as intelligent as his subject, but it is best if he is not too much dumber.) Yet more than cultural endowment and excellent prose is behind the high quality of their biographies.

What makes these two works so good is that in each one finds a sense of proportion and a sense of purpose. Painter's *Marcel Proust*, although it does a number of things besides, is dominated, and rightly so in my view, by a single fact: Painter's subject wrote the greatest novel of the twentieth century. Painter saw his task, then, as explaining how this came about; and in the course of doing so he finds himself explaining the novel as well; and because of the complex connections between Proust's novel and the events and relationships in Proust's life, explaining into the bargain how Proust used real people and actual events in his novel and how he transformed them into fodder for his imagination. Painter's biography is one long work of explanation, and since the interest in *Remembrance of Things Past* is inexhaustible—it is, at least, to me—so is the interest in George D. Painter's *Marcel Proust*.

Leon Edel's *Henry James* is a very different kettle of caviar. I have more than once attempted to account for what it is I so much admire about this long, persistently psychologizing work, when neither great length nor literary *shrinkerie* is my notion of a holiday at the sea. Nor is the criticism in Edel's work all that striking; it is always interesting, always intelligent, but more penetrating criticisms of James's books have been written than those that appear in Edel's biography. On the other side of the ledger, there is of course Henry James, about whom I love to read. Edel's book is as good as any book I have ever read about the organization of a writer's life, and no being was ever better organized for writing than Henry James. But more is involved.

Although artful biographies have been written of literary figures, books beautifully composed and shining with intelligence, there is no biography of our age that comes close to Leon Edel's *Henry James* as a work of art. Unlike any other modern biography I know, *Henry James* is a shaped work. Edel does wondrous things with time in his book, shifting back and forth with it, playing incidents and anecdotes for dramatic effect. Quotation is used with tact and always to a point, and never cited more lengthily than an incident being dealt with requires. Criticism is worked in quietly, supplementing but not interrupting the narrative. Edel demonstrates that the only entrée to a mind as fine as James's is through an understanding of its subtle psychological shadings. Even though one might disagree with discrete points or interpretations—was William James really as rivalrous in his feeling toward his younger brother as Edel makes him out to be? —the book is no more spoiled for its reader by this than a long novel is spoiled if one finds a character less than well drawn or a scene or two not altogether convincing. There is sweep to this biography, a sense of a life understood in its unity—unity of a kind that Henry James and the great nineteenth-century novelists assumed life to have. When James dies at the end of Leon Edel's fifth volume, one feels as if one has come to the close of a superior novel.

Lengthy though the Painter and Edel biographies are, authoritative though each seeks to be, neither, it strikes me, is definitive —and I intend that as a compliment. The urge to be definitive is the great hubris of the biographical craft. To want to write a life definitively, to have the very last word on it, to nail it down, to attempt to establish one's own literary immortality over someone else's dead body, this is a grievously mistaken impulse. It is this impulse that gives so many biographies their feeling of literary sprawl. Apart from wishing to be definitive, what can be the possible justification for writing books of more than five hundred pages on such figures as Katherine Anne Porter, Robert Graves, and Hannah Arendt? Yet definitive is the ultimate garland reviewers toss over the necks of biographers. This, even though almost every biography that has sought to be definitive in recent years has turned out to be, in some truly definitive way, a botch: Mark Schorer's *Sinclair Lewis*, Carlos Baker's *Ernest Hemingway*, John Unterecker's *Voyager: A Life of Hart Crane*, Joseph Blotner's *Faulkner*.

Hugh Kenner put the point interestingly when, in a recent

review in the *Times Literary Supplement* of Richard Ellmann's revised edition of *James Joyce,* he wrote: "But there can be no 'definitive' biography. Biography is a narrative form: that means, a mode of fiction. Many narratives can be woven from the same threads." I think that very intelligent yet also very dangerous. It strikes me as all too close to the thinking of Roland Barthes, who finds biography offensive because it involves "a counterfeit integration of the subject." There is a nihilism inherent in that notion, at least until one is able to supply an authentic integration of human character. One can say that autobiographers usually lie and biographers generally get it wrong, but one must insist on those qualifiers "usually" and "generally."

What remains at issue today is how a biographical portrait ought to be put together. Ought it to be composed, Seurat-like, with pinpoints of fact that taken together will add up to a large picture, or Van Goghishly, with large brushstrokes of interpretation? Harold Nicolson, in his book *The Development of English Biography,* felt that the hunger for facts, which he termed the scientific interest in biography, would win out. And it seems to have. Think only for a moment on the disparity, the madness really, of Lytton Strachey's writing a biography of Queen Victoria, who lived eighty-one years and gave her name to one of the great ages of man, that is briefer than Hilary Mills's biography of Norman Mailer. But to return to Harold Nicolson, who wrote:

> . . . the scientific interest in biography is hostile to, and will in the end prove destructive of, the literary interest. The former will insist not only on the facts, but on all the facts; the latter demands a partial or artificial representation of facts. The scientific interest, as it develops, will become insatiable; no synthetic power, no genius for representation, will be able to keep the pace.

It must be added that scientific biography, based as it is on a foundation and continual piling up of fact, tends to bring an air of dubiety to the biographical enterprise. Carlos Baker's *Ernest Hemingway* is as fact-ridden a modern literary biography as I have read—and inert. Biography, like fiction, is the art of selection. Even though biography is bound by fact, its truth is finally literature's kind of truth—truth completely comprehended not by the categories of right and wrong but by the categories of more and less persuasive.

If biography is bound by fact, it is also bound by time. Nicolson says that "no branch of literature has been more sensitive than biography to 'the spirit of the age,' " and that "the development of biography is primarily the development of the taste for biography." This is why every age rewrites the biographies of important figures, and why in literary biography there are nearly countless biographies of Stendhal, Samuel Johnson, Lord Byron. As it happens, the spirit of our age seems to call for building up factual material and the taste of the time for stripping down the pretensions of the mighty—including, sometimes, pretensions to dignity. Given this spirit and that taste, I can think of a number of biographies I would be willing to pay anywhere between $19.95 and $29.95 *not* to read: among them, biographies of Willa Cather (a lesbian?), Wallace Stevens (a nightmare marriage?), George Santayana (don't ask).

"Little demons of subtlety" Henry James called those critics— and, by extension, critical literary biographers—who seek to discover an author's hidden meaning. But the question arises, is meaning always hidden? Leon Edel has written that though the biographer must learn "to understand man's ways of dreaming, thinking and using his fancy," this "does not mean that a biographical subject can be psychoanalyzed; a biographical subject is not a patient and not in need of therapy." But I would go one step further to argue that many lives—let us call them "Sanforized"—are quite impervious to the notions of the shrink, and that these notions have little or no place in their biographies. Certainly it is the better part of biographical wisdom to know when they do and when they don't.

Where once literary biography was chiefly commemorative,

today it is largely explanatory. Today most people write literary biographies less to honor than to explain their subjects, although, to put the best face on it, honor is implied in the effort at explanation. To put the worst possible face on it, biographers are, in Elizabeth Hardwick's sharp phrase, "the quick in pursuit of the dead."

Although not a writer, Albert Einstein, who was nonetheless an artist in his own fashion, once noted: "The essential in the being of a man of my type lies in *what* and *how* he thinks, not in what he does or suffers." That is undeniably so, but who can honestly deny that he isn't also interested in what important men and women do and suffer? Whether or not we are entitled to know is quite another question, however, and the answer is not all that complicated. We are entitled to know all a dead writer's miserable little pile of secrets only insofar as knowledge of these secrets seriously alters or substantially enhances the reading of his work. If the revelation of such secrets in a literary biography doesn't work toward these ends, then, however great our pleasure, we are finally reading through a keyhole.

Literary biography presents a serious epistemological problem, which may be formulated thus: How much truth can we know about another person's life? When literary biography was less ambitious, when it was content to limn the shape of a writer's career, to account for his accomplishments, it could sail along blithely enough on its way, producing interesting and useful if somewhat limited material. But once literary biography began to play in deeper, choppier waters, diving beneath the surface to discover hidden motives, dark secrets, terrors, and traumas, it became at once more interesting and more dubious. The challenge for the biographer is greater because the risks of failure are greater. One has only to think about one's own hidden motives, dark secrets, terrors, and traumas, and about how unavailable they often are to oneself to know how unlikely it is that a stranger calling himself biographer should come into knowledge of them. Still, it sometimes happens. Yet now, as always, successful biography is what it was for Edmund Gosse, writing in the eleventh edition of *The Encyclopaedia Britannica,* "the faithful portrait of a soul in its adventures through life." When that portrait is indeed faithful and the soul great, biography is as splendid a literary form as any yet invented.

The New Criterion 1983

Is American Literature an Equal-Opportunity Employer?

I MAGINE, PLEASE, Alberto D'Andrea. He is twenty-two years old and is studying American literature at the University of Rome. He has never been to the United States, but as a boy he grew up, you might say, on American movies. This partly explains his interest in American literature; less consciously, perhaps, he was drawn to the study of American literature because of America's power in the world, for since World War II, when the United States emerged as a superpower, its literature has taken on a worldwide interest, resulting in institutions such as the University of Rome having a department of American literature. Thus far Alberto has studied the Puritans and the great New England writers of the nineteenth century; he has studied Melville, Twain, and James; he has, in a brisk survey course, read some of the novelists of naturalism and, in the twentieth century, Dos Passos, Hemingway, and Fitzgerald. Next term he is to take a seminar in contemporary writing in the United States, and in preparation for this seminar he has been able to get hold of a new book entitled the *Harvard Guide to Contemporary American Writing*.

Although his English is quite good, it nonetheless takes Alberto a full two weeks to slog through the more than six hundred pages of the *Harvard Guide*. Sometimes he thinks he will go a little mad trying to keep straight the names—oh, so many names —of American critics, novelists, dramatists, and poets (more than a hundred and sixty pages devoted to poets alone). These Barths and Plaths and Bellows and Blooms and Mailers and Malamuds and Millers (Arthur, Henry, Jason, Perry, and J. Hillis) refuse to sort themselves out in his mind. If the names remain a bit of a blur, in the end, owing to the way the *Harvard Guide* is organized, a general picture does begin to emerge, if rather hazily.

Contemporary American writing, young Alberto decides, is evidently a literature of great diversity. There is black literature, of course, of which Alberto has heard, with black writers on the attack against American society, and then further divided among themselves. There is women's literature, speaking from, as the critics in the United States say, another consciousness, "another, equally significant, area of existence." There are realists, naturalists, novelists of manners, and experimental novelists by the score. There are Southern writers, deep fellows these, writing on the theme of self and history and something called "the awful responsibility of Time." Then there are the Jewish writers—Alberto pictures them in yarmulkes and prayer shawls—dreamy figures, trying to flee the responsibility of tradition, family, civilization, so that they can enjoy sex a bit more.

If all these writers, with all their special concerns and points of view, have anything in common it is a grave unease in their own country. The *Harvard Guide,* Alberto cannot help but notice, claims over and over again that most American writers acutely feel a sense of powerlessness. In the words of one author discussed in the book, "America is a bitch." With his yellow-marker pen, Alberto D'Andrea draws a line under that sentence.

Alberto. . . . But enough of this young Italian, whom I have brought on stage in the first place because, reading through the essays that make up the *Harvard Guide to Contemporary American Writing,* I have had a difficult time imagining for whom the book might have been compiled. What purpose is this thick volume meant to serve? How, even, is it meant to be used? Is it to be read straight through? This is nearly impossible. Is it meant to be consulted in the way one does an encyclopedia? Nearly useless. Is it for the connoisseur in American literature? Too boring. The beginner? Highly confusing. The editor, Daniel Hoffman, remarks in his preface that the *Harvard Guide* is "a series of original essays by critics especially interested in the subjects and authors about whom they have chosen to write," and that these essays are intended, in Edwin Muir's phrase, as "a helpful intermediary between literature and the reader." Still, it is difficult to imagine who that reader might be—the mind goes all the way to Italy without quite finding him.

The *Harvard Guide* does fulfill another function, though not one that its compiler and contributors are well aware of. It provides literary history—or, more precisely, a substitute for literary history. Although A. Walton Litz omits mention of it in his survey of literary criticism in the *Harvard Guide,* one of the casualties of criticism in postwar America—and "contemporary" in this volume begins in 1945 and runs through 1978—has been literary history. No Van Wyck Brooks, no Vernon Parrington has emerged or is likely to. Such literary history as has been written must be dug out of biographies and criticism of the kind that Edmund Wilson was perhaps the last American critic to write; it can also be found in surveys of collective authorship such as the *Harvard Guide,* though here, too, one has to dig it out and piece it together, in the fashion of an archeologist.

Having pieced together the literary history of the past thirty-three years in the United States through the essays of the contributors to the *Harvard Guide,* one arrives at one of the most impressive omnium gatherums of literary cliché ever assembled. With but one exception—that of Nathan A. Scott, Jr. in his essay on "Black Literature"—each contributor pumps vigorously away at the old melodeon, as Mencken used to call the grinding out of clichés. In the case of one contributor, Gerald Weales, who writes the essay on "Drama," there was probably no help for it. American drama since 1945 has not been exactly exhilarating. There have been the posthumous plays of Eugene O'Neill; the works of the odd couple, Tennessee Williams and Arthur Miller; the complicated if not very interesting failures of Edward Albee after his early successes; the one-act plays of Sam Shepard; the one-play acts of various passing playwrights—and the rest has been British imports, Neil Simon, and trade-union negotiations. Weales has possibly published at least ten other versions of the essay he has now published once again in the *Harvard Guide*. But what is a theater critic to do? There's been no business in show business.

Along with Scott on "Black Literature" and Weales on "Drama," other contributors to the *Harvard Guide* and their subjects are: Alan Trachtenberg on "The Intellectual Background"; A. Walton Litz on "Literary Criticism"; Leo Braudy on "Realists, Naturalists, and Novelists of Manners"; Lewis P. Simpson on "Southern Fiction"; Mark Shechner on "Jewish Writers"; Josephine Hendin on "Experimental Fiction"; Elizabeth Janeway on "Women's Literature"; and Daniel Hoffman with three essays on poetry, "After Modernism," "Schools of Dissidents," and "Dissidents from Schools." Apart from Mrs. Janeway, all the contributors to the *Harvard Guide* are professors, though none is currently teaching at Harvard. The academy provides not only the dominant tone of the book, which is natural enough, but its organization as well, which is not natural at all. The *Harvard Guide* is organized, that is to say, rather like the curriculum of a university highly sensitive to public relations and worried about a ruckus with a touchy pressure group. By including essays on Jewish writing, black literature, and women's literature, the editor must have thought he was responding nicely to the time-spirit of the day.

The *Harvard Guide*'s categories of organization oddly—and badly—skew the material it sets out to cover. Saul Bellow is treated exclusively as a Jewish writer (and given a paragraph for his plays in the "Drama" essay), and Ralph Ellison exclusively as a black writer. Since each is a writer with serious pretensions to belonging to world literature, what point can be served in boxing them off in academic ghettos, except to diminish them? But the nuttiness of the *Harvard Guide*'s scheme of organization is seen to best advantage in the essay on "Women's Literature," where Mary McCarthy, Susan Sontag, and Lillian Hellman, like Russian female athletes who have failed to pass the hormone test to qualify for the Olympics, are ruled out of discussion for being inadequately feminist in their points of view. Throughout the book there are discussions of writers whose chief interest is that they fall conveniently into one or another category and who, but for this convenience, would scarcely be worth mentioning at all. By sheer allocation of space, Norman Mailer—included in the index under "Jewish writer," "novelist of manners," and also "experimental writer"—would appear to be the dominant figure of the age, and a stranger (our Italian student Alberto, say) might judge him America's most important postwar writer, when in fact he has only been the country's noisiest writer. Meanwhile, a quiet writer of great artistry, William Maxwell, who fits into none of the *Harvard Guide*'s existing categories—perhaps one ought to have been set up entitled "Good Writing"—goes quite without mention.

A *vade mecum* of this particular kind inevitably allows ample room for cavil. One is not used, for example, to see Mickey Spillane discussed with the dead (and deadly) earnestness that he is in Leo Braudy's essay on "Realists, Naturalists, and Novelists of Manners." To have Eleanor Roosevelt's memoirs brought into an essay on "Women's Literature" surely seems a case of scraping the outside of the barrel; and talking about the things that Joyce Carol Oates does better than Dostoyevsky, as Mrs. Janeway does in the same essay, shows evidence of having been hit over the head with the barrel. One wishes there were a plainer way of writing about Southern fiction than the swampy rhetoric, the literary equivalent of Senator Claghorn, that Lewis P. Simpson has had to resort to in his essay, which ends: "About all that can be said with assurance is that since the Southern novel had adhered closely to the novel's origin in modern historicism, the Southern novelist's imagination of the self's condition awaits further revelations of the congruence of self and history."

But these, as I say, are cavils. What cuts deeper is the absence of any serious attempt in the *Harvard Guide* to argue with or test any of the current cultural assumptions under which literary work is carried on in the United States. It is this that makes the book seem such a compendium of clichés—up-to-date clichés, to be sure, but clichés for all that. In his essay, "The Intellectual Background," the historian Alan Trachtenberg warms up the melodeon for much that is to follow. Trachtenberg begins with the standard revisionist version of the cold war and of the period up through the middle 1960s, which he refers to as "this phase of moralistic and anti-intellectual acquiescence." Against the energies of modernism—a word he uses in the loosest possible way —he sees those of "counter-modernism, resistance to the very idea of the modern. . . . It took the form of racism and sexism, resistance to redressing racial injustice and full equality to women. . . ." C. Wright Mills is approvingly quoted as saying that writers, artists, and professors have now become "employees," "dependent salaried workers who spend the most alert hours of their living being told what to do."

Really pounding away at the melodeon now, Trachtenberg misses nary a note: Robert Coles, the Uriah Heep of American left-wing social science, is praised for his " major undertaking in cultural psychoanalysis in the period, *Children of Crisis*"; there is the standard view of Paul Goodman (*Growing Up Absurd* is cited for its "voice of compassionate discontent and its unusual civic responsibility"); Norman O. Brown and Herbert Marcuse are admired as leaders of the "party of eros," though "many commentators have found that [Marcuse's] later thought tends to conflate art and politics and open the door to elitism. . . ." Trachtenberg concludes on a note of grandiloquent hedge: "Whether the imaginative writer will continue to hold his place of authority against the new media and against the cosmic fantasies fulfilled by reality itself remains to be seen." In short, as Adam said to Eve, while passing through the gates of Eden, "We're living in an age of transition."

With a background such as Trachtenberg's, what does the foreground of the *Harvard Guide* provide? Other of its contributors are not so overtly political as Trachtenberg, with the exception of Elizabeth Janeway, who, over the past decade, has gone from a pedestrian book reviewer to a zealous feminist ideologue. Yet, more literary than political though its contributors be, it is extraordinary how easily—and repeatedly—phrases come up describing the United States as "a madness-inducing society," "a disturbed society," "overstructured," a society dominated by "destructiveness, greed, and vulnerability," "a personal tragedy"; and, finally, in the essay on "Experimental Writing," Josephine

Hendin blithely remarks that Thomas Pynchon "indicts the capi-
talistic urge, the multinational corporation, the mega-cartel as
models of America, its allies and enemies, drifting toward cen-
tralized wealth and power."

Sometimes, as in these remarks on Pynchon, the critics are only
describing the views of the authors they are writing about. More
often, though, they seem to share these views. Certainly the critics
in the *Harvard Guide* only rarely engage their author's assumptions in argument. Increasingly over the years critic and author
are at one in their assumption. And this is true not just of literary
critics: in *The Culture of Narcissism*, Christopher Lasch, wishing
to demonstrate that American corporations make automatons,
zombies, prostitutes out of their employees, adduces as proof a
passage from Joseph Heller's novel, *Something Happened*. Like the
fly and the dunghill, left-wing sociology and left-wing fiction feed
upon and replenish each other.

The melodeon is never stifled for long in the pages of the
Harvard Guide, and one of its repeated high-C clichés has to do
with the decade of the 1950s, which, its contributors seem generally to agree, was a dreary decade indeed. Leo Braudy is at one
moment telling us that "The conservatism of the 1950's therefore
goes hand in hand with the great postwar consumer society, the
proliferation of the suburbs, and the expanding number of things
to buy," when Gerald Weales chips in at the next with his remark
that the fifties was "a decade famous for its blandness, its spirit of
conformity." After other comments of a similar kind, it is a bit
dispiriting to have Daniel Hoffman, as late as page 460, refer to
"the postwar period of seeming social and literary conformity."
Well, was it "seeming" conformity or the real thing?

Aside from the circumstance that the United States had a less
than greatly literate president in Dwight D. Eisenhower, the 1950s
was in fact a decade of literary production of an extremely high
quality. Not only were Faulkner, Hemingway, and Dos Passos;
Frost, Stevens, and Eliot; John Crowe Ransom, Marianne
Moore, and Allen Tate still alive and publishing, but Saul Bellow
and Ralph Ellison, Robert Lowell and Randall Jarrell, Elizabeth
Bishop and John Berryman, were coming into their full maturity

as artists; Lionel Trilling and Robert Penn Warren were at the height of their powers, and Edmund Wilson was still a powerful engine of literary creation. *Partisan Review,* potent and serious, had not yet turned into the journal got up in youth drag that it was to become. Literature had a dignity and a standing it has not since regained. And no one among the authors of the *Harvard Guide* seems to have noticed this; at least, none has chosen to mention it.

Literature, as Geoffrey Grigson once remarked, is always in a bad way, like government or politics or mankind. Granting this, one must go on to say that contemporary American literature seems in an even worse way than usual, though one gets almost no sense of this from the *Harvard Guide.* The closest one comes to it is an oblique nod from A. Walton Litz in his essay, "Literary Criticism," where he notes, apropos of the strange intellectual peregrinations of Harold Bloom and the critics who have come to be called deconstructionists, that "we are not confronted with contemporary writers of such overwhelming power that they command the critic's attention." Listen to what Litz is saying— that our writers are not good enough, or at any rate not interesting enough, for our critics. How did this come to be? Wedded to their clichés about the 1950s—Litz: "As the monolithic social and political attitudes of the 1950's gave way to the diversity and conflict of the 1960's, literary criticism also lost its monolithic appearance"—the contributors to the *Harvard Guide* are in no position to understand what has happened.

What has happened, I believe, is that American writers have never received so much attention or been so institutionally well supported—and never has contemporary literature seemed quite so beside the point, so peripheral, so trivial. This is not to say that good literary work isn't being done; it is, in discrete novels, volumes of verse, criticism, and especially in literary biography, which the *Harvard Guide* does not deal with at all. But literature *en bloc* seems to have lost its force, and no longer seems as central to serious culture or to the life of the nation as it once, and not so long ago, did. Since the *Harvard Guide to Contemporary American Writing* does not seem to have detected this, let alone spec-

ulated upon it, perhaps I can be allowed to fill in this ample gap
with a few ruminations of my own.

A good place to begin is by totting up the palpable changes
that have taken place in the conditions and circumstances of serious literary production since World War II. Among the most
obvious has been the enlargement of the freedom allowed novelists, poets, autobiographers, and biographers to write about the
sexual component of life, and in any language they choose. I say
enlargement of freedom but in fact this freedom is now quite
complete. James Jones, Gore Vidal, and Norman Mailer are
among the postwar writers who helped bring this about; but the
great figure here is Henry Miller, who paid the real price of
having his books banned from his own country. Yet greatly con-
venient to writers though it has been, this new freedom does not
seem to have resulted directly in any masterworks or marked any
towering advance in human understanding of the kind that literature at its best makes possible.

The postwar period has marked a change, too, in the relation
between American and European writing. During this time,
American writers ceased to gaze longingly on Europe, with its
older and denser culture, in the manner of Henry James and Edith
Wharton, and after them the writers of the generation of the
1920s. As form follows function, so often does literature seem to
follow political power. America, in literature, was where the action was—or at least seemed to be—and Europe for the first time
in matters literary gazed longingly at us (hence the department of
American literature at the University of Rome). For whatever it
may bode, this situation appears to be coming to an end. Flashier
American literary critics are now looking to France for models
and methods. The shedding of American feelings of literary infe-
riority vis-à-vis Europe appears, too, in the end not to have come
to much.

Far from feeling encouraged by a sense of new national grandeur, literature followed sociology and in the United States took
an ethnic turn. Black writing and Jewish writing were said, during this period, to be entering upon a golden age. We now know
this to have been largely bogus. The "unmeltable ethnics," as

Michael Novak styled the resurgence of ethnic feeling in the United States, melted quickly enough in literature. The essay, "Jewish Writers," by Mark Shechner, after many trite and a few quite false observations—Shechner's first sentence speaks of "a coherent and identifiable Jewish culture and religion [having] effectively ceased to exist"—takes up in detail only five novelists, the old Hart, Schaffner & Marx trio of Bellow, Malamud, and Roth, and adds Isaac Bashevis Singer and Norman Mailer. Shechner's own style has the taste of an older Jewish critical manner gone sour; his prose is a confection, reheated, of Irving Howe and Alfred Kazin, with occasional bebop touches. The Jew, he writes, with a characteristic overdramatized flourish, "has been obliged historically to turn the hyphen in his identity into the cutting edge of a sharp sensibility." Shechner is down on Malamud, high on Roth. But reading his essay one comes to recognize that the Jewish content in much contemporary writing—Singer and perhaps Malamud apart—is not very great. Find, for example, the Jewish element in a Norman Mailer, whom Shechner characterizes in the following terms: "To interpret the whole career as an exercise in consistency, one would have to note that at the bottom of all concerns is the obsession with power, usually at the point of conjunction between sex and politics where policy melts into potency and the arms race abuts the presidential orgasm." Such a sentence makes plain that there has not been all that much Jewish writing, but only a number of Jews, coming from a highly verbal culture, who write.

But contemporary American Jewish writers have not been as wounded by being lumped together as have black writers. The one unfailingly thoughtful and penetrating essay in the *Harvard Guide,* Nathan A. Scott, Jr.'s "Black Literature," offers an account of these wounds. Throughout his essay Scott mentions one after another promising black writer who has fallen silent, and the reason is that these writers are working under a pressure that other contemporary American writers have not had to face. They are caught between the Scylla of what has become white critical apathy and the Charybdis of black agitational militancy, and their craft has taken a terrific banging about. Scott praises the novelist

William Demby's *Beetlecreek* (1950), for example, for "its refusal of the automatisms of racial protest and the cogency of its construction," and of the characters of the novel he remarks that they "are not enlisted in the services of the sort of *roman à thèse* in which Negro writers have tended to make their chief investment."

Those few black novelists and poets who have held out, who have refused to abandon the stringent demands of literary art in favor of the easy anger of propaganda, have been read out by the black critics of the movement known as the Black Aesthetic, and of which a characteristic utterance is that of Harold Cruse: "Criticism of Negro writing is mainly the Negro's responsibility." Apropos of Richard Gilman, a white critic, having gone along with this view, Scott remarks that "it would seem surely that a profound collapse of faith in the indivisibility of the human family and in the unity of culture has everywhere become a notable feature of the period." Scott's essay lists some casualties: James Baldwin, who has pulled away from the reasoned penetration of his work in the 1950s, and who has since become a writer increasingly given over to the passions of hatred and comtempt; and writers such as Melvin Tolson, who have not succumbed to these passions but who have, unfairly according to Scott, never been "considered as something other than merely a special case of ethnic ferment." Scott closes his courageous essay on a note of complaint about the *Harvard Guide* itself: "There is an insurmountable impropriety involved in the discussion of black American writers under a special rubric reserved for them alone. But for the moment, given the carelessness with which the critical community canvasses their work, they must, as it would seem, be so treated, if any assessment of their accomplishment is to be guaranteed at all."

But of course the *Harvard Guide* allows a separate rubric for black literature because that is how it is done in the university. And here we come to one of the chief points about contemporary American writing, which is the increased importance to it of the university. Alan Trachtenberg mentions this, sanguinely and almost in passing, as "a phenomenon that indicates not only a new ground of acceptance for serious literature, a new audience among college students, but also, at an even deeper level, a new recognition of literature as itself a serious and legitimate form of knowledge—a form, that is, of idea as well as emotion; a form of *thinking* about common existence." This, though, isn't the half of it; it isn't even a hundredth part of it.

The principal, the major, the overriding and overwhelming fact about American writing between the end of World War II and the present is its nearly complete absorption by American universities. Even though a few novelists (Norman Mailer, John Updike, and William Styron), a few poets (James Merrill and Richard Howard), and a lone serious critic (Hilton Kramer) have remained outside the university, the preponderance of contemporary American writers now work in universities. More than this, contemporary writing has come to occupy a greater and greater part of the literary curriculum. Where once a young novelist might have learned about life working on a newspaper—as did Stephen Crane, Theodore Dreiser, Ernest Hemingway—he is now more likely to learn about it through a creative-writing program. Where once the world was a poet's workshop, today a poetry workshop is his world. A literary reputation is currently validated and certified above all by a writer's work finding a place in the contemporary curricular canon. For better or worse, the seat of contemporary literature is now the university.

Nor can there be much question that it has been for worse. An index to the health of our literature has long been the novel, and the novel, of all literary forms, seems to have come upon very lean days. Part of the reason for this, surely, is that increasing numbers of novelists and story writers are now university teachers, and thus locked away from their true subject, which is the great and very real world. That their true subject is lost to them, in turn, helps to explain the high production of experimental fiction. The novelists discussed in Josephine Hendin's essay, "Experimental Fiction," are many of them professors. Perhaps this is why their novels are so teachable; the problem is that they are not very readable. But then much of this fiction, it needs to be said, is not really intended for use outside an English department.

"Experimental fiction admittedly leaves out much of the joy

and nobility which exist in the real world," writes Professor Hendin, "but all art involves exclusion; no single work of art tells the whole truth about all experience." But why is this fiction, and so much else that passes for literary study in the university, so unrelievedly bleak in its views? (Not that cheerfulness is wanted, but if a writer is going to be glum, he ought at least to be interesting in his glumness.) The reason is that the professors who write and teach contemporary literature have swallowed the more dolorous views of modernism—in short, the wasteland outlook—and have accepted the normalization of alienation. Sentences encapsulating these views—little laboratory slides of despair—pop out all through the pages of the *Harvard Guide*. Here is one in Leo Braudy's hyper-ventilating style: "History was no longer a pattern of factually and philosophically analyzable causes; it was a nightmare, an allegory of good and evil, a metaphysical comic book." Here is Daniel Hoffman, explicating a bit of poetry and society along with it: "From his [Robert Lowell's] poems on the world about him we can infer that society itself is mad; the suffering poet in a mental hospital looms as a Promethean hero for our sick age." Nuggets of unearned nihilism of this kind are commonplace in the criticism devoted to contemporary writing, and the *Harvard Guide* is strewn with them.

The antinomian strain appears to nestle comfortably with the contemporary literary imagination. As contemporary writers are deemed not good enough for some of our critics, so is their country deemed not good enough for many contemporary writers. E. L. Doctorow, Robert Coover, Joseph Heller are the names of but a few of the better-known contemporary writers who require complete concordance with their politics to read them at all. There is no imaginative inquiry, no literary testing of the grounds of assumption in their works; as their novels open, the case on America is closed. Stendhal, in what has become a famous remark, once said that "Politics in a work of literature is like a pistol shot in the middle of a concert," but many contemporary American novelists and poets are so patently and thoroughly political that reading them is like being at a pistol range hoping to hear a note of music.

Yet another result of the absorption of contemporary literature by the university is the vast overproduction of criticism devoted to contemporary writers. Between the various guides and contemporary-authors series—Twayne, University of Southern Illinois, Minnesota Pamphlets (now Scribner's American Writers Series)—there is scarcely an American writer of any reputation (John Updike, Gore Vidal, Thomas Pynchon) who has not had at least one book-length study devoted to him, even though he might be very much in mid-career. It is all so vastly overdone, so thoroughly out of proportion. Literary journals offer no protection. A recent issue of *Parnassus* carries an article about the poet Adrienne Rich that is so idolatrous as to be unseemly applied to anyone still alive. *Salmagundi,* a journal that has published some good things over the years, recently ran an essay running to forty-two pages entitled " 'Shipwreck, Autochthony, and Nostos': An Approach to the Poetry of John Peck." Happening upon it, I wondered if this essay might be a parody—it begins with a quotation from Peck's doctoral thesis, and we later learn that he was born in Pittsburgh in 1941—but I have to report that it is not. Forty-two pages in a serious journal about a not very well-known poet who is not yet forty. Why? Reading much criticism of contemporary American writers one is reminded of the late Benjamin Sonnenberg's description of his work as a public-relations man: "I make very large pedestals for very small statues."

But even when the statues have rather more amplitude, the pedestals of contemporary American criticism have become extremely boring through reiteration. This is especially evident in the *Harvard Guide.* Simpson on Faulkner, Braudy on Dos Passos, Shechner on Bellow, Hendin on Nabokov, Hoffman on Stevens —one feels one has read all this before. And this is because, apart from a turn of phrase here or a twist of judgment there, one has. It has all been said before—over and over again.

Still the *Harvard Guide to Contemporary American Writing* does have one serious advantage, and this is that it causes one to think about the sweep of our literature over the past three decades. Despite the diversity of writing detailed in the *Harvard Guide,* despite the variety of talents at work among our writers, despite the enthusiasm of its contributors, one comes away feeling that contemporary American writing, taken as a corpus, is a good deal less than first-rate—that, in fact, we are currently in the midst of a distinctly second-rate literary era. By what measure can one determine this? I would invoke two measures. First, the presence of great writers. Second, the contribution that literature seems to be making to the life of the nation. On neither of these measures does contemporary American writing score high.

One might argue that the first measure, great writers, cannot be known—that this is a judgment available only to posterity. But one can have more than an inkling. Gravity is the quality that confers greatness in literature, even on comic literature; gravity has to do with spirituality, with high and undeflected seriousness, with recognition that literature provides the best record of the common humanity of all. It is immediately notable. Many contemporary Russian writers—Solzhenitsyn, Andrei Sinyavsky, Vladimir Voinovich—have it. So do V. S. Naipaul and Marguerite Yourcenar. But it is in very short supply in the United States just now.

As for the second measure, the contribution that contemporary literature seems to be making to the life of the nation, this, in the United States today, seems sadly negligible. Never have writers seemed so much to be writing for themselves. The old literary man's gambit here was to complain that readers are not sufficiently advanced, too philistine, not quite good enough. But there is a potentially ample public for serious literature in the United States; and one of the interesting phenomena of the postwar years has been the change in the fortunes of certain writers, once contributors to *Commentary* and *Partisan Review,* from small-public to large-public writers. (The watershed year was perhaps 1964, when Saul Bellow's *Herzog* and Mary McCarthy's *The Group* became best sellers.) But, increasingly, contemporary writers have cut themselves off from the lay public and have grown isolated and insulated. Critics have joined them rather than attempted to argue them back.

"In any period," F. R. Leavis once noted, "it is upon a very small minority that the discerning appreciation of art and literature depends." That small minority is in a condition of dishevelment today. Even though many writers have become celebrities and support for writing has never been so generous or the attention accorded it greater, American writing itself has never seemed less important, and more lost, than it does now. And it will take more than a *Harvard Guide* to help it find its way back.

Commentary 1980

It's Only Culture

F OR ALL THAT so many people extol the period in American life known with chronological inexactitude as the sixties, looking back upon it fondly as a time of unrivaled freedom and creative disorder—"Bliss was it in that dawn to be alive/ But to be young was very Heaven!"—I have never heard anyone of any seriousness extol its cultural achievements. There was the musical *Hair,* there were the Beatles, there was Pop Art, there were five or six notable movies, but of the creation of high art there was precious little. The *New York Review of Books* may have displayed on one of its covers a diagram of a Molotov cocktail, yet with the period's various cultural bombs not even that journal would have much to do.

It is puzzling, and the puzzle is compounded when one considers that the fifties, for all their advertised conformity, now appear a time of considerable achievement in the arts. There was Abstract Expressionism and the formation of the so-called New York School, there were a number of extremely impressive novels and an efflorescence of Jewish and other ethnic fiction, there were several splendid books of poetry, and there was a serious body of criticism. Putative freedom issuing in third- and fourth-rate art, putative conformity issuing in much first-rate art—are we in the presence of a paradox here? How does one account for this?

At least a partial answer might be found in the relationship between art and criticism in the two periods. To be sure, this relationship is one of immense complexity at all times. But of this complex relationship one thing can be said with a fair amount of confidence, and it is that art is primary. It is primary not only in the sense that art comes before criticism but primary also in the sense that art supplies the materials with which criticism has to work. So it is and so it has always been. Aristotle could not have written the *Poetics* without the art of Homer and the classical Greek dramatists to draw upon as models from which to formulate his critical theories. Criticism needs art more than art needs criticism, yet the two can exist and sometimes have existed in a roughly symbiotic relationship, each taking sustenance from the other. Criticism is propelled into thought by art, and art is reminded by criticism of what its true traditions, functions, and qualities ought to be. When criticism is doing its proper tutelary and evaluative job, art is in the position, to adopt a sports metaphor, of a confident and well-coached team.

Instead of performing the function of a coach, over the past fifteen or twenty years criticism has become a cheerleader. Jumping up and down, screaming on the sidelines, displaying its knobby knees and occasionally revealing itself to be wearing no pants under its short skirt, it has not only lost all semblance of control over the game but has become an off-the-field exhibition of its own. Meanwhile, out on the field, players shuffle in and out, every man for himself, each running his own eccentric patterns, while confusion reigns and the game all but falls apart. Such is the condition of art, specifically literary art, in our day.

How did the critics become cheerleaders? Who issued their short skirts? Who told them to expose themselves so boldly? These are questions one cannot help pondering while reading an odd but interesting new work of cultural criticism entitled *Panic Among the Philistines* by Bryan F. Griffin. Griffin feels that the times are hideously out of joint. In his view, the wrong artists have been praised in the wrong terms by the wrong critics; contemporary culture, insofar as it involves the meeting of art with criticism, he sees as an almost unprecedented case of worse coming to worst.

Panic Among the Philistines touches upon the movies, visual art, drama, and rock music, but its main emphasis is on literature. A couple of years ago Griffin published two articles in *Harper's* in which he smashed away at the number of literary reputations of the day, among them those of such novelists as John Updike, John Cheever, John Irving, Joyce Carol Oates, William Styron, and John Barth. This time out Griffin concentrates his fire on the critics and reviewers responsible for the inflated reputations of our day and for the low state of our culture generally. *Panic Among the Philistines* by and large scants the question of how the rot set in and dwells instead—interminably, it sometimes feels—on the rot itself.

Griffin has combed the cultural criticism published in the newsmagazines and the large metropolitan dailies, with an occasional side trip over to the *New Yorker* and the *New York Review of Books*. Through the relentless use of quotation, he has put together an anthology of wretched criticism that rivals *The Stuffed Owl*, D. B. Wyndham Lewis's anthology of bad verse. The philistines of Griffin's title are the critics—they are chiefly reviewers and journalists —who, even though culture is their bailiwick, are themselves really without culture, or who, if they ever had it, have forgotten what culture is supposed to be about. The panic of these philistines, according to Griffin, set in "at the time of the great crash of 1980," by which point "most knew that it was all over, but nobody wanted to say it, because nobody could afford to say it: there were long careers and swollen reputations at stake, and more than a few long books as well."

Panic Among the Philistines is an almost unrelieved chronicle of wretched cultural excesses. No one can accuse its author of not having done his homework, and there is a certain amount of satisfaction in watching him catch out the various Jack Krolls, Doris Grumbachs, John Leonards, and Walter Clemonses—reviewers and critics of middle and lower cultural echelons—in one after another ludicrous piece of empty cultural chitchat. There has been no want of such people, who in recent years have regularly pronounced the stupid to be significant and the loathsome to be amusing. Much of what they have written in newspapers and newsmagazines has since found its best use in wrapping fish, but there was something decidedly fishy about it even when it was still in the typewriter. It is useful to have it held up to ridicule now, to demonstrate how very badly it smells.

To give a sample of Bryan Griffin's *modus operandi:* he mentions, in connection with the publication of D. M. Thomas's novel *The White Hotel,* that Doris Grumbach "summed up all the fun with her increasingly tiresome trademark: 'What a splendid book!' " Then, in characteristic style, Griffin continues:

But the waters had grown higher and wilder, and it had become difficult to distinguish Ms. Grumbach's cries from those of the terrified competition. "I have not been so thoroughly enveloped by a book since reading *Garp,*" cried Laurie Stone of the *Village Voice,* trying to jump from one envelop to another without getting her thoughts wet in the process. She was having an awkward time of it, partly because Diane Johnson of *New West* was already hanging on to Mr. Thomas's Epic for dear life, just daring anyone to challenge her possessive ecstasy: "A great book . . . with Freud and the Holocaust and the erotic dreamings of a young woman," sang Ms. Johnson girlishly, keeping her head just above water: "a celebration of human consciousness and of the unconscious." "Very likely the best book to appear in 1981," snorted Ensign [Peter] Prescott of *Newsweek;* "Heartstunning," gasped [Christopher] Lehmann-Haupt of the *Times;* "I had found the book that would explain us to ourselves," sobbed Mr. Lehmann-Haupt's colleague [*sic*], Leslie Epstein, perhaps saying just a bit more than he'd intended to say. "Passionate, lyrical excess," panted young James Wolcott of *Esquire,* his little literary thighs pumping furiously as he tried (uncharacteristically) to keep up with the swim team. "A novel of erotic invention," thundered *New York* magazine, which had begun to take on water at an alarming rate. "Brutally explicit," promised the Book-of-the-Month Club. "Towers over virtually every other English-language work of fiction in the last two years," gasped *Publishers Weekly* weakly, and then everybody went under for the first time. They bobbed back up again, but they were beginning to look pretty soggy.

Ridicule, then, is Griffin's main weapon in *Panic Among the Philistines*. While on the one hand one feels that many of the people he ridicules richly deserve it, on the other hand one feels that ridicule does not truly get the job done. Bryan Griffin's style is a compound of two Toms: he writes with something of the knowingness about contemporary life of Tom Wolfe and the tendency to tirade of Thomas Carlyle. I use the word tirade with precision, for *Panic Among the Philistines* is a protracted composition marked by intemperate, vituperative, and highly censorious language. It has been said that civilization began when man first hurled an epithet instead of a spear, yet however bracing it may have been for Bryan Griffin to write the words, one wonders about the advisability of referring to John Irving as "schlock novelist John ('*Garp*') Irving." There are times, after all, when it is necessary to call a spade an implement extremely useful for digging.

It is a shame, really, for Bryan Griffin makes many a good point along his rather labored way. In a chapter entitled "The Important Subject," for instance, he takes out after reveiwers and journalists who on every occasion drag sex into print, seeing the way to good psychic health where mainly only prurience lies. Griffin argues that this crowd of cultural commentators have been a vacuous lot—with "no real beliefs, no standards, no purpose"— who have often used sex to fill their vacuum. The chapter begins with a quotation from Gay Talese: "Sex is so very important; it is probably the most important thing. What is more important? I know of nothing." Earlier Griffin quotes Pauline Kael, whose critical appetite for sex and violence the editors of the *New Yorker* seem not to have noticed, and of whom he writes:

It wasn't long before Ms. Kael's bizarre theories of violence began to get all wound up with her thoughts about Lust In The Back Row, and the results were just a tad embarrassing:

"Squeamishness—surely with terror and prurient churnings under it?—is the basis of this good taste," she sneered, just daring anyone to accuse her of prurient squeamishness. Nobody knew quite what she had in mind, but the ragged troops gave her one last weary cheer for having aligned herself four-square against Delicacy, Discrimination, Breeding, and Good Taste, the Four Horsemen of the Cultural Apocalypse.

That is tonally overwrought, but not far off the mark. The reviewers and journalists Bryan Griffin writes about in *Panic Among the Philistines* have been, as a group, singularly fearful of getting caught in public with their trousers up.

Griffin is very amusing on the language of the reviewers and critics who are the subject of his book. This is the language that I have come to think of as *blurbissimo*—sentences and phrases in reviews and columns that can be lifted and used for purposes of advertising. In *blurbissimo,* books and other cultural artifacts are always "important," "exceptionally important," "myth-shattering," "major," and "quite simply the most important, myth-shattering book by a major writer." In this language the dreariest of novels becomes "life-affirming" or "life-enhancing," and an album by a rock singer becomes "a major work by a major artist." In his book *Hype,* Steven M. L. Aronson notes that "hype differs from advertising—which it employs, along with public relations, as accomplices—in that it is not directly paid for." The hype of our reviewers, according to Bryan Griffin, conduces to convince us that, culturally, we live in a Golden Age, when in fact what surrounds us are zinc and lead.

If in American cultural life the worst has risen to the top, Bryan Griffin blames this, in part, on the rise of democracy and mass education, "with the mediocre crowding out the excellent, simply because there were more of the former than the latter." He writes:

By 1980, there were at least two artists in every garage and a philosopher in every pot. The museum basements were clogged with interchangeable 20th-century masterworks, the

library floors were piled high with last week's dazzling erotic
epics, the theaters were thick with thousands of rudderless
critics, the airwaves were cacophonous with the meaningless
gobbles of cut-out intellectuals and apprentice pundits; and
still the stuff came spewing out.

Most of the producers and the critics of culture, in his view, are
in some fundamental sense spiritually deficient people. "So we
are talking, in the final analysis, about losers," who "were losers
because they had lost themselves."

And why did these losers wish to exert so powerful an influence
on their culture? Griffin believes he knows:

> For the obvious reason: they were envious of whole-souled
> men and women, and jealous of the human spirit. Because
> they were bewildered by the deepest human emotions and
> aspirations—because they had no conception of what it was
> that men and women had been talking about and playing at
> for all those centuries—they *had* to remake the society if
> their own lives were to have any meaning. It is a natural
> human instinct to try to appease one's confusions by pre-
> tending that they are not confusions at all, but virtues. Peo-
> ple who cannot share in the common human spirit resent
> that spirit when they see it in others, and seek to destroy it,
> that they may feel whole themselves.

Bryan Griffin, it ought by now to be quite clear, is a moralist,
which to my mind is not a bad thing to be. But moralism does
have its limits, and these show up not always to good effect in
Panic Among the Philistines. As a moralist, he leans rather heavily
on the determinacy of character in human events. As he blames
the rise of the reviewers he contemns largely on their bad character, so does he say, toward the close of his book, that "we can't
have good art until we have good men." While there have been
good artists who have been good men, this nonetheless seems to
me a highly dubious statement. Tolstoy yearned to be a good
man—but was he? Was James Joyce a good man? Was Proust?

Kakfa? Thomas Mann? If we have to wait for good men before we have good art, I think we are safe in making plans for at least the next few weekends.

While moralism is a useful means of judging the middle- and lower-echelon reviewers and cultural journalists—for it does seem apparent that people of good character could not have written the things they have written—it does not account adequately for how they were able to rise to their positions of power over the culture. On this question Bryan Griffin is not much help, and in this respect *Panic Among the Philistines* resembles a chronicle of the bubonic plague that deals chiefly with the rats who carried it. One wants to know how these rats got past the city walls. What caused sanitary conditions to break down? Where were the city fathers? And how can future waves of plague be prevented?

In attempting to find the answers to these rather complex questions, I would begin with the rise of interest in culture generally, which was itself a result of the increase in enrollments in American universities. Sometime in the late fifties and early sixties greater numbers of people became more interested in the arts. The nature of this interest was a far from simple matter. It was hedged about with insecurity; it was associated with social status. But for all that, it was quite real. Culture became harder and harder to ignore; not to have seen the hot movie, not to have read the current best seller, not to have the obligatory opinion on the fashionable painters became a more and more difficult position for the college-educated and upwardly mobile to sustain. Confidence in the old comfortable philistinism was shot as businessmen began to be dragged off by their wives to see Beckett plays and young couples decorated their apartments with Chagall prints and posters. Culture for the millions was no longer a prophecy but a fact.

Newspapers and popular periodicals were not ahead of the populace here. With the exception only of theater critics, and perhaps in some cities of music critics, to write about culture for a newspaper was not a favored and was probably a dead-end job. Most movie critics were gentle flacks who in exchange for a few free junkets to the West Coast applauded in print Hollywood's latest creations. Outside New York, art critics were unknown except perhaps to local artists and museum directors. In Chicago, where the *Tribune* had a book section, books tended to be reviewed by English teachers at Notre Dame and Indiana. At *Time* and *Newsweek* both, the culture sections were known intramurally as "the back of the book," a phrase that at least in those precincts was heavily redolent of "the back of the bus."

But culture as a subject quite quickly got to the front of the bus. Sometimes, indeed, it has seemed to be driving the bus, or at any rate to hold substantial shares in the company. A few years ago one could scarcely go out among the educated classes without having seen the movie of the month and knowing, in addition, what Kael said and Simon said and Sarris said. Museum attendance is up enormously, and for special exhibits like the Vatican show one's tickets specify a time within a half-hour when one will be permitted entrance. Any list of the ten best-known people in Chicago would have to include the city's two movie critics. Money has lent an additional touch of glamour, for culture has become a high-stakes game, with millions floating around the table, and a writer can become a multimillionaire quicker than you can say four-book contract. E. M. Forster once envisioned a society in which everyone would be an aristocrat; if he were alive today he might have to change aristocrat to artist. Art in any case enjoys a prestige no longer quite available to aristocracy. For nearly two decades now art has been revered, "in," extremely fashionable.

The principles of fashion may in fact explain contemporary culture better than any other. It is by now a commonplace that ideas, like clothes and hairdos, are subject to fashion. And the two chief ideas that have come into fashion over the past twenty or so years—roughly the same period as the rise of Bryan Griffin's reviewers and journalists—have been sexual freedom and the loose bag of notions known as cultural liberalism, which include a wide tolerance for change mixed with a contempt for tradition and for the middle classes (from which, of course, most liberals come). There is a point of confluence between the spirit of liberalism and the spirit of fashion, and Kennedy Fraser, the *New*

Yorker's writer on fashion, though liberalism is not here her subject, makes my point when she writes: "Fashion is in ceaseless
pursuit of things that are about to look familiar and in uneasy
flight from things that have just become a bore. Pretending, fren-
ziedly, to market enthusiasm for novelty, in fact it sells disgust
for previous modes."

The fashionable mind is nothing if not neophiliac, or avid for
the new. It seeks not merely to go with the flow but to be out in
front of it, though not *too* far in front. As René König, in *The
Restless Image,* a most interesting study of the phenomenon of
fashion, puts it, the fashion snob "must always be ahead of his
time—as a matter of principle." Of clear distinctions, of questions
of good and bad, of how things really are, the fashionable mind
could hardly care less. It never asks of itself, what do I truly think,
what do I really believe, but instead, what ought I to think, what
can I get away with appearing to believe? Bryan Griffin is correct
when he says that the reviewers and journalists who are the subject of his book believe in nothing. They may think they have
politics, they may think they have opinions, but these, finally, are
a good deal less important to them than the dread prospect of
being out of harmony with their times. To quote René König
again: "The feeling of being in harmony gives a man a measure
of security religion can never give him."

Fashion has always been with us, but it only flourishes, indeed
sometimes dominates, in times and conditions of insecurity and
considerable status anxiety. The past two decades, with their great
change, their social turmoil, have been such a time; and the meeting of the college-educated middle classes with culture and intellectual things creates such a condition. If one habitually thinks of
fashion in connection with clothes, perhaps it is well to recall that
ideas and opinions about culture tend to be the clothing of the
intellectual life. The middle classes, who have now come to take
them up, have been rather in the position of the nouveaux riches
in their nervousness about getting things straight. Once culture
became so thoroughly subject to fashion, the function of the
reviewers and journalists of the popular press became to inform
them, in the realm of culture, what to wear and how to wear it.

One cannot help noticing that the reviewers and journalists in *Panic Among the Philistines* share many likenesses with the fashion press. (In Paris even the Communist press sends reporters to cover the shows of the leading couturiers.) Like the fashion press, these reviewers and journalists are, in effect, with the show. They are part, and an important part, of the mechanics of promotion. The idea of independence among them has neither been encouraged nor found to be enticing. As the fashion reporter is unlikely to pan the new show of a famous couturier, so is the modern reviewer unlikely to pan the latest product of the major novelist. After all, if he does so too often, he will not be invited back, he will lose his place as part of the show, he will henceforth no longer be an insider. Yet the relation between reviewer and famous novelist, like that between fashion reporter and famous couturier, is not necessarily cynical. As René König says: "Fashion not only makes the ordinary man giddy, it ultimately affects even the behavior of the critic and makes him its follower against his will."

Observers of fashion talk about "signal periods" and "trend setters." A signal period is the point that marks a new notion in fashion whose time has come; and a trend setter is someone who gives off the signal. I can think of no figure of our day to whose rise such terms better contribute understanding than Susan Sontag. What is of interest here, though, is how quickly the reviewers and journalists of the popular press pick up the signal, and consequently how drastically reduced is the time required for a new fashion in culture to take hold. Miss Sontag, for example, writes an essay on Camp in *Partisan Review,* and shortly thereafter Camp is discussed in *Time* and *Newsweek,* and not long after that on college campuses and in suburban homes. Of course, Miss Sontag has actually read Oscar Wilde and the other writers from whom she derived her notion of Camp, while the reviewers from *Time* and *Newsweek* have only read Susan Sontag, while the assistant professor or the suburban housewife has only read Jack Kroll of *Newsweek* or Frank Trippett of *Time.* Thus does a cultural notion diminish in substance as it heads toward bottom. Thus, too, does culture itself become thin and jittery.

It is the job of the reviewers and journalists on the cultural front to keep things jittery, which means to keep culture moving along at double time: to discover and popularize fresh notions regularly, to come up with new important writers, to give the impression that we are living in an exciting time for culture. As they say about executioners and garbage collectors and other unpleasant jobs, somebody has got to do it. Yet who gave them their jobs? Publishers and editors did. As H. L. Mencken years ago pointed out, publishers and editors chiefly acquire their ideas about the world from their own newspapers and magazines. Somewhere along the line, they decided—at the *New York Times,* at the *Washington Post,* at *Time,* at *Newsweek,* and elsewhere— that this was the going thing and that they would, well, go along with it.

Still, one wonders what a dignified woman such as Katharine Graham thinks when, as publisher of *Newsweek,* she reads the drama critic she employs complaining about the inadequacy of the lighting during a play featuring frontal nudity? Or what a serious man such as A. M. Rosenthal, executive editor of the *New York Times,* felt when, morning after morning, he arose to read in his own newspaper the incomprehensible gabble of his chief cultural correspondent, John Leonard. Only two possibilities occur to me, neither of them very complimentary. First: "I guess it sells." And second: "Oh, well, it's only culture."

It is only culture, yet culture, now that it is partaken of by millions, is becoming of even greater social significance. As such it affects not only social change but change in the attitudes and behavior of masses of people. (I shall spare readers my sermonette on the intrinsic worth of culture, though here is probably where it ought to come in.) No one can hope to direct culture, yet there is—or at least among intellectuals there used to be—an obligation to knock down everything in the realm of culture that is rubbishy and pretends to be otherwise. Today, however, the reviewers and journalists keep putting it all back up, making Sisyphus's job, in comparison with that of the serious critic of culture, seem like a sinecure.

Where, while all this has been going on, have been the guardians of culture, the critics and professors who are supposed to know what culture is and why it is important? A few have kept vigilant, repeatedly batting back all that is phony and trivial in the new culture. Some have simply ignored it. But many have gotten on the *Zeitgeist* express and have ridden with it. The new culture has infiltrated the universities, which for the most part have not chosen to argue with the set of assumptions currently available and so have allowed poorly taught courses in popular culture, second- and third-rate writers in residence, and a generally cheapened curriculum to pass undisturbed through their gates.

From the standpoint of the reviewers and journalists, of course, things do not look this way at all. On the contrary. They see themselves as brave voices singing out for advanced thought and exciting cultural innovation during the dark night of the Reagan administration and the Moral Majority. According to Griffin, their real panic comes from their awareness that their day is all but over. I quote him, while advising the reader to take 15 percent off for overstatement:

> By 1980, even the most persistent apologists for the old regime—the philosophical beneficiaries of the former establishment, the third-generation imitators and the elderly camp followers—had begun to understand that the long party was finally over, and that the giddy era of aberrant art and thought was about to be kicked aside as nothing more than that: one more aberration in the affairs of men, one more futile deviation from the human aim, one more wasted chance, one more century—a crucial one, this time—frittered away by half-souled harlequins disguised as full-hearted heirs of Athens. In its eleventh hour, Western culture had been led up the garden path, and abandoned in the brambles, one more time.

It would be nice to report that the demise of the reviewers and journalists of the popular press is at hand, but this seems doubtful. As the rock disc jockeys say, the beat goes on. One can still pick up the same magazines and newspapers and find the same cheerleading reviewers and journalists feigning the old phony excitement and continuing to treat unserious things with great seriousness. These reviewers and journalists are themselves peculiarly the product of the disruptions of the sixties, the interest earned on the capital from that nihilistic period in American life off which many people will no doubt continue to live through this decade. Seen from the perspective of today, the sixties were like a tidal wave that swept over America. The wave has begun to roll back, but in its wake the shore is revealed to be littered with broken glass, burned-out fires, dead animals, and all kinds of garbage. A lengthy period will be required before the beach is cleaned up and put back into use.

Commentary 1983

TWO | PORTRAITS OF NOVELISTS

Robert Stone:
American Nightmares

"THERE MUST in art, as in medicine and fashion," wrote Proust, "be new names." Robert Stone, the novelist, is such a new name. Not that Stone is quite so new as all that: he published *A Hall of Mirrors,* the first of his three novels, in the middle 1960s. But Stone's is a new name in the Proustian sense—in the sense that his reputation is in the ascendant. When lists of leading American novelists are brought out, he will henceforth be on them.

Who composes these lists? Nothing so interesting as a conspiracy exists. Certain telltale signs of elevation, though, do appear. Respectful reviews crop up in respectable places. Interviews are printed in which the coming man speaks of his work habits, then, portentously, of the contemporary condition. Blurb-masters sharpen their pencils. "Stone writes like a bird, like an angel, like a circus barker, like a con man, like someone so high on pot that he is scraping his shoes on stars," says Wallace Stegner, with the hollow exaltation that only one practiced in the blurby craft can command. Then there is the public changing of the guard: how ludicrous, notes the critic Richard Poirier in the *Chronicle of Higher Education,* to regard Mailer, Bellow, Styron, Roth, and Updike as our leading novelists, "given the presence of writers more powerful than all of them—except possibly Mailer—such as Thomas Pynchon and Robert Stone."

There is no shortage of reasons why the guard must change, why there must be new names. One is that the older guard is no longer felt to be good enough or interesting enough; what once seemed bright ideas soon come to seem rather haggard obsessions. Another reason is that the world hungers for new novelists out of as great an interest in novelty as in novels. *Time* and *Newsweek* do roughly two literary covers annually; the *New York Times* does four or five profiles of living writers, and they have already gone as far down as Joseph Heller, Joyce Carol Oates, John Irving. Fresh faces must be found.

Being photogenic is not the first consideration. Being a member of the right club can be, though, and sometimes this club is called Feminist, sometimes Jewish, sometimes Black. Novelists, like ethnic restaurants, can come to renown for the delicacies their works promise. Politics is frequently a consideration, as when a writer speaks to the issues, problems, questions of the moment in a way that critics and readers wish to hear them spoken of. And sometimes, finally, a novelist is brought forth for that oddest of all reasons—because he is very good at writing novels.

With *A Flag for Sunrise,* his most recent novel, there is no doubt that Robert Stone has arrived. But where, in this rather elaborate scheme, does he fall? By his own account, Robert Stone was born into a working-class family, of Scottish Presbyterian and Irish Catholic parents. He is a high-school dropout, a man who writes quite as much out of actual as out of bookish experience. Stone has been in the navy and in the Merchant Marine; he has put in his days among Ken Kesey, Neal Cassady, and other of the founding fathers of the drug culture and counterculture; later, as a civilian, he went to Vietnam on a journalist's visa. He knows wide stretches of America: the South, California, New York. He has lived abroad. Writing his novels, as it would seem, out of direct observation and instinct, Stone comports well with the old-fashioned idea of the novelist as primarily a man of wide experience. With his wispy hair, fullish beard, bulbous nose, he is even beginning a little to resemble Tolstoy.

It was Tolstoy who once said that sad people who do not know what they want in life should not write novels. Sad Stone is. No novelist today writes novels so unrelievedly bleak. Although there are flashes of wit in Stone's novels, each is in its own special way a dark book, the product of a dark imagination. Murder, madness, mayhem are the closing notes of his novels. Death when it comes is violent; torture is frequent; women, to put it gently, do not fare well. When one concludes a Robert Stone novel one knows one has been on a rough ride. One knows, too, that one has been reading a novelist of the highest ambition. In each of his three novels Stone has attempted a major statement: about the way we live, about America, about Man with a capital M.

One of the things people have always asked of novelists is that they know something the rest of us do not. By this I mean not only secrets of the heart, but information in a more specific sense. Be his book about a vicarage or a battleship, the novelist ought to know a setting, a kind of person, a corner of experience that comes as news to the rest of us. This news Stone supplies. His novels have to do with life in the netherworld—not the criminal underworld, though he touches on that too—the world of spiritually and sometimes physically broken human beings. "I got lost," says one of the characters in *A Hall of Mirrors,* and this might be said of almost every character in Stone's novels, from his sad Southern girls living on their wits to his washout priests to his pill-crazed sailors. Life has placed these characters *in extremis;* they live on the margin, friendless and miserable, out on the edge where life is dangerous and where one works without a net.

The world in which Stone's characters live out their days is utterly without tenderness of any kind. "If somebody ever tells you, Geraldine, that they need you," one character in *A Hall of Mirrors* says to another, "you tell them to buy a dog." Along with the high intake of pills and booze—in one way or another the majority of Stone's characters are hooked on one thing or another—the level of violence in this world is very high, and terror and fear are everywhere. A sailor hunting on speed blows his favorite hunting dogs apart with a shotgun; a young woman has her face pried open by an oyster knife; a girl's body shows up in a freezer; a madman is off on a child-killing spree; a nun is tortured and finally killed by a policeman using an electric cattle prod. Whether his scene be Central America or New Orleans, Vietnam or Los

Angeles. Stone makes of violence an elemental part of life, omnipresent and unavoidable.

None of this would be of great interest if Stone did not write so well about it. His prose has what Marianne Moore once called fiber: it is strong and flexible. He does landscapes and cityscapes with great artistry. He has keen ventriloquial qualities, and can speak out of the mouths and minds of a vast range of characters, from the lowly damaged to the highly cultivated. He has the novelist's gift of sympathetic imagination, especially for the down and out—something rather rare today among American novelists, so many of whom reserve their sympathy for those characters in their novels who are so clearly themselves. And he can persuasively describe the world for us as it is seen through a drug-induced perspective, as in this passage from his second novel, *Dog Soldiers:*

> Hicks drove on speed. His fatigue hung the desert grass with hallucinatory blossoms, filled ravines with luminous coral and phantoms. The land was flat and the roads dead straight; at night, headlights swung for hours in space, steady as a landfall—and then rushed past in streaks of color, explosions of engine roar and hot wind. Every passing truck left in its screaming wake the specter of a desert head-on—mammoth tires spinning in the air, dead truck drivers burning in ditches until dawn.

Taken collectively, Stone's novels show a clear line of development while working and reworking certain set patterns. In each of his three novels there is a character who survives, but whose survival marks him as a failure, for in these novels the brave are plowed under and only the uncourageous survive. All three novels have characters who can be described as hungry for justice, an appetite that Stone's survivors initially view with the greatest skepticism, not to say cynicism. In all three novels, too, the female characters are made to pay a frightful price for their entanglement in politics, crime, revolution. The narrative shape of Stone's novels is also similar from book to book: there is a rather careful setting up of scene and moral climate; a decision is made that triggers off a great rush of action; everyone is brought onto the page for a finale of devastation and death; and then each novel in its turn closes on an ironically bitter coda.

I have not yet said what Robert Stone's novels are about. *A Hall of Mirrors* (1967) is set in New Orleans against a background of racial tumult. *Dog Soldiers* (1975) is set briefly in Saigon, more lengthily in California, and it has to do with drugs and the *bizarreries* of the counterculture. *A Flag for Sunrise* (1981) is set in an imaginary Central American country, the scene of revolution and counterrevolution. The South in the sixties, Saigon and California in the early seventies, the Third World today—over his career as a novelist Stone has had a sharp sense of where the action is. And that action for him is inevitably political.

In his first novel Stone set out what has remained his subject. At a redneck rally in New Orleans, Rheinhardt, the book's hero (or anti-hero, as such characters were called then), who earns his living working for a right-wing radio station, announces what will be the theme of all Robert Stone's books:

> "The American Way is innocence," Rheinhardt announced. "In all situations we must and shall display an innocence so vast and awesome that the entire world will be reduced by it. American innocence shall rise in mighty clouds of vapor to the scent of heaven and confound the nations!"

When he makes this statement Rheinhardt's brain is floating in booze, mists of marijuana cloud his mind, but there is no question that he here speaks for his creator. This passage is an essential one in Robert Stone's work; from it much else follows.

The theme of innocence is announced in the very title of Stone's newest novel. "Everybody's after a new morning," Stone has said about it. "What do we have to run up and salute tomorrow. That is the meaning of the title." For its greater part the book is set in a Central American country called Tecan—"representative," Stone has said in an interview, "of all those places in the world, particularly in Latin America, that are beset by the

American presence and that are ill-governed." It is a country run by police bullies, ruled by a slightly mad dictator, and in thrall to North American interests. There is talk of turning the coastal part of Tecan into a resort paradise, which will bring many a jackpot to selected individuals, and nothing at all to the poor, which is to say nearly the entire population. It is a country lush with vegetation and ripe for revolution. It is one of those places, as a character in the novel describes them, "far from God, a few hours from Miami."

The organization of *A Flag for Sunrise* is episodic. The story is told through the thoughts of its four major characters: a priest named Father Egan, who runs a mission in the backwaters of itself backwater Tecan; Sister Justin, his assistant, a young American nun whose beauty is exceeded only by her moral earnestness; Frank Holliwell, an anthropologist who has helped the CIA in Vietnam, who is lecturing in the neighboring country of Compostela, and who is one of Stone's world-weary skeptics; and Pablo Tabor, a half-breed American, a Coast Guard deserter who spends his life high on pills and bristling with paranoia. A wide supporting cast includes CIA operatives, Third World priests, sadistic policemen, cold-blooded revolutionaries, gunrunners, and a Jewish fence of international reputation. The action of the book tends toward revolution. As generally happens in episodically told novels, through the labyrinth of cause and effect events inevitably draw the major characters together at the close. The novel has an element of the thriller to it, but thrills alone are not what Stone is after.

Terror arrives at the outset. In the novel's first episode Father Egan is scribbling away at a book that has been years in the writing—a book the Church is certain to reject but which is needed, he thinks, by "the masses so hungry for comfort in a violently dying world"—when he is interrupted by Lieutenant Campos, of the Guardia Nacional, who has come to fetch him. The lieutenant wishes to make a confession: he has murdered a young girl, an American hippie, whose body he has preserved in the freezer in his residence. He also wants Father Egan to dispose of the body for him, and with appropriate Church ritual. " 'I am not an animal,' Campos said. 'I believe there is a spiritual force. I believe in life after death.' " Campos is drunk at the time, but drunk or sober Father Egan knows himself to be up against a force brutal, barbarous, perverse. He is quite rightly terrified. Oughtn't he to report the murder to the authorities? But in Tecan Lieutenant Campos is the authorities.

This murder is not at the center of the novel, but it is meant to be illustrative of the sort of thing that goes on in Tecan, where people in power get away with murder. Scarcely is it any wonder that Frank Holliwell, when asked by the CIA to slip into Tecan to inquire about the activities of Father Egan and his assistant Sister Justin at the behest of the Tecan government, which suspects them of subversive activities—scarcely is it any wonder that Holliwell refuses to set foot in the country. Holliwell is, as other Stone heroes tend to be, "without beliefs, without hope—either for himself or for the world. Almost without friends, certainly without allies. Alone."

Sister Justin is in Tecan for reasons of conscience. She is a veteran of the civil-rights days, has been in a Mississippi jail. She runs the dispensary at the mission. But there is so little to do there that the mission has been ordered to close down. "I think you're very intelligent and moral and all good nunnish things," Father Egan tells Sister Justin. "You had an attack of self-righteousness and you decided to try the impossible." To imagine Sister Justin one might try to imagine an ideal reader of the old *Ramparts,* or of *Mother Jones.* She is someone who has not only bought the whole-earth catalogue of left-wing notions but is ready to die for them. Sister Justin is not prepared to leave Tecan, in fact, because she has signed on to aid, in any way she can, the revolution now in the works in that dark country.

As for Pablo Tabor, he is not someone who chooses to be in or out of Tecan. He is one of life's drifters, though he cannot drift very far without pills of one kind or another. Life and pills make Pablo paranoid. He is always worried, as he puts it, about being "turned around." His is an explosive paranoia. Death and disaster are his companions. He ties up with a gang of gunrunners who plan to supply the revolutionaries in Tecan. These plans go badly askew. Murder intervenes. Through a complicated concatenation of events, Pablo shores up in Tecan.

Well, to make a long novel short, Stone, through convincing enough artifice, pulls the strands of this ambitious work together. The parts mesh and fold and weave in and out. Many nice touches crop up along the way: interesting observations, deft descriptions, apt throwaway lines. Characters appear—the international fence Naftali among them—about whom one would have liked to learn more. Even though the novel goes soft in the middle and one begins to wish it were shorter, it is difficult not to be impressed with Stone's skills, the fecundity of his invention. Precisely for that reason one regrets all the more that *A Flag for Sunrise* is such a botch, such a sad and misguided failure.

The novel is rigged. Of course all novels are rigged, in the fundamental sense that they are artificial constructions, whose business it is, as it is the business of all literature, to turn facts into ideas. But Robert Stone works the other way round. For ideas he finds facts. He is imprisoned by his assumptions, and for a novelist few things can be more deadly. Reviewers have suggested that this novel of Stone's is Conradian, but it was Conrad who in *Nostromo,* wrote: "The wisdom of the heart having no concern with the erection or demolition of theories any more than with the defense of prejudices, has no random words at its command. The words it pronounces have the value of acts of integrity, tolerance, and compassion."

What are Stone's assumptions? He is still out to prove that "the American Way is innocence," and that "American innocence shall rise in mighty clouds of vapors to the scent of heaven and confound the nations!" Only those lines, first written in 1967 in *A Hall of Mirrors,* must now be altered, for in Stone's view American innocence has become a source of devastation, and the nations are now not so much confounded as destroyed by it. "Nothing is free," Stone has remarked in an interview, "and we've been getting our bananas, so to speak. . . . We've been sending in marines and pushing people around in Central America, and we're going to eventually have to pay the price for it."

A novelist is entitled to his opinions, but in his novels he has to earn them by demonstration, by convincing narrative. In the early pages of *A Flag for Sunrise,* it looks as if Stone will earnesly attempt this demonstration when, at lunch with a CIA man, Frank Holliwell is told, "Well, it's them or us, chum. Like always. They make absolute claims, we make relative ones. That's why our side is better in the end." It is a point to which Holliwell would seem, tacitly, to accede. But at the first opportunity, while lecturing in a country friendly to the United States called Compostela (compost, kids, get it?), he delivers a drunken talk about the thinness of American culture, the American worship of money—the standard stuff. "I think what is best about my country is not exportable," remarks Holliwell later in the novel. "What is best about America doesn't export," said Stone in his interview. But what either of them means by this cannot be known, for not a hint of a whiff of a shred of a trace of a clue about what is best about America has ever showed up in a Robert Stone novel.

Perhaps one day it will, but for now Robert Stone's view is roughly that of Sister Justin, who, thinking of the torturer and killer Lieutenant Campos, asks: "But was it not all of a piece—Campos on the coast, the President in his mortar-proof palace in the capital, the American interests that kept everything in place?" It is the standard view. It is a view that, brought to the writing of novels, gives us handsome young rebel priests and stout-hearted old revolutionaries without a glimpse of what Conrad, writing about revolutionaries, once called "the sinister impulses which lurk in . . . noble illusions." It is, in short, the view that comes with a one-year subscription to the *Nation*.

Can a novelist, even one with the most glittering gifts, command our attention when his ideas come to little more than the conventional wisdom? I doubt it, and Robert Stone would seem to doubt it, too. In a number of places in *A Flag for Sunrise* he attempts to deepen his subject, to cast out in deeper waters. Specifically, he wishes to invoke a vision larger than mere politics, a vision of cosmic evil. "There's always a place for God," says Holliwell during the question session after his drunken talk. "There is some question as to whether He's in it." Later in the novel, in Tecan, Holliwell goes diving, and, deep down along a sheer coral wall, terror stuns him. "Then Holliwell thought: It's out there. Fear overcame him; a chemical taste, a cold stone on the heart." What does Holliwell sense? "The thing out there must be feeling him, he thought, sensing the lateral vibrations of his climb, its dim primal brain registering disorder in his motion and making the calculation. Fear. Prey."

Is it a shark? Is it pure evil? Is it the death of American innocence? We are never told. Ambiguity is sometimes the mark of the highest poetry, but ambiguity fails here. Although metaphysical evil is a subject that comes up frequently in this novel for discussion, the problem is that it is just that—discussion. It is what Melville would have called "matter for psychologic theologians," and what Rheinhardt, from Stone's first novel, would have called "rebop," the jazz musicians' word for bull. Stone closes out this novel not just by implicating America in this metaphysical evil but by saying that America has been assigned to convey metaphysical evil to the world. Double rebop.

Unfortunately, Stone has convinced himself that he has a vision when all he really seems to have is a political point of view plated over with a thin layer of metaphysics. Richly endowed with literary gifts, he has chosen to offer them up on the altar of politics. What a sad demonstration of Karl Kraus's bitter aphorism, the one that runs: "Today's literature is prescriptions written by patients."

Commentary 1982

Why John Irving
Is So Popular

MBUSHING A Best-Seller" is the title Edmund Wilson
gave to a 1946 review of a novel by Anya Seton, but
clearly it is too late to ambush the novelist John Irving, who has already ridden into town, cleaned out the banks,
and ridden out again unharmed. After publishing three novels,
Irving rang the best-seller gong, and rang it with a sledgehammer
with his fourth, *The World According to Garp,* and then rang it yet
again with his fifth and most recent novel, *The Hotel New Hampshire.* These books have not been best sellers merely but thunderous best sellers. Three and a half million paperback copies sold
of *The World According to Garp,* weeks and weeks atop the best-
seller lists for *The Hotel New Hampshire,* both novels made into
movies. . . .

Yet all this is matter best left to the accountants. What is more
interesting, what distinguishes John Irving's recent novels from
the regular run of even thunderous best sellers, is that they are
not books meant for entertainment alone. They are written out
of serious intentions, and by and large they are read in a serious
way by their varied audience. My sense is that this audience
is fairly youthful, Irving's readers ranging preponderantly between their early twenties and their early forties, though not
exclusively so.

John Irving's admirers take his novels seriously, he most certainly takes them seriously, but how seriously ought serious people to take them? Fifty million Frenchmen can't be wrong, they

used to say before the establishment of the Vichy government; can five or six million American readers of John Irving? Of course they can, and over questions of serious art large audiences frequently are wrong. Yet they need not necessarily be. Right or wrong, however, the wide readership for John Irving's novels—mainly youthful, mainly middle class—is itself a phenomenon worth considering in its own right. But before considering the phenomenon of Irving's commercial success, let us consider the products that made the success a phenomenon—the novels themselves.

"Jubilant" is the word Mordecai Richler used to describe the quality of John Irving's talent. "America's most jubilant bestseller" reads the blurb atop the paperback edition of *Garp*. Jubilation, surely, is one of the effects Irving seeks as a novelist—a sense of joyousness, of exultation. Fittingly, he is a high-energy writer, who works in heavy brushstrokes, goes in for colorful effects, does not write the kind of careful novel in which, as Virginia Woolf once said of the novels of Jane Austen, "one slip means death."

In the contemporary novel, jubilation also implies comedy, comedy of a somewhat manic kind, and Irving, from the very beginning of his career, has been a comedian. The character T. S. Garp says, "Why did people insist that if you were 'comic' you couldn't also be 'serious'?" I am not sure that many people do insist this, for it is fairly common knowledge that there is a comedy that is at bottom highly serious. More about the quality of John Irving's comedy presently, but for now let it suffice to say that, as with the work of so many contemporary American novelists—Pynchon and Barthelme, Elkin and Roth, Coover and Barth—Irving's is riddled, is fairly bristling, with comic scenes.

Sex, too, is central to the Irving novel. Fancy fornication in one form or another is never far off in any of John Irving's novels, and it ranges from adolescent sex to lesbian love to couple swapping to incest. Fellatio in a car, both moving and parked, is another Irving *spécialité de la maison*. Comedy and sex often combine, and the result is generally scenes that are frenzied, hysterical, madcap, shading into slapstick in which lust leads to an Irving

hero being caught *in flagrante delicto.* The centrality of sex in
these novels is curious, in that Irving often goes well out of his
way to make plain his hatred of the sexual exploitation of women
and his sympathy for the general tendency of their liberation from
the old regime under which, presumably, women were treated as
sexual objects. More than one of John Irving's novels manages to
be both liberationist and pornographic. But then sex is perhaps
the only one of life's activities where one can eat one's cake and
have it, too.

The physical side of life generally gets a great deal of play in
the novels of John Irving. Sweat, secretions, smells, bumps,
lumps, rumps—all come in for their share of descriptive prose.
Although Irving is fecund in imagining incidents for his characters to run through, it is apparently a bit more difficult for him
not to create a narrator or at least one principal character who is,
as they say in the locker room, "in shape." Wrestling, running,
weight lifting, physical conditioning of one strenuous sort or
another is, in a way that is not quite made explicit, connected to
spiritual conditioning. But then perhaps the joggers of our day
do not need to have the connection made any more explicit.

One needs to be in a certain shape oneself to read a John Irving
novel; rather a strong stomach, specifically, is required for the
violence that is integral to his novels. Characters are set upon by
bears and other wild animals; body parts drop off people with a
more than fair regularity; bombings and rapes are provided: a
character from Irving's first novel, *Setting Free the Bears,* meets
his death through suffocation in a pit of human excrement, and
he, mind you, is a sympathetic character. In a notorious scene in
Garp, a car crash results in the loss of the following human inventory: one child, the eye of another, and one penis. But this is
lyrical stuff compared with another scene in the same novel in
which (in the course of a story within the larger story) a man is
disemboweled while committing a rape. John Irving is not unaware of the heavy dosage of violence in his novels, and in his
latest, *The Hotel New Hampshire,* his narrator remarks of the
book's ending, "I know it's not nearly violent enough to please
some of the friends and foes from our past. . . ."

It was only with the fourth of his novels, *The World According to Garp,* that John Irving began to talk thus to his readers, to refer to his own works within his works. Roughly three-quarters of the way through *Garp,* for example, Garp, the narrator, tells us that he is planning to write a novel called *My Father's Illusions,* which turns out to be not the title but one of the principal themes of Irving's next novel, *The Hotel New Hampshire.* In *Garp,* too, the narrator is supposed to have written an earlier novel entitled *The Second Wind of the Cuckold.* Irving never wrote such a novel, though the phrase—"If cuckolds catch a second wind, I am eagerly waiting for mine"—is found embedded in the last line of Irving's previous novel, *The 158-Pound Marriage.* One autobiographical parallel follows another in Irving's recent novels, and these are often followed by little sermonettes about the need to disregard "shitty autobiographical associations that make those rabid readers of gossip warm to an occasional fiction." And again: "Usually, with great patience and restraint, Garp would say that the autobiographical basis—if there ever was one—was the least interesting level on which to read a novel." Setting down a rug, then pulling it out from under a reader, this is what academic literary critics, who are infinitely patient men and women, like to call novelistic playfulness.

Although no doubt Irving would detest the notion, there is a strong sense in which he is an academic novelist. He is a former student at the University of Iowa Program in Creative Writing, and while you can take the boy out of the Program in Creative Writing you can't always take the Program in Creative Writing out of the boy. Two of Irving's five novels—*The Water-Method Man* and *The 158-Pound Marriage*—have academic settings. But more is involved than scenes and settings. In the very first of Irving's novels, *Setting Free the Bears,* which has to do with freeing the animals from the Hietzinger Zoo in Vienna, one already senses certain school-learned touches, bits, ironies. Having set a good part of this novel during World War II, Irving has one of his characters remark late in the novel, that his teacher, a Jew, "was enraged that I should be so pretentious as to dash through the war with so little mention of the Jews. I tried to explain that he should really look at my autobiography as what is loosely called fiction—a novel, say." Irving often goes in for these Chinese-box effects—characters are writing books or shooting films within his books—and this game-playing, rather than telling a story straight out, is one of the standard marks of the academic novelist at work.

More important than John Irving's academic roots, however, is that his writing seems very much of a special generation. In *Setting Free the Bears,* Siegfried, the hero of the novel, who in 1967 is twenty-one years old, remarks: "What I mean is, we're at an interim age at an interim time; we're alive between two times of monstrous decisions—one past, the other coming." This quotation may make John Irving seem a political writer, but he isn't, at least not in any obvious or direct way. What he is, I think, is a generational writer—a writer attractive to readers of a certain age. It is the young—or rather the youngish—to whom he appeals. His novels exert their greatest pull on those people who are undecided about growing up: they are college-educated, getting on and even getting up in the world, but with a bit of the hippie-dippie counterculture clinging to them still—yuppies, they have been called, the initials YUP standing for young urban professionals. A friend who is a professor at my university's law school, for instance, has told me that many of the younger law professors among his colleagues are nuts about the novels of John Irving. Not that this constitutes a CBS/*New York Times* poll, but I have never before heard of young law professors being nuts about any novelist. Why? What's the attraction?

Irving's second novel, *The Water-Method Man,* is about a graduate student in German at the University of Iowa, who only reluctantly accepts the roles of husband and father. Fred "Bogus" Trumper is his name, extreme passivity his game. The passive hero, or hero as passive, has by now become a tradition of sorts in contemporary American fiction. We have had a Dangling Man and an Invisible Man, and to these Irving adds a Water-Method Man. The title refers to a method of treatment that the novel's hero undergoes for the difficulty he has in urinating: drinking lots and lots of water. *The Water-Method Man* is the most convoluted of Irving's novels—his hero is doing a translation of an old German epic for his dissertation, while at the same time a documentary film is being made of his life—and also easily the most boring. A great many little academic games are being played out in it: dead ducks appear, people sleep with tropical fish tanks around them, the hero retells the story of *Moby-Dick* to his child —in short, there is plenty of symbolism to go around.

Certain elements appear in the pages of *The Water-Method Man* that will be hallmarks in John Irving's novels to come: the broad joke is carried a bit beyond much too far (the squeamish are advised to pass up the urological jokes and horror stories that run throughout); the rather persistent dropping off of human body parts begins in earnest; the hero turns out to be a wrestler; the main characters arrive, as they invariably do in an Irving novel, in Vienna; adorable children appear who must be protected from the world's cruelty; and, finally, there is a celebration of the flesh (the last clause in the novel reads, "Bogus Trumper smiled cautiously at all the good flesh around him"). And, too, as with all of Irving's novels, whatever the suffering and death that have gone before, the ending is somehow upbeat. But then wasn't it William Dean Howells who said that what the American public wanted above all was a tragedy with a happy ending?

The 158-Pound Marriage is Irving's best-formed novel. Its subject is wife and husband swapping, with an occasional bout of *ménage à quatre* and a single detour into lesbianism. Of the four principals, two are writers, one a teacher and wrestling coach, one an Austrian brought up by a captain of the army of the USSR during the occupation of Vienna. It is the most sex-ridden of Irving's novels, even though at one point its narrator says that "sex is only a temporary cure." In the pages of *The 158-Pound Marriage* it has to do until something better comes along. Nothing better does. Reading this novel one is inclined to agree with one of the two wives, who, near the close, remarks, "I think we were just *f——ers!*" Something new has been added for the first time in Irving's work, an element that will henceforth appear in all his novels; for the first time discussions of fiction appear in the middle of his fiction. "Edith and I agreed," that narrator says, "that when the subject of fiction became how to write fiction, we lost interest. . . ."

Mutilation of various kinds continues in *The 158-Pound Marriage*. Men without legs, a man with a hole in his face, a dancer with a part of her foot missing supply some of the novel's notable subtractions; children are also wounded in a blood-drenched shower-door accident, but afterward, if memory serves, all parts are present and accounted for. At this point in one's reading in John Irving's novels one begins to wonder about all these wounds, rips, tears, broken bones, and vitiated organs. There arises the question, to adapt a phrase of Henry James's, of the disfigurement in the carpet.

It did not arise too urgently because John Irving's standing as a novelist was not itself an insistent question. His first three novels gave him the reputation of an interesting but minor writer. ("Garp," thinks the hero of Irving's next novel, *"hated* the reputation of 'small but serious.'") Commercially, he appeared to be one of those novelists who would eventually have to be published by an outfit like the Fiction Collective. Then, in 1978, along came *The World According to Garp,* a success both critical and commercial. People not only bought this, Irving's fourth novel, they read it; they not only read it, they loved it. "Joyous and outrageous," wrote the critics, "full of vitality and grace," "rich and humorous," "brilliant," "overwhelming," "superb," "wonderful," "absolutely extraordinary."

Extraordinary *The World According to Garp* is. So loaded down with incident and invention is the novel that its plot beggars recapitulation. Briefly, it is an account of the life and times of a youngish novelist, T. S. Garp, the fatherless son of a well-born woman who, quite without consciously wishing it, becomes a feminist leader and heroine. Garp's wife is a university teacher, who teaches among other things a course in narrative technique, but it is Irving who attempts to show how much technique a narrative can have. His novel contains two separate short stories and the first chapter of another novel, *The World According to Bensenhaver*, which will make Garp himself a hugely best-selling novelist, even as, we now know, *The World According to Garp* made John Irving a best-selling novelist. Bears, wrestlers, Austria, by now old Irving standbys, put in their appearances. Instructions about writing and book reviewing are provided between bouts of sex (and sex, for Garp, "was always an act of terrific optimism"). Garp quotes Marcus Aurelius one moment, and the next—most unAurelianly—boffs one of his children's baby-sitters. Mutilation fans will not be disappointed. One of the principal characters in the novel is a former tight-end for the Philadelphia Eagles who has had a sex-change operation. A group of militant feminists— the Ellen Jamesians—cut out their tongues. ("But Garp . . . felt the whole history of the world is self-mutilation.") There is a bit of couple switching, also an assassination. The novel has an epilogue, in which two characters agree that "Garp was a man with remarkable energy."

The World According to Garp is not so much salted as drenched in sex and violence, but so is the world drenched in sex and violence, and so, too, in recent years have a large number of novels been drenched. The sex and violence in *Garp* do not, in any case, go very far toward explaining the novel's immense popularity, for these are to be had in ample supply elsewhere. In *The Water-Method Man* a passage runs: "You should always tell stories . . . in such a way that you make the audience feel good and wise, even a little ahead of you." This implies that a best seller can be rigged, but here, too, there are reasons for doubting, for if it were so easily do-able it would be done more often. In the pages of *Garp,* Garp's editor feeds his authors' manuscripts to a cleaning woman at his publishing firm: "She did not like most things, but when she said she liked something, it meant to John Wolf [the editor] that nearly everybody else was at least sure to be able to read it." A valuable woman, clearly, every publishing house ought to have one, but I fear she exists only in John Irving's imagination.

No, when a book such as *The World According to Garp,* a book with serious literary pretensions, catches on so epidemically with the public, something else, something deeper than pat formulas for constructing best sellers is involved. In the book *Bestsellers,* which investigates the popular fiction of America and England during the 1970s, John Sutherland makes the point that vastly popular novels need to be considered from two points of view, the economic and the ideological. The economic has to do with the way a book is marketed. Of the ideological, Sutherland writes: "The bestseller expresses and feeds certain needs in the reading public. It consolidates prejudice, provides comfort, is therapy, offers vicarious reward or stimulus. In some socially controlled circumstances it may also indoctrinate or control a population's ideas on politically sensitive subjects. In other circumstances, especially where sexual mores are concerned, it may play a subversive social role."

"Ideological" has to be understood here in its loosest sense; certainly it does in considering the case of John Irving, for Irving is not, in any reasonable sense of the term, a radical or ideologue. On the contrary, in his novels he has demonstrated real disdain for people whose lives are controlled by their politics: the Ellen Jamesians in *Garp* and a group of Austrian radicals in his more recent novel, *The Hotel New Hampshire,* are equally detested by their author. The ideological freight carried by John Irving's recent novels is not, then, political in the strict sense, but is instead to be found in Irving's attitudes, point of view, what he himself calls his vision.

The young T. S. Garp, considering his own early writing, thinks: "What I need is *vision,* he knew. It will come, he repeated to himself. . . ." Has John Irving's vision come? His novels are an extraordinary jumble, of the sentimental and the violent, of the cute and the loathsome; reading them one sometimes feels one is reading a weird collaboration between J. D. Salinger and John Hawkes, a strained effort to be, simultaneously, adorable and gruesome. In *Bestsellers* John Sutherland says that best-selling fiction tends to divide ideologically between the emancipated (Erica Jong, for example) and the traditional (James Michener, for example). In a strange yet evidently commercially successful way, John Irving's latest novels tend to combine the emancipated and the traditional, the effect of which is to make his readers feel advanced in their views yet fundamentally sound in their emotions.

For instance, while disdaining the wilder side of women's liberation in *Garp,* Irving views it very kindly. As a writer, T. S. Garp stays home, does the cooking and cleaning, and is generally, not at all to his displeasure, the model househusband. John Berry, the narrator in *The Hotel New Hampshire,* plays, quite comfortably, a roughly similar role in that novel. Yet the one character is an ardent wrestler, the other a serious weight lifter—traditionally masculine, one might even say *macho,* types. John Irving prides himself on his endless invention—"Garp," he writes, "was a natural story teller; he could make things up, one right after another. . . ."—but his real invention is in the creation of these heroes. They are extremely sensitive (Garp lies down next to his young son to smell the freshness of the boy's breath in his sleep), yet when it is required of them, brutally tough (John Berry, in *The Hotel New Hampshire,* kills a man with a bear hug). These John Irving heroes, these sweet bruisers, are also permanently puerile, young men whose chief experience occurred in adolescence—it's downhill after your middle teens, says a character in *The Hotel New Hampshire*—and who have been able to arrange things so that, whatever their chronological age, they never quite have to leave adolescence.

The Hotel New Hampshire rode high upon the best-seller lists for a very long stretch. The *New York Times,* in a capsule comment on the book in its best-seller list, described it as "Life with an eccentric family." That description as aptly fits *The Brothers Karamazov,* so perhaps a better one might be, "Winning formula well in hand, John Irving strikes again." Although Lily Berry, the daughter of the family in this novel who is herself a best-selling novelist says, "My God, the next book has got to be bigger than the first," in fact *The Hotel New Hampshire* is not quite so vast in its canvas as *The World According to Garp.* It is about a family whose father harbors utopian illusions about running a hotel that will provide perfect hospitality, hospitality with slight psychological overtones. "People have to grow their own way," Father says. "We provide the space." Many of the same symbols and themes, incidents and concerns, appear here as in *Garp* and Irving's earlier novels: the Austrian interlude, the bears, the physical conditioning, the sidebar discussions of fiction ("Life is serious but art is fun"), the mutilations. The appeal, too, is similar. At the heart of this novel, as of *The World According to Garp,* is the allure of family.

As in *Garp,* so in *The Hotel New Hampshire,* family becomes a fortress of a kind into which one withdraws with one's children for protection against the cruelty of the world. Rape, in both novels, is a big item (". . . rape, Garp thought, made men feel guilt by association"). Rape is indeed at the very center of *The Hotel New Hampshire;* the rape and recovery from rape and revenge for rape of Franny Berry are the incidents that bind the novel together. At the novel's close, the narrator and his wife—formerly a lesbian so homely she preferred to go about in a bear costume (I'm not making this up; John Irving did)—move into a final hotel that they use as a rape crisis center.

The Hotel New Hampshire is pro-family and anti-rape. If these views do not simply take your breath away, let me go on to say that in all of John Irving's novels, discerning good from evil is never a problem; like every other moral question, it never really comes up. There are good folks and there are bastards in these novels, and one hardly needs a program to tell one from the other. Good folks can go under, but bastards get it in the neck—and in the nether regions. ("It was not one of Garp's better points: tolerance of the intolerant.") As the narrator of *The Hotel New Hampshire* puts it: "The way the world worked was *not* cause for some sort of blanket cynicism or sophomoric despair; according to my father and Iowa Bob, the way the world worked—which was badly—was just a strong incentive to live purposefully, and to be determined about living well." Now here is advice your local young law professor and a happy few million others can live with comfortably.

Commentary 1982

Bernard Malamud
Goes Ape

WHEN DO WE give up on a novelist? Sometimes, if it be foul enough, a single sentence will do the job. I was able, for example, to fling across the room in good conscience the novel in which the following sentence appeared on page 12: "And anyway, what can be more romantic than self-denial—your basic Dante and Beatrice trip?" This was fairly easy to do, for the writer, though long a professional, was a first novelist. He has never written a second novel, so I assume that other people, perhaps later than page 12, also sent his book sailing.

But what if the writer has acquired a reputation as a serious and highly accomplished artist, thought in some quarters to be a major novelist, a modern master even? What if, more complicated still, he has given you pleasure, insight into the working of the human heart, and other rewards in the past? What if he writes one poor book, then a second, then yet a third? At what point do you concede, however regretfully, that this writer no longer speaks to you, and walk away?

Bernard Malamud is now in his late sixties. His has been a career not without its compensations. He has won a Pulitzer Prize and two National Book Awards, and at a time when the latter meant something. Not that Malamud's rise was anything like meteoric. He did not publish his first novel, *The Natural,* until he was thirty-eight. *The Natural* plays off all the old baseball legends against Arthurian and other myths, and does so in a way that is both charming and serious. Although it was a first novel, the book sets out most of the themes, motifs, and character types its author would work with over the next few decades. The hero of *The Natural,* Roy Hobbs, is a loner, the first in what will be a fairly heavy traffic in Malamudian hard-luckers who can usually be counted upon to fade and fall within sight of the finish line. Suffering is at the heart of this novel, its point and its purpose. As one of his lady friends tells Roy Hobbs: "We have two lives, Roy, the life we learn with and the life we live with after that." Good advice, for those who can take it, which not all Malamud heroes can.

While there was more than a dash of Ring Lardner in *The Natural,* and a touch or two of Nathanael West, the dominant style was Malamud's own, and this was most impressive. Anchored in realistic detail, it was nonetheless able to fly off into the regions of the fantastic at the drop of a comma. By means of this style Malamud could see the comedy of his characters while retaining his—and engaging our—sympathy for them. Here, for example, is the early Malamud style, that supple instrument, describing the change in a character from *The Natural* named Pop Fisher, a baseball manager who has been a perennial loser, as his team finally begins to look like a winner:

> His hands healed and so did his heart, for even during the tensest struggle he looked a picture of contentment. And he was patient now, extraordinarily so, giving people the impression he had never been otherwise. Let a man bobble a hot one, opening the gate for a worrisome run, and he no longer jumped down his throat but wagged his head in silent sympathy. And sometimes he patted the offender on the surprised back. Formerly his strident yell was everywhere, on the field, in the dugout, clubhouse, players' duffel bags, also in their dreams, but now you never hear it because he no longer raised his voice, not even to Dizzy's cat when it wet on his shoes.

There are no Jews in *The Natural;* or at least no Jews to whom being a Jew has any importance. The point is worth making because being a Jew, its responsibilities and the consequences of not living up to those responsibilities, became central to Malamud's work over the next decade or so.

During this same time—roughly 1953 through 1965—writing by American Jews took on a special interest. Extraordinary works about Jews, with Jewish scenes and settings, had appeared before: Abraham Cahan's *The Rise of David Levinsky* (1917), Henry Roth's *Call It Sleep* (1934), Meyer Levin's *The Old Bunch* (1936). Books by and about Jews had also been thumping best sellers: Herman Wouk's *Marjorie Morningstar* (1955), Myron S. Kaufmann's *Remember Me to God* (1957), Jerome Weidman's *I Can Get It For You Wholesale* (1937). But suddenly, toward the middle 1950's, writing by Jews living in America came to seem serious and absolutely central. Looking back upon it, I believe the watershed moment may have been the publication in 1953 of Saul Bellow's translation from the Yiddish of I. B. Singer's story "Gimpel the Fool" in *Partisan Review.* Or it may have been connected with the rise of Bellow's own career, marked by the supercharged prose of *The Adventures of Augie March* (1953). Around this time, too, Philip Roth, in his middle twenties, began producing the stories later collected in *Goodbye, Columbus.* After "Gimpel," I. B. Singer's work, once largely restricted to Yiddish editions, began increasingly to appear in English translation, with Singer eventually becoming a regular contributor of fiction to the *New Yorker.* If one did not live in the United States, but knew it only through the fiction published and critically discussed in the country's serious journals, one might have concluded that America was predominantly a nation of Jews.

To this effulgence of American Jewish writing Bernard Malamud contributed heavily. "In Bernard Malamud," the critic Ihab Hassan wrote, "we find further testimony that the urban Jewish writer, like the Southern novelist, has emerged from the tragic underground of culture as a true spokesman of mid-century America." This is a bit overheated—"tragic underground of culture?"—but it was the standard kind of criticism that American

Jewish writing received, much of it from American Jewish critics. The Jew was suddenly everywhere written about as "moral exemplar," "the representative figure of the twentieth century," and other happy clichés; and often these clichés were jumped up a step higher when it was announced that the Jew was also Everyman.

Yet it must also be said that if the work of any contemporary American Jewish writer encouraged such ethnic theorizing, it was Bernard Malamud's. Although writing about recognizably Jewish types, Bellow seemed more interested in general intellectual and philosophical than in Jewish questions, and Roth seemed more interested in sociological and psychological matters than in Jewish ones. But the ethical import of being a Jew was Malamud's subject.

The Assistant, Malamud's novel of 1957, is about little other than the question of what it means to be a Jew. I won't recapitulate the details of this carefully made yet exceedingly cheerless novel, except to say that it is saturated with pain and filled with the dignity of suffering. To be a true Jew, for Morris Bober, the book's exemplary character, is "to do what is right, to be honest, to be good." It is also, according to the rabbi who delivers the eulogy over the dead Bober, to suffer and endure, "but with hope." Hope is decisive for Malamud. The more interesting among his characters are those who have suffered. But their suffering, to have meaning, must not only be understood but cherished ("My past is meaningful to me," says a character in Malamud's story, "The Lady of the Lake," "I treasure what I suffered for") and qualified by hope for better things ahead. Such is the whole meaning of the close of *The Assistant,* whose chief non-Jewish character, Frank Alpine, converts to Judaism and submits himself to a circumcision.

The importance of suffering, the need for hope no matter how heavy the burden of suffering, the necessity of not shutting one's heart to the suffering and hopes of others—out of these cards Bernard Malamud built the splendid literary house that is *The Magic Barrel,* the book of stories that won the National Book Award for 1958. *The Magic Barrel* marked a rise in Malamud's reputation. Most people who read the book did not merely like it—they loved it. And much there is in it to love. Each story in the book shimmers with implications. Malamud seems to have found the perfect plots to give unforgettable flesh to his themes. Comedy and grief rub shoulders, as when an immigrant Jew addresses the Lord: "My dear God, sweetheart, did I deserve that this should happen to me?" Malamud's stories come out of the Yiddish tradition of storytelling, from the way they open ("Feld, a shoemaker," or "Kessler, formerly an egg candler," two of the stories begin) to the way they can ignite suddenly into fantasy (in "The Loan," the baker Lieb relates that "one day out of misery, he had wept into the dough. Thereafter his bread was such it brought customers in from everywhere"), to the way their particulars rise off the page into universal significance. And, finally, the book reveals Malamud to be a moralist, an intricate and subtle and unpredictable one—which is to say, a moralist of the most interesting kind.

A New Life, Malamud's novel of 1961, exhibited both a continuation of and a number of departures from his previous work. Among the notable departures is the fact that this novel is more firmly anchored in time and place than Malamud's earlier books. Apart from the few stories in *The Magic Barrel* set in Italy, Malamud's novels and stories had been located in some unnamed lonely America of the mind; the time at which they took place was unclear and of less than paramount interest. In *A New Life,* however, both time and place are significant: the novel is set in a third-rate university in the Northwest, in an Oregon-like state that the author calls Cascadia; and its time is the early 1950s, the period of the most heightened activities of such organizations as the House Un-American Activities Committee. *A New Life* is, in one of its aspects, a political book, though political well after the fact, the novel after all having been written in 1961.

Into this atmosphere of provinciality and political conformity, Malamud inserts one S. Levin, bearded, passionate, a trifle *meshugah*. Levin is part traditional Jewish *shlimmazel* (in the classic formulation, the *shlemiel* is the man who spills his soup, the *shlimmazel* the man on whom he spills it), part characteristically Malamudian. The Malamudian part has to do with his past. The emotion of Levin's life, he tells us, has been humiliation. Loneliness is his lot. His father was a thief; his mother insane; he himself, although now only thirty, is already an ex-drunk. "All my life I've been engaged in wanting," Levin says. The person he says it to is someone he wants, the wife of the man who will be the new chairman of the English department in which he works as an instructor, a newcomer, an outsider. This woman is also his lover; and therein hangs a tale.

But not, alas, much of a tale—or not as impressive a tale as one might have hoped for from the author of *The Magic Barrel*. Two things seem to be at stake in *A New Life:* first, the control of the English department, over which there is a struggle between the forces of conformism and reaction (represented by an interest in teaching freshman composition) and those of humanism and the higher seriousness, in which Levin, an ardent believer in the gospel of the Humanities, is enlisted; and, second, the outcome of Levin's love affair on which ride his hopes for a new life. While working these matters out, Malamud provides a good deal of landscape writing; expresses many corny political sentiments (students "must either be the best—masters of ideas and of themselves—or choose the best to lead them; in either case democracy wins"); and puts S. Levin through a number of failed erotic adventures. Bright patches there are in *A New Life;* laughs, too. Yet the novel seems, for the first time in a work by Bernard Malamud, thin. It sags in its middle. Lengthy though *A New Life* is, its substance feels light, while the stories in *The Magic Barrel,* though brief, have ballast. More, in fiction, is frequently less.

If there is something a bit trivial and finally clownish about *A New Life,* no such thing can be said of *The Fixer* (1966). This novel, it will be recalled, is based on the 1913 Mendel Beiliss case. Beiliss, an obscure Russian Jew employed in a Kiev brick factory, was framed by the anti-Semitic group called the Black Hundred for allegedly killing a twelve-year-old Russian boy and using his blood in the preparation of Passover matzoh. If Beiliss were found guilty, it would mean that Christian blood was indeed used in the preparation of matzoh, and hence all consumers of matzoh would by association be guilty. Thus, in the pathetic person of Mendel Beiliss, the Russian Jewish community, indeed all Jews everywhere, stood on trial.

There is a natural gravity to this subject, and Malamud proves in every way up to it. The difficult materials of *The Fixer* are handled with great artistic tact. So serious is the subject that there isn't room for the least literary exhibitionism, and none is allowed. The phrase *tour de force* for once applies. For more than a hundred pages Malamud has his hapless hero, who is given the name Yakov Bok, alone in his cell attempting to make sense of the outrageous events of his life (and of life in general) with a mind stocked only with a few shreds of Spinoza, a fragment or two he remembers from the Torah, and years of dreary *shtetl* experience—and Malamud is able to bring this off without the least trace of *longueur*. "It is not easy to be a free-thinker in this terrible cell," says Yakov Bok, who at the novel's end—and it ends, rightly, just as the trial is about to begin—thinks, "there's no such thing as an unpolitical man, especially a Jew. You can't be one without the other, that's clear enough. You can't sit still and see yourself destroyed."

The Fixer was not only an artistic but a critical and a commercial success. With this book, one reviewer wrote, "Malamud moves on to the stage of world literature." "A literary miracle," said *Newsweek,* with the kind of breathless idiocy that passes for praise in some literary quarters. The novel won a Pulitzer Prize and a National Book Award; a movie was made out of it. Malamud meanwhile was given an academic imprimatur, and soon essays about his work with such titles as "Four Versions of Pastoral," and "Comic Vision and the Theme of Identity" began to appear in the journals. If Malamud was not yet hanging around the house awaiting a call from Stockholm, he nevertheless had every reason to think himself among the major writers of our day.

Malamud continued to produce books of stories—*Idiots First* (1963), *Pictures of Fidelman* (1969)—but the reputation of the writer of his current stature would henceforth depend on his production of novels. (Why this should be is by no means clear, except as it can be explained through the requirements of publishing and publicity.) And the first novel that Malamud produced after *The Fixer* was *The Tenants*. The year of its publication was 1971, and its subject was, in part, race relations. In this novel two writers, Harry Lesser, a neurotically slow worker, and Willie Spearmint, an undeveloped black with only raw power, are living in a New York building awaiting the wrecker's ball. Each is trying to complete his novel.

Already, you might say, a mistake. Unless you happen to be Henry James, writing about being a writer is almost always a mistake, like poems about poems or paintings in which someone is painting. Such as it is, the drama of *The Tenants* mainly has to do with whether the two writers will complete their manuscripts. Racial feelings mix with rivalry and these are further complicated by Harry Lesser's interest in Willie Spearmint's white lady friend. Whatever the novel's symbolic intent, it is spoiled because the details seem so wrong. A woman character says of Willie Spearmint, "He belted me in the eye and left." John O'Hara used to maintain that no educated woman ever says "half-a-buck," and I believe no educated woman ever says "belted" either. More, though, than small details are off. Tonally, the novel sounds wrong. Malamud does not quite seem up to the violence of his black writer. No character in the novel is worthy of one's sympathy, so among them all one divides one's antipathies. Saddest of all, for the first time in a book by Bernard Malamud, you don't want to turn the page.

How can a really good writer write a really bad book? He can choose the wrong subject. He can—which is much the same thing—misgauge his own talent, and allow his literary ambition to exceed his literary equipment. He may become unfocused morally, the world suddenly seeming more complicated to him than once it did and hence less susceptible of being dealt with by his art. However serious he is as an artist, he may nonetheless come to take himself too seriously. In the case of Bernard Malamud, with *The Tenants* a new heaviness set in, and it was not the weight of authority.

Dubin's Lives (1977), Malamud's next novel and also his longest, is about a professional biographer, a husband and father who in his late fifties has a bout of eleventh-hour adolescence and sets out to prove the adage about there being no fool like an old fool. Which is to say, at fifty-six William Dubin falls in love with a girl of twenty-three. There is every reason to think that Bernard Malamud would not agree with this brief summary of his nearly four-hundred-page novel. My guess is that he views this novel as a profound investigation of middle age, and that he sees his biographer, William Dubin, as a quester, a man ardent not to let life slip away from him. "My God," Dubin thinks, "how long does this romantic hunger—residue of old forms, habits, daydreams—haunt the blood?" As a biographer Dubin is the author of other people's lives, and now he wants to live his own or, more precisely, make up for what he has missed in life: "Middle age, he thought, is when you pay for what you didn't have or couldn't do when you were young."

The earlier Malamud would have made fine ironic hay of this, and spun it into interesting moral material. The late Malamud takes it straight. "With this girl I know the flowering pleasure, heathen innocence, of the natural life," biographer Dubin thinks. And: "One recovers of youth only what he can borrow from the young." Yet again: ". . . the fountain of youth is the presence of youth." Cliché of clichés, we are talking, in *Dubin's Lives,* about a bloody midlife crisis. But the crisis is not only William Dubin's; it is also Bernard Malamud's as a novelist. Signs of this novelistic crisis are that Malamud's language has begun to fall apart—"presently" is misused, "into" (as "into an affair") crops up again and again, "experience" is used as a verb—his self-indulgent and boring descriptions of landscape go well beyond the permissible, and winters in the novel seem longer than they do in life; Malamud's writing about sex, earlier always witty, here becomes chiefly embarrassing. Worst of all, William Dubin is a selfish, charmless man, and it is far from clear that Malamud is aware of this. This is what makes reading *Dubin's Lives* such a chore. As Jane Austen puts it in *Mansfield Park:* "'The indignities of stupidity, and the disappointments of selfish passion, can excite little pity." And, one might add, less interest.

Why do novelists seem to feel the need always to be changing

—to be, in the cant word, "growing"? Did Tolstoy feel this? Did Dickens? Is this a contemporary phenomenon? Is it chiefly an American one? No one, surely, can accuse Bernard Malamud of disobeying the dictum to change, of ignoring the urge to innovate. Now, after the straight realism of *Dubin's Lives,* he has turned, in his latest novel, *God's Grace,* to fantasy. *God's Grace* is a book whose setting is "after the thermonuclear war between the Djanks and Druzhkies." Only one human being has survived, Calvin Cohn, a paleologist who was at the bottom of the sea when the weapons were fired. A World Flood follows the Day of Devastation—the capital letters are Malamud's—and Calvin Cohn, along with a chimpanzee named Buz, is left to reconstitute civilization and to discover why God would permit such destruction. Ah me, as a mother in Sybille Bedford's novel *A Legacy* says to her young daughter, "There is nothing so fatal as a good vast subject."

In *God's Grace* Calvin Cohn shores up on an island where vegetation exists but no animal life (though he will later discover more chimpanzees, an ape, and some baboons). The novel's early pages have some of the pleasing excitement of Robinson Crusoe, with Cohn setting up house on the island. Then Cohn discovers that the chimpanzee Buz has been trained to talk. Soon the other chimpanzees show up, attesting to God's "cosmic absent-mindedness" and, more important, the novelist's need to keep his story going. Cohn sets out to renew life by establishing a community among the chimpanzees and the ape and himself—one that is more civilized, founded on sounder principles, than the one that has just destroyed itself, apparently with God's willingness, in a nuclear devastation.

Naturally, this plan will come to grief. Despite Calvin Cohn's lecturing the chimps on the best thought of the Bible, Freud, Kierkegaard, Ortega y Gasset, despite his holding a seder for them to honor God and his impregnating the one female chimpanzee on the island, the animals revert to type—human type, that is. They become, in other words, competitive, aggressive, divisive, finally vicious. But the novel goes bad before the chimpanzees do. Once the chimpanzees are allowed to speak, *God's*

Grace takes on something of the quality of a television situation comedy, with symbolism added. Much of the humor in the novel is of the kind known as faintly amusing, but then chimp humor, on the scale of wit, is roughly three full rungs down from transvestite jokes. Someone once defined charm, negatively, by saying that if you think you have it, you don't. In *God's Grace* one feels Malamud thinks he has it.

Poor Malamud, the larger he strains to become, the smaller his talent begins to appear. In *God's Grace* he sets out to understand the ways of God, which is quite a project. In his earlier fiction, when a shoemaker, a grocer, a "fixer" spoke, one felt one could hear God in the background; in this novel, where God does speak, all one can hear is the reedy voice of a novelist. *God's Grace* is meant to be Malamud's *A Guide to the Perplexed*. Maimonides, though, is better, the Maimonides who, in what might serve as a gloss on Bernard Malamud's earlier work, wrote: "But just as the human intellect is incapable of grasping God's thoughts, so too our thoughts are unable to understand the wisdom and righteousness of His dispensations and operations. But when the time comes that the Lord wishes to chastise someone, He offers him the possibility of acting contrary to the Torah in order to inflict a just punishment on him. If a man is not ready for punishment, the Lord lets him sin so that he will be ready." Of the perplexing mystery of what causes a novelist to be transformed from a central to a now almost negligible figure, Maimonides, so far as I know, does not speak.

Commentary 1982

John Updike:
Promises, Promises

I N HER MEMOIR, *A Backward Glance,* Edith Wharton
speaks of the advantages of not being considered
promising. It was better, she thought, at least in her
own case, "to fight my way to expression through a thick fog of
indifference." Fighting his way through "a thick fog of indifference" has not quite been John Updike's problem in his career as
a novelist. From his earliest novels Updike has had powerhouse
critics behind him, among them Mary McCarthy, Arthur Mize-
ner, Stanley Edgar Hyman, lauding him, cheering him on, ac-
claiming his promise.

Edith Wharton also speaks in her memoir of the disadvantages
of being regarded as too promising, saying of those so considered
that in middle age they often "sat in ineffectual ecstasy before the
blank page or the empty canvas." This, as we know, has scarcely
been John Updike's problem either, for now, twenty-four years
after the publication of his first novel, *The Poorhouse Fair,* he has
published fully twenty-five more books. Yet in a curious way, just
as John Updike remains boyish in personal appearance and manner, his reputation has remained oddly boyish, too; now at fifty
years old he still seems to be considered promising.

There are two jokes about John Updike. One is that he is an
underacheever. The other is that he is an overacheever. The confusion between Updike and the late John Cheever stems of course
from the fact that both have been writers long associated with the
New Yorker and both have written extensively about suburban

upper-middle-class life. But the confusion cannot be real to any-one who has read the two of them. Updike, for one thing, has taken up many subjects aside from the suburban one; for another, he has been by far the more productive writer; and for a third, he has been the more literary, in the sense of having read widely in the work of his contemporaries and taken a serious interest in the more sheerly aesthetic aspects of prose fiction. If ambition, pro-ductivity, and absorption in the ideas of one's day are to be counted, then John Updike is a overacheever.

But if we are to judge by greatness of theme, or seriousness of purpose, or largeness of spirit, is John Updike still an over-acheever, or is he an underacheever or perhaps something else altogether? I fell away from John Updike's fiction with *Rabbit Redux* (1971), the second of what is now a trilogy of novels about the character Harry Angstrom. Until then Updike was a novelist I had read without particularly esteeming. He was—and remains —so obviously, so ardently, so determinedly a stylist. He was also so clearly the coming man, so full of a promise that never quite seemed to come to fulfillment. *Rabbit Run,* for example, the first of three Harry Angstrom books, was a novel with an interesting idea at its center, that of a young man whose greatest glory (as a high-school athlete) is behind him at eighteen, yet the book grew diffuse, chaotic, and finally failed in a wash of violence at its close. *The Centaur,* Updike's attempt to stretch a contemporary novel upon a classical myth, *à la* James Joyce, seemed to me misfired, a bad idea taken all the way out. *Of the Farm,* a novel about a young man torn between the rivalrous claims of his wife and mother, was interesting but small. Between these novels Updike turned out an impressive flow of short stories, literary criticism, light verse. He became a large-public writer, in Wyndham Lewis's phrase, with the publication of *Couples,* a novel about sexual cus-toms in the suburbs. As I recall, I did not quite finish reading *Couples*. It wasn't the sex that put me off—it was the conversation afterward.

Except for a hundred or so pages of *Rabbit Redux,* which I put down as improbable in its violence, I pretty much stopped reading the novels of John Updike. Promises, promises, of Updikean promises I had had, for the present, enough. Still, quite without my readership, John Updike's reputation continued to grow. When *Rabbit Is Rich* (1981) won the American Book Award, the National Book Critics Circle prize, and the Pulitzer Prize, the last named, in its citation, praised the novel as "a fulfillment of Updike's fabulous promise." *Time* put Updike on the cover of its issue of October 18, 1982, and inside ran a story about him entitled "Perennial Promises Kept." Had I decamped too soon?

"Updike," *Time* noted, "is ubiquitous." And so of late he has seemed. His books fill the mass paperback racks. In *Bech Is Back,* the hero, a Jewish writer named Henry Bech, has finally written his "long-awaited" novel. No one has ever had to wait very long for a John Updike novel. Yet it is a bit unclear if anyone, apart from his publishers, is waiting at all. Perhaps it is owing to his high, his almost excessive, productivity, which eliminates the pleasure of awaiting a fresh Updike work, but I do not get the sense that people love John Updike's work or that they bring certain hopeful expectations to it, as readers still do to the novels of, say, Saul Bellow or V. S. Naipaul—the hope that they will come away with fresh knowledge of the world or insight into themselves. Even John Updike seems to be a bit bored by the phenomenon of John Updike. "In novel after novel," he recently told a *New York Times* reporter, "the amorous get together, there's the romantic failure, the economic struggle—God, we've all done it so many times."

Bored Updike may have grown, but fatigued never. Since I ceased to read him he had, it seems, written five novels—not to mention books of stories. I decided to pick him up with a novel of 1976 entitled *Marry Me.* This is a book in which Updike takes up his old suburban subject, which I understand to be yearning among the upper-middle class. In *Marry Me,* Jerry Conant, a commercial artist and a married man with three young children, has an affair with and struggles over the question of whether to marry a woman, also married with three young children, who is part of his and his wife's social circle. Such drama as the novel has is about his waverings, his tugs of conscience. Much domestic detail is presented: many bedsheets are rumpled, a good deal of bread is toasted and buttered.

So is a good deal of the prose toasted and buttered. The hero of *Marry Me* cannot even urinate without Updike describing "his diminishing arc of relief." Updike simply cannot pass up any opportunity to tap dance in prose. Toward the novel's close, as it shambles to its denouement, one must still clamber over—as an adoring reviewer put it in the *Boston Globe*—"the famous style." Thus, debarking from a plane in France, the novel's hero Updikistically notes: "The air was soft, clean, and somehow fractionated, Cubistically portioned and dislocated by the diagonal rays of a tepid sun." In Updike there is always time to type out a bit of tapestry.

Style is worth dwelling on a moment longer, for John Updike is perhaps above all considered a stylist, the *primo don* of contemporary American prose. "I notice as I write," he has said, "it comes out as sort of Updike prose. . . . It's always mine, and there's no way I can seem to get around it. Isn't it funny you only have one voice?" With that style Updike can make elaborate metaphors, strike resounding rhythms—"Skating, Ruth flew and, flying, she was free"—and chisel small but interesting observations, such as this upon a minor character in *Marry Me:* "His anxious face had forgotten the attempted suavity of its blurry little mustache."

Can one write too well? I shouldn't have thought so, and yet style, understood as sheer prettiness of phrasing, can cover up the absence of having anything very pressing to say—or even anything to say at all. With Updike it appears to be the case that the less he has to say the more he turns on the style—charm being intended to substitute for substance. Unfortunately, it is usually not an adequate substitute.

Finally nothing more improves style than actually having something to say, but in *Marry Me* it is far from clear that Updike has anything at all to say. Jerry Conant, the hero, is a great ditherer, but then, in working out this novel's plot, so is its author. "Plot has always been a great worry to me," Updike told an audience at Skidmore College, "because I don't think that life falls into plots, it does not end quite the way books do." Maybe, and maybe not. But then neither does life fall into such old-style ladies'-magazine dialogue (" 'But love must become fruitful, or it loses itself,' "), such sententious observations ("Ruth disliked, religiously, the satisfaction he took in being divided, confirming thereby the split between body and soul that alone can save men from extinction"), such hilariously unintentional comic lines (" 'I'm a Judaeo-Christian, just like you are,' Ruth said") as this extraordinarily flat novel provides. Of moral conflict there is none, of interesting characters there are none, of acute observations there are none. There is only prose, working on nothing, exhibiting itself, as if to say: "Look Ma, no thoughts."

Why would a novelist write such a book? Perhaps because he had had an experience—Updike some years ago did go through a divorce—and felt, as contemporary novelists tend to do, that no experience, God forfend, should be wasted. This same explanation might do for John Updike's next novel, *The Coup* (1978). Updike was a Fulbright Fellow in Africa, and it must have seemed a shame to him not to attempt to turn the experience into literature. *The Coup* is set in an imaginary African nation called Kush, ruled by a Marxistical Islamic leader named Colonel Hakim Félix Ellelloû, a man who has four wives, goes about the streets of his country in disguise, and was educated in the United States. Do I give away the tone and tenor of *The Coup* if I note that Colonel Ellelloû attended McCarthy College in Franchise, Wisconsin?

It is not quite so simple as that, though very nearly so. *The Coup* is intended, I suspect, as a satire, of the a-plague-on-both-your-condominiums sort, with plenty of contumely to go round for both East and West as they meddle in and destroy the cultures of the Third World. I say "I suspect" because it isn't always clear quite what Updike intends. Not only does he lash out more savagely at the West—which, naturally enough, he knows better than he does the East—but his prose once more gets in the way. Be they African leaders or Toyota dealers, John Updike heroes all sound very Updikean ("Isn't it funny you only have one voice?"), and Updikean, ventriloquated through Colonel Ellelloû, sounds like this: "I even knew how she would make love: with abashed aggression, tense in her alleged equality of body, primed like a jammed bazooka on the pornographic plastic fetishes and sexual cookbooks of her white tribe and yet, when all cultural discounts are entered, with something of graciousness, of helpless feeling, of a authentic twist at the end. . . ."

It is no accident (as the old Marxist polemicists used to say) that this quotation happens to concern sex. Sex has come more and more to fill the pages of John Updike's novels. It is rather surprising, really, that the feminist thought-control police haven't paid these books a visit. When they do so they will find that the women in an Updike novel turn out to be most notable for their legs, breasts, lips, and—as our tender-hearted author himself might put it, in one of his soggier metaphors—damp shady places. In *The Coup,* for example, Colonel Ellelloû is given four wives chiefly because, as near as I can make out, this allows Updike to illustrate four styles of fornication.

What is all the sex doing in John Updike's novels? Is it screwing merely? I would say that it is screwing mostly but not merely. Without its descriptions of sex a novel like *The Coup,* thin enough as it is, would scarcely exist. Although Updike has read a bit of West African history and looked into the Koran and even been to Africa, none of this seems to go very far in moving his novel along. Satire doesn't take him much farther: " 'America is downright loveable,' " an American diplomat in the novel says, " 'America loves all peoples and wants them to be happy, because America loves happiness.' " Heavy thinking—"It may be, Ellelloû reflected . . . that in the attenuation, desiccation, and death of religions the world over, a new religion is being formed in the hearts of men . . . a religion whose antipodes are motion and stasis . . . whose ultimate purpose is entropy"—no, heavy thinking isn't much help either. That would appear to leave only overwriting and sex, and overwriting about sex.

Is it permitted to complain about sex in novels this late in the day? One would have thought all this was settled decades ago. In "On the Treatment of Sexual Detail in Literature," an essay of 1912, the English philosopher F. H. Bradley allowed that stunted natures, to whom it is not given "to take and enjoy art and literature for what they really are," might be wrongly stimulated by sexual description in books and paintings. But, Bradley concluded with great passion, "What is not tolerable is that stunted natures set up their defects as a standard. It is an outrage, it is sheer blasphemy, when they bring the divine creations of literature and art to the touchstone of their own impotence, their own animalism, and their own immorality." Bradley later had second thoughts, and, in a note appended to his essay, he wrote: "And it must be admitted against the novel that, retaining to a greater or lesser extent the aspect of a tale of adventure, it, to speak in general, is prone to exalt the adventurous aspect of sexual love, which is not really the aspect which in life possesses most moral importance." Still, Bradley's general point stands: literature must not be restricted in its freedom because of the effect this freedom might have on brutish readers.

F. H. Bradley acknowledged that sexual detail "may tend to exalt one-sidely one side of human nature, and possibly depress others." But what he overlooked is what the freedom to write about sex in detail might do to novels and novelists. Aesthetically it has had, I think it fair to say, a generally poor effect on the novel. Among other things, it allows writers, whenever they feel their plots slowing down, to drop their characters into bed. For many contemporary novelists these bedtime moments are the great moments in their books. William Gass, in *On Being Blue,* remarks that as readers we want "the penetration of privacy. We want to see under the skirt. . . ." Is this so? Difficult to say, but what is not difficult to say, what Gass in fact says in his essay, is that "writers remain unduly responsive to it."

Some writers more than others; but enough, I think, to formulate one of those grand dichotomies, like Philip Rahv's division of American writers into Palefaces and Redskins. Today, I believe, the real division is between novelists who are grown-ups and novelists who despite chronological age have managed to remain boys and girls. The way you can tell the boys and girls is in their interest in purveying sex in the greatest possible detail. Not that grown-up novelists are uninterested in sexual relations

—Isaac Bashevis Singer, a grown-up, has said that he considers nothing quite so interesting to him as a novelist—but rather that they view the actual details as a private matter. Boy and girl novelists, by contrast, are always lifting skirts, dropping trousers, adjusting ropes and pulleys, hooking up dry-cell batteries, bringing in zebras, passing out towels, what have you.

By this standard Norman Mailer is an excellent boy novelist, and so is Philip Roth; Erica Jong and Francine du Plessix Gray are two good girl novelists; one could make a lengthy list of others. The chief way you can tell the boys and girls from the grown-ups is that in the novels of the former, sex—plain and fancy fornication—is not merely an ornament but absolutely crucial. Without the heavy dosage of sexual detail, their novels wouldn't quite exist.

John Updike is certainly a boy novelist in the sense that many of his novels are unthinkable without their elaborate sexual detail, but he is a boy novelist in other senses, too. In *The Coup,* Colonel Ellelloû, recalling his education in America, notes: "I perceived that a man, in America, is a failed boy." If there is a preponderant emotion running through Updike's novels it is that of boyish yearning, or more precisely the yearning once more to be a boy. In *Rabbit Is Rich,* Harry Angstrom, at his son's wedding, thinks: "Life, just as we first thought, is playing grownup." But the playing, the pretense, is thin, and in John Updike novels men do tend to be boys. Other boys seem either not to notice or to mind; in fact, they greatly approve. The boys who do the book reviewing in this country widely, even wildly, praised *Rabbit Is Rich,* the third of Updike's novels about Harry Angstrom, the book that won the Pulitzer and other prizes.

Rabbit Is Rich might as easily have been entitled *Rabbit Is Babbitt* (X-rated). In the novel Harry Angstrom, now in his late forties, runs his deceased father-in-law's Toyota agency in the town of Brewer, Pennsylvania. He has been married to Janice Springer now for twenty-three years; they live in his mother-in-law's house; their only son, Nelson, is a student at Kent State. Harry is a careful reader of *Consumer Reports.* He has a 42″ waist and is a Rotarian. He is financially well-off; in a middle-aged sort of way, relatively content. The novel is set in 1979: the gas short-ages have begun in earnest, American hostages are locked away in Iran. Through the 400-odd pages of the novel Rabbit rumi-nates on the decline of America, on the bittersweet goodness of the old days, but mainly on—in the old locker-room phrase—getting laid. "The trouble with you, champ," says one of Rabbit's car salesmen, "is you have screwing on the brain."

Even though the lengthiest of Updike's recent books, *Rabbit Is Rich* is easily the most readable. The reason, I suspect, is that in Harry Angstrom Updike is in real touch with his subject. He isn't in complete touch with it: Rabbit's days at the Toyota agency aren't very convincing in their detail, but then it is difficult to recall an American novelist who has been convincing on the work his characters do since Theodore Dreiser and Sinclair Lewis. Still, the yearning that Rabbit feels as he drives through the town in which he grew up, noting changes and desecrations, calling up boyhood memories, can be very moving. So, too, are the sad exchanges between Rabbit and his hopeless son, and the desola-tion Rabbit feels at being unable to find any meaning in life. All sorts of interesting bits, lovely touches, aptly captured minor characters—a hip clergyman, a sleek home-improvements sales-man, Rabbit's sour mother-in-law—are in *Rabbit Is Rich*. Some-how, one feels, this ought to be a better book than it is.

John Updike knows all about Harry Angstrom, even down to his teeth, which now, in middle age, are jacketed in gold inlays. But it is hard to believe that Updike finally cares for Rabbit, just as it is hard to believe that he cares very much about the decline of American power that he continually alludes to in this novel. They seem merely things to write about. Why, for example, does he deal so perversely with Rabbit, who he more than once hints might be homosexual? (" 'I think he's queer,' " his son Nelson says, and in Rabbit's sex fantasies, Updike writes, "The woman's sensations seem nearer to him than the man's"). Why does he make Rabbit so irreducibly sexual a being, whose every thought, every action, every motive begins and ends in sex? "The aim of my fiction," John Updike has said, is to "let literature concern itself, as the Gospels do, with the inner life of hidden man." But the inner life, in Updike's fiction, seems increasingly to be located in the scrotum.

In *Bech Is Back,* sex looms less large, and this for a not very complicated reason: it is about a writer, and the writing life is something that John Updike knows well, better even than he knows the life of Harry Angstrom. The writer as a public figure, as celebrity and grist for academic mills, is in fact the subject of two brief Updike novels, written more than a decade apart. Both are about Henry Bech, a blocked New York Jewish writer whose reputation has continued to rise even as his literary output has remained exactly the same.

Reading *Beck: A Book* (1970) and *Bech Is Back* (1982) one after the other, one senses something interesting at work. When *Beck: A Book* was published, American Jewish novelists were riding high; Jewish and novelist seemed almost linked words; and consequently there was more than a touch of acid in Updike's portrait of Henry Bech, who seemed a character created out of the idiosyncrasies of a number of Jewish novelists. *Bech: A Book* was an extended parody, but from time to time an edge of real nastiness cut through, as when an aristocratic English woman says to Bech, " 'You American Jews are so romantic. . . . I hate the "pity me" in all your books' "; or when, mocking Bech's sterility as a writer (as opposed to his own fecundity?), Updike refers to those honorable literary failures who "rather endear a writer to the race of critics, who would rather be reassured of art's noble difficulty than cope with a potent creative verve." Much mockery of the New York intellectual milieu was tossed in—Bech wrote for *Commentary,* which "let him use a desk"—and another character refers to the New York intellectuals' "heady mixture of art for art's sake and Depression funk."

In *Bech Is Back,* though, the abscess of nastiness has largely drained. As the novel begins, thirteen years have passed, and Bech has maintained his silence; indeed he has won the Melville Medal "awarded every five years to that American author who has maintained the most meaningful silence." In the seven loosely joined stories that comprise *Bech Is Back,* Henry Bech marries, is goaded by his Gentile and suburban wife into writing *Think Big,* a sloppy blockbuster best seller, and loses such privacy as he had remaining to him. Jabs are made from time to time at critics and reviewers. Some of the bits are finely done. Updike is very funny on the changing of the guard in American publishing, where old-style line editors have been replaced by new-style marketing impresarios. Many a nice throwaway line pops up: Bech "had the true New Yorker's secret belief that people being anywhere else had to be, in some sense, kidding."

But something rather more interesting has happened between *Bech: A Book* and *Bech Is Back,* and this is that Updike has gone from mockery of Henry Bech to affection for him. In the process Bech, one of America's leading Jewish novelists, has come to seem decidedly less Jewish, and more a member of another minority group: writers on whom society makes endless demands. "The writer's duty to society, Bech had said, was simply to tell the truth, however strange, small, or private his truth appeared." Yet society wants more than truth, to hear *Bech Is Back* tell it; it wants interviews, autographs, photographs, television talk-show appearances, all of which, in this novel, Henry Bech supplies. Not the least ironic touch in *Bech Is Back* is in the line: "Bech was photographed by Jill Krementz, caricatured by David Levine, and interviewed by Michiko Kakutani." For the jacket photograph of John Updike in this book is by Jill Krementz, a fresh caricature of him by David Levine accompanies the favorable review of the book in the *New York Review of Books,* and around the time of the book's publication Updike was interviewed for the *New York Times* by Michiko Kakutani. Ah, me, there goes life imitating art imitating life imitating art imitating life again.

The chief point of both *Bech* books is the tragicomic one that, as novels have become less important in the United States, novelists have come into greater public demand. Updike may speak of the writer's only duty being to tell his own "strange, small, or private" truth, but this truth has itself become stranger, smaller, and more private all the time. Such, for all his own early promise, have John Updike's own truths become, dealing as they for the most part do with ornate sex and social clichés got up in velvet metaphors. In his heart Updike may even know that his own high reputation and success are part of the general swindle, and *Bech Is Back* may be his form of admitting it. If so, that would constitute a strange, small truth that it is nonetheless well to have made public.

Commentary 1983

Ann Beattie
and the Hippoisie

A FEW YEARS AGO I spent three days as a visiting writer on the campus of a liberal-arts college. The campus may have been small, the college in the hills of Ohio, but the English department, whose paid guest I was, ran an absolutely up-to-date operation. Among its members were a black, a Jew, and Asian woman, a homosexual, a combat-booted feminist, and a young woman whose socio-political provenance I did not immediately make out. When I inquired about this woman of the young teacher who had been assigned as my guide, a man who had himself recently been denied tenure—and to be denied tenure at such an institution is always a splendid inducement to speak plainly about it—he replied, "Oh, you mean Ruthie. Ruthie is from the sixties."

"From the sixties"—the locution, I thought, was most interesting. "From the sixties" sounds rather like from the Ukraine, or at least from another country. The sixties do seem like another country—a country of a different time, a different spirit, but a real country nonetheless. Certainly its denizens are readily enough identified. Take Ruthie. In her early thirties, she was dark, chunky, and wore her hair in a Caucasian version of an Afro. She carried a backpack over a coat made out of the hide of some unidentifiable beast, a coat with string fringes and badly in need of a cleaning. She drove a Volkswagen bug, yellow, its back seat cluttered with books, Kleenex boxes, a large bottle of jug wine. Car and woman had a packed look, as if they might, without too great notice, take off for either coast. She was self-declared as a poet. She might have been a character in an Ann Beattie story, although I hadn't yet read Ann Beattie, and so could not have known this.

I first heard of Ann Beattie, in fact, at another gathering of Ann Beattie characters, this one rather more prosperous. It was at a dinner given by a couple who were then living together. She was a historian who had recently been appointed to the director-ship of a newly established women's program at a Midwestern university. He had an unfinished dissertation at Harvard and worked at intellectual odd jobs in and around the social sciences: a bit of teaching, a bit of consulting, a bit of time put in with public agencies. The other people there that evening, my wife and myself excepted, had been students in universities in the middle and late sixties and early seventies, a cause among them for some pride. A good deal of energy went into the preparation of the dinner, and a great deal of talk—about the bread, the wine, the pasta, the fish, the pastry—accompanied its digestion. Former hippies at least in spirit, these people took kindly to bourgeois habits while retaining adversary points of view; "the hippoisie" was the name they only half-jokingly gave to themselves. For a number of people there that evening, Ann Beattie was their writer, and to call them Ann Beattie characters would not, I suspect, have hurt their feelings.

I have now read Ann Beattie, her two novels and the three volumes of short stories that comprise her collected work to date. This is no small output for a writer still in her middle thirties. There are fifty of these stories. I believe I may have read some of them earlier when they first appeared in the *New Yorker*. I say "I believe" because I am not always certain. Reading them in her books I experienced a sense of *déjà lu*. Have I read them before, or have I instead read stories like them for I am told that Ann Beattie already has a number of imitators? (One line of dialogue I do clearly remember having read earlier. It runs, "Name me one thing more pathetic than a fag with a cold," and is uttered by a homosexual.) Ann Beattie's novels and stories do make an effect: they depress, even when they have what ought to be happy endings. Yet they somehow do not stay with one; they seem to seem to slide off the page; one story melts into another, and the whole finally dissolves in the mind, like one of those small blue pills some of Ann Beattie's characters require to get through the day, a downer.

As I read through story after story of Miss Beattie's, I asked myself why these stories—stories written by a writer with a true command of prose style and a deadly eye for right details—were at once vaguely depressing and distinctly forgettable? I have, for example, been reading Miss Beattie's latest collection of stories, *The Burning House,* and turning back to the book's table of contents I notice that I cannot connect stories to titles. Was "Afloat" about the woman about to have a child with a man to whom she is not married? Is "Playback" about the young man who works for an advertising agency? Is "Desire" the story in which everyone gets stoned, or in which the woman's husband leaves her for another man? Beats me.

As for the depression, well, one is used to depression in modern fiction, which provides many laughs but very few smiles. One is used to it in traditional literature, too. *Anna Karenina* comes down with a bump. But however depressed that great book leaves you, you do feel you have got something for your sadness. The depression that comes with reading Ann Beattie is of a different order, and not just because she isn't Tolstoy. It is depression at reading about the sheer hopelessness of her characters' lives; from these lives, they learn nothing and neither do we. Nor, by design, are we supposed to. In one of the stories in *The Burning House* it is said of a six-year-old girl: "She used to like stories to end with a moral, like fairy tales, but now she thinks that's kid's stuff."

Miss Beattie has a real subject, and a highly interesting one. Her subject is the fate of her own generation, the generation that was in college and graduate school in the late sixties and early seventies. This generation, as everyone knows, grew up in the shadow of the Vietnam War, and it was the first to have a free hand with sex and drugs, to know splendor both in and on the grass. I recall, in the middle sixties, a *Partisan Review* symposium, those occasions on which intellectuals are invited to say things they are sure to regret later, in which nearly all the participants had a good word for the young. Everyone agreed that this was to be a generation of great promise. The members of this generation felt that they were promising, too, but they also felt that they were, in some odd and never quite defined way, promised. Promised what? Because of their own intrinsic superiority, moral and intellectual, they felt they were promised a freer and richer and happier life than any known before here in America and possibly on earth.

But the world of the sixties ended neither with a bang nor with a whimper but, it would seem from Ann Beattie's fiction, with an album. "Rachel cried when she heard Dylan's *Self-Portrait* album, because, to her, that meant everything was over." In the story "The Lawn Party" from the collection *Secrets and Surprises* (1979) we read: "When Janis Joplin died Elizabeth cried for six days." A character in Miss Beattie's first novel, *Chilly Scenes of Winter* (1978), remarks of his sister: "You could be happy, too, Sam, if you were nineteen in 1975, and you hadn't had your eyes opened in the 60's." In the same novel another character says: "Everybody's so pathetic. What is it? Is it just the end of the 60's?" And a character in *Falling in Place* (1980), Miss Beattie's most recent novel, remarks: "There were a lot of things for which graduate school did not prepare you." One of them being, the reader is tempted to answer, the rest of life.

About all of Ann Beattie's fiction there is something of an after-party atmosphere. Her stories begin after the sixties binge is done and gone. No mention is made of the Democratic convention of 1968, of the marches and protests, of any other of the momentous happenings of those years. In one of her stories a maimed Vietnam veteran appears, in another a woman's brother is mentioned as having been killed in Vietnam, and in yet another a veteran is said to be unable to stop talking about Vietnam. Yet Miss Beattie does not hammer away at Vietnam or speak of politics except obliquely, though a foul air of things gone wrong hovers about her characters and their world. Anxiety, disappointment, despair, these are the pollutants in the Beattie atmosphere, and both characters and readers are made to choke on them.

Already in *Distortions* (1976), her first book of stories, the general pattern of Ann Beattie's fiction is set. *Distortions* is very much a young writer's book, and hence rather more experimental than the more mature Ann Beattie's fiction will be. The book's opening story is about a marriage of dwarfs. Another story is done in short takes, rather like blackout sketches. "Wesley has gaps between his teeth," one such take begins; "Janie Regis' hair is all different colors," the next one picks up. Another experimental story is entitled "It's Just Another Day in Big Bear City, California," a title which is almost a story in itself. But the less experimental Ann Beattie's stories are, the better. Taken by themselves, some of the straighter stories are quite impressive—"Wolf Dreams," for example, written when Miss Beattie was only twenty-six. Nearly all the stories show a high degree of professional polish. The dialogue always feels right; the interior monologue, too, seems on target. The flat style, a Beattie trademark, is already in use in *Distortions,* as in this opening passage from a not very good story entitled "Hale Hardy and the Amazing Animal Woman":

> Hale Hardy went to college because he couldn't think of anything better to do, and he quit because he couldn't see any reason to stay. He lasted one and a half years. He did not exactly quit; he was thrown out. When that happened he went to visit his sister Mary, who was living with another girl, Paula, who was being supported by some dude. Hale didn't know the dude's name, or why his sister was living there. He just went.

That passage reveals more than the style of Miss Beattie's fiction; it reveals the peculiar will-lessness of her characters. Passive agents, they do not act but are acted upon. "The important thing," one character in a story in *Distortions* advises another, "was to know when to give up." Here is a note Ann Beattie has held through all her books. The first story in *The Burning House* ends thus: "What Ruth had known all along: what will happen can't be stopped. Aim for grace."

Amazing Grace. If grace is what Ann Beattie's characters aim for, very few achieve it. But then they don't aim very carefully. Not much in life interests them. Politics doesn't—though they are all convinced that America is hopeless—neither conventional politics nor emotional politics. "There aren't any answers," says a Beattie character. "That's what I've got against woman's liberation. Nothing personal." Although people have love affairs, once a couple moves in together, the end is in sight. Sex is no big deal. Miss Beattie rarely describes it. Detailed description tends to be reserved for getting stoned. Few relationships endure. Work is pointless. Things fall apart; the center, hell, in Ann Beattie's fiction not even the fringes seem to hold.

In a diary entry of 1945 Noël Coward wrote: "Read Elizabeth Bowen's new short stories; exquisite writing but a trifle too inconclusive." Perhaps it is well that Coward did not live to read Ann Beattie's stories. Miss Beattie specializes in the inconclusive; inconclusiveness, in her fiction, is quite deliberate. It is part of her method. E. M. Forster once wrote that the king died and then the queen died is a story, but the king died and then the queen died of grief is a plot. Miss Beattie does not go in much for plot. Her work is, in some respects, anti-plot. In the story "Greenwich Time" in *The Burning House* a man is at the house of his former wife and her current husband; the house was one he once lived in with his wife. Now he is alone in it with his young son and the maid. His ex-wife and her husband are late—unusually late. Generally they are home long before now. It is worrisome. Yet why they are late, whether they will eventually arrive home safely, these are things we never learn. Instead, "Greenwich Time" ends with the maid telling the man that, though he may have been dispossessed from this house, she is still his friend. "Then they stood there, still and quiet, as if the walls of the room were mountains and their words might fly against them." That's it. End of story. Cut and print that (the *New Yorker* did, originally).

Chekhov instructed that if a gun appears on the wall in a scene in the first act of a play, before the play is over the gun will be fired. Not in Ann Beattie's stories; more likely the wall will disappear. This is again by way of saying how little interested she is in plot in the conventional sense. What her fiction strives to achieve is not development of character, accounts of motivation, or moral resolution—no, what she strives to achieve are states of feeling. This she often succeeds in doing. Thus in a story such as "A Reasonable Man," from the collection *Secrets and Surprises,* she can show what a woman feels who is mismarried and on the edge of nervous breakdown—loneliness, frustration, anxiety, quiet terror—and you will feel it, too. Attempting to capture states of feeling, as opposed to doing so within the construction of careful plots, is of course a great aid to composition, which helps explain why Miss Beattie has been so prolific. What is less clear is why the states of feeling her stories reveal are always those connected with sadness and loss.

Another problem arises: the states of feeling Ann Beattie strives for, workable though they may be within the brief compass of a short story, are not sufficient to keep a longer work afloat. This is why her novels, in my view, sink. The first of them, *Chilly Scenes of Winter,* is about two young men, veterans of the sixties, who are now in their late twenties. One is a Phi Beta Kappa who hasn't the money to go to law school, so instead has to settle for a job selling men's jackets. The other has a government job that bores him stiff, a mother who goes in and out of mental hospitals, and a love for a woman with whom he had an affair but who is married to someone else and about whom he cannot stop thinking. The novel's title is also the title of a song by a group called the New Lost City Ramblers and Cousin Emmy.

The winter in question is that of 1974–75, the scene of such action as there is Washington, D.C. Very little sense of the city of Washington comes through. The characters are not described elaborately. What does come through, though, is that the characters in this novel are under a malaise. It is almost as if they had come back from a war, except they haven't. " 'The goddam 60's,' Charles says. 'How'd we end up like this.' " What, exactly, went wrong? A number of things, it turns out. The country, the United States, seems partly to blame: it provides no good work, it throws up characters like Richard Nixon, it is killing off its wildlife.

Parents, partially, are to blame as well; at least most parents in Ann Beattie's fiction as in *Chilly Scenes of Winter,* have troubles that they seem to pass on to their children: divorce, alcoholism, madness. The old dreams, from Norman Rockwell to the legend of Scott and Zelda Fitzgerald, are dried up and dead. Things are grim. "Unhappiness," said the young Henry James, "is a disease," and Ann Beattie's characters have caught it.

Perhaps I make this sound slightly grimmer than it is. Miss Beattie has a sly sense of humor. From time to time she will toss an interesting flake into her fiction, such as, in *Chilly Scenes of Winter,* the young woman who is making up her mind to be a lesbian, and who says of a friend in California: "She claimed she screwed Peter Fonda on the kitchen floor in an all-night health food restaurant, but I don't believe it." The novel's hero thinks perhaps he ought to move to California but then concludes that, at twenty-seven, "he is too old for the West Coast." The two principal characters in the book have longish exchanges—conversations are not quite what they are—about food, their pasts, their futures, that are Beckett-like in their comic hopelessness.

And yet a dark doleful cloud hangs over everything. At the close of *Chilly Scenes of Winter,* the married woman whom the hero of the novel loves, and about whom he ruminates at great boring length, leaves her husband and returns to our hero. "A story with a happy ending," he says. But that seems unlikely. Why mightn't she leave him again? Why mightn't he soon grow tired of her? Why not any of a thousand possibilities—in fiction that is so weightless, where events occur without cause and life has no lessons to teach, anything can happen. If Ann Beattie's fiction makes a single point it is this: the one thing you can depend on is that there is nothing you can depend on.

"It's selling you such a bill of goods to tell you that you should get married and have a family and be secure. Jesus! What your own family will do to you." So says a woman in *Falling in Place,* mother of three, whose husband, an advertising executive of forty, is having an affair with a young woman of the sixties generation currently resident in a small apartment along Columbus Avenue. *Falling in Place* is Ann Beattie's first novel about subur-

ban, upper-middle-class family life, and that life—surprise, surprise—turns out to be hell. Not that the book is exclusively
suburban. The cast of characters includes another assortment of
sixties casualties. Among them are dropouts from Bard College;
pilgrims from the West Coast; a drug dealer worried about Three
Mile Island ("No way drugs explain why this is a bad world");
and a woman graduate student teaching high school in the summer who "was born the year *Howl* came out, but she still felt sure
that she was one of the people Ginsberg was talking about." In
Miss Beattie's fiction there are, finally, two classes of people—
those who came of age in the sixties and those who didn't, and
those who did are better.

The interesting characters in *Falling in Place,* however, are the
children. The advertising man and his wife have three: Mary, a
fifteen-year-old who is mad for Peter Frampton and who responds to everything she doesn't care for—which covers a great
deal—with the phrase, Suck-o; John Joel, her younger brother,
detached, a compulsive eater, who spends a lot of time reading
violent comics or perched in a tree in his yard; Brad, the baby,
who lives with his grandmother. Their father wants to leave their
mother but cannot quite bring himself to do so. A friend at his
advertising agency tells him, "The real killer was when you married the wrong person but had the right children." Mary and
John Joel, it must be said, are not the right children. They loathe
each other, and such denouement as the novel provides comes
about when John Joel, quite by accident, shoots and wounds his
sister.

This act forces the hand of their father, who can barely grasp
what he feels to be the enormity of it, and who because of it
determines to leave his wife at last. Only—and this seems to me
a decisive only—he, the father, does not know that the shooting
was an accident. He acts on incomplete knowledge, and Miss
Beattie, in the course of the novel, sees no need to complete it for
him. That characters get things wrong, that their vision of events
is more than a little occluded, none of this seems to matter. The
world, Ann Beattie seems to be saying, goes sourly on its way.
Things fall in place.

I say the world goes sourly on its way, but some might argue that *Falling in Place* is a relatively sunny novel. The father of these children goes off with his lady friend. His wife, without him, will have a better chance to pick up the pieces of her own shattered life. His children, being young, presumably will pull themselves together. Another couple in the novel—an Abbie Hoffman type minus the genius for publicity, and the graduate student born the year *Howl* was published—settle in after troublous days. Near the novel's close, a young man, a practicing magician, remarks: "It's a rotten world. No wonder people want answers. No wonder they want to have parties and get distracted. Sometimes something nice happens, though."

But not very often. How could it in a world seen through such dark glasses? As *Chilly Scenes of Winter* finishes off work, *Falling in Place* does the job on family. The surrounding culture provides no relief; there menace chiefly lurks. Join the magician in *Falling in Place* in his interior monologue: "He knew the real world was the Pentagon . . . and he was at least thankful that he was not involved in the real world." Cop a thought from the advertising man in the same novel: "It was true that someone could dress very conventionally and still be evil: Nixon with his jacket and tie walking on the beach, for example." (What would so many contemporary American novelists do without good old Dick Nixon still there to kick around?) Without work, without family, without support in the culture, what, really, is left for knowing people but such pleasure as can be taken on the run and the hope for some measure of personal salvation through awareness?

Awareness of what? Awareness, I believe Ann Beattie wants us to know, of what a dreadful crock life is. Philosophy resides in composition, and the method by which Miss Beattie creates her stories and novels tells much about their author's view of the world. There is, to begin with, the causelessness in her fiction. Her characters are seldom allowed to know why things happen as they do, and without such knowledge there cannot be any deliberate action. It is for this reason that almost every Ann Beattie character is so passive and, finally, so depressing. What, after all, can be more depressing than to be certain that one has no control whatsoever over one's destiny? Destiny, in the grand sense, simply does not exist in Miss Beattie's fiction. Her characters neither know about it nor seem to care about it. All that they do know is that they are living in the shade of a malaise; since this malaise is rather vague, so are the reasons for their unhappiness. Can it be, one sometimes wonders, that the reason they are so unhappy is that they do not feel happy enough—that they feel life has reneged on its promises?

What is more, as they grow older, it continues to do so. Certainly, Miss Beattie's fiction grows more and more cheerless. The first two stories in her collection *The Burning House* bring forth a brain-damaged child and a brain-damaged adult. The word "cancer" pops into the discussion fairly regularly. The intake of pills seems greater: yellow Valium, blue Valium, green Donnatal, reds. In one story a child is read to from the works of R. D. Laing, and in another a woman thinks, "Children seem older now." Many is the miscarriage and no fewer the abortions. Meanwhile, the sixties themselves begin to fade: Dennis Hopper—the usual prizes for readers who remember that name—puts in a cameo appearance in one story in *The Burning House,* and in another, set in Virginia, it is said that "Art Garfunkel used to have a place out there." People sit around and tell where they were when John F. Kennedy was shot. But I had better stop—this is beginning to get me down.

What does Ann Beattie think of all this? I happened to note that *The Burning House* is copyright under the name Pity & Irony, Inc. I don't know if that denotes a tax shelter or a self-regarding literary criticism. Miss Beattie pities her characters, true, but in the end her irony does not go very far. In her fiction it is not always easy to distinguish author from subject, dancer from dance. Her identification with her characters is nearly complete. In the biographical note to *The Burning House* she is made to sound like nothing so much as one of them: "She occasionally teaches writing at the University of Virginia and lives, with her dog, in New York City." Ann Beattie is a generation writer, and that is a severe limitation. Milan Kundera, in his novel *The Joke,* has one of his characters say: "The very thought of a generation mentality (the pride of the herd) has always repelled me." But a more severe limitation is that, while she knows a good deal about life's phenomena, she chooses to deny life's significance. In so doing, she ends by denying significance to her own work, for literature is finally about the significance and not the phenomena of life. At this point in her career, Ann Beattie is the chief purveyor of her own generation's leading clichés—the L. L. Bean of what passes for sixties existentialism.

Commentary 1983

How Good Is
Gabriel García Márquez?

H ow good is Gabriel García Márquez? "Define your
terms," I can hear some wise undergraduate reply.
"What do you mean by *is?*" Yet I ask the question in
earnest. Over the past weeks I have been reading García Márquez's four novels and three collections of stories—all of his work
available in English translation—and I am still not certain how
good he is. If I were to be asked how talented, I have a ready
answer: pound for pound, as they used to put it in *Ring* magazine, Gabriel García Márquez may be the most talented writer at
work in the world today. But talent is one thing; goodness, or
greatness, quite another.

Valéry says somewhere that there ought to be a word to describe the literary condition between talent and genius. In writing
about García Márquez, most contemporary American literary
critics have not searched very hard for that word. Instead they
have settled on calling him a genius and knocked off for the day.
Thus, John Leonard speaks of "the genius of the mature García
Márquez"; Alfred Kazin speaks of "the sign of Márquez's genius."
A writer in the *New Republic* casually compares him with Proust
and Joyce. "Classic" and "master" are two other words that pop
up with a fair regularity in discussions of García Márquez.

In sum, no novelist now writing has a more enviable reputation. His is of course an international, a worldwide reputation—
one capped by the Nobel Prize, won in 1982 at the age of fifty-
four. The Nobel Prize can sometimes sink a writer, make him

seem, even in his lifetime, a bit posthumous. But with García Márquez it appears to have had quite the reverse effect, making him seem more central, more prominent, more of a force. Before its initial appearance, the revived *Vanity Fair* magazine, which published García Márquez's slender novel *Chronicle of a Death Foretold* in its first issue, ran what seemed like countless ads displaying the author's beaming mustachioed countenance, so that by now it may be fair to say that Gabriel García Márquez is, in North America, a household face.

In Latin America, Gabriel García Márquez has been a household name and face since 1967, when his famous novel *One Hundred Years of Solitude* was first published in Buenos Aires. This novel is said to have sold more than six million copies and to have been translated into more than thirty languages. Writing about its author in 1976 in the *New Yorker,* Alastair Reid noted: "The book was immediately moved by reviewers beyond criticism into that essential literary experience occupied by *Alice in Wonderland* and *Don Quixote.* Invoked as a classic, in a year it *became* a classic, and García Márquez, to his discomfort, a literary monument." I cannot vouch for the discomfort, but otherwise Reid's account appears accurate. Mario Vargas Llosa, the very able Peruvian novelist who has written a lengthy critical study of García Márquez, said of this remarkable novel: "*One Hundred Years of Solitude* is one of those rare instances of a major contemporary work of literature which everyone can understand and enjoy." That, too, seems to be largely true, except that the first time I attempted to read *One Hundred Years of Solitude* I thought it quite brilliant and stopped reading it at page 98 (of 383 pages in the paperback edition). A number of intelligent people I know have gone through a similar experience in reading the book. All thought it brilliant, but felt that anywhere from between eighteen to fifty-one years of solitude was sufficient, thank you very much. I shall return to what I think are the reasons for this.

As for Gabriel García Márquez himself, he proves a highly complicating factor in the appreciation of his own novels. He was born in 1928, in Colombia, in the coastal town of Aracataca, was raised for the first eight years of his life by his grandparents, and later studied law at the University of Bogotá. He lived for a spell in Europe, as many Latin American intellectuals and writers seem to do, chiefly in Paris and in Rome, working as a journalist for various papers and for a time for Fidel Castro's Cuban news agency, *Prensa Latina.* A very political character—he describes himself as "an emergency politician"—García Márquez is without equivocation a man of the Left, and if not an orthodox Marxist, still indisputably devoted to the cause of Castroite revolution in Latin America. He has recently been called (in the *New York Times Magazine*) "the most active of the continent's writer-politicians, frequently to be seen in the company of world leaders from Managua to New Delhi."

Not long ago García Márquez told an interviewer from *Playboy:* "I feel myself *Latin American* in the broadest sense. As such, I use my international reputation to conduct what might be called extra-official diplomacy. I have friends, at high levels, in governments in Europe and Latin America." Fidel Castro is among these friends, and in this same *Playboy* interview García Márquez talks about supplying Castro with books whenever he goes to Cuba. Of Castro he says, in a line that to me sounds like no one so much as Woody Allen, "The man knows *everything* there is to know about seafood."

Lots of lines quite as zany as that seem to arise in connection with Latin American literary life. For example, in the same article in which García Márquez is described as "the most active of the continent's writer-politicians," the author of the article, Alan Riding, chief of the *New York Times* Mexico City bureau, notes, with a straight face: "Since the revolution [in Nicaragua], some fifty poetry workshops have sprung up in the army, police, and the trade unions, and even in peasant organizations." Now why does that line seem vaguely ludicrous? And why, moreover, is it only about a country in Latin America that one would dare to attribute so insubstantial an item to revolutionary progress?

Short of going to Latin American countries on extended visits, how does one find out anything about them? Whom does one trust? *New York Times* reporters capable of prattling on about fifty new poetry workshops in Nicaragua? American novelists—Robert Stone, Joan Didion—who have put in cameo appearances in one or another Latin American country and then returned to write about it? Academic experts, the kernels of whose true information are not easily freed of their ideological husks? Perhaps native writers? On this last count, I have recently read a most charming novel set in Lima, Peru, *Aunt Julia and the Scriptwriter,* by Mario Vargas Llosa, which gives us a portrait of daily life— corrupt, incompetent, sadly provincial though it is—very different from that which Gabriel García Márquez supplies. Whom is one to believe?

So many oddities crop up. How, for example, explain that García Márquez had his famous novel, *One Hundred Years of Solitude,* a book that he has claimed is an argument for change in Latin America, published in Argentina, universally regarded—to hear Jacobo Timerman tell it—as the most repressive of Latin American countries? How for that matter explain the emergence of Latin American literature to a place very near contemporary preeminence? How does one reconcile these various paradoxes, contradictions, confusions? It may be that finally, in reading about Latin America, one has to settle for the virtue that Sir Lewis Namier once said was conferred by sound historical training—a fairly good sense of how things did *not* happen.

Such a sense becomes especially useful in reading a writer like Gabriel García Márquez, who is continually telling us how things did happen. What he is saying is not very new. He speaks of the depredations upon the poor by the rich, upon the pure by the corrupt, upon the indigenous by the colonial—standard stuff, for the most part. But how he says it is new and can be very potent indeed. So much so that Fidel Castro is supposed to have remarked of him, "García Márquez is the most powerful man in Latin America." When presented with that remark in his *Playboy* interview, García Márquez responded that if Castro "did say that, I'm sure he was referring to me as a writer, not as a political man."

But are the lines so easily drawn? In her recent book, *Salvador,* Joan Didion ends a brief account of a televised Señorita El Salvador contest by writing that "it occurred to me that this was a contest in which winning meant more than a scholarship or a screen test or a new wardrobe; winning here could mean the difference between life and casual death, a provisional safe-conduct not only for the winner but for her entire family." Miss Didion then quotes a passage from García Márquez's surreal novel about unmitigated evil, *The Autumn of the Patriarch,* and closes by noting that "I began to see Gabriel García Márquez in a new light, as a social realist." Here perhaps is what Fidel Castro had in mind when he called García Márquez the most powerful man in Latin America.

None of this power would exist, of course, if García Márquez were not a considerable artist. Literary artists make us see things, and differently from the way we have ever seen them before; they make us see things *their* way. We agree to this willingly because in the first place they make things interesting, charming, seductive, and in the second place they hold out the promise of telling us important secrets that we would be fools not to want to know. The first paragraph of García Márquez's first novel (novella, more precisely), *Leaf Storm,* begins thus:

—Suddenly, as if a whirlwind had set down roots in the center of the town, the banana company arrived, pursued by the leaf storm. A whirling leaf storm had been stirred up, formed out of the human and material dregs of other towns, the chaff of a civil war that seemed ever more remote and unlikely. The whirlwind was implacable. It contaminated everything with its swirling crowd smell, the smell of skin secretion and hidden death. In less than a year it sowed over the town the rubble of many catastrophes that had come before it, scattering its mixed cargo of rubbish in the streets. And all of a sudden that rubbish, in time to the mad and unpredicted rhythm of the storm, was being sorted out, individualized, until what had been a narrow street with a river at one end and a corral for the dead at the other was changed into a different and more complex town, created out of the rubbish of other towns.

One senses, straightaway, that one is in the presence of the real thing here. (Gregory Rabassa's translations, considered as English writing, seem to me, as to everyone else who has commented on them, absolutely first-class.) Sweep and power are readily available to García Márquez; so, too, are what seem like endless lovely touches, such as a man described as "lame in body and sound in conscience." In "The Handsomest Drowned Man in the World," a charming tale about a time when people had hearts capacious enough for the poetic, the way is prepared for a man "to sink easily into the deepest waves, where fish are blind and divers die of nostalgia." The movements of a woman in the story "There Are No Thieves in *This* Town" have "the gentle efficiency of people who are used to reality." A man in the story "One Day After Saturday" is caught at an instant when "he was aware of his entire weight: the weight of his body, his sins, and his age altogether." García Márquez's stories are studded with such charming bits: a woman with "passionate health," a man with a "mentholated voice," a town "where the goats committed suicide from desolation," another man with "a pair of lukewarm languid hands that always looked as if they'd just been shaved." García Márquez, as Jimmy Durante used to say of himself, has a million of them.

This fecundity of phrase was not always so readily available to García Márquez. Today his fame is such that his very earliest works are being reprinted and translated—most of them are in the collection *Innocent Eréndira and Other Stories*—and these early stories are dreary in the extreme: dryly abstract, bleak, cut-rate Kafka, without the Kafkaesque edge or the humor. As a novelist, García Márquez seems to have come alive when he began to write about the coastal town he calls Macondo and—the two events seem to have taken place simultaneously—when, by adding the vinegar of politics to his writing, he gave it a certain literary tartness.

García Márquez has claimed William Faulkner as a literary mentor, and the two do have much in common. Each has staked out a territory of his own—Yoknapatawpha County for Faulkner, Macondo and its environs for García Márquez; each deals lengthily with the past and its generations; and, finally, each relies on certain prelapsarian myths (Southern grandeur before the American Civil War, Latin American poetic serenity before the advent of modernity and foreign intervention) to bind his work together. There is, though, this decisive difference between the two writers: Faulkner's fiction is almost wholly taken up with the past, while that of García Márquez, as befits a politically minded writer, generally keeps an eye out for the future.

Immersion in the work of such writers provides one of those experiences—perhaps it might be called moral tourism—exclusive to literature. By reading a good deal about a place rendered by a powerful writer, in time one comes to feel one has walked its streets, knows its history and geography, the rhythms of its daily life. Only certain writers can convey this experience through the page: Balzac did it both for Paris and French provincial towns; Faulkner did it; Isaac Bashevis Singer does it for Jewish Poland; and García Márquez does it, too.

Macondo—read enough Gabriel García Márquez and you will come to feel you know the town. The almond trees, the failing movie theater, the bells tolling out whether or not that evening's movie is censored by the Church, the fly excrement, the brothel providing modest conviviality and certain relief, the billiard hall, the dead mice, the sea and the dock where ships stop but rarely, the mayors either corrupt or stupid and usually both, the endless rains of October, the air thick with flying ants, the fog of mosquitoes, the streets either dusty or muddy, the houses where widows hole up for decades, where men walk out and meet their humid deaths by stabbing, where the dentist without a degree has his office, the old Arab section where the Syrians set out their wares on tables on market days, where the mail comes only on Friday—Macondo, you can't miss it, it's the next town up from Riohacha.

Viewed in retrospect, the Macondo stories—they are found in *Leaf Storm and Other Stories* and *No One Writes to the Colonel and Other Stories,* and the town is also the setting for the novel *In Evil Hour*—appear to be an elaborate warm-up for the novel *One Hundred Years of Solitude.* They seem to be sketches, trial runs, dress rehearsals for the big novel ahead. In these stories names will appear in passing—like Colonel Aureliano Buendía, one of the heroes of *One Hundred Years*—almost as if they were coming attractions. Then, working the other way around, incidents occur in *One Hundred Years* that have been the subjects of whole stories in the earlier volumes. To know fully what is going on in García Márquez one has to have read the author in his entirety. In these stories the stages in García Márquez's literary development are on display, rather like specimens inside formaldehyde-filled jars showing progress from zygote to fully formed human. One reads these stories and witnesses his talent growing, his political ardor increasing. In these stories, too, García Márquez shows his taste for that blend of fantasy and hyperbole, exhibited in a context of reality, that is known as magic realism.

Magic realism is the blotting-paper phrase that has absorbed much critical ink on the subject of Latin American fiction. A blurring of the magical with the real, it works differently in different hands. In Demetrio Aquilera-Malta's novel *Seven Serpents and Seven Moons,* for example, a pirate screws out his eye to take a closer look at someone; or a wooden Jesus Christ will leave his crucifix to bum a cigarette, then climb back up on the cross. Thus are the mythical and the real, the ethereal and the mundane, mated and mixed. The ideological is often included as well. In García Márquez's story "Big Mama's Funeral," an account of the death of a woman of fabled wealth, the woman dictates to a notary the following list of her "invisible estate":

> The wealth of the subsoil, the territorial waters, the colors of the flag, national sovereignty, the traditional parties, the rights of man, civil rights, the nation's leadership, the right of appeal, Congressional hearings, letters of recommendation, historical records, free elections, beauty queens, transcendental speeches, huge demonstrations, distinguished young ladies, proper gentlemen, punctilious military men, His Illustrious Eminence, the Supreme Court, goods whose importation was forbidden, liberal ladies, the meat problem, the purity of language, setting a good example, the free but

responsible press, the Athens of South America, public opinion, the lessons of democracy, Christian morality, the shortage of foreign exchange, the right of asylum, the Communist menace, the ship of state, the high cost of living, republican traditions, the underprivileged classes, statements of political support.

She didn't manage to finish. The laborious enumeration cut off her last breath. Drowning in the pandemonium of abstract formulas which for two centuries had constituted the moral justification of the family's power, Big Mama emitted a loud belch and expired.

"What I like about you," says one character to another in the García Márquez story "The Incredible and Sad Tale of Innocent Eréndira and Her Heartless Grandmother," is the serious way you make up nonsense." Serious nonsense might stand as a blurb line for *One Hundred Years of Solitude*. E. M. Forster remarked that at a certain age one loses interest in the development of writers and wants to know only about the creation of masterpieces. Certainly *One Hundred Years of Solitude* has everywhere been so acclaimed. The novel is a chronicle of six generations of the Buendía family, founders of the village of Macondo. It recounts such extraordinary happenings as Macondo's insomnia plague, its thirty-two civil wars, banana fever, revolution, strikes, a rain that lasts five years, marriages, intermarriages, madness, and the eventual extinction of the Buendía line with the birth of an infant who has a pig's tail and who is eventually carried off by ants.

"*One Hundred Years of Solitude* is not a history of Latin America," García Márquez has said, "it is a *metaphor* for Latin America." With that quotation we are already in trouble. What can it mean to say that a novel is a metaphor for a continent?

Before one attempts to ascertain what it might mean, tribute must be paid to the sheer brimming brilliance of *One Hundred Years of Solitude*. "Dazzling" does not seem to me in any way an imprecise word to describe the style of this novel, nor "epic" any less imprecise a word to describe its ambitions. Its contents cannot be recapitulated, for in its pages fireworks of one kind or another are always shooting off. Disquisitions on history, memory, time wind in and out of the plot. Yellow flowers fall from the sky marking a man's death; a heart-meltingly beautiful girl ascends to heaven while folding a sheet, a girl whose very smell "kept on torturing men beyond death, right down to the dust of their bones." Everything is grand, poetic, funny, often at once. A man suffers "flatulence that withered the flowers"; a woman has "a generous heart and a magnificent vocation for love." Then there is Colonel Aureliano Buendía, of whom García Márquez writes:

> Colonel Aureliano Buendía organized thirty-two armed uprisings and he lost them all. He had seventeen male children by seventeen different women and they were exterminated one after the other on a single night before the oldest one had reached the age of thirty-five. He survived fourteen attempts on his life, seventy-three ambushes, and a firing squad. He lived through a dose of strychnine in his coffee that was enough to kill a horse. He refused the Order of Merit, which the President of the Republic awarded him. He rose to be Commander in Chief of the revolutionary forces, with jurisdiction and command from one border to the other, and the man most feared by the government, but he never let himself be photographed.

The novel's ending loops back upon itself brilliantly, so that at the close the last of the Buendía men, sitting in his room at the beginning of a cyclone, has finally deciphered a coded Sanskrit manuscript that tells the history of the Buendías, including the end of the family and of the town of Macondo in a cyclone. Here is a sense of an ending—with trumpets.

And yet—why do so many readers seem to bog down in this glittering work? Part of the difficulty seems to me technical, part psychological. *One Hundred Years of Solitude* is peculiarly a novel without pace; it is, for its nearly four hundred pages, all high notes, service aces, twenty-one-gun salutes. In a novel, such non-stop virtuosity tends to pall. To use a simile to describe a novel that its author describes as a metaphor, reading *One Hundred Years* is like watching a circus artist on the trampoline who does only quadruple back somersaults. At first you are amazed to see him do it; then you are astonished that he can keep it up for so long; then you begin to wonder when he is going to be done, because frankly you'd like to see something less spectacular, like a heavy-legged woman on an aged elephant.

Unless, that is, you sense a deeper meaning beneath all this virtuosity. And here it must be said that there has been no short-age of deep readings of *One Hundred Years of Solitude,* a novel which, if critics are to be consulted, has more levels than a zig-gurat. There are those who think that the true meaning of the novel is solitude, or, as Alastair Reid puts it, "We all live alone on this earth in our own glass bubbles." There are those who think that the novel is about writing itself; thus, D. P. Gallagher, an Oxford literature don, writes that "one of the novel's funda-mental aims is to tell us something about the nature of contem-porary Latin American writing on which we shall see that it acts as a kind of interpretative meditation." There are those who are fascinated with the book's allusiveness; an acquaintance of mine, a great García Márquez fan, said, "Don't you suppose you really have to know a good deal about South American Indian myth to know what's going on in the novel?" There are those who believe that the stuff of myth ought not to be looked at too closely; thus John Leonard, who can always be counted upon for the flashy phrase, says, apropos of the writing of García Márquez, "dreams redeem." Then there is García Márquez himself, who has given a clear political reading to his own novel, commenting, in an inter-view, "I did want to give the idea that Latin American history had such an oppressive reality that it had to be changed—at all costs, at any price!"

Modern taste in literature runs to interesting ambiguities. "Lit-erature is the instrument neither of a whole thought nor of an organized thought," wrote Valéry, in a sentiment for which

Schlegel prepared the ground more than a century before when he wrote, "the freedom of the poet shall suffer no law to be imposed upon it." But how much freedom ought to be allowed? If we are unwilling to hold literature to a certain standard of intellectual responsibility, are we not ultimately refusing to take it seriously?

A case in point is García Márquez's use of numbers in *One Hundred Years of Solitude*. For the most part he uses them to hyperbolic effect by exaggerating with comic precision. Thus the great rain storm in Macondo lasts "four years, eleven months, and two days"; one of the Buendía daughters during school holidays brings home seventy-two classmates and nuns; note, too, the numbers used in the passage quoted above on Colonel Aureliano Buendía. But in a key section of *One Hundred Years,* a strike of banana workers, precision gives way to imprecision: "more than 3,000" striking workers are murdered by federal troops, their bodies carted away in a train "with almost 200 freight cars and a locomotive at either end and a third one in the middle."

When queried about this number, García Márquez readily owned up to the exaggeration built into the figure, saying:

There were very few deaths. If 100 people had been killed in 1928 it would have been catastrophic. I made the death toll 3,000 because I was using certain proportions in my book. One hundred wouldn't have been noticed. I was also interested in achieving a certain imagery: I wanted the bodies to be taken away in a train, a train such as the ones that were loaded with clusters of bananas. I did research and found that to fill such a train, you'd need at least 3,000 bodies. Three thousand in 1928 would have been *all* the residents of the town.

But if García Márquez owns that the number of people killed was at most 100, perhaps, allowing for exaggeration, it was in reality twenty, or even ten. Who knows? Along with magic realism, Gabriel García Márquez has given us another new literary-critical label, "political realism," which, in its own way, is itself quite magical.

If *One Hundred Years of Solitude* leaves any doubt about the political intent of García Márquez's mature work, *The Autumn of the Patriarch* wipes that doubt away. When García Márquez says that *One Hundred Years* is a metaphor for Latin America, he is of course putting a political interpretation on his own novel. The *The Autumn of the Patriarch* is neither metaphor nor symbol but a direct representation of a strong political point of view. The novel is about the life of a dictator, the type of *el caudillo,* in an unnamed Caribbean country, though to put it that way is rather like saying that Joyce's *Ulysses* is about a Jew walking around Dublin one day in June 1904.

The dictator in *The Autumn of the Patriarch* lives for more than two hundred years, his demise, *à la* Mark Twain, being often reported but much exaggerated. He has been in power—he has been *the* power—longer than anyone can remember, and his is the greatest solitude of all: that of the unloved dictator perpetuating his unearned power. This man, who himself can neither read nor write, is described, examined, and prosecuted with the aid of a novelistic technique as relentlessly modernist as any in contemporary fiction.

The Autumn of the Patriarch is divided into six chapters, but that is the only division in the novel, and the only concession to the reader's convenience. The book has no paragraphs, and while the punctuation mark known as the period may show up from time to time, the novel's sentences are not what one normally thinks of as sentences at all. A sentence might begin from one point of view, and before it is finished include three or four others.

The structure of the novel is built upon what García Márquez has called "multiple monologue," but on the level of sentences it works along the lines of the following:

They did not spread the news immediately that time either, contrary to what he expected, but many prudent hours passed with clandestine investigations, secret agreements, among the heirs of the regime who were trying to gain time by denying the rumor of death with all manner of contrary versions, they brought his mother Benedición Alvarado out into the commercial district to show that she was not wearing a mourning face, they dressed me in a flowered dress like a chippy, sir, they made me buy a macaw-feather hat so that everybody would see me happy, they made me. . . .

And so on.

This is García Márquez working out of the James Joyce tradition, attempting, through literary technique, to capture on the page, with Joycean ambition, the whole of life. The effects García Márquez achieves are brilliant, often breathtakingly so, though often, too, as in all militantly modernist writing, one has the feeling that art is imitating art rather more than nature. But between Joyce and García Márquez there is a difference: James Joyce, though scarcely anyone's notion of a large-hearted man, loved his characters; while Gabriel García Márquez, nearly everyone's notion of a large-hearted man, reveals for his an unsurpassed loathing.

One of the small shocks of this novel is to see the most complex modernist techniques put to the most patent political purposes. Now it must be said that García Márquez did not invent the Latin American dictator. Trujillo, Batista, Perón, Hernández Martinez, Duvalier (dare one add the name Fidel Castro?)—one could put together a pretty fair All-Star team, though these boys are bush league compared with what Europe and Asia in this century have been able to produce.

García Márquez's portrait of the dictator in *The Autumn of the Patriarch* is an amalgam of Latin America's dictators, minus the great seafood man Fidel and with a touch or two of Franco added. As a picture of squalor, rot, and bestiality, it is devastating. The devastation is in the details, of which the endlessly inventive García Márquez is never in short supply. Let one incident suffice here. The dictator learns he has been betrayed by the one crony

he thought reliable; shortly after learning of this betrayal he invites to dinner the main military men of his regime,

> . . . and then the curtains parted and the distinguished Major
> General Rodrigo de Aguilar entered on a silver tray stretched
> out full length on a garnish of cauliflower and laurel leaves,
> steeped with spices, oven brown, embellished with the uni-
> form of five golden almonds for solemn occasions and the
> limitless loops for valor on the sleeve of his right arm, four-
> teen pounds of medals on his chest and a sprig of parsley in
> his mouth, ready to be served at a banquet of comrades by
> the official carvers to the petrified horror of the guests as
> without breathing we witness the exquisite ceremony of
> carving and serving, and when every plate held an equal
> portion of the minister of defense stuffed with pine nuts and
> aromatic herbs, he gave the order to begin, eat hearty gentle-
> men.

The Autumn of the Patriarch is about more than politics alone
—time and the nature of illusion are motifs played upon artfully
throughout—but politics give the novel its impetus and are finally its chief subject. These politics are highly selective, predictable, more than a trifle clichéd. Octavio Paz has said that García
Márquez, as a political thinker, "repeats slogans." As a novelist,
he can make these slogans vivid, even funny, but they remain
slogans. For example, the attacks on the United States in this
novel come through the dictator's continuous dealings with a
stream of U.S. ambassadors of perfectly Waspish and quite forgettable names—Warren, Thompson, Evans, Wilson—who in
the end succeed in swindling him out of the very sea. Americans,
the Catholic Church, politicians, all, in the mind and in the novels
of Gabriel García Márquez, are swindlers. Liberals or conservatives, it does not matter which, they are crooks, every one of
them. Which leaves—doesn't it?—only one solution: revolution.

So talented a writer is García Márquez that he can sustain a
longish tale on sheer storytelling power alone, as he does in his

most recent book, *Chronicle of a Death Foretold*. It has been said of García Márquez that he combines the two powerful traditions of Latin American writing: the left-wing engagé tradition of the Communist poet Pablo Neruda and the modernist mandarin tradition of Jorge Luis Borges. In this slender novel it is the Borges side that predominates. The book is about a plot on the part of twin brothers who are out to avenge their family's honor against a young man who they mistakenly believe has deflowered their sister, thus causing her husband to return her in shame to her family the morning after the wedding night. In fact, the brothers wish to give the young man every chance to avoid their slaughtering him, so they bruit it about the town that they are looking for him, which ought to give him sufficient opportunity to escape his fate. Through a most unusual absence of the usual concatenation of circumstances, no one is able to warn the young man, and so, because the brothers feel compelled to carry on a barbarous tradition, he is massacred at the door of his own home.

As always with García Márquez's work, there are wondrous fine touches throughout. After the murder, one of the brothers, in talking about his repeated stabbing of the young man, says, "I felt the way you do when you're galloping on horseback." The victim, a fastidious gent, falls with his entrails in his hands—this is a most gory tale—but then, in the words of an eyewitness, "He even took care to brush off the dirt that was stuck to his guts." Magic realism crops up in details little and large. After the murder the despoiled virgin and disappointed bride, now living in another town, writes almost two thousand letters to her husband-of-one-night, who never reads any of them, yet seventeen years later, fat and now losing his hair, returns to live with her. The tale is told with such subtle organization and such complete fluency that García Márquez can insert anything he wishes into it; and indeed the narrator does insert mention of his marriage proposal to his own wife and a brief account of his youthful dalliances with prostitutes. Such is the easy mastery of this novel that the reader is likely to forget that he never does learn who actually did deflower the virgin. *Chronicle of a Death Foretold* is a handsomely written and inconsequential book of a kind that offers ample leeway for deep readings, and one that could have been composed only by a hugely gifted writer.

"Intellectuals consider themselves to be the moral conscience of society," García Márquez is quoted as saying in the *New York Times Magazine,* "so their analyses invariably follow moral rather than political channels. In this sense, I think I am the most politicized of them all." Yet, oddly, in García Márquez's fiction morality is rarely an issue; García Márquez himself seems little interested in moral questions, or in the conflicts, gradations, and agonies of moral turmoil. The reason for this, I suspect, is that for him the moral universe is already set—for him, as for so many revolutionary intellectuals, there are the moral grievances of the past, the moral hypocrisies of the present, and, waiting over the horizon, the glories of the future, when moral complexity will be abolished. The moral question is, for García Márquez, ultimately a political question. Outside of his politics, García Márquez's stories and novels have no moral center; they inhabit no moral universe. They are passionate chiefly when they are political; and when they are political, so strong is the nature of their political bias that they are, however dazzling, flawed.

Thus, to return to where I set out, a short answer to my question—how good is Gabriel García Márquez?—is that he is, in the strict sense of the word, marvelous. The pity is that he is not better.

Commentary 1983

Mailer Hits Bottom

O N PAGE 421 of Norman Mailer's new novel, *Ancient Evenings,* my eyeballs glazed like a franchise dough-nut, I came across the following line, spoken by the Pharaoh Ptah-nem-hotep to Menenhetet II, the character who for the most part narrates this more-than-700-page book: "To tell too little is becoming your sin." That caught my attention, as did, earlier, this line: " 'Yes,' said my great-grandfather, 'and I have observed that most of those who are so fortunate as to have been given the great member of a god often show an uncontrol-lable lack of patience.' " Long before that moment I had thought to throw this small tombstone of a novel against the wall—pa-tience, let me speak plainly, never having been my long suit. But I forbore, and instead, in all-too-brief intervals among the multi-ple acts of buggery and other sexual permutations that festoon the novel's pages, allowed my mind to formulate reverse blurbs: "Insomnia sufferers, your cure is at hand." "Gives the argument for censorship a whole new lease on life." "Extremely repulsive, utterly loathsome."

My pleasure in *Ancient Evenings* was not, then, unbounded. Yet when a talented writer writes a truly wretched book—and I believe *Ancient Evenings* to be wretched in a big-time way—all sorts of interesting questions arise. First among them is, why did he do it? This might be followed by, how could he have lost his self-critical bearings so completely? What in the intellectual envi-ronment of the day encouraged him on his crash course? When did his wagon jump the track in the first place? And, finally, was there something in his general line of thought that made artistic disaster inevitable?

Many would deny the chief premise behind these questions—that is, that Norman Mailer is a talented writer. Certainly he has written more that is bloated, foolish, and simply junky than any other serious writer of our time. He has specialized in making a public buffoon of himself, and acted in ways that reveal a deeper strain of self-deception than is usually permitted a man who stakes out for himself the claim to being a major novelist. Writing empty books, running for mayor of New York City and performing other clownish antics, aiding in the parole of a killer who, once out of prison, soon killed again, and generally leading a public life best fitted for the People section of *Time* magazine—Norman Mailer must have plenty to occupy his thoughts on modern evenings in Brooklyn Heights.

Still, when he is working well, Norman Mailer has impressive gifts. I was sharply reminded of this while reading *The Executioner's Song* (1979), his lengthy account of the life and execution of the murderer Gary Gilmore. In that book Mailer reveals himself as a man of enormous sympathy—and the best kind of sympathy, imaginative sympathy, the sympathy that a writer shows for the people he writes about by being able to enter into and successfully convey their interior lives. Again and again in *The Executioner's Song*—a book not without its flaws, which I shall get to presently—Mailer displays this power of getting inside the minds of people whose circumstances in life are so very different from his own: the arthritic mother of a killer, a successful Mormon lawyer, a police squealer. Mailer can portray the chaos in the life of a nineteen-year-old girl, unmarried with two children, and no prospect of any kind—and make you believe in her, feel for her, wish her life were not so hopeless as you know it will be.

But if expenditure of imaginative sympathy has always been one of the great things that novelists do, it is not what Norman Mailer is famous for. He is famous instead for creating his own literary persona, that of an autobiographical journalist more than a novelist, a kibitzer known for pushing himself to the center of the stage, above all a personal voice, savvy, logorrheic, always and endlessly self-dramatizing. Here is a sampler from *Advertisements for Myself* (1959):

> Like many another vain, empty, and bullying body of our time, I have been running for President these last ten years in the privacy of my mind, and it occurs to me that I am less close now than when I began. Defeat has left my nature divided, my sense of time is eccentric, and I contain within myself the bitter exhaustions of an old man, and the cocky arguments of a bright boy. So I am everything but my proper age of thirty-six, and anger has brought me to the edge of the brutal. In sitting down to write a sermon for this collection, I find arrogance in much of my mood. It cannot be helped. The sour truth is that I am imprisoned with a perception which will settle for nothing less than making a revolution in the consciousness of our time. Whether rightly or wrongly, it is then obvious that I would go so far as to think it is my present and future work which will have the deepest influence of any work being done by an American novelist in these years.

Today this style seems pretentious in the extreme, feverish, self-parodying—"the edge of the brutal," "sour truth," "imprisoned within a perception"—yet it did not seem so then. It seemed then, in fact, rather seductive; it found many inferior imitators, among them not a few overheated academics. For a time, critics tended to praise Norman Mailer in quite Maileresque terms. In reviewing *The Armies of the Night,* Mailer's account of a 1967 anti-Vietnam war march on the Pentagon, Richard Gilman, in the *New Republic,* wrote:

> All the rough force of his imagination, his brilliant gifts of observation, his ravishing if often calculating honesty, his daring and his chutzpah are able to flourish on the steady ground of a newly coherent subject . . . history and personality confront each other with a new sense of liberation.

A new sense of liberation—the admiration for Norman Mailer during the late 1960s and the early 1970s certainly owed a good deal to that. But let us return briefly to the passage from *Advertisements for Myself* and check it for prophetic accuracy. Mailer was quite wrong about his influence as a novelist. Apart from two not very distinguished works, *An American Dream* (1964) and *Why Are We in Vietnam?* (1967), Mailer ceased writing novels. Instead he wrote an ample amount of journalism to which he would append the word novel in subtitles. *The Armies of the Night,* for example, carries the subtitle "History as a Novel, The Novel as History," and, later, *The Executioner's Song* is subtitled "A True Life Novel." It was not Norman Mailer the novelist, then, but Norman Mailer the journalist and public figure who did help make, in his phrase, something akin to "a revolution in the consciousness of our time." That does not seem to be in question. What is in question is the nature, or quality, of that revolution.

Along with Paul Goodman, Norman O. Brown, and a number of lesser figures—flacks, really—Mailer was one of the key men responsible for releasing the Dionysian strain in American life. To be sure, they had help from pot and other drugs, from the new sexual freedom, from rock music, and from the Vietnam War. Mailer was the premier journalist of this era. Whatever he wrote about—John F. Kennedy, the anti-war movement, our national political conventions—he pumped up with his self-dramatizations. Wherever Norman Mailer was, to hear Norman Mailer tell it, there was "the existential moment." He often referred to himself, in his own writings, in the third person, the better to mock yet also to push himself forward. A characteristic passage: "Yes, Mailer had an egotism of curious disproportions. With the possible exception of John F. Kennedy, there had not been a President of the United States nor even a candidate since the Second World War whom Mailer secretly considered more suitable than himself. . . ."

Yet he could on occasion shoot off observations of real power. In his coverage of the 1968 Democratic convention in Chicago he provided a portrait of Hubert Humphrey that could make anyone who cared for Humphrey wince at its deadly, and devastating, accuracy. There is a very moving moment in Mailer's *The Armies of the Night* where he describes the radical hippie contingent before the Pentagon exchanging stares with the young military policemen, each group seeing in the other its fantasies of the devil. No, had Mailer been less talented he could not have brought off what he did.

Nevertheless, read today his journalistic books all seem terribly overcooked—almost comically so. Crossing the line of MPs at the Pentagon in *The Armies of the Night,* Mailer has himself exclaim:

> "I won't go back. If you don't arrest me, I'm going on to the Pentagon," and knew he meant it, some absolute certainty had come to him, and then two of them leaped on him at once in the cold clammy murderous fury of all cops at the existential moment of their making their bust—all cops who secretly expect to be struck at that instant for all their sins—and a supervising force came to his voice and he roared, to his own distant pleasure in new achievement and new authority—"Take your hands off me, can't you see? I'm not resisting arrest."

And so on, into the dark night of the syntactical soul. A point that is worth making about this is that Mailer could not have been in danger for a moment. Someone unknown, someone without fame or funds, might have risked a blow over the head, but not a famous writer. There are, after all, existential moments and existential moments.

Feverish times get feverish writing, and this Norman Mailer through the 1960s was able to supply by the yard. Yet even before the tumult of the sixties, Mailer was a writer who seemed to flourish in tumult. His first novel, *The Naked and the Dead* (1948), was published when he was twenty-five, and though it was a great commercial success, it was also very much a young man's book— meant to be daring in its political views, its brave use (for the day) of blue language, its portrayal of low life. Right from the start Mailer had set up shop as an *enfant terrible*. Now past sixty years old, he seems ever after to have been locked into the role. Thirty-five years as an *enfant terrible* leaves one a *vieux terrible,* which is a much more tiresome, not to say tiring, role to play.

Part of the terribleness of this particular *enfant* has been his penchant for literary violence. In much of Mailer's work some form of fascism, political or spiritual, looms as the great American danger, yet Mailer himself is almost invariably more fascinated than repelled by it. An incarnation of this fascist spirit appears in *The Naked and the Dead,* in the character of Sergeant Croft, a man whose very being is violent. The identification between Mailer and Croft is very strong, as Kenneth S. Lynn has recently remarked in *Commentary,* and as Croft only comes alive through the opportunity for violence, so does Mailer's prose come most alive in describing Croft.

In time, violence began taking an ideological turn in Norman Mailer's writing. Nowhere did this become more clear than in an infamous essay he wrote in 1957 entitled "The White Negro." The essay acquired its infamy because in it Mailer, in the course of explaining the phenomenon of a type of the social outlaw known as the hipster, appeared to condone murder. The offending passage, which came armored in parentheses, is the following:

(It can of course be suggested that it takes little courage for two strong eighteen-year-old hoodlums, let us say, to beat in the brains of a candy-store keeper, and indeed the act—even by the logic of the psychopath—is not likely to prove very therapeutic, for the victim is not an immediate equal. Still, courage of a sort is necessary, for one murders not only a weak fifty-year-old man but an institution as well, one violates private property, one enters into a new relation with the police and introduces a dangerous element into one's life. The hoodlum is therefore daring the unknown, and so no matter how brutal the act, it is not altogether cowardly.)

So far as I know, Norman Mailer has never apologized for this passage, or for any part of this essay. It is scarcely likely that he could have done so, for "The White Negro" has running through it the blueprint for Norman Mailer's own artistic career. For this reason it is worth briefly summarizing.

Behind the essay are the assumptions that, what with its concentration camps and atomic bombs, ours has been a particularly murderous century. In American life, according to Mailer, the great enemy is conformity, which is, in ways never really explained, subtly totalitarian. Much Maileresque exaggeration now comes into play: "A stench of fear has come out of every pore of American life, and we suffer from a collective failure of nerve." Nor is there any shortage of dubious statement: "A totalitarian society makes enormous demands on the courage of men, and a partially totalitarian society makes even greater demands, for the general anxiety is greater" (tell it to Solzhenitsyn). "The shits," Mailer announces, "are killing us."

Onto the scene comes the hipster, or, as Mailer once refers to him, "the American existentialist." He is a great disrupter—part psychopath, but one who seems in some way to have generalized his psychopathology sufficiently to know that his true enemy is a society that perpetually threatens to deaden his instinctual life. It is only through great risk, through living in the present, through engaging death, that the hipster maintains his poise and his authority:

> It is this knowledge which provides the curious community of feeling in the world of the hipster, a muted cool religious revival to be sure, but the element which is exciting, disturbing, nightmarish perhaps, is that incompatibles have come to bed, the inner life and the violent life, the orgy and the dream of love, the desire to murder and the desire to create, a dialectical conception of existence with a lust for power, a dark, romantic, and yet undeniably dynamic view of existence for it sees every man and woman as moving individually through each moment of life forward into growth or backward into death.

Mailer remarks that, at a modest estimate, there are ten million Americans who are more or less psychopathic, yet "probably not

more than one hundred thousand men and women who consciously see themselves as hipsters, but their importance is that
they are an elite with the potential ruthlessness of an elite, and a
language most adolescents can understand instinctively, for the
hipster's intense view of existence matches their experience and
their desire to rebel."

It is one thing to understand the psychopathology of the hipster, another to sympathize with it. Mailer sympathizes with it—
completely. How could it be otherwise when, though he never
says so outright, he nonetheless clearly sees himself as the artistic
arm of the hipster enterprise? The following passages from "The
White Negro," meant to apply to the hipster, make much more
sense when understood as expressing the underlying assumptions
of Norman Mailer's own career as a writer:

> Given its emphasis on complexity, Hip abdicates from any
> conventional moral responsibility because it would argue
> that the results of our actions are unforeseeable, and so we
> cannot know if we do good or bad. What is consequent
> therefore is the divorce of man from his values, the liberation
> of the self from the Super-Ego of society. The only Hip
> morality . . . is to do what one feels whenever and wherever
> it is possible, and—this is how the war of the Hip and the
> Square begins—to be engaged in one primal battle: to open
> the limits of the possible for oneself, and for oneself alone,
> because that is one's need.

> . . . it takes literal faith in the creative possibilities of the
> human being to envisage acts of violence as the catharsis
> which prepares growth.

> A time of violence, new hysteria, confusion, and rebellion
> will then be likely to replace the time of conformity.

In Mailer's view, as man and as artist, you either move forward
or you die—and as for man and artist, so for society. Such a view

allies Mailer thoroughly with the notion that art must always be about the business of transcending previously established boundaries; it must smash icons, loosen the hold of settled morals, everywhere shatter complacency. The artist is most useful when he is most disruptive. As a writer, Mailer sees himself as destructive for the public good.

Fairly early in his career Mailer took for his model Ernest Hemingway. In prose style and in the general texture of their minds no two writers are more unalike, but what Mailer acquired from Hemingway, along with a lot of cheap boxing metaphors to describe his artistic career, was the notion of the novelist as perpetually in competition, both with his peers and with the writers of the past. ("So, mark you. Every American writer who takes himself to be both major and *macho* must sooner or later give a *faena* which borrows from the self-love of a Hemingway style.") But he also took the notion that a major writer must also be a major public personality. ("Let any of you decide for yourselves how silly would be *A Farewell to Arms* or, better, *Death in the Afternoon,* if it had been written by a man who was five-four, had acne, wore glasses, spoke in a shrill voice, and was a physical coward.") Hemingway, it must be said, was much better at this than Mailer. While Norman Mailer has indeed managed to become a major public personality, the personality he has over the years projected has not been one of cool courage ("grace under pressure," in the old Hemingway formulation) but instead one of chaos and confusion—of a somewhat muddled man straining to seem spiritually larger than he is.

From Hemingway, too, Mailer seems to have absorbed the additional notion that writing, no less than life itself, entails taking terrible risks. Of course the idea that the best life is the life lived dangerously does not begin in the mind and work of Ernest Hemingway. "Believe me!" noted Nietzsche, "The secret of reaping the greatest fruitfulness and the greatest enjoyment from life is to live dangerously." And early in *Ancient Evenings* Mailer has his chief character announce: "In its true exchange, one cannot gain a great deal unless one is willing to dare losing all. That is how the loveliest plunder is found." But the notion that *writing* is a dangerous activity beautifully suits Mailer's sense of self-dramatization.

Such, then, has been the bulky baggage of ideas that Norman Mailer has dragged through his career: the artist must transcend all previous boundaries; he must be a disturber of the peace; he must regularly be making fresh breakthroughs; he must establish a public celebrity that will lend added luster to his work; he must see himself in perpetual competition with all other writers, in a kind of artistic-intellectual Mr. Universe contest; and, finally, he must recognize—and through his writing realize—that the life of the artist is fundamentally a most dangerous life, filled with risk and daring and the search for unknown treasure, a form of deep-sea diving of the mind.

Whatever the intrinsic merit of these notions—and I, for one, do not think there is much merit in them—they are dangerous above all to writers. Among other things, one cannot sustain a long literary career on them. It is noteworthy in this connection that those writers who *(mutatis mutandis)* did seem to work under such assumptions died, perhaps mercifully, young: Byron, Baudelaire, Rimbaud. Those who live long lives—Henry Miller comes to mind—become *vieux terribles*. A strong argument could be made that these same notions have done serious damage to Norman Mailer's own literary career. Not once but twice he has undergone a decade-long hiatus between novels. This probably should not surprise; after all, to shock, to break through, to live dangerously—a man cannot figure to do this year in and year out.

At the end of his first ten-year hiatus Mailer produced a novel entitled *An American Dream* (1965). He produced it, moreover, under extraordinary conditions. He wrote it in eight installments, for *Esquire,* under the pressure of magazine deadlines—the way, as the author himself modestly pointed out, Dostoyevsky and Dickens wrote many of their novels. But Dostoyevsky, but Dickens, *An American Dream* is not. It is instead a Maileresque fantasy with a hero, one Stephen Richards Rojack, who is the kind of man Mailer no doubt imagines himself to be. Along with being the "one intellectual in America's history with a Distinguished Service Cross," Rojack is a former United States Congressman, a television celebrity, a professor of existentialist psychology, author of *The Psychology of the Hangman,* a better than middling boxer, and a sack-artist of Olympian caliber. For intellectual provender, *An American Dream* offers a murder, a buggery, and a good deal of chatter about the CIA and the Mafia. Its message, put into the mind of Rojack, who goes off scot free after killing his wife, is this: "Comfortless was my religion, anxiety of anxiety, for I believed God was not love but courage. Love came only as a reward."

Mailer has taken his share of critical bumps over a long career, but at the same time there has also been a steady claque of admirers, always ready to justify, to find a deeper significance, to stand in articulate awe of his shoddiest work. Thus of even so puerile a novel as *An American Dream,* one claqueur, the critic Richard Poirier, could—and did—write that this novel showed "that there is clear indication that if he [Mailer] so chose he could write any kind of novel that literature has made available to us." Poirier went on: "What he wants to do, however, is something altogether more daring. He wants to show that the world of the demonic, the supernatural, the mad is not simply the reverse side of the world that sets the normal standards by which these other conditions are defined as abnormal. Instead he wants to suggest that these worlds are simultaneous, coextensive."

Ah, we sleep deep tonight. Criticism stands guard.

No one can ever accuse Norman Mailer of being lazy. His problem, as a writer, has never been that of getting his bottom in his chair and his chair up to the desk; rather it has been getting out of his chair—of stopping. In 1967 Mailer published *Why Are We in Vietnam?,* a novel that was not directly about Vietnam but rather about Texans in Alaska hunting bears from helicopters and chewing up the landscape with powerful weapons. He lavished his prose upon political conventions, heavyweight fights, Marilyn Monroe, graffiti, astronauts, the new feminism. He became first a celebrity, then a celebrity bore. It became very easy to cease reading Norman Mailer, to cease taking him seriously.

When *The Executioner's Song* appeared in 1979, I felt that

undergoing exploratory surgery was a more pleasant prospect than reading this more-than-1,000-page book. I was wrong. True, *The Executioner's Song* would not suffer for being cut by a few hundred pages, but it is nonetheless a remarkable book. It tells those of us of the middle classes, who get most of our information about American life from books, newspapers, and television, something about which we are likely to know very little: the not-quite-rooted white lower-middle-classes of the Western states who tend to live on time-payments and food stamps, off six-packs and fast food, in trailers or cinder-block homes and motel-like apartments. And it tells us about it extremely well—entering into it, as I have said, with an imaginative sympathy that greatly enlarges our understanding.

This is the milieu of Gary Gilmore, the killer who in Utah refused to appeal his death sentence, which was eventually carried out in January 1977. Gilmore was then thirty-five and had spent eighteen of his last twenty-two years in jails. Out of jail a very short while, he murdered, twice, both murders connected with robberies. To one of his victims Gilmore claims to have said: "Your money, son, *and* your life." He then shot him, point blank, in the back of the head. He slaughtered his second victim in the same manner. In *The Executioner's Song,* Mailer recounts these murders and the events leading up to them and those following after them, going back into the life of Gary Gilmore, of his girl-friend, of his and her relatives, jailers, cellmates, prosecuting and defense attorneys, and everyone else connected with Gilmore. It is an extraordinary work of journalism—so extraordinary that it becomes, in my view, literature.

Mailer's method in this book is close to what in fiction used to pass under the label of naturalism. The author intrudes as little as possible; his task is to show how environment affects character and character leads out into destiny, from which emerges, when it is effectively done, a picture of a man in society, or at least a segment of society. Mailer's writing in *The Executioner's Song* is artfully unadorned; it is a plain controlled prose served up in short paragraphs:

It came down on Nicole what an expression like "horrible loss" really meant. It was throwing away the most valuable thing in your life. It was knowing you had to live next to something larger than your own life. In this case, it was knowing that Gary was going to die.

She began to think there was not even a minute when she stopped loving him, not for a minute. Not a minute of her day in which the guy was not in her mind. That she liked. She liked what was inside her. But it was spooky. She would take in a breath and recognize that she was falling more and more in love with a guy who was going to be dead.

But Mailer is really telling two stories here. Along with the story of Gary Gilmore's life and death, he is also telling the story —the distinctly and wretchedly contemporary story—of the elaborate negotiations involved in the "literary rights" to Gilmore's life. This story centers on a journalist named Lawrence Schiller, a former *Life* photographer, whose specialty it has become to purchase, organize, and sell off the literary rights to the lives of the notorious. Schiller had acquired the rights to Lenny Bruce's story from Bruce's widow, he had acquired the rights to Susan Atkins's life (in the Charles Manson case), he was the man who secured the last interview with Jack Ruby, and now he had moved in on the Gary Gilmore story. The mechanics of Schiller's operation are fascinating—selling off an interview with Gilmore to *Playboy,* a few photographs to this or that scandal sheet, something to the newsweeklies, bits and pieces to the European press, interviews with family members to ABC. Schiller himself is an interesting character, a man highly sensitive to being called scavenger and worse. Mailer treats him most gingerly but goes into his dealing with the utmost thoroughness. Well, almost utmost thoroughness. The only deal he does not mention is that which Schiller must have cut with Norman Mailer that made possible the writing of *The Executioner's Song.*

The Executioner's Song is additionally interesting because of the light it throws both on the past and on the future of Norman Mailer's career. Gary Gilmore was declared by the state of Utah to be technically and hence legally a psychopath, rather than a psychotic, and his psychopathology very tidily fits the definition of the psychopath hipster in Mailer's "The White Negro."

In that essay, as I have noted Mailer remarks that no one has yet projected himself into "essential sympathy" with the psychopath. This Mailer does in *The Executioner's Song*. The projection, indeed the identification, of Mailer with Gary Gilmore, though it does not ruin the book, is nonetheless very great. Gilmore, at times, comes off as the very type of the artist. His parole officer, in Mailer's words, thinks, "They were about the same age, but Gilmore . . . looked much older. On the other hand, if you put up a profile of what an artist of thirty-five might look like, Gilmore could fit that physical profile." Gary Gilmore actually turns out to have been quite a good draughtsman. He was a prison autodidact; one of his favorite novels was J. P. Donleavy's *The Ginger Man*. He did not like television. He was fearless. (His final words to his executioners were "Let's do it.") He was, in several respects, many things that Norman Mailer, at least in his theoretical writings, would seem to wish the artist, Norman Mailer, to be—except, of course, dead.

But what saves *The Executioner's Song* is that it does not include any of Norman Mailer's theorizing. It is descriptive, naturalistic in the mode of James T. Farrell and John Dos Passos—writers Mailer much admired when he was a young man. Mailer's talent, in my view, lies in this mode. That may seem like a put-down but is not intended as one. The methods of modernism, with very few exceptions, have not been successful in the novel. Although *The Executioner's Song* is not a novel, it is the best of Norman Mailer's books, the one that seems most likely to be readable ten or twenty years from now. Mailer, to repeat, is best when he is descriptive, when his imaginative sympathies are engaged. He is at his worst when he is being Norman Mailer, the modern thinker. He is, that is to say, a serious writer except when he is thinking, and the trouble is that over his long career he has been thinking a very great deal.

In *Ancient Evenings,* unfortunately, Mailer is thinking nearly full time. Although his new novel is set in the twelfth and thirteenth centuries B.C.E., for the most part in the reigns of the Egyptian Pharaohs Ramses II and Ramses IX, Mailer is mostly concerned with his standard obsessions—ambition, sex, telepathy. To which one can now add reincarnation, though this came up in *The Executioner's Song,* where time and again Gary Gilmore remarks that in his current life he feels he is paying for the sins of an earlier life and time and again he remarks upon his confidence in yet another life to come. Mailer, too, has come to believe "that we're not here just one time, and I don't have any highly organized theology behind that—it's just a passing conviction that keeps returning."

Ancient Evenings is chiefly about the four lives of one Menenhetet I, who has been thrice reincarnated and who during his first life was charioteer to the great Pharaoh Ramses II, and later governor of his harem and guard of his two queens. The greater part of *Ancient Evenings* is taken up with this Menenhetet I recounting his life under Ramses II, and doing so for Pharaoh Ramses IX on the long night of the festival known as the Night of the Pig, when one may tell the Pharaoh unpleasant truths. The narration gets complicated, for sometimes Menenhetet tells his own stories, at other times we learn about things through his great-grandson, Menenhetet II, who has gifts of telepathy and who, through these gifts, tells us what other people in the novel are thinking.

The architecture of *Ancient Evenings* is highly elaborate. The novel begins in a tomb, where the spirits of Menenhetet I and Menenhetet II first encounter each other. After forcing the spirit of his great-grandson to perform fellatio upon him—are you still with me?—he informs him (and us), lengthily, about the theogony of the Egyptian gods: Ra, Amon, Maat, Osiris, Isis, Set, Horus, and, as a baseball announcer in my town has it, "all that gang." Mailer has obviously swotted up the subject of ancient Egypt for this novel, studied *The Book of the Dead,* stuffed himself with such facts as are available on Egyptian methods of embalming, on religious ritual, on daily life. He has tossed into the stew a belief in telepathy and reincarnation, in neither of which Egyptians of the ancient world quite believed, and added ornate sets of his own devising. I do not know enough about Egypt to judge whether he has got this material down correctly—though it is comforting to note that at the court of Ramses IX they use the word "hopefully" quite as ungrammatically as do so many American undergraduates and television journalists—but I do know that as a subject, ancient Egypt presents certain very real problems.

The first of these problems is that reincarnation can wreak havoc on the fundamentals of plotting. One of the nice things about death, for a novelist, is that it brings plots to a close. But under reincarnation, if you die, that is only the beginning—your troubles have only started. It is worth noting that Menenhetet talks almost solely about his first life. If he had gone into similar detail concerning his second, third, and fourth lives, Mailer would have had on his hands a novel well in excess of 2,000 pages.

No one, surely, can have wished *Ancient Evenings* longer than it is now. Even among the novel's admirers, you can hear, in the midst of their praise, the groans of fatigue this book has brought on. Thus Walter Clemons, in *Vanity Fair:* "Whatever you decide about it, and I warn you it can be hard going. . . ." Thus Brigitte Weeks, in the *Washington Post:* "But it is not easy to stay afloat in a flood, and despite all the glitter and the magic, the imaginative gymnastics, this reader, at least, sometimes felt as if she were going under for the third time." Thus Peter S. Prescott, in *Newsweek:* "Stupefying the book may be. . . ." Thus Harold Bloom, in the *New York Review of Books:* ". . . if you read *Ancient Evenings* for the story, you will hang yourself."

Part of the problem is Mailer's Egyptology. If he has learned about some bit of Egyptian lore or craft, not wishing to be wasteful, he lays it on us. He will stop, for example, to expatiate on Egyptian methods of rock cutting. Too often the novel reads like something devised by Mel Brooks's Two Thousand Year Old Man—though he'd have to be three thousand years old—but without the jokes. Not that some of these items aren't finely done. Mailer's account of the battle of Kadesh is splended; and so is his account of the embalming of Menenhetet II, as the spirit of the man being embalmed details it. Yet *Ancient Evenings* is finally a

novel altogether without pace. As Menenhetet I explains the gods
to Rama-Nefru, the Pharaoh Ramses II's second queen, he notes,
"A haze was over my eyes." Friend, I thought, you are not alone.

Mailer has said that his novel is about magic and that it reflects
his interest in the very rich. But the real subjects, once again for
Mailer, are power and sex, and apart from the battle of Kadesh,
all the big moments in the book have to do with sex. It is a sign
of the deep poverty of Norman Mailer's imagination that the only
climax he can imagine in any human relationship is really just that
—a sexual climax. Everything in his novel builds up to someone
penetrating someone else in one orifice or another, usually with a
good deal of humiliation involved for one of the parties, a sense
of triumph for the other. Tender feelings rarely come into play;
love, never.

Sex, its contemplation or enactment, must take up more than
half of *Ancient Evenings*. Without it the novel would not even be
a bad *National Geographic* article. Since no one else has pointed it
out, may I be the first to announce that the sex in *Ancient Evenings*
is extremely repulsive? Mailer has wrought a courtly language for
this novel, which he combines with a certain (as he imagines it)
antiquity of phrasing, so that orgasms are described as "coming-
forth"; so that, preparatory to buggering a thief, Menenhetet II
notes, "No door could have withstood my horn"; so that Menenhetet remarks of his mother, "The fresh seed of my father was the
finest lotion she had ever found for her face"; so that Nefertiri,
first queen to Ramses II, says to Menenhetet I, "I will make love
to you tonight by all three of My mouths." And here is Ramses
II having at Menenhetet I:

> I heard a clangor in my head equal to the great door of a
> temple knocked open by the blow of a log carried forward
> at a run by ten good men, it was with the force of ten good
> men that He took me up my bowels, and I lay with my face
> on the stony soil of the cave while a bat screamed overhead.

Buggery and sodomistic rape seem to be the central sexual
experiences of *Ancient Evenings*. With the bracing humorlessness

of modern criticism, Peter S. Prescott, in *Newsweek,* notes: "Mailer, we know from past novels, has thought long and hard about anal rape, but here he outdoes himself." While Harold Bloom, in the *New York Review of Books,* chimes in: "In *Ancient Evenings* [Mailer] has emancipated himself, and seems to be verging upon a new metaphysic, in which heterosexual buggery might be the true norm." (The true norm? Can this be true, Norm?) The connection between buggery and excrement is not shirked in this loathsome book in which excrement is intended to have magical, even divine, properties. "Certainly," says Menenhetet I, "I came to the sad conclusion that excrement was as much a part of magic as blood or fire, an elixir of dying Gods and rotting spirits desperate to regain the life they were about to lose." There is much more of this kind of blather about, as Menenhetet II puts it early in the novel, "the sinuosities of shit." So much of it, in fact, that another admirer of the novel, George Stade, wrote in the *New Republic:* "If you do not buy [Mailer's] notions of magic and the unconscious, of course, you will simply feel that Mailer and his novel are full of shit." To answer a two-clause sentence in two parts: I don't, and therefore I do.

Why would Mailer write a novel so empty, so inert, so pretentious? Breaking through again, I fear. But breaking through to what—and why does he have to go all the way back to ancient Egypt to do it? Apart from the Cecil B. De Mille sets, the chit-chat about the significance of feces, and an untested recipe for successful reincarnation (impregnate a woman at the exact moment one is dying), *Ancient Evenings* is, for Norman Mailer, pretty much business as usual. I think he wrote an empty, inert, pretentious novel because, given the theories to which he is hostage, it is no longer possible for him to write a good novel.

Not that this has stopped critics from finding deep significance in *Ancient Evenings.* Professor Stade reads the book as "an on-and-off metaphor for the repressed unconscious." Mr. Prescott sees the book's "message (if it has one) . . . to be that the concentration of power at the top of the pyramid unhinges all stability: to rule all is to fear everyone." But the most ingenious reading comes from Harold Bloom, author of *A Map of Misreading,* who holds that "Mailer too wishes us to learn how to live, in an America where he sees our bodies and spirits as becoming increasingly artificial, even 'plastic' as he has often remarked." Professor Bloom, also the author of *The Anxiety of Influence,* finds Ernest Hemingway in *Ancient Evenings,* for he reads Hemingway into the character of Ramses II and Mailer himself into that of Menenhetet I, adding that "to have been bumbuggered by one's precursor is a sublime new variant on the sorrows of literary influence." Clearly, a critic's work is never done.

But then, in our era, neither is a novelist's. Since the publication of *Ancient Evenings,* Norman Mailer has been promoting his novel with furious energy. Through an endless round of interviews and a general media blitz, Mailer, with the aid of certain critics and reviewers, has pushed very hard to make his new novel seem important—so much so that one realizes that not long ago a new novel by Norman Mailer would have seemed an important literary event in its own right. Now it seems merely another media event—one more yelp in the contemporary racket—a novel that needs all the outside help it can get. "If it's no good," Mailer has said of this novel in more than one place, "I'm no good." That may be putting the case more starkly than is necessary, but then, one suddenly begins to think, perhaps it is true. Could a good writer have written so foul a book?

Commentary 1983

What Does
Philip Roth Want?

THERE IS, as the folks in the head trades might say, a lot of rage in Philip Roth. What, one wonders, is he so angry about? As a writer, he seems to have had a pretty good roll of the dice. His first book, the collection of stories entitled *Goodbye, Columbus,* published when he was twenty-six, was a very great critical success; in brilliance, his literary debut was second in modern America perhaps only to that of Delmore Schwartz. ("Unlike those of us who came howling into the world, blind and bare," wrote Saul Bellow in *Commentary,* "Mr. Roth appears with nails, hair, and teeth, speaking coherently. At twenty-six he is skillful, witty, and energetic and performs like a virtuoso.") After two further novels, *Letting Go* (1962) and *When She Was Good* (1967), he wrote *Portnoy's Complaint* (1969), a *succès fou,* a tremendous hit both critically ("It's a marvelously entertaining book," wrote Theodore Solotaroff, "and one that mines a narrow but central vein more deeply than it has ever been done before"), and commercially (it was a best seller of a kind that removes a writer permanently from the financial wars). One recalls the protagonist of Saul Bellow's *Henderson the Rain King,* regularly muttering, "I want! I want! I want!" Philip Roth, who at an early age had critical attention, wealth, and celebrity, continues to mutter, "It isn't enough. It isn't enough. It isn't enough."

What does Philip Roth want? For one thing, he wishes to be recognized as a great writer, the natural successor to Gogol and

Chekhov and Kafka. He wishes also to have the right to strike out against the bourgeoisie—particularly the Jewish bourgeoisie —and to be adored for his acute perceptions of it. And he wishes to have appreciated what he takes to be the universal application of his own experience as it has been transformed by the imagination in his several novels. Recognition, adoration, appreciation— all this would be his if people would only understand what his work is really about. Or so he believes, and so he would have us believe. But thus far all too few people do understand. In fact, they don't seem to understand at all.

Not that Philip Roth, in his many interviews about his work, has neglected to enlighten them. The Roth *modus operandi* is to publish an interview around the time each of his new books appears, or shortly thereafter, and in these interviews meticulously explain what the book is about, what the influences behind it have been, and what its place is in the Roth canon. Sometimes other writers interview Roth; on occasion he interviews himself. In some cases—*Our Gang* (1971), *The Breast* (1972), *The Great American Novel* (1973)—the interviews are rather better than the novels. (Did you read the novel? No, but I saw the interview.) One thing is clear: Philip Roth is far and away the most generous critic we have of the writings of Philip Roth.

It may be useful to keep this in mind because when reading the novels of Philip Roth one discovers that he is not all that generous to anyone else. Make no mistake, he is an immensely talented writer. He is always very readable. He has a fine eye for the detail and texture of social scenery. He has a splendid ear and an accompanying gift of mimicry, which allows him to do the Jews in a thousand voices. He is famously funny, dangerously funny, as Mel Brooks once characterized the kind of humor that can cause strokes from laughter. He has a most solid literary education. Philip Roth has in fact everything but one thing: a generous spirit. Reading through his work, however, one begins to wonder if, in the case of the novelist, this one thing may not perhaps be the main thing.

Randall Jarrell once wittily defined a novel as "a prose narrative of some length that has something wrong with it," and there has certainly been no shortage of critics ready to declare various things wrong with Philip Roth's novels. Many a rabbi took to his pulpit to denounce the treatment of Jews in *Goodbye, Columbus.* *Letting Go* was in more than one quarter found sententious, Henry James on the graduate-school level, a point nicely caught in "Marjorie Morningstar, Ph.D.," the title of John Gross's *New Statesman* review of the novel. Reviewing *When She Was Good* in *Commentary* (November 1967), Robert Alter noted of the characters in this, Roth's third book, that "Humanity is divided into those who are hateful and those who are merely contemptible. . . ." At the close of a review of Roth's slender novel *The Breast* (1972), Frederick Crews offered a two-for-one critical sale, writing in a single sentence: "In a sense *The Breast* is a more discouraging work than the straightforwardly vicious *Our Gang* [Roth's 1971 travesty of Richard Nixon]."

Philip Roth, then, has taken his critical lumps. But the deepest and unkindest cut of all came from Irving Howe, who, in an essay in *Commentary* entitled "Philip Roth Reconsidered" (December 1972), quite consummately eviscerated all Roth's work. Howe pointed out that Roth's "great need is for a stance of superiority," that one reason his stories "are unsatisfactory is that they come out of a thin personal culture," that "the cruelest thing anyone can do with *Portnoy's Complaint* is to read it twice," that such literary narcissism as Roth has displayed throughout his career "is especially notable among minor artists, with whom it frequently takes the form of self-exemptive attacks on the shamefulness of humanity," and so on and on. When Howe is done, he has allowed that he thinks well of a single Roth short story, "Defender of the Faith."

I used the word "eviscerate" to describe this essay; its effect was as though Dr. Howe, working over the corpus of Roth's work, had removed all the patient's major organs, leaving only a small portion—that one short story—of the spleen. This essay, as we shall see, has left Philip Roth in the spiritual equivalent of intensive care for the more than a decade since it was written.

I have said that Philip Roth is always very readable, but I have recently learned that (as Howe pointed out) he is not very rereadable. Trial by rereading is a tough test for a novelist, and I am not sure exactly what it proves, except of course that it is obviously better to write books that can be reread with pleasure than not. (Ezra Pound once distinguished between journalism and literature by saying that literature could be read twice.) Roth, on a second reading, begins to seem smaller; one starts to notice glancing and low blows. In *Goodbye, Columbus,* for example, a cheap point is scored off Mrs. Patimkin, the mother of the family of rich and vulgar Jews who it is fair to say are the target of the novella, because she has never heard of Martin Buber. "Is he *reformed?*" she asks. The assumption here is that people who do not know the name of Martin Buber are swine, like people who listen to the recordings of Kostelanetz and Mantovani. The term for the thinking behind this assumption is intellectual snobbery, and of a fairly low order. In the novella Brenda Patimkin remarks to Neil Klugman, its protagonist, "Why do you always sound a little nasty to me!" This seems to me a good question.

Or, again, in rereading *When She Was Good* I discovered myself feeling an unexpected rush of sympathy for that novel's main character, the moralizing and man-destroying Lucy Nelson. For all that Lucy Nelson is mean-spirited and endlessly judgmental, throughout the novel there is someone meaner and even more judgmental on her tail—her creator, the author. The novel is relentless, ending with Lucy Nelson's death in the cold, a chilling performance in every sense. Mighty is the wrath of the Lord; but the wrath of Roth, for those of his characters on whom he spews it—from the Patimkins to Lucy Nelson, to Jack and Sophie Portnoy, to assorted lady friends in various of the novels, to the critic Milton Appel in the recent *The Anatomy Lesson*—is not so easily borne either.

A highly self-conscious writer, the early Philip Roth no doubt felt the weight of his own crushing moralizing. True, in his first book he was moralizing against moralizing—yet it was still moralizing. Moral tunes were the ones he had been trained to dance to. "I was," Roth has written, "one of those students of the 50's who came to books by way of a fairly good but rather priestly literary education, in which writing poems and novels was as-

sumed to eclipse all else in what we called 'moral seriousness.' "
The year before, in an interview with himself, he announced: "I
imagined fiction to be something like a religious calling, and
literature a kind of sacrament, a sense of things I have had reason
to modify since." What may have caused Roth to modify his sense
of moral earnestness was the unrelieved gloom in which it issued
in such novels as *Letting Go* and *When She Was Good*. Roth's early
fiction was about what he construed to be the coercive forces in
life—family, religion, culture. At some point he decided that
among those coercive forces he had to add another: his own
literary moral seriousness.

Near the end of the 1960s, that time of many liberations, Philip
Roth achieved his own with the publication of *Portnoy's Complaint*. Toward the middle of *Goodbye, Columbus* the hero notes:
"I am not one to stick scalpels in myself"; henceforth, Roth's
heroes will comport themselves as if taking acupuncture with
scalpels. Of course, to blame the guilt of Alexander Portnoy, a
guilt beginning in ceaseless masturbation, issuing in an adult case
of raging sex fever, and closing in impotence—to blame this guilt
on Portnoy's Jewish middle-class upbringing was certain to put
Roth in solid with the Jewish friends he had already made
through *Goodbye, Columbus*. Dwelling on masturbation, fellatio,
cunnilingus, and other features of what H. L. Mencken once
referred to as "non-Euclidean sex," the novel was deliberately in
atrocious taste. It read rather like a more literate and extended
Lenny Bruce skit. It was meant to cause the squeamish to squirm,
the righteous to rave—and by and large succeeded in doing so.
If Berkeley was what happened to the university during the sixties, Andy Warhol what happened to contemporary art, *Portnoy's
Complaint* was what happened to American Jewish fiction.

For Philip Roth, *Portnoy's Complaint* was evidently, in one of
the cant phrases of the day, a breakthrough. Suddenly, the sexual
subject, with all its taboos shattered, was now fully his to command; suddenly, in his use of material and language, he was little
boy blue. He had also developed a new tone, a detached intimacy
such as a practiced analysand might adopt with his therapist.
Psychoanalysts—variously called Spielvogel, Klinger, and other

German names—will henceforth appear in Roth's novels, while Roth himself will come to view the psychoanalytic as an important mode of apprehending reality. Roth's explanation of the meaning of *Portnoy* reflects this clearly enough, when he says, in yet another of his interviews, that the book, "which was concerned with the comic side of the struggle between a hectoring superego and an ambitious id, seems now, in retrospect, to have realigned those forces as they act upon my imagination."

I myself prefer not to hear novelists using words like superego and id. Whatever aid they may bring to the suffering, however necessary they may be to the discourse of therapeutic workers, they are death on art, and on no art are they more deadly than fiction. Novelists do better to speak of morals and desire, of conscience and soul. The later Roth has, I believe, shed his true-believer views of psychoanalysis; in his most recent novel, *The Anatomy Lesson,* he seems to have shucked them off nearly altogether. But he has retained certain of the habits of the analysand—classically conceived, as they say down at the Institute—not the least of which is an unshakable belief in the importance of sex and an implacable confidence in the significance of one's own splendid self.

Although I have not taken an exact count, it strikes me that, along with John Updike and Norman Mailer, Philip Roth is a hot entry in the sweepstakes for the most fornication described within the pages of a single body of serious work. (Edmund Wilson once grouped a number of novelists of the thirties as "The Boys in the Back Room"; Updike, Mailer, Roth, and perhaps William Styron, all writers with a puerile interest in sex, might be thought of as The Men in the Boys' Room.) By now a practiced hand, Roth can describe sex as easily as Dickens could describe London, though the views Dickens offers are more interesting. Roth has mastered his technique to the point where he can advance his plots through dialogue while keeping his characters *in flagrante*. All this is by design. Roth has said that the direction his work has taken "since *Portnoy's Complaint* can in part be accounted for by my increased responsiveness to, and respect for, what is unsocialized in me."

Yet it isn't the sheer volume of sex in Roth's novels that is troubling; one feels, rather, that sex is one of the few subjects left to him, and that it has now begun to qualify as an uninteresting obsession. Like cityscapes to Bellow, so bedscapes to Roth; one senses he could do them in his sleep, and after a short while one wishes he would. I. B. Singer is a novelist quite as concerned with sex as Philip Roth, but, it seems to me, with a decisive difference. In Singer's fiction, the pleasures of sex mix with the terrors of guilt and sin, and somewhere off in the distance you feel perhaps God is watching. In a Roth novel, sex has to do with a writer paying respect to his "unsocialized side," and somewhere off in the distance you can hear a pen scratching.

You hear a pen scratching because, as a novelist, Philip Roth has lived for some while pretty close to the autobiographical bone. The relationship between fictional representation and autobiographical sources is endlessly complicated, and can usually only be properly understood by a literary biographer willing to spend decades with his subject. How much of Stendhal is in Julien Sorel, how much of Balzac in Lucien Chardon, how much of Tolstoy in Levin? The more contemporary the age, the more complex, and the more crucial, the question seems to grow. How much James Joyce in Stephen Dedalus, how much Proust in the Marcel of *Remembrance of Things Past,* how much of Kafka in Joseph K? The closer we get to our own day, the smaller the gap between the fictional and the autobiographical seems to be. A remark by E. R. Curtius goes a good way toward explaining the impetus behind this phenomenon. "Since Chateaubriand's *René,*" Curtius writes, "literature has preferred to deal with the conflicts of the individual, the shipwreck of ideals, the disillusionment of the heart, the quarrel with society." All the items Curtius mentions, from the conflict within the individual to the quarrel with society, cry out to be dealt with directly, shorn of the mediating screen of fictional representation. And dealing directly with such things in fiction often means dealing with them in a highly autobiographical manner.

This is a touchy point for Philip Roth, who again and again has accused his critics and readers of confusing his life and his work. The confusion set in with a fine vengeance, he claims, with *Portnoy's Complaint,* when "a novel in the guise of a confession was received and judged by any number of readers as a confession in the guise of a novel." In an essay entitled "Portnoy's Fame— and Mine," Roth has told how, not long after the enormous success of *Portnoy's Complaint,* when Roth himself had become a gossip-column item, at one point romantically linked (I believe the phrase is) with Barbra Streisand, the rumor circulated that he had had a nervous breakdown—which, as he notes, given the original confusion between the author and the protagonist of *Portnoy's Complaint,* makes a certain amount of sense, madness being the end preordained for onanists.

Time and again, in interviews and essays and now even in his fiction, Roth has gone on insisting that he is not, in his novels, writing about Philip Roth, except through the transmutations of art. "That writing is an act of imagination," says Nathan Zucker- man in *The Anatomy Lesson,* "seems to perplex and infuriate every- one." Roth has spoken of readers getting a "voyeuristic kick" from reading his autobiography into his books. I think "voyeuris- tic kick" is exactly the correct phrase, and my first response to it is that, if a writer doesn't wish to supply such kicks, perhaps he would do better not to undress before windows opening onto thoroughfares.

Yet one wonders if voyeuristic kicks are not precisely at the heart of Roth's recent novels (as well as those of other contem- porary novelists). In an odd conjunction of circumstances, while novels seem to mean less and less to the way people live, at the same time a number of novelists have become celebrity figures: through television appearances, magazine interviews, gossip sheets. These novelists can hardly be unaware of their celebrity, however much they may say they do not like it, and they also ought to be aware that readers—and quite intelligent readers, too —will see the novelists' lives in their work, especially when the writer has taken so little trouble to disguise himself. If there is anyone in the world who believes that the hero of Saul Bellow's *The Dean's December* is anyone other than Saul Bellow, I should like to meet that person and have the opportunity to sell him some mining stock. If there is anyone who believes that young Stingo in *Sophie's Choice* is not the young William Styron, that person brings a freshness and an innocence to his reading that I believe borders on insanity. It is a cheap thrill but nonetheless one very much for the taking, this reading of gossip about famous novelists in—of all places—their own novels.

In short, it is the novelists who make this gossip, these voyeuristic kicks, possible in the first place. If they don't wish so to be read, the way out is through invention, imagination, fresh creation, greater subtlety. Another prospect, however, is simply to give way, to write about oneself almost straight-out, to cultivate the idiosyncratic vision, to plow away at one's own obsessions, becoming a bit of a crank, something of a crackpot, and risk being a minor writer indeed. Alas, I think this is the path that Philip Roth has set himself upon.

After *Portnoy's Complaint* Roth wrote two satires, the one about Richard Nixon, *Our Gang,* and *The Great American Novel,* about baseball. Such works are known as *jeux d' esprits;* when they fail, as these two do for being excessively heavy-handed and insufficiently funny, they are also known as regrettable. There followed *The Breast* (1972), in which David Kepesh, a professor of English—surprising that Roth didn't make him a CUNY linguist —wakes up in a hospital to find himself turned into a breast. Kepesh feels that he got into this fix through reading fiction. He has been teaching Kafka and Gogol. "The books I've been teaching—they put the idea in my head." He asks: "Why this primitive identification with *the* object of infantile veneration?" Perhaps, he thinks, "Success itself! There is what I couldn't take—a happy life!" Other theories are tried out. Kepesh's psychoanalyst is consulted. To no avail. The reason David Kepesh has become a breast remains unknown both within the story and outside it. With *The Breast,* Philip Roth's problem has officially become identifying Philip Roth's problem.

At this point Roth's fictional works, like runny cooked vegetables on a plate, begin to bleed into one another. Three Roth protagonists come on the scene: Nathan Zuckerman, Peter Tarnopol, and, not yet breastified, David Kepesh. A Chinese-box effect sets in. In *My Life as a Man* (1974) we are presented with a story written by Peter Tarnopol about the sexual adventures of the young Nathan Zuckerman; this Nathan Zuckerman will return as the author of a shocking best-seller about sexual liberation entitled *Carnovsky*, which sounds like nothing so much as *Portnoy's Complaint*. But back at *My Life as a Man*, Peter Tarnopol's editor asks him: "Is that what you're up to, or are you planning to write Zuckerman variations until you have constructed a kind of full-length fictional fugue?" By now, Philip Roth has written three books about his Nathan Zuckerman character. All that remains to complete the circle is for Peter Tarnopol to write a novel in which David Kepesh is teaching a year-long honors seminar on the novels of Philip Roth.

These characters have a number of qualities in common: they are bookish (two are writers, one a teacher of writing), Jewish, single, past or current analysands and hence mightily self-regarding, great prizers of their personal freedom (two have had disastrous first marriages, one, Nathan Zuckerman, has had three marriages about two of which not much is said), fearful of a great deal but above all of personal entrapment. Their characteristic response is to whine and complain. Much of their time on the page is spent in the effort of self-analysis through which they hope to arrive at self-justification. Oh, yes, one other thing: for the above-mentioned reasons, none is in any way easy to sympathize with.

Reading these novels, one begins to sense with what pleasure a psychoanalyst must look forward to knocking off at the end of the day. It's a small world, that of the patient—it has, really, only one person of importance in it. So, too, with Roth's novels which feel so terribly underpopulated, confined, claustral. One admires their sentences, picks up on their jokes, notes the craft that went into their making, and finishes reading them with a slight headache and a sour taste in the mouth. One puts them down, finally, in not so different a condition, one assumes, from the psychoanalyst picking up his briefcase, sighing, and flicking off the light in the office; only, unlike the analyst, one has not been so well rewarded for the day's work.

Not that these novels are without brilliant passages and portraits. In the second section of *My Life as a Man,* the section
entitled "Courting Disaster (or, Serious in the Fifties)," Nathan
Zuckerman contracts a mistaken marriage for chiefly literary reasons. To escape his own cozy Jewish middle-class upbringing, to
meet experience such as it is met in literature, he is drawn to a
sad, broken woman, a perfect mismatch, chiefly because "she had
suffered so much and because she was so brave." But this section
of the novel, so beautifully done, is blown when, after many
nightmarish years in the marriage, Zuckerman runs off to Italy
with his very young stepdaughter. The appropriate reference is
made to Nabokov. Roth and his characters have books on the
brain, and not only great literature but criticism into the bargain.
Zuckerman says of himself: "Where Emma Bovary had read too
many romances of her period, it would seem that I had read too
much of the criticism of mine."

In his later novels, Roth regularly measures himself against the
great literary figures of the past, attempting to discover with
whom among them he belongs. Peter Tarnopol is a great admirer
of Flaubert, though at one point in *My Life as a Man* he notes:
"I'll try a character like Henry Miller, or someone out-and-out
bilious like Céline for my hero instead of Gustave Flaubert—and
won't be such an Olympian writer as it was my ambition to be
back in the days when nothing called personal experience stood
between me and aesthetic detachment." David Kepesh has a case
on Kafka, and in *The Professor of Desire* pays a visit to the aged
prostitute in Prague to whom Kafka was said to bring his custom.
(No one ever said Philip Roth wasn't inventive.) In *The Anatomy
Lesson* Nathan Zuckerman recalls his undergraduate experience of
the magisterial, and majestic, presence of Thomas Mann lecturing
on literature at the University of Chicago, and gauges how far his
own artistic aspirations have fallen since that time. The way other
people look to religion and philosophy, Roth and his heroes look
to literature. "Literature got me into this," says Zuckerman in
one of the sections of *My Life as a Man,* "and literature is gonna
get me out." Thus far, it must be reported, it hasn't.

"Moral delinquency has its fascination for you," says Dr. Klinger, David Kepesh's analyst, and so it does for Philip Roth. In Roth's later novels, though, moral delinquency has almost exclusively meant sexual delinquency. Roth himself, in an interview published around the time of *The Breast,* formulated the moral war of his characters as "between the ethical and social yearnings and the implacable, singular lusts for the flesh and its pleasures." Yet in this particular war Philip Roth is in the embarrassing position of one of those Japanese soldiers holed up on a Pacific island, still polishing his boots and cleaning his rifle, who hasn't yet heard that the war between ethical and social yearnings and sexual appetite is long over. Ethical and social yearnings lost and sexual appetite promptly departed.

More and more of Roth's subject is falling away from him, like the hair on Nathan Zuckerman's head in *The Anatomy Lesson.* In *My Life as a Man* this same Zuckerman is said to have written a novel, filled with "moral indignation," entitled *A Jewish Father.* Roth himself, in such portraits as those of Mrs. Patimkin, Aunt Gladys, Sophie Portnoy, and others has been putting together a bitter volume that might be entitled *World of Our Mothers.* Now, however, that generation, in whose rage for order Roth read repression and perhaps unintended but nonetheless real malevolence, is old and dying and hardly any longer worth railing against. Even Roth appears to have recognized this, and some of the few touching moments in his later fiction—the scenes with David Kepesh's widowed father in *My Life as a Man,* memories of Nathan Zuckerman's mother in *Zuckerman Unbound* and *The Anatomy Lesson*—are tributes to the generation of his own parents.

When a writer has used up all other subjects within the realm of his experience, one subject remains—that of writing itself. Philip Roth's last three novels—the Zuckerman trilogy—are about precisely this subject. The first, *The Ghost Writer,* much of which takes place at the home of the ascetic writer E. I. Lonoff, is about the toll in loneliness and self-abnegation that the writing life exacts. Being a Roth novel, *The Ghost Writer* is not without its comic touches, or without its attempts to *épater les juifs.* In the latter category, the Zuckerman character imagines bringing home

Anne Frank as his wife—the one sure way to please his parents, who are already aggrieved at what they construe to be his abetting of anti-Semitism by publishing stories about the seamier side of the family. Playing Anne Frank for laughs is Roth the bad boy at it again, attempting to make the Jews squirm. He cannot seem to help himself on this score. He can't leave it alone.

Zuckerman Unbound, the second Zuckerman novel, is about the wages paid for large-scale success in America, in this case paid out to Nathan Zuckerman for writing his shocking best seller *Carnovsky*. The coin in which these wages are paid is that of the unwanted company of hustlers, intrusive idiotic publicity, and family misunderstanding. Here again one begins to feel many autobiographical teases. Did Roth's parents react to *Portnoy* as Zuckerman's did to *Carnovsky?* Does Roth feel the same petulance about publicity as Zuckerman? "Never trust the artist. Trust the tale," pronounced D. H. Lawrence. Yet the more it becomes apparent that there is little to choose between tale and teller, the more one ends up trusting neither. Part of the burden of *The Anatomy Lesson,* it seems to me, is that Roth may no longer trust either himself.

A long while ago Philip Roth removed the fig leaf; now, in *The Anatomy Lesson,* off—or nearly off—comes the mask. In this novel Nathan Zuckerman is suffering a great unexplained pain in his back and neck. So great is the pain that he cannot write. He can, though, while settled on his back upon a rubber mat on his living-room floor, carry on love affairs with four different women. But these affairs do not absorb him nearly so deeply as does an attack written on his work by a Jewish intellectual critic he once admired by the name of Milton Appel that appeared in the magazine *Inquiry*. Not many people will need to know this, but Milton Appel is another name for Irving Howe and *Inquiry* is intended to be *Commentary*. A few details have been shifted here and there, some with an almost pathetic indifference: Howe's essay on Roth appeared in *Commentary* in December 1972, Appel's on Zuckerman in March 1973. (What extraordinary transformations art can make!) I am sure a number of characters are invented, touches and twists are added, nothing is quite as it was in life, but at its center this is a *roman à clef*—one that is being used, through gross caricature and straight insult, to repay an old wound.

It is also a *roman* of clay. The only points of interest have to do with the sense it conveys that Philip Roth himself may feel he can go no further in this vein. He has written himself into a corner and up a wall. "There's nothing more wearying," Zuckerman tells a friend, "than having to go around pretending to be the author of one's own books—except pretending not to be." Elsewhere he remarks: "If you get out of yourself you can't be a writer because the personal ingredient is what gets you going, and if you hang on to the personal ingredient any longer you'll disappear right up your [orifice deleted]." And later he adds: "Chained to my dwarf drama till I die. Stories now about Milton Appel? Fiction about losing my hair? I can't face it." Neither, for much longer, I suspect, can we.

When, with *Portnoy's Complaint,* Philip Roth's career took its turn toward investigating the inner life, Roth must have thought he was on his way to becoming the Jewish Gogol, the American Kafka. But it has not worked out. Roth's fictional figures lack the requisite weight; they aren't clown-heroes out of Kafka or Gogol who have somehow been tricked by life, the butt of some towering cosmic joke. A character who is having love affairs with four women and wishes to get his own back at a literary critic—this is not, as Philip Roth the teacher of literature himself must know, exactly a figure of universal significance. No, it has not worked out. *Portnoy's Complaint* ended on the couch, with the psychiatrist remarking to Alex Portnoy, "Now vee may perhaps to begin. Yes?" *The Anatomy Lesson* ends with Nathan Zuckerman, determined to give up writing for a career in medicine, helping the interns in the hospital in which he himself is a patient. I should have preferred to see it, too, end in a psychoanalyst's office, with the analyst announcing to Portnoy-Tarnopol-Kepesh-Zuckerman-Roth: "Now, vee are concluded. Vee haf gone as far as vee can go. Yes?"

Commentary 1984

Miss Ozick Regrets

O<small>N MORE</small> than one occasion Edith Wharton was called "a Henry James in skirts," a remark that chagrined, irritated, and finally infuriated her. If only someone had said the same thing of Cynthia Ozick, the comparison would have made her day. As a young woman Miss Ozick had a real thing for Henry James. I use the vague, gossip-column word "thing," but Miss Ozick tells us that, at age twenty-two, near-sighted, departing from graduate school without a Ph.D., she actually "became" Henry James—and not the young, still hesitant Henry James, groping for the essentials of his art, but the elderly bald Henry James, the high priest of fiction, the figure whom Leon Edel refers to, appositely, as the Master.

What Cynthia Ozick is talking about here is a very virulent case of the Jamesian virus—another, earlier sufferer was Willa Cather—whose chief symptoms are an unrelenting dedication to the craft of fiction and the belief that nothing is so important as literature, life itself seeming but wan and shabby by comparison. This virus can hit anywhere; it first struck Miss Ozick when she was a seventeen-year-old bookworm reading between deliveries in her father's drugstore in the Bronx. At that time, in that place, she read James's story "The Beast in the Jungle" and decided, then and there, that "Here, here was my autobiography."

Miss Ozick recounts this Jamesian phase in her life in a brief essay entitled "The Lesson of the Master," in which she not only takes up her misbegotten infatuation with James as a priest of art but her sad misreading of James, whose true view, as she has come to see, is not that one must deny all for art but instead that one must live life to the fullest. "I mistook him" writes Miss Ozick, "I misheard him, I missed, absolutely and irrevocably, his essential note."

In another of her essays, Miss Ozick once again strikes the note of regret:

> In my twenties I lived the life of the elderly Henry James. In my thirties I worshiped E. M. Forster for the lure of his English paganism. Fifteen years went into a silent and shadowed apprenticeship of craft and vision. When at last I wrote a huge novel I meant it to be a Work of Art—but as the years ground through that labor, it turned, amazingly and horribly, into a curse. I discovered at the end that I had cursed the world I lived in, grain by grain. And I did not know why. Furthermore, that immense and silent and obscure labor had little response—my work did not speak to the Gentiles, for whom it had been begun, nor to the Jews, for whom it had been finished. And I did not know why. Though I had yearned to be famous in the religion of Art, to become so to speak a saint of Art, I remained obscure.

The "huge novel" referred to in this passage is her first, *Trust* (1966). She also refers to it, in an essay otherwise having to do with feminism ("Previsions of the Demise of the Dancing Dog"), as "an enormous novel, the writing of which had taken many more years than any novel ought to take." *Trust* must be reckoned Miss Ozick's pledgeship to the fraternity of literature, and it was not, as she avers, an easy one. It is an exhausting novel, it is also a badly misshapen and sadly misconceived one. It is a book filled with lengthy opaque paragraphs, heavy-handed symbolism, vast stretches of overwriting, flat jokes (most of them involving puns), and a general over-richness such as can cause one's mental teeth to ache.

In a reconsideration of Truman Capote's *Other Voices, Other Rooms*, Miss Ozick called the book "the novel of someone who wanted, with a fixed and single-minded and burning will, to write a novel." Her own *Trust* is just such a novel, by a writer who was herself stuffed with literature. One can read back into it—with its talk of the Holocaust, radical politics, the death of Europe, the social classes, muses, literary puzzles, the meaning of money—nearly every literary preoccupation of the years during which it was written. Yet it contains flashes of brilliance as well, such as this nice distinction between Materialists and Idealists:

> He's reading Materialism and Idealism. What it means, you see, is that there are two sorts of philosophers, Materialist and Idealist. One thinks the world is bad and really there, the others think the world is good and not really there. The Materialists—the ones who think the world exists but is bad —believe in God, but hate Him for creating a bad world; and the Idealists—the other camp—are atheists who would love God if only they believed in Him.

"Two things are equally boring in art," the poet Howard Moss has written, "a lack of skill and too much of it," and in *Trust* Miss Ozick managed to demonstrate both simultaneously.

Cynthia Ozick's plight was not an uncommon one among young writers: a flaming desire to write combined with nothing much to say. By the time *Trust* was published, however, she was thirty-eight—not quite still young. Like many writers of her generation, she may well have been, if not over-educated, then over-impressed with the importance, not to say the sacredness, of literature. It is not easy to get much work done with such characters as Henry James, E. M. Forster, T. S. Eliot, and Virginia Woolf hovering about one's head. The trick may reside in somehow at the same time incorporating and shaking off such influences. Complicated stuff. As Miss Ozick says at the end of her Henry James essay, "Influence is perdition."

As late as 1970, in a paper delivered at a conference in Israel, Miss Ozick, almost by the way, could note: "I am a writer, slow and unprolific, largely unknown. . . ." But she would not be slow or unprolific or largely unknown for very much longer. Something happened to change all that. The dam burst: stories, a number of extraordinary essays, a novel all flowed forth. Suddenly, Cynthia Ozick's number came up: she won a Guggenheim Fellowship and something financially more rewarding called a Mildred and Harold Strauss Living Award from the American Academy and Institute of Arts and Letters. She was now the subject of profiles in such places as the *New York Times Magazine*. (Do you suppose they are called "profiles" because, after one has submitted to one, it is difficult to look one's friends straight in the face?) What all high-school girls of my generation sedulously avoided, and what all writers quite as sedulously seek, Cynthia Ozick now had: a reputation.

Although Miss Ozick never tells us how exactly it came about, what happened to her as a writer is fairly clear from the evidence she supplies in her essays. What happened is that she acquired a point of view. Cynthia Ozick's point of view is Jewish. Not that she wasn't Jewish all along, but now she became a Jewish writer. Miss Ozick may be the only prominent writer in America who is prepared to let that adjective appear before that noun. "I am not a Jewish writer; I am a writer who is a Jew," Philip Roth has said. I believe that, on more than one occasion, Saul Bellow has said something similar. In declaring themselves thus, these writers by no means wish to hide or even play down their Jewishness; not a bit. What they are doing is trying to preserve their writing from the label (the accusation?) of parochialism. They are Jews, but their writing, they wish to affirm, is part of Western civilization. Cynthia Ozick apparently wishes no part of such distinctions. She considers herself, she wishes to be known as, she is, a Jewish writer.

What does it mean to be a Jewish writer? Those Jews who like to claim as many vaguely distinguished figures as possible for the Jewish people—the cultural and intellectual equivalent of Jewish kids who can name eleven Jewish American League third-basemen—might wish to list, say, Woody Allen, Norman Mailer, and Susan Sontag as Jewish writers. One can easily imagine their arguments for doing so. Woody Allen's work demonstrates the rich complexity—self-reflexive yet casting a suspicious eye outward—that has long characterized Jewish humor. Mailer's restless questing for new styles, his ceaseless plumbing of the depths of alienation, offer a near-perfect parable of the modern Jew in the Diaspora. Susan Sontag's tireless energy for making distinctions, her ability to turn an argument first this way, then that, resemble no other activity so much as that of talmudic study. Such dumb stuff has constituted the substance of a great deal of talk about "Jewish writers."

Cynthia Ozick is different. She calls herself a Jewish writer because, first, she has given up "the religion of Art," and, second, takes seriously the Jewish covenant and its commandments. What is more, she believes that it is only through taking such a turn that writers who are Jews have—or, rather, that their work has —a chance to survive. Excluding only those two half-Jews, Montaigne and Proust, Miss Ozick maintains that "there are no major works of Jewish imaginative genius written in any Gentile language, sprung out of any Gentile culture." Especially do minor writers who are Jews, in her view, fall quickly into oblivion when they try in effect to pass in Gentile culture; here she cites the case of Isaac D'Israeli, now forgotten as a man of letters and remembered at best as the father of the first prime minister of England of Jewish ancestry. "The fact is," she says, "that nothing thought or written in Diaspora has ever been able to last unless it has been centrally Jewish."

But then how strictly Miss Ozick means us to take her notion of "the Jewish writer" becomes a bit unclear when she claims, in the same essay, that the nineteenth-century novel, at its pinnacle, was "a Judaized novel," adding: "George Eliot and Dickens and Tolstoy were all touched by the Jewish covenant; they wrote of conduct and of the consequences of conduct; they were concerned with a society of will and commandment." Miss Ozick is here defending the novel, and literature generally, against those who view it as having no ideational but only aesthetic interest. Still, in asserting the importance of the Jewish point of view and then citing George Eliot, Dickens, and Tolstoy as exemplars— isn't this rather like leavening your bread and calling it matzah, too?

Although not a systematic or analytical thinker, Cynthia Ozick can be a provocative, even a startling one. She is impressively unpredictable. Just when one thinks one has her locked into a fixed position, she springs free. For example, *Art & Ardor* contains three essays on feminism. Two of them—"The Hole/Birth Catalogue," which is an attack on the Freudian notion that anatomy is destiny, and "Previsions of the Demise of the Dancing Dog," which is an attack on the clichés about female literary sensibility—are fairly standard feminist fare. The third essay, "Literature and the Politics of Sex: A Dissent," however, must have given fits to the editors of *Ms.* magazine, where it originally appeared. In this essay Miss Ozick disavows the label "woman writer"—as, interestingly, she doesn't disavow that of "Jewish writer"—and sets out the claims, with admirable clarity and fine passion, of imagination over politics. "Politics," she declares, "begins with premises; imagination goes in search of them." She delivers a terrific chop to the ideological turn that feminism has taken, when she writes: "Now we are enduring a feminism so far advanced into 'new truths' that it has arrived at last at a set of notions indistinguishable from the most age-encrusted, unenlightened, and imprisoning anti-feminist views." And she closes by maintaining that women who write, like all writers, need not worry about fighting for freedom—in their imaginations they already have it.

Cynthia Ozick, then, is a Jewish writer who is also a woman; but, in addition, she is a writer of stories and novels who is also an essayist. Many a novelist has performed handsomely as an essayist; and at present among women in particular there are a number of writers—Mary McCarthy, Elizabeth Hardwick, Susan Sontag, Renata Adler, Joan Didion—who, so to speak, go both ways. The proper and highest and most academically kosher critical principles call for a critic to ignore a novelist's essays when confronting his fiction. Yet in Cynthia Ozick's case this becomes difficult to do, not only because she often remarks penetratingly upon fiction in her essays but because it may well be that she is a better essayist than novelist. (So, incidentally, are the five women mentioned between my dashes two sentences above, though none, I suspect, would be pleased to hear it.)

Brilliant, quirky, profound, outrageous—these are some of the adjectives I would haul into service to describe Cynthia Ozick's quality as an essayist. Her brilliance, when she is writing at the top of her bent, is very bright indeed, as in her portraits of Virginia Woolf and Edith Wharton. The Virginia Woolf essay is an instance of brilliance combining with quirkiness, for it turns out to be really quite as much an essay on Leonard Woolf as on Virginia, and it asks, among other rude but interesting questions, what was a nice Jewish boy like Leonard doing in a place like Bloomsbury? The flow of essayistic observation is constant and high: "Candor," she notes apropos of Leonard Woolf, "is often the mode of the obtuse person." Miss Ozick rates Virginia Woolf higher than I do, and she also rates John Updike higher than I do, but she is the sort of writer with whom you do not have to agree to find interesting. In writing about Updike's *Bech* books, for example, she notices that Bech, a Jewish character, is one of the few of Updike's characters who has no theological life; he is, as she wittily says, "a secular/neuter."

If Miss Ozick has flaws as an essayist, these include a tendency, given the wrong subject, to abstraction that almost instantly turns into intellectual Excedrin headaches 51 through 163, and another tendency to wing it on the spirit of imagination alone. For an example of Cynthia Ozick at her most impenetrable, one cannot do better (do worse?) than her essay "Literature as Idol: Harold Bloom," a title whose arrhythmic sound is matched by prose that must have something to do with the imitative fallacy, for in this essay Miss Ozick has taken an unreadable critic and written unreadably about him—a case, perhaps, of letting the punishment fit the crime. But why should I, an innocent reader, have to sit in a cell with such abstruse prose upon my lap?

Aldous Huxley once defined the art of Montaigne, the first great practitioner of the essay form, as "free association artistically controlled." Of her own essays, Miss Ozick writes: "The only nonfiction worth writing—at least for me—lacks the summarizing gift, is heir to nothing, and sets out with empty pockets from scratch." I think she is mistaken about her own gifts here. Two such essays in *Art & Ardor* in which she "sets out with empty pockets from scratch" are "The Riddle of the Ordinary" and "The Biological Premises of Our Sad Earth-Speck," and each quickly falls into deadly abstraction and what I think of as undocumented and hence unpersuasive grandiosity. In my view, Miss Ozick's best essays are those in which she writes about artists, for she has the soul of an artist herself, and entry to the souls of other artists is not barred to her.

Clearly Cynthia Ozick thinks of herself as an artist—a writer of stories and novels. She prefers fiction to essays for, among other reasons, the sense of adventure and risk that the former provides. "Fiction is all discovery," she has written, "discovery plotted— fallen into, rather—by character: first the writer's, and only then the characters'. Even failure is worthwhile—so much has been dared: scaling an edge to find out something 'new,' 'true'—inherent, immanent, encoded—that was unsuspected at the start, and by the end seems both ingenious and right." This is a bit more abstract than is necessary, but one knows what Miss Ozick means: in an essay one is aware of one's destination, in a story one is astonished at having arrived where one has. This sense of astonishment is often shared by Cynthia Ozick's readers, though here, it must be said, astonishment does not always imply satisfaction.

Cynthia Ozick is an original. There is no one now writing quite like her, nor is she quite like anyone else (pressed, I suppose one could tickle out traces of Bernard Malamud, I. B. Singer, and Saul Bellow). Unlike the case with so many contemporary fiction writers, for the most part her creative sources do not seem patently autobiographical. She does not write in yesterday's bedclothes, which is to say that, although she can be a sexy writer— see, for two examples, her stories "The Pagan Rabbi" and "Puttermesser and Xanthippe"—sex is not at the center of her fiction. As she once said in a memorial essay about Maurice Samuel, "He revered language, but he loved idea more," so is she, passionate about language though she obviously is, even more passionate about ideas in fiction. "For me," wrote Vladimir Nabokov, "a work of fiction exists only insofar as it affords me what I shall bluntly call aesthetic bliss. . . ." Miss Ozick is far from inattentive to aesthetic bliss, but for her, as she puts it in the preface to *Bloodshed and Three Novellas* (1976), "a story must not merely *be,* but mean," and in the same preface she adds: ". . . I believe stories ought to judge and interpret the world."

I admire Cynthia Ozick's sense of artistic vocation, I admire her prose, I admire her views on the point and purposes of fiction —I admire almost everything about her, in fact, but her stories. I hope I am appreciative of all of them; I know I am impressed by many of them; and I confess to having been amazed by a few. But for all that I am appreciative, impressed, even amazed by Miss Ozick's fiction, in the end I am usually left unsatisfied by it. Why, I ask myself, why?

For a time I thought that the difficulty with Cynthia Ozick's fiction was that she simply didn't know how to end a story successfully. I thought of her art as comparable to that of a very considerable chess player of my imagining. This player is a man with astonishing openings, stunning defenses, a player who can make knights and bishops and even pawns do things one had scarcely realized they could do, a player with all the moves but one—namely, the ability to work his opponent into checkmate. The analogy is not quite neat, for Cynthia Ozick's stories do end, but their endings seem to fall far short of what has gone before. They seem to end ineptly. Or, to switch analogies from chess to bullfighting, many an Ozick story seems to me rather like a bull-fight in which the matador works the bull with the greatest subtlety and elegance, and then, at the moment of climax, drops the bull with a grenade.

Take as an example the title story from the volume *Levitation, Five Fictions* (1982). It is about a husband and wife, both novelists, who give a party. The husband makes his living as an editor. "His manner was powerless," Miss Ozick writes, in one of her lovely touches, "he did not seem like an editor at all." He is a Jew; she, the daughter of a minister, is spiritually if not technically a convert to Judaism. As novelists, the one principle they agree on is never to write about writers. They agree on other things as well.

Both husband and wife are absorbed by questions of social-literary power; both recognize their own powerlessness.

About their own lives they had a joke: they were "secondary-level" people. Feingold had a secondary-level job with a secondary-level house. Lucy's own publisher was secondary-level; even the address was Second Avenue. The reviews of their books had been written by secondary-level reviewers. All their friends were secondary-level. . . .

Meanwhile, to their party they invite a number of "luminaries." Miss Ozick names names: Irving Howe, Susan Sontag, Alfred Kazin, Leslie Fiedler; Norman Podhoretz, Elizabeth Hardwick, Philip Roth, Joyce Carol Oates, Norman Mailer; William Styron, Donald Barthelme, Jerzy Kosinski, Truman Capote. None shows up. Instead the usual crowd does. People divide up to talk about different subjects: theater and film in the dining room; Jews, among them a refugee, are discussing Jews in the living room. The wife thinks how intense Jews can be. "They were intense all the time; she supposed the grocers among them were as intense as any novelist; was it because they had been Chosen, was it because they pitied themselves every breathing moment?"

Details in this story are concrete, anchored in the particular. We have those names of living writers. We have little bowls of potato chips, carrot and celery sticks; the husband eats the last olive. Everything in place, all set—all right, hang on. The living room begins to levitate. The talk by Jews about Jews is apparently causing this to happen. "The room was ascending. . . . It was getting free of her [the wife], into loftiness, lifting Jews." While this is happening the wife has an illumination about a scene in a city park, in which Sicilian dancers and an anthropologist from the Smithsonian figure prominently, but whose point is to remind her "how she has abandoned nature, how she has lost the true religion on account of the God of the Jews." Coming out of her illumination, the wife realizes that she is tired of hearing about the Holocaust. She "decides it is possible to become jaded by atrocity. She is bored by the shootings and the gas and the camps, she is not ashamed to admit this. They are as tiresome as prayer." She returns to the dining room, where the secondary-level people are talking about secondary-level things. At the story's close, the husband and the refugee are "riding the living room." The story's final two sentences are: "Their words are specks. All the Jews are in the air."

I may sound more like a landlord than a critic here, but I react to this story by asking, "Madam, what is that living room doing on the ceiling? Madam, I implore you, get those Jews down, please!" I recognize that Miss Ozick is reaching for something deep and special here. Can she be referring, metaphorically, to the inherent *luft*iness of Jews, to the spirituality that can set them apart, especially when they speak of themselves among themselves? No doubt she is, and she is no doubt referring to more as well. But the atmosphere up there, in that living room aloft, and in the story "Levitation," finally seems extremely thin. I prefer my Jews grounded. An artist, I realize, may do with her art what she likes. Yet a reader may say that it isn't enough.

But then I seem to like least those of Cynthia Ozick's stories that she herself likes best. The title story in *The Pagan Rabbi and Other Stories* (1971) is about what its title advertises: a brilliant young rabbi who goes pagan, makes love to a dryad (" 'Scripture does not forbid sodomy with plants,' I exclaimed"), and eventually takes his own life. "The Pagan Rabbi" is a piece of dazzling writing; to render an account of lovemaking with a supra-human being believable, as Miss Ozick does here, is no small trick of craft. It is all almost too glittering, too astonishing. It is virtuosity unfettered. And yet it puts one in mind of nothing quite so much as a sentence from Miss Ozick's own criticism: "In literature it is perilous to be too original in one's premises—one ends not with a novel but with a fairy tale."

In the title story of *Bloodshed and Three Novellas,* Jules Bleilip, a lawyer who is currently working as a fund-raiser, goes off, out of curiosity, to visit a female cousin who has married into a hasidic community in a new-made town outside New York. Most of the members of the community are survivors of the death camps or children of survivors. A secularist himself, a man "whose vocabulary was habitually sociological," Bleilip is both repelled by these religious refugees and lured toward them because he "supposed they had a certain knowledge the unscathed could not guess at." Although the community has a rebbe, he doesn't, we are told, specialize in miracles. The Jews are there to study, uninterruptedly, in their own way. Bleilip is taken that evening to a *minyan* that the rebbe attends. After the *minyan,* during the study hour, the rebbe rises to speak. He is a man of about fifty, wearing a worker's cap; two of the fingers and all of the nails are missing from one of his hands, the result, we learn later, of a freezing experiment conducted upon him at Buchenwald. As always with Miss Ozick, the details are strong and feel true: "Bleilip reversed his view and saw that the rebbe was their child, they gazed at him with the possessiveness of faces seized by a crib, and he too spoke in that mode, as if he were addressing parents, old fathers, deferential, awed, guilty."

The rebbe speaks to the matter of the sacrificing of bullocks and goats during the days of the Temple, concluding bitterly, "For animals we in our day substitute men." Then he turns on Bleilip, questions his motives for being in the room. He, the rebbe, claims that his despair has been transferred to him from Bleilip—"Everything . . . you heard me say in a voice of despair emanates from the liver of this man." Presently he asks Bleilip to empty his pockets, and when he does so Bleilip is revealed to be carrying a toy pistol. Then, later, after the closing prayer session, the rebbe asks—demands, really—that Bleilip remove the contents of his coat pocket, which turn out to include not a toy but a real pistol. There is an exchange between the rebbe and Bleilip in which Bleilip confesses that he did once kill a pigeon with this gun and in which the rebbe remarks: "It is characteristic of believers sometimes not to believe. And it is characteristic of unbelievers sometimes to believe." Does Bleilip ever believe? " 'No,' Bleilip said; and then: 'Yes.' " " 'Then you are as bloody as anyone,' the rebbe said. . . ." and returns Bleilip's pistol to him "for whatever purpose he thought he needed it."

Throw a pebble into a pond and nine sages can't find it. Write a story such as "Bloodshed" and at least one literary critic—me—

cannot figure it out. "Bloodshed" is, I realize, meant to be a wisdom story, but its wisdom eludes me. I find it baffling, but I am baffled in a half-irritated and not in a fascinated way such as would stimulate me to unravel what I find puzzling about this story. Rightly or wrongly, I feel the muddle is not mine but the author's. "Levitation," "The Pagan Rabbi," "Bloodshed"—are these examples of the new "liturgical" fiction, the new "literature attentive to the implications of Covenant and Commandment," that Cynthia Ozick has set herself to write? I must own that I, for one, find these stories willed and schematic (even where I cannot precisely figure out the scheme). Dazzling in parts, they seem extraordinary as sheer literary performance, yet, because the parts do not cohere and come alive as a whole, less than first-class as literature. Cynthia Ozick's most Jewish stories remind me in fact of the Catholic stories of Flannery O'Connor—both seem to me ambitious, impressive, yet finally, somehow, static.

I prefer Cynthia Ozick's stories written in a more realistic mode: "Envy; or, Yiddish in America," about the travail of an aging Yiddish poet desperately searching for a translator, to "Puttermesser and Xanthippe," about a middle-aged civil servant who devises a golem that brings about a temporary reform of New York City; "The Doctor's Wife," about an older physician whom everyone is trying to marry off, to "The Refugee's Notebook," about (among other things) sewing-harems on another planet. I like Miss Ozick's work least, that is to say, when she is readiest to let her imagination rip; I like it best when she brings her Jews down to earth.

Ad astra, or toward the stars, is the motto of Joseph Brill, the protagonist of *The Cannibal Galaxy,* Cynthia Ozick's second novel and her first one in some seventeen years. A French-born Jew, a survivor who was hidden first in the basement of a convent, then in a peasant's hayloft during World War II, Brill emigrates to the American Midwest, where he founds, and is made principal of, a day school that teaches a dual curriculum, made up of equal parts of the Jewish and French traditions, which reflects his own upbringing and education. " 'My two aunties nurtured me,' he often explained, 'my Torah *Tante* and my Parisian *Tante,* each the heiress of an ancient line.' " He, Brill, has the highest standards. An astronomer by training, "he was drawn," we are told, "to heights of every kind." And: "He was maddened by genius. He respected nothing else." This Joseph Brill is the most filled-out and interesting character of all of Cynthia Ozick's fiction.

T. S. Eliot once said that the best method for being a critic is to be very intelligent, but intelligence doesn't hurt in a novelist either. *The Cannibal Galaxy* is a book brimming with intelligence, and one into which much sheer learning has been poured. Add to this a good deal of craft and a great deal—at moments perhaps too great a deal—of style. It is not, in the glib phrase of the day, "a good read"; instead it requires—and in my view largely repays—careful reading. Words are put under heavy pressure in this novel; ideas come wrapped in epigrammatic, often poetic language. Miss Ozick has mastered the manner of sliding neatly from the mundane to the grand and back again. The engines of her art here are at full throttle.

The Cannibal Galaxy is, above all, a work of style. Idiosyncratically, characters appear with "long wrists," "leathery lobes," "clever nostrils." A male teacher at Brill's school has "an altogether pretty nose conscious of its duty." One of his Parisian boyhood friends, now an aged art critic, has "a wrinkled wattle that made Brill think of an emptied-out testicle sac." Occasionally such descriptions are pushed a mite too far. Some of the mothers of Brill's students are "nervous divorcées, scratching at their little moles," when moles do not, I believe, itch. In the classroom we hear "the high and rugged beast-laugh of small children," when beasts do not, with the exception of hyenas, possess laughter. Students' opinions wind and wind, "like elongated spittle," when . . . but enough.

If Miss Ozick lapses into occasional overwriting, it is perhaps owing to the structural needs of her novel; this is a book written with great economy. In only 161 pages she provides the chronicle of a complicated man's life and the institution, his school, that will give it such meaning as it is to have. Time is handled with delicate care. Miss Ozick will linger over certain key episodes in Joseph Brill's life—his early education, his hiding out in the con-

vent—and then let a single sentence register the passage of a
decade. The overwriting is often compensated for by the elegant
writing, of which there is a plenitude: " 'What is the Enlightenment?' Rabbi Pult said. 'Joseph, the Enlightenment engendered
a new slogan: There is no God, and the Jews killed him. Joseph,
this is the legacy of your Enlightenment.' " Always an interesting
prose writer, Cynthia Ozick has become, when she is going well,
a remarkable stylist, as I believe this passage about Joseph Brill's
wanderings, during the day of the rounding-up of Jews in Paris,
amply demonstrates:

> Sweat spilled from behind Joseph's ears down into the well
> of his collarbone; it was July. He hurtled himself back to-
> ward home for some clothes to take with him; then suddenly
> grew sane; it was folly to go back. Instead he ran, he ran
> nowhere; he ran. There were mobs moving toward the Seine
> and its bridges; he veered, and ran the other way. His throat
> roared with a burning; his ribs were in agony. He discovered
> that he was praying for his three older sisters—only what
> seemed to be prayer of the lung was merely panting and
> throat-pain. In his new sanity he admonished himself to
> come to a halt. His legs would not obey. Then he ordered
> them to show dignity, fearlessness, to slacken, to stroll, to
> saunter, to walk. At a cruelly casual pace, the blood gyrating
> in his neck, he wandered through Paris, himself its prey. . . .

The central drama of *The Cannibal Galaxy* begins when Principal Brill, as he is known to everyone connected with his school,
realizes that among his school's students is the daughter of Hester
Lilt, a European writer of truly philosophical weight, a "primary
thinker," who not only resembles Mme. de Sévigné, a heroine of
his boyhood, but who herself, a pure intellectual, was "free of
event because she was in thrall to idea." Having Beulah Lilt to
educate, the daughter of a not widely recognized but nonetheless
authentic powerful thinker, is the great opportunity of Principal
Brill's pedagogic career. The girl, it turns out, does not test well;
the psychological counselor does not view her as promising.

What is more, she lives up to—or, rather down to—these bleak estimates of her ability. She is irretrievably dull in the classroom; on the playground she slavishly follows the school's most popular girl. The girl is given every chance; radical accommodations are made to encourage her. All to no avail. Her mother takes it all calmly enough. But Principal Brill, seeing his great chance pass him by, is cast into a slough first of perplexity, then of despond.

Ad astra, seeking the heights, hoping for genius, the high road upon which Joseph Brill has set himself has seemed to lead nowhere. Cast down, Brill thinks to pull himself up by a late marriage. "I want my own son. I want someone to say kaddish for me when I die—I want to be normal," he exclaims. He marries one of the school secretaries, a rather commonplace woman much younger than he. They have a son, Naphtali by name, who early shows the greatest intellectual quickness, power, promise. Hester Lilt and her daughter return to Europe. Time passes. Eventually, Brill, now full of years, is eased out of his principalship. He retires to Florida. He becomes a television watcher, and one day, over his television screen, whose face appears but that of Beulah Lilt. The negligible little girl has grown up to become a famous Parisian painter and, more than that, a theoretician of the new avant-garde. Interviewed about her girlhood in America, she has no recollection of Principal Brill's school. Brill's own son, meanwhile, has become a business-administration major at Miami University. (Such a bright boy, one would have thought he could have got into the Wharton School.) Joseph Brill's life, in brief and in sum, is a sad and fairly complete failure.

It was Cynthia Ozick who wrote, "A story must not merely *be,* but mean." What does *The Cannibal Galaxy* mean? The title refers to "those megalosaurian colonies of primordial gases that devour smaller brother galaxies," and Brill thinks of Hester Lilt as such a cannibal galaxy. On the last page of the novel, he speaks of her having spoiled his life: "In hindsight he knew he had been ambushed by Hester Lilt." But how had she ambushed him? Is this only Brill deluding himself? Is the novel instead about the unpredictability of education? Is it saying that true ability is sometimes hidden, only to flame up later at mysterious bidding (as with

Beulah Lilt), while young stars that glow brightest often fizzle out early (Naphtali majoring in business; one of the brightest girls in the school doing no better than returning to it as a teacher)? All this comes under the category of "interesting—if true." Yet its truth isn't persuasively presented in this novel. How after all did Beulah Lilt grow into this figure of radiant intellectual power? And then one wonders, why is Joseph Brill's life made to come to so little, why is this extremely intelligent and largely altruistic man brought so low? Was he insufficiently patient with Beulah Lilt? Is he to be damned for lowering his sights toward the close of his life? There is an air of unexplained vengefulness hovering over the harsh fate dealt out to Joseph Brill, and it throws this gorgeously written novel into doubt.

I seem to have been continually patting Cynthia Ozick on the back while slapping her in the face. But in one of her old churches, which I still attend, where they celebrate the religion of Art, we learn that only truly interesting writers are capable of greatly disappointing. I hope Cynthia Ozick will write a great many more essays, and I hope, too, she ceases to write fantastical fiction. She is a writer who only flies with her feet securely on the ground.

Commentary 1984

The Sunshine Girls:
Renata Adler and
Joan Didion

AS AN EDITOR of an intellectual magazine, I once asked a noted—as these gents seem always to be called—British psychiatrist to write an article for my magazine explaining the phenomenon of depression. The phenomenon was evidently not a highly puzzling one for him, for the noted British psychiatrist wrote in his article—I summarize but I do not simplify—that those people are most likely to be depressed who were not frequently hugged in their infancy. This explanation did not go down well with me, and I fear I instructed the noted British psychiatrist, in the most polite language, to go hug his article, for the reductionism of his thinking, not to put too fine a point on it, greatly depressed me.

What I meant by the phenomenon of depression was rather more complex and not something to be so readily puréed in the Cusinart of conventional Freudian psychology. By depression I meant that spiritual, perhaps psychological condition that causes us—some of us more than others, yet almost all of us at one time or another—to dwell on the darkest side of things. What I wanted to know was whether, generally speaking, depression was in effect the common cold of the mind or spirit, something we all lapse into every now and then, usually to emerge not too much the worse for wear; or whether when depressed we are in fact seeing the world in the dark cheerlessness that—given the basic data: birth, struggle, disease, and death—represents reality perceived in its truest clarity. This is what I wondered when I solicited the noted British psychiatrist, and I wonder about it still.

I do not have the attention span to sustain a lengthy depression, but I have of late been reading two novelists who do: Renata Adler and Joan Didion. I think of them as the Sunshine Girls, largely because in their work the sun is never shining. If weather reports were offered in novels, in their novels the forecast would almost always be gray, mostly cloudy, chill winds, with a strong chance of rain. They seem, these two writers, not really happy unless they are sad. They keep, to alter the line from an old song, a frown on their page for the whole modern age. Muriel Spark once wrote an interesting book entitled *Girls of Slender Means*. Miss Adler and Miss Didion are slender women who write slender books heavy with gloom. Let us look, then, to their means as novelists in the hope of discovering to what end they lead us.

Along with their gloom, Miss Adler and Miss Didion share an expertise at self-promotion, albeit of a subtle kind. The New Criticism used to advise avoiding the author and concentrating on the work, but this was before the advent of personal journalism and the author's publicity interview. Both Miss Adler and Miss Didion send themselves out to the world as nervous, rather fragile characters. "She scrutinizes and edits her speech ceaselessly," writes a reporter, interviewing Miss Adler for the cultural pages of the *New York Times*, "cutting off thoughts with 'Oh, that's a blind alley,' or 'No, that's not true.' And faintly but noticeably, her hands often quiver." Miss Didion, in such works as her recent *Salvador*, makes plain her difficulty with migraines, is usually photographed in sun glasses, writes about the nightmarish quality of author publicity tours.

Two delicate ladies, one might think. But if so, what is Miss Adler doing so regularly as a subject in *Women's Wear Daily*, her single gray braid over her shoulder, or as subject of the fashion photographer Richard Avedon, while Miss Didion, who has written big-money screenplays, apparently holds her own on the coast among some fellows who, as they say out there, "play hard ball." Depressed these women may be, nervous and fragile they may seem, I nonetheless take them to be two tough cookies.

Of the two, Renata Adler is the less practiced novelist. She has written, in fact, two novels but no narratives. *Speedboat,* her first novel, and *Pitch Dark,* her second, are both composed for the most part of short, journal-like entries, which, in the modernist spirit, a reader has rather to assemble on his own. *Speedboat,* published in 1976, was much praised; it won the Ernest Hemingway Award for best first novel of the year in which it was published. Reading it today, one notices certain affinities with the work of Ann Beattie: a flatness of expression meant to convey a deep spiritual fatigue. On the formal level, the novel seems Barthelmystically influenced, though without Donald Barthelme's intellectual playfulness. Here is a characteristic passage:

> A young professor from Iowa, who was in the city for a lecture series on Wordsworth and the Lake Poets, spoke of his closeness to his own students, with several of whom he had had affairs, although he did not believe, in the academic context, in shacking up. He was preoccupied with his brightest student, a girl, with whom, during office hours, he engaged in—he wished there was an Anglo-Saxon word for it —fellatio. I said I thought it was sort of a metaphor for education, wasn't it? Then I thought I had gone too far. But no. He said, "Exactly." We all watched the "Eleventh Hour News," which went on, of course, at the Twelfth Hour. Jim and I drove out to the country. It was very late. We stopped for coffee at an all-night dairy-and-diner on the way. A man got out of a truck, came in, ordered a milkshake, put his wallet on the counter, and mumbled something. Then he left, looking angry. "He asks me for a package of rubbers," the man being the counter said. "I mean, this is a *dairy.*" When our car broke down near the highway exit to the farm, a boy with a sign reading BOSTON trotted over. He thought we were slowing to give him a lift.

Miss Adler is not telling a story in *Speedboat;* instead she is trying to create a feeling through the thoughts, incidents, and odd happenings that occur to the presence at the center of her book, Jen Fain, who is a working journalist also teaching a film course at a school that resembles the City University of New York. The feeling she is trying to create is one of dislocation, disorientation, depression. "There doesn't seem to be a spirit of the times," Jen Fain remarks on the second page of the book. Miss Adler, though, will soon enough supply one. On that same page she has her character remark, "I think sanity, however, is the most profound moral option of our time." And at the bottom of the page, awaking at the apartment of one of her men friends, she is told, " 'Just stay here. *Angst* is common.' " We are, you might say, off and limping.

Manhattan Transfer, John Dos Passos called his novel of New York life in the early 1920s; *Manhattan Transference,* Renata Adler's account of New York life in the early 1970s might be called, for even though Miss Adler is no lover of therapeutic culture, the world she describes in *Speedboat* is a highly neurotic one. "Sometimes it seems that this may be a nervous breakdown—sleeping all day, tears, insomnia at midnight, and again at four A.M. Then it occurs to me that a lot of people have it." In *Speedboat* disconnection is a way of life. Rats roam the halls; a Doberman pinscher attacks an old woman. Jen Fain reports: "I knew a deliverer of flowers who, at Sixty-ninth and Lexington, was hit by a flying suicide. Situations simply do not yield to the most likely structures of the mind." And: "There are some days when everyone I see is a lunatic." These passages pile up, and all are written, in the spiritual if not the grammatical sense, in the passive voice.

Having said all this, I must go on to say that I do not find *Speedboat* boring. It ought to be, but it isn't. Perhaps it isn't because, though the book offers none of the traditional pleasures of the novel, it does offer pleasures of a different kind. When it begins to hum, Miss Adler's is a lively mind, which throws off interesting insights. "Lonely people," she writes, "see double entendres everywhere." In a brilliant passage she talks about what she calls "the Angry Bravo," which is what goes on when, in her example, an audience cheers *No, No, Nanette* when in fact behind their cheers is rage at *Hair* or whatever is the going triumph of the day. She is also clever on the unseriousness of certain artists and intellectuals. In a scene in which no names are given, an Indian lady whom I take to be Mrs. Gandhi is told by a poet whom I take to be Allen Ginsberg, "I think in this country we need to disburden ourselves of our, our burden of rationality." To which Miss Adler offers the capping comment: "He sat down. It did not seem exactly India's problem."

The world depicted in *Speedboat* is that of unattached youngish people for whom money is not a serious problem but finding a purpose in life is. They I won't say bound but at least crawl into one another's beds, less it seems out of passion than out of the need for comfort and solace against a cold world. They are distanced from life. Boredom is among their deadliest enemies. They have endless time to spend thinking about themselves. (" 'Self-pity' is just sadness, I think, in the pejorative," says Miss Adler's Miss Fain.) Therapy is no help. "In every city, at the same time, therapists earned their living by saying, 'You're too hard on yourself.' " There is a slightly frenetic stylishness about their lives. "Elaine's was jammed"; a man invents a drink called "Last Mango in Paris" (reminiscent, this, of a man in an Anthony Powell novel who invents a drink that he calls "Death Comes for the Archbishop"). Nothing quite holds. Jen Fain avers: "The radical intelligence in the moderate position is the only place where the center holds." But of those who write or argue or say that the center will not hold, I always wonder how they know they are standing in the center—or anywhere near it.

It doesn't take long for *Speedboat* to run out of gas. The book provides no forward motion, nothing in the way of momentum. In a snippet of conversation reported in one of Miss Adler's paragraphs, a man says: "Janine, you know I'm very tired of your *aperçus*." So in time does one grow tired of Miss Adler's, which, in a book without any narrative force, could, any one of them, as easily appear on page 14 as on page 203. Cause and effect, narrative order, nothing seems to matter. "It all ends in disaster anyway." But then Miss Adler is forthright about not having a story to tell. Toward the close of *Speedboat,* she writes: "There are only so many plots. There are insights, prose flights, rhythms, felicities. But only so many plots."

Friend, here's the bad news: you want to call yourself a novelist, you're going to have to find a plot.

Pitch Dark, Renata Adler's recent novel, does appear to be setting out to tell a story: that of the break-up of an eight-year love affair between another journalist, Kate Ennis, and a married man referred to as Jake. But the story turns out not to be much of a story. As the dust-jacket copy has it, ". . . *Pitch Dark* moves into new realms of feeling." This book, too, peels off into aperçuistical paragraphs; it is interested in making disconnections. It is about, as the narrator of this non-narration says, "my state of mind." This second book of Miss Adler's is more modernist, more avant-garde, in intention than *Speedboat*. The practical consequence is that, within its pages, more puzzles are offered, more elaborate games are played.

Like all contemporary works of modernist intention, *Pitch Dark* is highly self-reflexive—that is, it often talks about itself. Thus, two-thirds through the book Miss Adler writes:

> But will they understand it if I tell it this way?
> Yes, they will. They will surely understand it.
> But will they care about it?
> That I cannot guarantee.

The way that *Pitch Dark* is told is aslant, through indirection. "Do I need to stylize it, then, or can I tell it as it was?" Miss Adler stylizes it, in my view. At the forefront of her book is the affirmation that stories can no longer be told. "For a woman, it is always, don't you see, Scheherazade. For a man, it may be the Virginian. There he goes then, striding through the dust of midday toward his confrontation. Here I am, of an evening, wondering whether I can hold his interest yet a while."

Throughout *Pitch Dark* lines repeat, meant to convey a refrain-like resonance. "But you are, you know, you were, the nearest thing to a real story to happen in my life," is one such line; "Did I throw the most important thing perhaps, by accident, away?" is another. We cannot know for certain who is saying these lines, Kate or Jake. But the lines recur, as do, among others, these two: "The world is everything that is the case," which is from Wittgenstein, and "And in the second place because," which is the first line of a Nabokov story. Both these lines are there to establish the modernity of Miss Adler's narrator's mind as well as to establish the modernity of her own intention in this book. Of the Wittgenstein line, an epigrammatic couplet by the poet Donald Hall seems particularly pertinent here:

The world is everything that is the case.
Now stop your blubbering and wash your face.

For there is a certain high-tone blubbering going on in *Pitch Dark*. In its pages Miss Adler has the portentousness knob turned all the way up. "As much as this is the age of crime, after all, this is the century of dislocation," Kate Ennis notes. "Not just for journalists or refugees; for everyone." As for the novel's weather report, it is given on page 79: "I stand, in pitch dark now, and in heavy rain.

Miss Adler never does get around to telling the story of Kate Ennis's long love affair with Jake. Instead she shows the sad after-effects of its break-up. Accounts of events, she believes, are lies. What is important are moods, feelings, symbols. So we are given an account of a raccoon who slowly dies of distemper on the stove of Kate Ennis's country house. Is this meant to stand in for the symbolic death of her love affair? So we are given a lengthy, deliberately paranoid account of a trip through Ireland. Is this meant to stand in for Kate Ennis's feeling of utter disorientation after the prop of her love affair is pulled out from under her? So the same lines repeat and resound throughout the book. Miss Adler succeeds in giving her novel a highly claustral feeling. Reading it one feels rather as if one is being asked to play handball in an empty but very small closet.

Bleak, psychologically inconclusive, bereft of the normal pleasures of storytelling, *Pitch Dark* has nonetheless enjoyed a pretty good run in both the popular press and from critics. In part, I suspect, this derives from the autobiographical atmosphere of the novel. In the course of an adulatory piece about her in *New York* magazine Miss Adler has implied—and perhaps more than implied—that the love affair that she has not really written about in *Pitch Dark* is one that she herself has gone through. Then there is a celebrity sheen playing about the book's pages. Kate Ennis is often aloft, en route to one or another island; in Ireland she stays at the house of a former American ambassador to that country. There is also the attraction of gossip. "One morning, in the early nineteen-eighties, Viola Teagarden filed a suit in a New York State court against Claudia Denneny for libel. Also named as defendants were a public television station and a talk-show host." We all know who Viola and Claudia are, do we not? Withholding such obvious names is a fine advance on name dropping.

As for the critical appreciation of *Pitch Dark,* here Miss Adler has what I think of as the moral minority on her side—that select group of critics who worry about not lending approval to avantgarde endeavor. Roger Shattuck, for example, writing in the *New York Review of Books,* has remarked that "Adler has created in *Pitch Dark* a sense of form that could be called cubist." Professor Shattuck plays that old shell game of modern criticism, switching genres, in which the critic has to guess under which genre the work lies. "Adler, like many of her contemporaries, abjures fusion, practices simple removal," he writes. "The resulting minimalist genre should properly not be called a novel, for it answers radically different expectations, brings other rewards." Better yet, the book has allowed Professor Shattuck to erect what he calls "the innarratability principle," which has to do with the inability —or, more precisely, unwillingness—of certain modern writers to tell their story straight out.

But to return to the old, perhaps boring, narratability principle, would it be too rude to suggest that Miss Adler has let slip away an extremely interesting story? The story of being a married man's mistress, told from the point of view of the mistress, is after all neither a common nor an unpromising one. What is it about women who enter into lengthy affairs with married men? What do they have to gain? What is it they are afraid of? Why are they so ready to put themselves almost automatically in second place or below? But then this is a story Renata Adler, given her view that accounts of incidents are lies and that narrative contains the seeds of its own falsity, could never tell. She is among that band of contemporary writers who evidently do not agree with Oscar Wilde's statement: "It should be our faith that everything can be expressed in words."

Joan Didion, my second Sunshine Girl, is vastly superior as a novelist to Renata Adler. To begin with, she really is a novelist— that is, she has no bias against telling stories and she is interested in lives outside her own. Her vision is dark, her views are bleak, but she is richly talented. That she is a novelist to the bone became clear a little more than halfway out in her first novel, *Run River* (1963), where the book's heroine, Lily Knight McClelland, finds herself seated next to a sailor on a Greyhound bus from San Francisco:

> From San Francisco to Vellejo she sat next to a sailor who was going to meet his girl in Salt Lake City. She lived with her folks in Salt Lake but Frisco, he explained, was their lucky town. They had met there, in a gin mill on Market Street, four days before he shipped out in 1943. When she promised to wait had been the A-1 moment in his life, and the second A-1 moment had been a week before on the U.S.S. *Chester* when he got his first sight in two years of the Golden Gate Bridge. . . . Lily began to cry, struck by the superiority of his appreciations to her own, and the sailor said wait a minute, hold your horses, it wasn't sad, honey, it was like women crying at weddings. . . . When the sailor got off at Vallejo to wait for the Salt Lake express Lily wished him good luck and watched him covertly through the window. He was sitting on his duffel bag reading a comic book and eating a Milky Way, and she wanted to get off the bus

and give him her garnet ring for his girl, but did not know how to go about it.

Run River is set in the countryside above Sacramento among the families of the landed gentry and is the only novel I know, since those of John Steinbeck, to present life in California with the kind of density of detail that makes it seem real. It takes in three generations; it talks about Dekes at Stanford and Pi Phis at Berkeley and the pre-World War II days of convertibles and Glen Miller albums. The range of human types is wide, not least interesting among them the father of Lily's husband, of whom Miss Didion writes: "Everett had once explained that his father referred to all Mexicans and to most South Americans—including the President of Brazil, who had once been entertained on the river—as goddamn wetbacks and to all Orientals as goddamn Filipinos. . . . Easterners fell into two groups: goddamn pansies and goddamn Jews."

At the heart of the novel is a tragic love between a husband and wife. This love is made tragic by the wife's penchant for lapsing into rather empty affairs, one of which ends in a murder of one of her lovers by her husband. The plot begins with the murder, flashes back for the better part of the book, and closes on the very real if highly complex love between husband and wife. Published when Miss Didion was only twenty-nine, *Run River* has something of the feel of Faulkner to it—"I think nobody owns land until their dead are in it," one character says—and rather good Faulkner at that.

A note of despair plays through *Run River* yet somehow does not take over the book. The density of novelistic detail covers it over, the devotion to complexity of presentation lends it an affirmative feeling. But Joan Didion, in her next three novels, has not returned to density of detail, and complexity has become, in her work, less something to demonstrate than to talk about. Her second novel, *Play It As It Lays* (1971), is her Hollywood book, but it might have been more accurately entitled *Fear and Trembling, and the Sickness Called the West Coast*. The philosophy behind it has been called, I believe, freeway existentialism.

Maria (pronounced Mar-AY-ah), the character in the center of
Play It As It Lays, is a film actress whose career is in eclipse and
whose marriage to a coming young director is shot. She has a
daughter in a mental institution, has had an abortion, is on bar-
biturates. "From my mother," she announces early in the novel,
"I inherited my looks and a tendency to migraine. From my father
I inherited an optimism which did not leave me until recently."
Along with migraine, she suffers dread. She feels the "peril, the
unspeakable peril, in the everyday." Looking for some order in
life, she finds none. Instead her portion in life is unrelieved, im-
mitigable anxiety. "All along she expected to die, as surely as she
had expected that planes would crash if she boarded them in bad
spirit, as unquestionably as she believed that loveless marriage
ended in cancer of the cervix and equivocal adultery in fatal accidents to children. Maria did not particularly believe in rewards,
only in punishments, swift and personal."

With *Play It As It Lays* Miss Didion acquired, as a novelist, a
new in-group: those people who no longer believe in cause and
effect, who feel, as a knowing Hollywood figure puts it to Maria,
that they know something because "we've been out there where
nothing is." Or, as Maria herself says, on the final page of the
novel: "I know something Carter never knew, or Helene, or
maybe you. I know what 'nothing' means, and keep on playing."
Along with nothing, Miss Didion knows a thing or two about
the Hollywood life about which she writes. She knows how
agents think and talk; she knows the distinction between a tan
acquired at a health club and one acquired during an entire life
spent in season. Yet the question arises, why would a writer be
drawn to the subject of a rather inarticulate young woman having
a nervous breakdown in expensive surroundings? The inadequate
answer is, I fear, because she is a Sunshine Girl, drawn to the
dark and the hopeless in human affairs.

Miss Didion's third novel, *A Book of Common Prayer* (1977), is
set among the ruling family in a country called Boca Grande—a
country with no history and where everyone lives in cinder-block
houses. The story is told by one Grace Strasser-Mendana, a North
American trained as an anthropologist who studied under Krober

and worked with Lévi-Strauss but who has lost her faith in her own method, "who stopped believing that observable activity defined anthropos." She married into Boca Grande's ruling family, and is now dying, at a fairly leisurely pace, of cancer. She has also, she says, "been for fifty of my sixty years a student of delusion." The story she has to tell is about Charlotte Bogart Douglas, whose eighteen-year-old daughter Marin is a revolutionary student on the run from the FBI. Charlotte has come to Boca Grande to await the arrival of her daughter—or, as the narrator puts it, "located herself at the very cervix of the world, the place through which a child lost to history must pass."

With *A Book of Common Prayer* we are in V. S. Naipaul country, the Third World in turmoil and collision with Western things it can neither live with nor without. There is a hotel in which nothing works, a French-named restaurant serving wretched food, swimming pools without chlorine, while off in the mountains the guerrillas may or may not be forming for attack. Except that, unlike Naipaul, Miss Didion is playing this subject for dark laughs. Although she scores greatly off the grotesque right-wing family that rules Boca Grande, a family that stages various coups against itself, she does not do so from a left-wing perspective. Charlotte Bogart's first husband is a left-wing academic intellectual, her second husband a radical lawyer roughly cut from the model of William Kunstler, yet the second husband can say to the first: "Something I've never been able to understand is how you happen to know more Trotskyists than Trotsky did." Agents provocateurs appear in Boca Grande, but "the main mark they leave is to have provided employment for the many other people required to follow them around and tap their telephones." No, the politics of this novel are neither of the conventional right- nor left-wing variety. They are more radical than either; they are the politics of despair.

Here the visions of Renata Adler and Joan Didion begin to mesh—so much so that one could gently lift sentences from *A Book of Common Prayer* and insert them into *Speedboat* or *Pitch Dark,* or vice versa, without, I suspect, anyone noticing. For example: "I am less and less sure that this story has been one of delusion." Or: "What an odd notion it was that fiction was just a matter of getting facts completely, implausibly wrong." Or: "I am less and less convinced that the word unstable has any useful meaning. . . ." Or: "I guess I'm just neurotic." The first and third sentences are Miss Didion's, the second and fourth Miss Adler's. Despair, in the contemporary novel, doesn't have a great deal of range: it speaks, you might say, in one voice.

One up on T. S. Eliot's "The Hollow Men," Miss Didion's novels usually end on both a bang and a whimper. Charlotte Bogart Douglas is killed in yet another of Boca Grande's habitual coups d'état. The narrator reports: "The moment and circumstances of her arrest are matters of record but the moment and circumstances of her death remain obscure. I do not even know which side killed her, who held the Estadio Nacional at the moment of death." One had scarcely anticipated less. But in the end one feels as Keats reported feeling upon viewing a painting by Benjamin West entitled "Death on the Pale Horse": ". . . in this picture we have unpleasantness without any momentous depth of speculation excited, in which to bury its repulsiveness."

Democracy, Joan Didion's most recent novel, is, as its narrator, a woman calling herself Joan Didion, calls it, a "novel of fitful glimpses." It is Miss Didion's richest novel since *Run River.* By richest I mean that there are riches on every page: lovely details, sharp observations, risky but always interesting generalizations, real information—many of the things that I, for one, read novels in the hope of discovering. "Let the man build you a real drink," one character says to another, and with that single sentence, a sentence of a kind for which Miss Didion has a splendid knack, she calls up a whole way of life, in this instance that of the business-class country-club stage of culture.

Miss Didion can build you a real character, too, and *Democracy,* slender though it is as a novel, is filled with interesting characters, major and minor. Of Billy Dillon, the administrative assistant of Harry Victor, the husband of the heroine of *Democracy,* a left-wing politician who made an abortive run for the presidency during the Vietnam War years, the demographics of whose "phantom constituency were based on comfort and its concomitant uneasiness"—of this Billy Dillon, Miss Didion writes: "Killer mick, Harry always said about Billy Dillon, an accolade." Jack Lovette, a high-rolling international operative who early understood "war itself as a specifically commercial enterprise," is a man of "a temperamental secretiveness, a reticence that had not so much derived from [his] occupation as led him to it."

At the center of *Democracy* is Inez Victor, the wife of Harry and the lover of Jack Lovett and the most interesting of Joan Didion's female characters. A daughter of the rich business class in Hawaii, beautiful, beautifully connected, she worked after college as a docent at the National Gallery, an under-editor of *Vogue,* put in a year at Park-Bernet. With Inez Victor we are of course in the world of *Women's Wear Daily* and *Rolling Stone,* the celebrity world of the beautiful and the bored. Hers is a name that crops up with a fair regularity in the Style section of the *New York Times* or *Washington Post.* She is a woman who has everything but happiness. Her husband refers to her "quite unpalpable unhappiness." Miss Didion notes: "In retrospect she seemed to have been most happy in borrowed houses, and at lunch." Like all Joan Didion's heroines, she has a wide "capacity for passive detachment." (Charlotte Bogart Douglas, in *A Book of Common Prayer,* feels a sense of "separateness," which is much the same thing; Lily Knight McClelland, in *Run River,* feels perpetually disconnected; and Maria, in *Play It As It Lays,* feels nothing but all of the above.) But Inez Victor's passive detachment, in Miss Didion's hands, can render interesting effects:

> Inez said the 3:45 A.M. flight from Honolulu to Hong Kong
> was exactly the way she hoped dying would be.
> Dawn all the way.

Democracy is doing two things at once. It is telling the love story of Inez Victor and Jack Lovett, and it is providing an account of the fradulence of public life, in its political and celebrity realms, and both are subtly done. Its criticism of left-wing politics, in the person of Harry Victor, is devastating. As Jack Lovett says, "You people really interest me. . . . You don't actually see what's happening in front of you. You don't see it unless you read it. You have to read it in the *New York Times,* then you start talking about it. Give a speech. Call for an investigation. Maybe you can come down here in a year or two, investigate what's happening tonight." But it won't do to slip Miss Didion into a political box. She doesn't much like what has happened in America. Yet she doesn't much like it anywhere else either. Set for the most part during the Vietnam years, her novel, perhaps intended to bring Henry Adams's novel *Democracy* (1880) up to date, dwells on the decline of American power and the decay of American life. But then Miss Didion is, by temperament, drawn to decline and decay.

Good as *Democracy* is, one cannot help feeling it would have been better if Miss Didion had left out the character called Joan Didion, the novelist. Throughout the novel, this Joan Didion drops in to tell you about the difficulties and limitations of narrative. "This is a hard story to tell," she says at one point; "I am resisting narrative here," she says at another. "Consider any of these things long enough," she remarks, "and you will see that they tend to deny the relevance not only of personality but of relevance." There is a sense in which, because of the fragmented way she tells her story, Miss Didion must have felt called upon to bring her own novelistic problems into the book. Yet one also feels that she is pleased by the modernist note that this device demonstrates.

Why make narrative seem so difficult? The trick used to be to make telling a story as straight and smooth as one could. Now it seems to be to make it as tortuous and jagged as possible. I think Miss Didion would have done better, to borrow a phrase, to have played her story as it lay, and not to have undermined it with accounts of the unreliability of narrative.

With its deconstructionists in literary criticism, its ordinary-language and other philosophers, and its novelists, our age may one day come to be known in intellectual history for its role in the advancement of techniques to prove that reality doesn't exist.

Along with their natural gifts of dark temperament, our Sunshine Girls, Renata Adler and Joan Didion, are joined in this enterprise. It is more than a mite depressing.

In search of comic relief while reading the novels of Miss Adler and Miss Didion I happened upon Nietzsche's little book *Schopenhauer as Educator*—one must take one's laughs where one can find them—where I came upon the following remarkable explanation of why such novels, and the general train of thought they represent, are so depressing:

> Basically, you see, cheerfulness is only to be found where there is victory, and this applies to the works of all true thinkers as it does to every work of art. Even if the content is terrible and serious as the problem of existence itself, the work will have an oppressive and painful effect only in those cases where the half-thinker or half-artist has spread the haze of his inadequacy over it; whereas nothing better or more cheering can happen to a man than to be near those victorious persons who, because they have thought the deepest thoughts, must love what is most alive, and finally, like the wise men they are, turn to the Beautiful. They really *talk*, they don't stammer or gossip; they really live and move, unlike other human beings who lead such a strange mask-like existence. For this reason when we are near them we feel, for a change, human and natural and have an urge to shout out as Goethe: "How marvelous and precious is a living thing! how real and truly adapted to its condition!"

Recall that Nietzsche is here talking about Schopenhauer, the darkest of all modern philosophers. There is a plain pessimism and there is heroic pessimism—and of plain pessimism, of the kind Renata Adler and Joan Didion dispense, we have had quite enough. Let, please, the sunshine in.

Commentary 1984

THREE | THE OLDER CROWD

The Ordeal of
Van Wyck Brooks

T O B E K I N D to the dead and hard on the living is no useful principle in life but an excellent one in literary criticism. Although he never enunciated it as such, this was essentially the principle, the program, upon which Van Wyck Brooks as a literary critic operated. Thus far no one has thought to apply the principle to Brooks himself. Visiting England in the last years of his life, Van Wyck Brooks was struck by the statue of Thomas Hardy in Dorchester, which caused him to remark to his wife: "England remembers her great literary men. In America they're forgotten by the next generation." Brooks died in 1963 at the age of seventy-six, and the corpus of his work, moldering in the dry boneyard of literary history, has grown quite as cold as the corpse in his grave.

To hear some tell it, *rigor mortis* had set in on Brooks's work several decades before his actual death. As early as the 1920s, Brooks's contemporary Paul Rosenfeld, in what is for the most part an essay celebrating Brooks's early achievement, ends on a warning note: will Van Wyck Brooks set out on new paths of literary discovery, or will he remain, sedentary, locked into the house of the past? "The man has brought a great freshening," Rosenfeld wrote, "and he is already a small classic. And yet, the dominance of the sitting position would mean defeat. It would be a great defeat for all America." In 1924, when he received the *Dial* award for his contribution to literature, Mary Colum cited Brooks as belonging to "the highest order of critics." In a letter

Sherwood Anderson told him, "you must realize what an inciter to flame in others you are." Brooks was not yet forty when recognition of this kind came rolling in. The general view among literary intellectuals in the United States was that, if America did not yet have a major literature, it did have, in Van Wyck Brooks, a major critic—and that was a start. Before Brooks was fifty, he was already written off as no longer central, out of it, altogether a back number. What went wrong?

Received opinion has it that what went wrong was Van Wyck Brooks himself. Once a slashing critic of American literature and culture, he had, the common view held, mellowed to the mush of chauvinistic nostalgia as a literary historian. In the early 1920s Paul Rosenfeld wrote that no other writer had Brooks's "depth of insight into the nature of American life and of human life in general, the erudition, the sense of the function of art, and the knowledge of psychology"; but in the 1930s Malcolm Cowley, F. W. Dupee, and F. O. Matthiessen had written disapprovingly of Brooks, Cowley remarking that he had "withdrawn from the battle." As the decades sailed past, things for Brooks's reputation did not get better but worse. In 1941 Dwight Macdonald, never noted for the light touch, weighed in with a reference to Brooks as "our leading mouthpiece for totalitarian cultural values." The line on Van Wyck Brooks had been fixed and, once fixed, has remained to this day unchanged. The line, in a single sentence, is: when he was young he was very, very good, but when he was old he was horrid.

"A point of view . . . ," the early Van Wyck Brooks wrote, "inevitably makes the critic a champion and a man of war." Although Brooks would later contend (rightly) that his central concerns remained unchanged throughout his career, his point of view did change, and change radically, in mid-career. The early Van Wyck Brooks—the Brooks essentially of *America's Coming-of-Age, Letters and Leadership,* and *The Ordeal of Mark Twain*—was a white-hot excoriator, a critic who set out to prove that American literature was thin nearly to the point of being non-existent. (Whitman was the one American writer he had good things to say about, though even here he provided strong qualifications.) As he viewed it, the Highbrow and the Lowbrow—the first devoted to the plane of theory, the second to that of action—were separated by a gulf never bridged in American culture. Business "occupied the center of the field" in America, absorbed the best minds: "The highest ambition of Young America is to be—do I exaggerate?—the owner of a shoe factory." Such idealism as there was in America was unattached, cut off from the nation's chief preoccupations, blown about by the winds of irrelevance.

"*A focal center*—that is the first requisite of a great people," Brooks wrote in *America's Coming-of-Age*. And that, he found, was precisely what the United States did not have. Nor did it have "one thinker strong enough to create a resisting background in the vague element of American life." Gloomy though Brooks painted the picture of American culture, he did leave a small light bulb burning. The final chapter of *America's Coming-of-Age* begins with a quotation from J. B. Yeats: "The fiddles are tuning as it were all over America." Slim though the hope for creating a genuine culture in America may be, as yet it is not impossible.

> To leave behind the old Yankee self-assertion and self-sufficiency, to work together, think together, feel together, to believe so fervently in the quality of standards that we delight in prostrating our work and our thoughts before them—all that is certainly in the right direction.

Socialism is thrown into this vague hopper of hope. "Socialism from this flows as light from the sun." A metaphorician always, Brooks ends: "I have heard of seeds which, either planted too deep or covered with accretions of rubble, have kept themselves alive for generations until by chance they have been turned up once more to the friendly sun."

Orphic and vatic, written in a prose with true flow, it is no puzzlement why Brooks's early books appealed so to young American writers and intellectuals. They were, in effect, a call to Pioneers, O pioneers. Nothing that had come before them, they were instructed, was of much value. A clear enemy, business culture, was limned. A job remained to be done: the bridging of the Highbrow and Lowbrow elements in American life, which could best be accomplished through literature. A community of common interest was established. As for that "one thinker strong enough to create a resisting background in the vague element of American life," perhaps he had already arisen—Van Wyck Brooks himself.

In *The Ordeal of Mark Twain* (1920) Brooks set out to demonstrate the baleful effects of life in America on a revered American writer. The book argued that Mark Twain was a divided writer, riven up the center of his life between the triumphant literary career that should have been his and the dominant business values of the culture in which he lived—the latter providing a soil in which Twain's natural genius could only shrivel. "The Lincoln of our literature," as William Dean Howells called Twain, came out in Brooks's version little more than a dreary Van Buren or Buchanan. The writer who might have been an American Rabelais or Swift had been ground down by society into a lecture-hall comedian, a tame humorist, a defeated man.

In *The Ordeal of Mark Twain* Brooks used psychology to explain what he deemed to be the dualism, or double personality, of Twain. He would later disavow the use of psychology in literature—"Our age of psychology," he remarked in his notebooks, "is not an age of interest in human nature"—but too late to prevent its being used against him. Those who have put writers on the couch shall themselves be put on the couch. Couched Brooks has certainly been, for from here on out in his career nothing other than literary psychoanalysis has occurred to critics to explain Brooks's radical change in point of view. This change grew out of his work on *The Pilgrimage of Henry James* (1925), after which Brooks went mad. Nervous breakdown is the parlor phrase but madness is what Brooks suffered. James Hoopes's *Van Wyck Brooks* provides for the first time the details of Brooks's long bout with madness, and they are shattering. Put through the wringers of various sanatoria in the United States and in England ("houses of the dead," as he described them in his *Autobiography*), set to pathetic regimens of balancing balls, enforced recreation, carpentry, and naps, Brooks, for five years, from 1926 through 1931, feared starvation, live burial, being chased by a Hindu with a knife. He ate grass; he rolled in the snow, hoping for pneumonia; in one of the most pathetically inept attempts at suicide on record, he broke the crystal of his wristwatch and tried to do away with himself by eating the glass.

"Chronic melancholia" was the label Jung, when consulted by letter, affixed to Brooks, citing his condition as "a terribly hard case for treatment, if possible at all." Earlier, at the nadir of despair, as he recounts in his *Autobiography,* he thought of his youthful writing with "rage and shame." "I was pursued especially with nightmares in which Henry James turned great luminous menacing eyes upon me. I was half aware, in connection with him, of the division within myself, and with all the bad conscience of a criminal I felt I had viewed him with Plato's 'hard little eye of detraction.' "

In his *Autobiography* Brooks devotes a scant though searing eleven pages to his breakdown in a chapter entitled "A Season in Hell." Professor Hoopes gives the episode a chapter of twenty-three pages, and much earlier space to adumbrating the fall that is to come as well as later space to its consequences. The breakdown is also at the center of William Wasserstrom's *The Legacy of Van Wyck Brooks* (Southern Illinois University Press, 1971). It has quite become the figure in Brooks's carpet. Rolled out, the tapestry that emerges tells of a courageous young Van Wyck Brooks stopped in his tracks at mid-career by self-doubt, then, after surviving his mental crash, shoring up against his ruins a new-found, and psychically necessary, optimism about life and letters in the United States. After his breakdown, the argument runs, Brooks was no longer willing, if indeed able, to look on the dark side; that way lay danger of the most real kind. The result was that Brooks's early trenchancy gave way to the belletristic writer of the later phase, the critic against the American grain turned into the historian of the usable past who wrote all too smoothly with the American grain.

While persuasive up to a point, psychology, in Professor Hoopes, and in Professor Wasserstrom before him, too often stands in for literary and political history. Maladies and motives quite aside, the younger Van Wyck Brooks had painted himself into a tight corner. In his early books he had argued that the air of American life supplied insufficient oxygen for writers to breathe. In *The Pilgrimage of Henry James* he argued that exile from America condemned a writer to a loss of roots, and hence of the possibility of natural growth. The conclusion of the Brooks's book on James was that after *The Bostonians* (1886) James had simply run out of his American material and was left to create a "vast arachnid of art, pouncing upon the tiny airblown particle and wrapping it round and round." Remaining in America, the writer would suffocate; fleeing America, as did James, deracination awaited. Damned if you do and damned if you don't; and double-damned if you are a critic whose subject is American literature.

An impressive performance by a younger scholar, Professor Hoopes's biography provides much new material about Brooks's youth and first marriage and the strains under which he wrote. While Professor Hoopes slips into the psychological mode, his book is not of the kind that Vladimir Nabokov, that scourge of Freudians and others of the Viennese delegation, labeled a "psychoplagiarism." Too often, though, the scholar has the upper hand over the artist in Professor Hoopes, and here perhaps the explanation lies in that he does not have a clear point of view about his subject. Sympathetic to Brooks's travail, impressed by his early accomplishments, he nevertheless presents the by now standard view. His biography serves chiefly to amplify and reinforce the received opinion about Van Wyck Brooks, and this, though scarcely Professor Hoopes's intention, is to leave Brooks without a saving remnant and his career a dead issue in American literature.

Is there a saving remnant? Not long after his madness Brooks began work on *Makers and Finders,* his five-volume study of the literary life in America. Working on *Makers and Finders,* according to Brooks, "saved my life." He had, according to Professor Hoopes, "felt for a long time that he must cling to America to preserve his personality from disintegration." When one explains

Brooks by psychology the tendency is to explain him away. Thus the entire latter half of Brooks's career, in the standard view, is seen as a failure of nerve. Literary cowardice is the verdict, quite understandable for psychological reasons to be sure, but cowardice all the same.

Everything that has been said against Brooks's *Makers and Finders*—that it does not always distinguish between major and minor figures, that it is sometimes difficult to know when the point of view is Brooks's or that of the writer he is discussing at the moment, that it shies away from the darker corners of American literary life (Melville's despair, for example, or Whitman's homosexuality)—is true. But it is not the whole truth. The reading of some 400 books and 2,600 pages of Brooks's prose went into *Makers and Finders.* The first serious inventory of American literature, it contains more than a few serious literary discoveries: Edmund Wilson, in *Patriotic Gore,* would avail himself of at least one of them for his own splendid essay on John De Forest, the nineteenth-century novelist who had been altogether neglected before Brooks rediscovered him. When Brooks had been an undergraduate at Harvard a single course in American literature had been taught; and taught with maximum condescension by Barrett Wendell. American literature was looked upon, in America itself, as a dependency of English literature. Owing in no small part to Brooks's efforts, this situation has altogether changed.

A great gallimaufry of a work, filled out with portraits of genius and even more by the variegated bulk of lesser genius, *Makers and Finders* is doubtless not literary history as it should (by academic standards) be written; but it is literary history that can be read. One of Brooks's chief criteria for inclusion in his history was style, "which writers must have to rank as writers—whether they possess 'form' or not—the one indispensable mark of the significant in letters. . . ." What binds *Makers and Finders,* and keeps it very much alive today, is Brooks's own style. Light on analysis though it is, the work holds interest through its evocation of atmosphere and the brilliance of its portraiture. Brooks is, as Edmund Wilson noted of him, "most interested in extracting from a writer's work, no matter how coarse in text or how insipid in tone, a sort of precious quintessence, in imparting to it the sheen of his own fine prose." Whatever Brooks's shortcomings as a critic—his blind spots, his prejudices, etc.—he was a literary artist, and this alone guarantees that his work will outlast other critics who have been merely correct.

Not that Brooks was so very incorrect. While his point of view had changed, his principal concern had not. "*A focal center*—that is the first requisite of a great people," he had written in 1915, and from 1932 till 1952, in *Makers and Finders,* he attempted to supply that center. Defending his literary history from its many critics, he rejoined that he had written it in the hope of connecting "the literary present with the past, reviving the special kind of memory that fertilizes the living mind and gives it a sense of a base on which to build." His effort was a model of mistiming, for Brooks set out to provide a literary center at a time, the 1930s, when the dominant strain in American literary life ardently desired that such center as there was would not hold. Malcolm Cowley, F. W. Dupee, and F. O. Matthiessen, derogating critics of *The Flowering of New England,* the first published volume in the *Makers and Finders* series, were fellow travelers all, an important point that goes without mention in Professor Hoopes's study. In the same fashion, Professor Wasserstrom criticizes Brooks for joining up with "the ideology of the American grain," as if the reigning ideology among American intellectuals over at least the past four decades were not—as it indubitably has been—precisely against the American grain.

Brooks was well enough aware of his standing, or lack of standing, in his later phase. In an entry from *From a Writer's Notebook* he wrote:

Every writer who has lived long and passed through several phases acquires a public that is attached to each one of these phases; and each of these publics thinks that the writer ought to remain in the phase that it finds sympathetic. Once a literary radical, he should always remain one; once an authority on this or that, he should never be anything else. Every one of these publics is determined that he shall not grow an inch beyond the phase in which it liked him, and no matter how self-consistent he is or how natural his growth has been, there will always be some public that regards him as a traitor.

Another entry from the same book notes: "How many of them [Americans] repeat Daumier's phrase, 'One must be of one's time'; how few can have said with Ingres, 'But suppose my time is wrong?' " Brooks felt his time was wrong, profoundly so, and he said it out, over and over again. This took courage, for the saying of it cut him away from the herd, leaving him very nearly alone.

Specifically, what Brooks felt had gone wrong was the dominance of formalism in literary criticism and the enshrinement of modernism in literature. In taking on both he anticipated by more than three decades what are only now beginning to emerge as the major literary issues of our day. I take these issues to be: is literary criticism strangling on the umbilical cord of its own increasingly arcane analysis—an analysis of a kind that places it at further and further removes from life? And is it not merely that modernism is overrated as a body of literature but, more important, that it represents a dead stop to literature's once central place in the strivings of men?

With asterisks and hysterics Brooks took up the fight against modernism in a book entitled *The Opinions of Oliver Allston* (1941). Had he not published this book, his reputation might have been other than it is—that of a man who had done important work when young and later became a literary fuddy-duddy instead of what it has turned out to be: that of a literary reactionary. In this book Brooks made the distinction between what he termed Primary and Coterie writers. "A great writer," he noted, "is a great man writing, not a mere artificer or master of words—and was this not the fact that our time had forgotten? . . . A great man writing is one who bespeaks the collective life of the people, of his group, of his nation, of all mankind." One did not always have to say this, Brooks continued. "In times when it was understood, one might affirm the fact by implication; but the great critics had affirmed it, either by statement or implication—human values underlay their literary values." The emphasis of modern criticism, he found to be "wholly on 'form.' " This was the time of the New Criticism, "whose guardian angel is Eliot and whose John the Baptist is I. A. Richards."

Literature, under the modernists, had turned inward; it was, Brooks held, defeatist, doubting the value of life and literature along with it. While the modernists "contributed something to the study of form, they reduced the dimensions of literature to the area of the school yard." In this they were abetted by modern criticism, which specialized in what Pound called "excernment," or the paring down of literature into canonical works. Had not Eliot deemed *Hamlet* an artistic failure and Milton beyond the pale? Were not Henry James's famous prefaces of value chiefly as instructions for writing Jamesian novels? Did not Gertrude Stein attempt to empty literature of literary content, confining it to verbal and rhythmic gymnastics? Were Valéry, Rimbaud, Mallarmé truly writers of the first class, primary writers? Brooks not only named names; he attached epithets. Proust was "a spoiled child"; Joyce "the ash of a burnt-out cigar"; Eliot and James "Little Jack Horners." The leading critics of the day—John Crowe Ransom, Allen Tate, Yvor Winters—"evaded the whole world of values"; they "provided a learned game for students to play."

The furor such remarks aroused may be easily imagined. It was as if Brooks had attacked the Founding Fathers before the American Legion. But then it was precisely the Founding Fathers he had attacked—the Founding Fathers of modern literature. The legion of its followers rose up. He was accused of savagery. Brooks had vastly overstated his case, and overstatement invites overstatement in response. In his list of primary writers, only a single contemporary appeared: Thomas Mann. He, Brooks, was said to be against the modern. Stalin was against the modern in art; so, too, was Hitler. Ergo, for Dwight Macdonald, Brooks was "our leading mouthpiece for totalitarian cultural values."

Yet, wild though Brooks's attack was, if one were to stop the clock now, he appears to have proved more correct in the generality of his remarks than not. Can anyone today claim that literary criticism is of interest anywhere outside English departments? And for good reason. It is, as Gibbon remarked of certain books of Roman jurisprudence, "interesting to few and entertaining to none": written in a "style equally devoid of elegance and simplicity." One picks up a recent book on La Rochefoucauld by Philip E. Lewis, the editor of the journal *Diacritics,* and, in the preface, confronts the following sentence:

> The advent of "poststructuralist" theses in philosophy, the remarkable development of discourse analysis and, more generally, of a linguistics of performance, the elaboration of a problematics of textuality, and the burgeoning research in the field of semiotics have begun to steer critical inquiry toward a theoretical horizon in which the processes of language and writing can no longer be conceptualized in terms of forms and themes and their tensions and connections.

Although good work continues to be done in both the novel and poetry, neither, it can fairly be said, occupies the central place it once did. Attempting to make do on the legacy of modernism, literature and criticism today live in penurious state.

Rumblings, though, are beginning to sound. In his Nobel lecture, Saul Bellow remarked: "What would writers do today if it would occur to them that literature might once again engage those central energies: if they were to recognize that an immense desire had arisen for a return from the periphery, for what was simple and true?" Prescriptions, as Bellow says, are futile, but he does add that the attitudes and ideas of the modernists, which are now the enshrined orthodoxy of writers and critics, "are everywhere and no one challenges them seriously." By doing so thirty-five years ago Van Wyck Brooks greatly lessened his reputation. Perhaps one day before too long it will instead redound to his honor.

"In reality," as Brooks formulated criticism of the kind he wrote, "books are bred by men, men by life and life by books through a constant interrelation and cross-fertilization, so that an element of social history can scarcely be dispensed with in any account of literary phenomena and forces." A return to Brooks's conception of literary criticism, however unlikely, would be most welcome. "Nothing," Santayana wrote, "is more barren than art that is interested in itself rather than its subject." In his work Brooks never forgot that the subject of all important art, and hence of all important criticism, is life. In the living chain of literary tradition he came to revere, his own career is a substantial link.

Times Literary Supplement 1977

Living for Literature:
Edmund Wilson

T
WO ANECDOTES illustrate the extraordinary unity of
Edmund Wilson's life, providing what is, in effect, a
perfect set of bookends to a life that was itself a uniform collected edition. The first, circulated in T. S. Matthews's
autobiographical volume *Name and Address,* reports that Edmund
Wilson's mother, when her son was quite young, wishing to
divert the boy from his inordinate bookishness, bought him a
baseball uniform. Wilson promptly put the uniform on, and went
out of the house to sit under a tree, where he read a book. The
other, which appears in no book but instead traveled the often
sour New York literary grapevine, had it that, late in his life,
Edmund Wilson received a telephone call from an editor at *Time*
magazine, informing him that he had been chosen as a cover
subject and that presently a reporter would arrive at his ancestral
home in Talcottville, New York, to interview him. Wilson, according to the story, told the *Time* editor that he would be awaiting the reporter on the lawn of his home with a shotgun in hand
and, should the man come within shooting distance, he could
expect to be plugged. The only thing wrong with these anecdotes
is that, alas, both are apocryphal. Apart from the inconvenient
fact that neither actually happened, they are altogether true—true
in the sense that they are splendidly in character.

Strong though the impress of Edmund Wilson's character was,
his life, rather like his fiction, lacks real dramatic quality. Events
there were aplenty: his experience in the First World War, his

jobs in journalism, a brief breakdown, the death of a wife, four marriages in all, a Marxist phase, trouble with the United States Internal Revenue Service, fallings-out with old friends, crankish last years. Yet these seem mere ripples in an otherwise unbroken current. Again like his fiction, his life was for the most part taken up with the working-out of a handful of ideas. But the tools with which to work them out were there from the outset. It is remarkable how little his prose changed over the course of his lifetime: a prose whose goal was never pyrotechnics or showmanship of any sort but always force and a clarity leading to precision of formulation. From the outset, too, he had the great and unexplainable gift of authority—no doubts, no hesitation, what he had to say he said straight out and well and confidently. At twenty he wrote of Boswell to a friend: "He was the true creative genius, which always feels more than it knows."

Yet for all the evenness of Edmund Wilson's literary career, it has, since his death in 1972, been rather difficult to get him into clear focus so as to take his proper measure. At his death he seemed mammoth. But with publication of the first volume of his notebooks and diaries, *The Twenties,* with their chillingly mechanical interest in sex—in one notebook entry he jots down, "I addressed myself to her bloomers"—he seemed to have shrunk. Now his *Letters on Literature and Politics,* edited by Elena Wilson, his wife, restores him to size once again, and what is more, fills him out, giving him a dimension that before now was somewhat muzzy.

Long before his death, Wilson was wrapped in mummy rags, the epithet Man of Letters branded upon his forehead. America's Great Man of Letters or America's Last Man of Letters, these were the mothballs thrown at Wilson by the generation of critics —Harry Levin, Alfred Kazin, Irving Howe—that came after his own; they are meant to be honorific, and are, but nonetheless they still give off a musty odor. Daniel Aaron, a longtime friend of Wilson's, takes this same general line in his introduction to the *Letters:* "But he belonged to the American family of Matthew Arnold. . . ." He also views Wilson as "the moral and intellectual conscience of his generation." If this were so, he certainly did a bum job of it, for the generation of Edmund Wilson's literary contemporaries was notable for going under in a sad wash of alcoholism, insanity, literary sterility, and early death. Closer to the truth to say that Wilson was his own conscience and an uncompromising professional writer.

Edmund Wilson's father was a cultivated and brilliant lawyer given to periodic bouts of despondency followed by breakdown, and his mother a stern woman carapaced in deafness. Whatever separate virtues they passed on to their only child—discipline, stability, high standards—in combination they tended, as Leon Edel has written, to starve the young "Bunny" Wilson of human intercourse, forcing him to seek companionship in bookish things and to acquire a voracious appetite for print. Unfortunate in some respects though he may have been in his parents, the scale was balanced by Wilson's teachers, in whom he was extremely fortunate, chief among them Alfred Rolfe, a teacher of Greek at the austere Pennsylvania preparatory school Wilson attended, and Christian Gauss, a teacher of Romance literature and language at Princeton. Wilson later wrote splendid essays in tribute to both men, each of whom not only early recognized his fundamental seriousness but stood as models of intellectual strength and cultural breadth.

Not that Wilson did not bring strength and breadth of his own to the Hill School and to Princeton. Yet for years one's picture of the young Edmund Wilson had been framed by a phrase, "the shy little scholar of Holder Court," from the essay "My Lost City" by his Princeton classmate F. Scott Fitzgerald. If there was ever anything shy about Edmund Wilson, his youthful letters betray no trace of it. He knew what he wanted to do with his life right off ("my single aim has been literature"); his candor was never reined in by tact—shortly after leaving Princeton he congratulates Fitzgerald on a poem that "possesses a depth and dignity of which I didn't suppose you capable"—and he was, in all, an almost bristlingly aggressive young man very certain of his own high worth. He would seem unbearable but for the fact that about his own worth he was not wrong.

Edmund Wilson was never—and is not yet, and probably will

not soon be—officially revered in American universities, at least insofar as reverence can be gauged by courses devoted to him or classroom hours given over to his books. The reasons for this are not hard to find. His qualities are not teachable; they can merely be asserted: wide curiosity, utter seriousness, comprehensive reading, a shaping imagination, prose that without being at all idiosyncratic was nonetheless manly and personal. Wilson put his own case plainly enough:

> The implied position of the people who know about litera-
> ture (as is also the case in every other art) is simply that they
> know what they know, and that they are determined to im-
> pose their opinions by main force of eloquence or assertion
> on the people who do not know.

Yet if Wilson has any academic standing it has chiefly to do with his connection with the 1920s, the last—and here one must allow for inflation in the phrasing—golden age of American lit-erature. By courtesy of longevity he became the last living link with the 1920s, and as a young man he was very much in the thick of it. In the literary histories of the decade he pops up again and again, here putting up Hemingway as an original and important talent, there putting down T. S. Eliot's turn toward religion. Frequently he appears in the guise of a literary cop, signaling stop and go to novelists and poets. The poet Maxwell Bodenheim described him thus, as "a fatuous policeman, menacingly swing-ing his club." Hart Crane decried his influence, remarking on his propensity to "hatch little squibs of advice to poets not to be so professional as he claims they are." E. E. Cummings—of whom Wilson, in his severest constabulary tone, writes in one of his letters, "that young man is very half-baked and needs correction rather than encouragement"—called the young Edmund Wilson "the man in the iron necktie."

One of the many good things about Elena Wilson's edition of her husband's *Letters* is that it allows one to glimpse Edmund Wilson with his club laid by and his iron necktie off. (In *The Twenties* he was on view with his trousers frequently down, but

the necktie remained on.) Sober as befits a judge, and coldly
formal by intention—as a young man he shrugged off Christian
Gauss's suggestion that he write a *confession d'un enfant du siècle,*
saying, "That kind of thing is really repugnant to me, and I expect
to become more and more objective instead of more and more
personal"—even the most ardent of his admirers might have said
of him as he in one of his letters writes about Henry Adams: "I
esteem him without being very crazy about him." Yet the repeated demonstrations of lively good humor in his letters help to
take the chill off Wilson's character. In his letters he describes
Gide as "the fairies' Dostoyevsky"; Eliot as "the Aquinas of the
Criterion"; speaks of selling *Axel's Castle* to the movies, "with
Adolphe Menjou as Proust and the Marx Brothers as Joyce."
Always more than a bit of the village atheist, he asks a friend to
be sure to return a borrowed copy of *Histoire d'O,* for he always
makes a point of reading it aloud to his family every Christmas.
Truman Capote in his party-giving phase, Wilson remarks,
"wants to be the feminine Elsa Maxwell."

On the American literary scene of the 1920s Wilson's *Letters*
give off many a pungent whiff. The sense their aroma arouses is
that of nostalgia—nostalgia even for a world one has never
known. Although it may not have seemed so to those who lived
through it—Wilson among them, who complains that he feels
more sophisticated than "the rest of the intellectual and artistic
life of the country"—literary culture was thicker then than now,
more palpable, more full of excitement and promise. Wilson's
own coign of vantage on the decade was from two editorial
chairs: the first, that of managing editor of *Vanity Fair,* a product
of the smart journalism of the time that lingers on today, rather
shabbily, in the magazines *Esquire* and *New York* and the recently
revived *Vanity Fair;* the second, that of literary editor of the *New
Republic,* a job procured for him by Walter Lippmann. The bold
little scholar of Holder Court quickly set himself up in a position
of superiority to his contemporaries and one of equality with his
elders. For the better part of the 1920s a bachelor of the arts, his
letters record the ragged end of his love affair with Edna St.
Vincent Millay—"old Dr. Wilson's last words on the chief mael-

strom of his early years"—and of nights given over to "a little serious drinking."

Beginning in the 1920s and ending only at his death, his letters are full of literary advice to friends and acquaintances. On this count, his candor had all the delicacy of a whiplash. To Elinor Wylie he starkly writes: "I didn't like your T. S. Eliot thing. . . ." He informs his Princeton classmate John Peale Bishop that, at *Vanity Fair,* he is editing a manuscript by Paul Rosenfeld in which he is "letting off several quarts of surplus metaphor." He reproves H. L. Mencken for using the word "jejune" inexactly. He does not hesitate to tell Christian Gauss that he has been reading two of Gauss's favorite poets, Byron and Baudelaire, and finds them both disappointing. Two of his prime whipping-boys are Malcolm Cowley and F. Scott Fitzgerald. Of a review by Cowley for the *New Republic* he writes: "Your capacity for doing these trivial things well is astonishing." (Later he will liberally apply the lash to Cowley for clinging well beyond the bounds of normal obtuseness to Stalinism.) Fitzgerald is regularly tied to the mast, his shirt stripped back, after each of his literary productions, including *The Great Gatsby.* After due congratulations ("in some ways the best thing you have done—the best planned, the best sustained, the best written"), he notes: "I wish, in your next, you would handle a more sympathetic theme." The Lord giveth, and the Lord taketh away.

With trembling fingers writers among his friends must have pried open fresh letters from Edmund Wilson, yet surprisingly few broke with him. He was forever correcting writers, straightening them out, pointing up thinness, misusages, and factual errors in their work—the most amusing of the scant number of footnotes Mrs. Wilson provides is appended to a letter to Waldo Frank and reads: "Seven pages of criticisms, corrections, and errata ommitted"—and they took it. Perhaps they recognized that there was something quite impersonal about such candor, something objective and distant—and all the more valuable for that. Then, too, if Wilson could lay on the lash he could also, in crisis, be counted on to apply the balm. His letters to friends who have suffered breakdown are written with the authentic sympathy of one whose own emotional passport had itself been stamped by that hellish country. His letters to friends upon the death of wives —again something he had himself undergone—pass the severe test of true condolence, never veering into the specious wisdom of sentimentality.

But a distinction needs to be drawn between Edmund Wilson's letters to men and his letters to women. His letters to men are forthright, not to say abrasive and tactless. (To a professor who has written a study of Wilson's own career, after pointing out a number of mistakes, he writes: "Though I doubt whether your book will ever get into a second printing, I may note that there are misprints on pages 18, 47, 49.") To women he was charming, affectionate, even gallant. His letters to Louise Bogan, a poet of fragile but very real talent who came in for more than her share of troubles, are uniformly touching. In a letter written in his seventy-fifth year to a correspondent named Mary Meigs he signs off "Good night, my dear," rather as if he were tucking a daughter in bed. It may seem understatement to say of a man who married four times that he was susceptible to women, but Wilson's letters to women show yet another hitherto unknown side of him—a gentleness one would not have supposed to have existed.

On a side that is known to have existed, Wilson's Marxistical phase in the 1930s, the *Letters* help fill out the picture previously glimpsed, but one expects this to be further filled out with the publication of *The Thirties,* the volume of diaries and journals next scheduled for publication. As with the Depression, so with Edmund Wilson's radicalism; there is, in his letters, no early warning that it is on its way. True, he writes to John Peale Bishop in 1928 that the Sacco-Vanzetti case "revealed the whole anatomy of American life," and claimed to mark the beginning of his disagreements with Herbert Croly, the editor of the *New Republic,* over the case; but earlier, when John Dos Passos asked him to join in formal protest, he demurred. Wilson's flirtation with Communism—he never became a member of the Party—has been likened to a Boston virgin getting on the streetcar. Amusing, that, but not quite true. When he fell, he fell, and on the way down uttered as many lunkheaded statements as any other literary intellectual who took the plunge. The *Letters* record the usual litany of radical folderol: the empty manifestoes, the playing at being an American Plekhanov ("one ought to identify the interests of the petty bourgeois with the proletariat," etc.), the statements that one would have to spend one's life living down. "One doesn't want to give aid and comfort to people who have hopped on the shootings in Russia as a means of discrediting socialism," Wilson wrote to John Dos Passos, in a line that can do service for an entire anthology of idiotic remarks that could easily be extracted from the writings of literary intellectuals during the 1930s.

The question is, how seriously ought Edmund Wilson's politics to be taken? While Wilson himself obviously took them very seriously, no one else is obliged to, except, of course, where they affected his literary judgments. Sometimes they did, as in his noting in a letter of 1932 that "the literature of Marxism . . . corresponds more or less to the literature of the Enlightenment before the French and American Revolutions. . . ." But for the most part, what in later years he said about Swinburne can be said of him—that it is pleasant "to read again about somebody who is occupied entirely with literature (one can't take his politics seriously)." Perhaps the best way of viewing it is to note that Edmund Wilson never had a proper adolescence and that he had a delayed one in the 1930s. (He would have a second adolescence in the 1960s, but for different reasons.) Placing him at a remove from life, his bookishness set him up for his days of political duncery, but his bookishness was also his salvation.

On this score Lionel Trilling has recounted a telling anecdote. In the early 1930s Trilling's own spirits were down because he was working at turning his dissertation into a book on Matthew Arnold, a book that no one seemed to want at a time when everyone else was swept up with radical politics. Then, at a political meeting, Trilling ran into Wilson in the men's room of the New School for Social Research in New York—impossible not to picture them, the past half-century's two most important American critics, trough to trough—and Wilson "asked me how my book was getting on, and not merely out of politeness but, as was clear, because he actually thought that a book on Matthew Arnold might be interesting and useful. He wanted to read it. It is impossible to overestimate the liberating effect which this had upon me. . . ."

For others, to whom the effect of Edmund Wilson was not so direct, he stood as an embodiment of the literary life. It was not only that his own literary roots were sunk in the rich soil of the 1920s, or that he wrote on such various subjects in prose of uniformly confident cadence. It was crucial that he was not a professor; he earned his living by literature: he lived in, on, and off it. This lent him, at a time when the university was taking over literature, added luster. Although for a time, in financial need, he attempted to land a job teaching and over the years put in a stint or two at it, he later came to regard teaching for writers as a "crutch." The problem before him was how to occupy oneself thoroughly with literature and make a living out of it "without turning it into a business." Part of his solution was to become very savvy in his dealings with editors and publishers. He sensed the often subtle relationship between writers and their editors and publishers—between, that is, producers and purveyors— and, as a producer, he made sure he had the upper hand.

Wilson's letters to editors and publishers will permanently endear him to anyone who has tried to make a living from writing. What a joy it is to watch him thwack out at Maxwell Perkins for Scribner's stinginess to him: "your apparent assumption that Scribner's has been remarkably generous with me in general moves me to expatiate on this subject." He accuses F. W. Dupee, then an editor at *Partisan Review,* of "developing all the symptoms of the occupational disease of editors—among them, thinking up idiotic ideas for articles that you want writers to write instead of printing what they want to write." He instructs Helen Muchnic: "You must get over the instinctive idea that publishers are doing you a favor or have anything in mind but their own gains." He chides Katharine White, of the *New Yorker,* for misconstruing a story of his then friend Vladimir Nabokov: "a truly alarming condition of editor's daze." Later he writes to William Shawn, in protest against the *New Yorker*'s tendency to hold back pieces for months and even years, "I write my articles as a journalist in the expectation of getting printed fairly promptly." On the basis of these letters alone, Edmund Wilson ought to be adopted as the tutelary saint of the Author's Guild.

The *New Yorker* was Wilson's salvation as a professional writer. He signed on with the magazine in 1943, taking over from Clifton Fadiman as regular book reviewer. The *New Yorker* gave him ample space, paid at high rates, and was splendidly suited to the method he had earlier devised—and utilized for *Axel's Castle* and *To the Finland Station*—of first publishing his work as articles in magazines and then reworking them into books. The *New Yorker* could also afford his expensive habit of heavily rewriting his work on galley proof. Eleven sets of proof, he informs one of his correspondents, were pulled before his articles on the Dead Sea Scrolls appeared. In return he gave the *New Yorker* dollar value— and, as usual, free criticism on the way it ran its shop: see his letter to Katharine White lambasting its editorial procedures, style, and fiction—and his death has left a hole in that estimable magazine that will never be filled.

Not the least fascinating aspect of these letters is the ladder they provide to the window of their author's study. Of special interest are Wilson's reading habits. Edmund Wilson was the Brillat-Savarin of reading, and turning the page was for the former as lifting the fork for the latter. The Marquis de Sade, he noted in his essay about him, was the only writer he could not abide to read at breakfast. Here he writes to Max Eastman: "Did you ever notice that it makes you sick to read Marx in too prolonged doses?" At forty-one, he reports to his friend Morton Zabel: "I'm fortunate in never having read *War and Peace* before, as I've been going through it in the evenings and go to bed feeling as if the house were all full of people." At seventy-two he goes on a Balzac binge, and at seventy-three remarks: "In the course of my program of getting through, before I die, all the celebrated books I haven't read [I have] been reading Macaulay's history." Always getting up a new foreign language—Russian, Hebrew, Hungarian—he regrets, toward the end, being too old to learn Chinese.

It is comforting to learn that there are gaps in his reading—gaps and strong antipathies. His dissent on Kafka is famous, but he apparently thought no better of Thomas Mann. Graham Greene and Aldous Huxley he did nicely without, writing of the latter, "he bores me to death." "I think it is awful" is his judgment of Tolkien. *Under Western Eyes* "confirms my doubts about Conrad at the time years ago when I gave up reading him." F. R. Leavis could not have been pleased to have his opinion of D. H. Lawrence: "I've always been meaning to read Lawrence's novels —other than *Lady C*—but have not got round to it. I met him once and thought him ill-bred and hysterical, and his writing mostly affects me in the same way." More surprisingly, he admits "I never could read Hazlitt."

If a pattern is to be discerned in this grab-bag of opinions, it is one that reveals the absence of a strong philosophic dimension to Wilson's mind. Pointing up his own idea of what literary criticism ought to be in a letter to Christian Gauss, he remarks: "There is also the philosophical kind too, of course. But it happened that the more or less historical kind has always been the kind I wanted to write." His antipathy to such writers as Kafka, Conrad, and Mann is perhaps best explained by his dislike not only of the mystical but of the mysterious as well. His preference was always for the concrete over the abstract—a preference exemplified by his anti-religious feeling: "I think we have got to learn to get along without religion." As a practicing critic, he believed in explicitness and deplored the elliptical; *approfondi* is a repeated approbative term in his youthful letters. Upbraiding John Peale Bishop for the metaphysical maunderings and "phoney" Spenglerian gloom he finds has seeped into his poetry, he offers in their stead his own unblinking view: "But the life of man, if profoundly explored, is in itself a complete reality."

If the absence of a philosophical strain was Wilson's weakness, this weakness led into his strength. His was a historical rather than philosophical imagination: "metaphysics," he wrote, "is the poetry and fiction of people who do not produce concrete images." Concrete images are what his own best work is about. His aim as a literary critic was to gain "a history of man's ideas and imaginings in the setting of the conditions which have shaped them," and this was altogether consonant with his temperament. When he was working well, which was most of the time, his criticism became strong narrative blended with the dramatic play of ideas—and the result was literature, potent, compelling, built to endure.

In his last years, Edmund Wilson fell into a furious anti-Americanism. In *A Piece of My Mind* (1956) he wrote that he read *Life* magazine and no longer recognized the country depicted in its pages. But the shock of recognition, for him, came with the tax collector. An editor of the *New Republic* though he once was, the fact seemed to have escaped him that one had to file income tax, and he had failed to do so for a number of years. His debt and fines were considerable, and he was made to suffer a lien placed on his earnings and other harassments. He wrote a book about it, *The Cold War and the Income Tax* (1963), in which he recorded his astonishment that a substantial part of one's taxes actually went for defense. With the tax collector on his back the former Sovietophile now became a great enemy of centralization and nationalization.

Wilson's complaints about America were, in his letters, but a paragraph's distance from his complaints about his tax problems. Thus, in 1963, he writes to Dos Passos: "The Americans at the present time are being tyrannized over by the federal government in a way that ought to give them more cause for complaint than the colonists had against the Crown, but they seem to take it lying down." Then in the following paragraph, he writes of hoping to spend the next winter in Europe, "but I don't know whether we'll have been left enough money by that son of a bitch —Uncle Sam." He turned radical again, not altogether in a conventional left-wing way—he remained pro-Israel, for example— but rather in the crankish literary man's tradition of the older Henry Adams. His view of the Soviet Union and the United States was the commonplace and mistaken one that holds the two countries were more alike than different, and he pronounced a plague on both their houses. But his curses against the United

States were much more elaborate and energetic. Articles about the machinations of the CIA set him spuming with indignation. He supported H. Stuart Hughes, a supporter of unilateral disarmament, for the Senate. He talked about becoming a Canadian citizen.

A distillation of the politics of Edmund Wilson's later years can be found, in all their crudity, in the introduction to *Patriotic Gore,* which is, interestingly enough, his best book. As sustained an exercise in political obtuseness as that introduction one seldom comes across. It is cut-rate Hobbesianism, replete with zoological metaphors, comparing nations to sea slugs, schools of fish, and grasshoppers. Writing to Alfred Kazin about his introduction he announced: "No clear line can be drawn between man and the other animals." Suddenly discovering great likenesses between Bismarck, Lenin, and Lincoln he felt, of his introduction, that he was getting well beyond politics and morality.

Yet, though Edmund Wilson thought that the main body of *Patriotic Gore* handsomely illustrated the contentions of his introduction, the fact is that it provided a direct refutation to them. One comes away from that extraordinary book's more than 800 pages—a dazzling literary performance—more impressed than ever with the strength and dignity of human character when put to the test. In his elegant portraits of Lincoln, Grant, Alexander H. Stephens, Justice Holmes, and the novelists, poets, and diarists who lived through the Civil War, Wilson pays high tribute to the spirit and endurance of men and women in crisis in a way that not all the editorializing of his introduction can subtract from. In 1937 Wilson wrote to Christian Gauss: "I wanted to cite Dante as an example of a great writer whose political ideas were completely mistaken. . . ." A quarter-century later, in *Patriotic Gore,* he furnished another example—himself—of the same phenomenon. Literature, fittingly in his career, triumphs over politics.

As rich as any collection one is likely again to see, Wilson's *Letters on Literature and Politics* does all that such a collection should: it records a chronicle of the time in which a writer lived;

reveals its author in the full idiosyncrasy of his character, weaknesses and strengths alike; recounts the story of a man's life in the conditions that shaped it. As one reads Edmund Wilson's letters, one's understanding of him increases without one's admiration for his immense achievements in the least diminishing.

Times Literary Supplement 1977

Gray Eminence
with a Blue Pencil:
Max Perkins

WHAT DOES A publisher's editor do? Anything, one opinion holds, an author will allow—and then a little more. Nothing, a contrary opinion holds, but send the manuscript down to the printer. Some editors are of the first kind: hot-handed and rambunctious. Some editors are of the second kind: world-wise and word-weary. (One of the characters in Paula Fox's *The Widow's Children* is a publisher's editor who feels a twinge of nausea at the sight of a printed page.) Most editors, of course, fall betwixt and between these two extremes. Betwixt and between is the publisher's editor's true terrain. Representing the author to the publisher and the publisher to the author, he is the middleman in what is often a struggle between adversaries. That few publishers have ever done enough for their authors and that few authors have ever come up to the expectations of their publishers is axiomatic. The editor, as the man in the middle, must lie to each about the splendid intentions of the other.

"An editor," E. B. White has written, "is a person who knows more about writing than writers do but has escaped the terrible desire to write." In contemporary publishing an editor is also a person who is hired for his putative literary taste and then, once on the job, is rarely allowed to indulge it. Much of his professional energy, certainly, is siphoned off in keeping his authors and the publisher happy. When it comes to the need for praise, authors, who in this sphere do not know the meaning of the word fulsome, like it applied not with a trowel but a crane. In a business riskier than most, publishers require assurances of reward of a kind not otherwise available this side of hell. Both the praise and the assurance must come primarily from the editor. Between the stroking of egos and the stoking of greed, the publisher's editor spends the greater part of his days, with evenings and weekends left free for reading and tinkering with manuscripts.

Not the pleasantest of jobs, that of publisher's editor, nor, except at the higher reaches, particularly well paid. Yet it continues to hold great allure. To announce that one is "in publishing" is, in the United States, to announce a commendable thing—to wear the badge of culture. Forget for a moment that *Publishers Weekly,* the trade journal of the American publishing business, might run an item (as it not long ago did) with the headline "In One Month, Four Books on Incest to be Published," to work in publishing is still deemed to be in the service of literature. Freshly minted English majors send in to publishers their hopeful résumés—"other interests: writing poetry, filmmaking, classical guitar"—in a supply that greatly exceeds the demand. Should one of them be fortunate enough to land such a job, what does he expect it to be like?

Oh yes, it is understood that one cannot start at the very top. Working at the beginning with a certain amount of literary dross—how-to manuals on sex, say, an encyclopedia of house plants—is perhaps inevitable. But slowly, through the combined force of good taste and sure commercial instinct, progress will be made in the firm. Then one will bring in and see properly published those neglected poets whom one adores, work with those novelists—organizing, inspiring, emotionally supporting—who will change the literary consciousness of the age, present to the public those writers who have dangerous but indubitably necessary things to say. The picture is clear enough: it is that of the gray eminence with a blue pencil.

The gray eminence with the blue pencil is the conventional picture of Maxwell Perkins. Although the young man or woman who nowadays aspires to go into publishing may never have heard the name, his or her imaginings owe much to the legend of Maxwell Perkins. As Clarence Darrow is to law, as William Osler is to medicine, so Perkins is to publishing: an exemplary type made flesh. If testimonial be needed, here it is from Thomas Wolfe, in the form of the dedication to his novel *Of Time and the River:*

To
Maxwell Evarts Perkins

A great editor and a brave and honest man, who stuck to the writer of this book through times of bitter hopelessness and doubt and would not let him give in to his own despair, a work to be known as "Of Time and the River" is dedicated with the hope that all of it may be in some way worthy of the loyal devotion and the patient care which a dauntless and unshaken friend has given to each part of it, and without which none of it could have been written.

It says much that this dedication by Thomas Wolfe—"the Primo Carnera of writers," as the always invidious Ernest Hemingway called him—required editing: it was cut down from an original version running to three pages. It says even more that, before his next novel, Wolfe left Perkins and the publishing firm of Charles Scribner's Sons with much bad feeling, it having been bruited about that Thomas Wolfe was a creature of Maxwell Perkins's editorial pencil. But the dedication limns, in broad strokes, the legend of Max Perkins as friend, supporter, and quietly painstaking literary craftsman. Along with Thomas Wolfe, other of Perkins's authors were F. Scott Fitzgerald, Ernest Hemingway, Ring Lardner, and John P. Marquand. These authors have given Perkins the reputation of chief editorial overseer of American fiction in the 1920s, though his career as an editor at Scribners began in 1914—he had started there in 1910 in the advertising department—and ended with his death in 1947. If one wishes to view the Perkins legend in full flower, one cannot do better than read a two-part profile of Perkins published in the *New Yorker* in 1944 by Malcolm Cowley, the great publicist of

American writing in the 1920s and perpetrator of many of its reigning myths.

Is the legend of Maxwell Perkins any more than that—a legend, a collection of stories that, though comely enough, have little of truth in them? Three collections of Perkins's letters to authors have thus far been published in the United States—*Editor to Author* (1950), *Dear Scott/Dear Max: the Fitzgerald-Perkins Correspondence* (1971), and *Ring Around Max: the Correspondence of Ring Lardner and Max Perkins* (1973)—but apart from making clear Perkins's unflagging devotion to Fitzgerald, they do not make clear much else. An editor, granted, is the man behind the arras in literary production, but Maxwell Perkins's letters to his authors, many of them banal and aphoristic in a bland way, make him sound rather too much like Polonius: "The book belongs to the author"; "I believe the writer, anyway, should always be the final judge"; "the function of a publisher in society is to furnish a means by which anyone of a certain level of intelligence and ability can express his views"; and so on.

Along with these letters, Malcolm Cowley's mythopoeic profile, limited mention in Van Wyck Brooks's autobiography, Thomas Wolfe's account of the writing of *Of Time and the River* in *The Story of a Novel,* walk-on parts in the biographies of other writers, and a fistful of anecdotes, not all that much is known about the career of Maxwell Perkins. This absence of knowledge had been filled in by a full-blown biography of Perkins. *Max Perkins: Editor of Genius* by A. Scott Berg carries its author's point of view in its subtitle. Although there might seem something askew in so ample a book devoted to the life of an editor—is someone now at work on a biography of Proust's proofreader, Joyce's printer, Eliot's stationer?—in the instance of Maxwell Perkins, so great is the legend that has grown up round him, the effort nearly seems worth it.

I say nearly, for A. Scott Berg's biography is not all that it might have been. Adulation courses too heavily through its pages. The author attended Princeton, the school of F. Scott Fitzgerald, where his biography found its first life in the form of a 250-page undergraduate essay, and, as was perhaps inevitable, A. Scott is too much in thrall to F. Scott and the cast of 1920s literary characters. Among other things, the ambiguous character of publishing, arising from the clash of business methods applied to cultural artifacts, is too little appreciated by Mr. Berg. A touch of cynicism about a business as cynical as publishing—cynicism along the lines of Albert Jay Nock's remark that "a good book, from a publisher's point of view, was a book as nearly as possible like another book which had sold a great number of copies"—would have provided a welcome leavening.

Still, Mr. Berg has labored long and produced, if not a work of biographical art, a goodly amount of useful information about Maxwell Perkins. He has turned up a cache of letters written by Perkins across the span of more than a quarter of a century, which are the record of an epistolary love affair, unconsummated, with a woman named Elizabeth Lemmon, who was still alive at the time of this biography. "My Aspern Papers," Miss Lemmon calls her letters, and she has permitted Mr. Berg, who is no publishing scoundrel, full use of them. These letters greatly aid him in rounding out his portrait of Max Perkins as a Yankee gentleman, a man maniacal for work who was unhappy in his marriage and, as the nature of his love affair with Miss Lemmon more than implies, a monument to New England repression. But of greater interest than the portrait of Perkins's character is the account Mr. Berg provides of Perkins's editorial procedures. From it can be drawn a more balanced picture than the legend has hitherto allowed of the strengths and limitations of a very good editor as well as much of general interest about the job of publisher's editor itself.

Maxwell Evarts Perkins was well-born—on the Evarts side his grandfather was President Hayes's Secretary of State and twice a United States Senator; his Perkins grandfather was an art critic and friend to the Brownings and Longfellow—but not well off. His father died when Perkins was still an adolescent; he went to Harvard, but in a condition of shabby gentility, with an Evarts uncle picking up the tab for his membership in a Harvard club. Van Wyck Brooks, who had grown up in the same Wall Street suburb of Plainfield, New Jersey, as Perkins, was a boyhood friend and his roommate at Harvard. Perkins wrote for the Harvard *Advocate,* the college literary magazine, but in his studies concentrated not on literature, but on political economy. Unlike most of the friends in his set, Perkins was not able after graduation to go off on a year-long tour of Europe, the equivalent at the time of graduate school for the children of the American rich. Instead he went to work as a junior reporter on the *New York Times.* Not long afterward an old-boy-network letter from Professor Barrett Wendell—"He has in him the right stuff. He is really the sort one can depend on"—to Charles Scribner II landed him the job of advertising manager at Scribners. The job at Charles Scribner's Sons enabled him to marry the woman who was to bestow upon him five daughters and much conjugal unhappiness.

After four years as advertising manager, Perkins was made an editor at Scribners. Although Charles Scribner was not so culturally purblind as Anthony Powell has recently described the English publisher Gerald Duckworth—"His interest in books, anyway as a medium for reading, was as slender as that of any man I have ever encountered"—nonetheless the Scribners firm was staid, if not hidebound. Its best-known authors were Edith Wharton, Henry James, and John Galsworthy. The firm's principal editor, William C. Brownell, held to a severe editorial credo: "I don't believe much in tinkering, and I am not *suffisant* enough to think the publisher can contribute much by counseling modifications." Under this regime Maxwell Perkins did not flourish, nor even particularly distinguish himself. His chores, as Mr. Berg describes them, were perfunctory ones: proofreading, arranging anthologies, raking grammatical errors out of manuscripts.

Maxwell Perkins's ticket out of obscurity was F. Scott Fitzgerald. The Irish journalist Shane Leslie, a Scribners author, sent in to Scribners the manuscript of the young Fitzgerald's first novel, then entitled "The Romantic Egotist." The manuscript went through the firm, down the editorial chain of command, gathering uniformly censorious comments along its way. Perkins alone espied quality in it, and wrote to Fitzgerald suggesting that, after making some substantial revisions, he resubmit the novel. This Fitzgerald did, but with no improved result the second time round. Perkins then suggested that Fitzgerald try his luck with other publishers. Fitzgerald did so, only to have his manuscript meet with cold rejection. After still further editorial advice from Perkins—who now counseled, among other changes, a shift in the narration from first to third person—Fitzgerald resubmitted the novel yet again to Scribners. When at an editorial meeting the novel (now entitled *This Side of Paradise*) looked to be going under for a third and final time, Perkins, to his honor, put his own job on the line in speaking out on its behalf: "If we're going to turn down the likes of Fitzgerald," he announced. "I will lose all interest in publishing." Because in speaking thus Perkins was felt to represent the younger editors in the firm, this was sufficient to win the day for publication of the novel.

But only the day would have been won, the victory would have been otherwise quite an empty one, had not *This Side of Paradise* gone on to become a best seller, running into several printings in the first months after its publication. Had the novel not caught commercial fire, Perkins doubtless would have been packed off to editorial Siberia, there to live out his days editing gardening manuals and assembling cookbooks. Which says a good bit about how an editor, then as now, acquires power in a publishing house. Trade publishing is the name of the game, and its terms are those of trade: show a profit or go under. Maxwell Perkins accepted these terms and succeeded under them. This is worth emphasizing, if only because Mr. Berg implies something rather different. "Perkins," he writes, "sought out authors who were not just 'safe,' conventional in style and bland in content, but who spoke in a new voice about the new values of the post-war world. In this way, as an editor he did more than reflect the standards of his age; he consciously influenced them and changed them by the new talents that he published."

Not quite so. Mr. Berg's assessment makes Perkins out to be an editor with an ear finely attuned to the inevitably discordant singing of the avant-garde. In fact, the only modernist writer he published was Hemingway—whose work, along with that of Ring Lardner, was brought to his desk by Fitzgerald—and then only the best-selling Hemingway, beginning with *The Sun Also*

Rises. Perkins took his share of risks, but these were commercial risks; he was, from the beginning and throughout his career, an editor of large-public books. Pound and Eliot and Stevens, Kafka and Proust and Joyce, he did not seek out; it is entirely possible that he never heard of them, or if he had heard of them did not know what they were about, till it was all explained to him, in a long and laborious letter from Edmund Wilson, in which Wilson set out the plan for *Axel's Castle* for Perkins's editorial approval. Wilson, too, was brought to Perkins by Fitzgerald, though he was not to remain at Scribners for long.

As for Mr. Berg's assertion that Perkins "did more than reflect the standards of his age," it could as easily be argued that in some respects he reflected the standards of an age earlier than the one he lived in. He was, for example, much exercised about blasphemy, and it is instructive to witness him attempting to persuade F. Scott Fitzgerald to tone down the attack against the Bible of a character in Fitzgerald's second novel, *The Beautiful and the Damned:*

> It is here that the question of the public comes in. They will not make allowances for the fact that a character is talking extemporaneously. They will think F. Scott Fitzgerald is writing deliberately. Tolstoi did that even, and Shakespeare. Now you are, through Maury [the blaspheming character], expressing your views, of course; but you would do so differently if you were deliberately stating them as your views.

While Maxwell Perkins was neither a persistent hunter of new talent nor of a spirit well in advance of his age, where he can be counted an innovator is in his editorial methods. As far as is known, he was the first of the publisher's editors to stride boldly into the jungle of a manuscript and machete an editorial clearing: offering alterations in the plots of novels, providing plans for radical reorganization, suggesting subjects for stories and entire books, and in the case of some of his authors—Thomas Wolfe most famous among them—rolling up his sleeves and doing much of the work of revision himself. Such aggressive editing, in which the editor frequently became a collaborator on a book, called for the most delicate tact. Tact often blended into flattery. Whether through conscious cunning or pure instinct, Perkins sensed the need for praise on the part of writers, and filled that need handsomely. Note in the paragraph above his casual linking of F. Scott Fitzgerald's work with that of Tolstoy and Shakespeare. When he was suggesting revisions, Perkins's tact was consummate: he could counsel radical cuts in a manuscript by telling an author that these portions interfered with "the harmony of the narrative"—which is rather like a surgeon informing a young woman that the amputation of both her arms would have the beneficial result of calling attention to the sensuality of her shoulders.

Although Maxwell Perkins worked with a great many authors, and had nearly a score of books dedicated to him, Mr. Berg rightly concentrates the better part of his biography on Perkins's relationships with his three most famous writers: Fitzgerald, Hemingway, and Thomas Wolfe. Others of Perkins's authors of lesser literary standing, though great commercial value, were Marjorie Kinnan Rawlings, Taylor Caldwell, Erskine Caldwell, and James Jones. But it is from his work with Fitzgerald, Hemingway, and above all Wolfe that Perkins's own high reputation derives. Of the three, Perkins editorially did the least for Hemingway, the most for Wolfe, and, despite his generous devotion, was unable to save Fitzgerald from himself. In Fitzgerald, Hemingway, and Wolfe, Perkins had a boozer, a bully, and a baby: even for writers, these three were very shaky *hombres*.

In a letter to Wolfe, Fitzgerald referred to Perkins as "our common parent," and later he wrote to Perkins: "What a time you've had with your three sons, Max. . . ." Not only were these "sons" prodigal, they were rivalrous into the bargain. Hemingway wrote to Perkins to report that Wolfe's *Of Time and the River* was "something over 60 per cent shit," and Fitzgerald remarked that Wolfe had "no right to glut people on whole meals of caviar." Hemingway always had a bad word for Fitzgerald and for that matter for all his "overassed and underbrained contemporaries." Wolfe was a madhouse unto himself, one of the earth's walking wounded: anti-Semitic, muzzy-headed Marxist, shattered by the least criticism, touchier than a fresh burn.

Heavy baby-sitting responsibilities were, for Perkins, part of the complete editorial service. Despite his own disinclinations, Perkins found himself having to clean up after Wolfe's drearily messy love affairs; locked between Scott and Zelda Fitzgerald in their perennially tumultuous marriage; the recipient of stories about Hemingway, drunk, using a freshly caught 514-pound tuna as a punching bag. Meanwhile other writers—Edmund Wilson for one, the older Sherwood Anderson for another—left Scribners because they felt that they were not getting enough of Perkins's attention. To Elizabeth Lemmon, though to no one else, Perkins wrote: "I'm so fed up on contention and struggle with irrational people." "A sturdy drinker," his friend and fellow editor at Scribners, John Hall Wheelock, called Perkins, and the reasons why he needed to drink—sturdily, steadily—are not far to fathom.

To Fitzgerald, Perkins rendered the services of friendship well beyond the call of editor, even making personal loans. Perkins knew his man—of Fitzgerald toward the end he said: "If he will only begin to dramatize himself as the man who came back now, everything may turn out rightly"—but knew as well there was little he could do to help him. Perkins's chief function as Hemingway's editor was to listen to his criticism when it came. Two of Hemingway's poorest books, *The Green Hills of Africa* and *To Have and Have Not,* were produced under Perkins. It is somewhat unclear whether Perkins knew these to be bad books; but even if he did, he knew that so bristling a character as Ernest Hemingway, combining as he did bullying arrogance and pathetic insecurity, was not to be fiddled with, editorially or otherwise. The moral would seem to be that the best of editors cannot prevent the worst of books.

But the ultimate editorial relationship was that between Perkins and Thomas Wolfe. Perkins served Wolfe as editor, friend, father-figure, novelistic subject-matter, scapegrace, and, after death, literary executor. Over the years Perkins did everything for Wolfe but his dental work. His efforts upon Wolfe's baggy monster of a novel, *Of Time and the River,* are famous. Stories went the rounds that the original manuscript was delivered to Perkins's office at Scribners in a truck. In *The Story of a Novel* Wolfe himself gauged the length of the manuscript to be "about twelve times the length of the average novel or twice the length of *War and Peace.*" Perkins placed it upon the chopping block that was also his desk, cutting away fat and gristle. Thomas Wolfe had a love affair with language that was not always requited. Perkins knew this as well as anyone. "The Book," he wrote to Wolfe's agent, "will contain too many adjectives, and much repetition of a sort, and too much loud pedaling. Those are faults that Tom won't dispense with yet."

The editing was done in the evenings, in Perkins's office and with Wolfe on the premises. An introductory chapter running to 100,000 words was largely lopped off; other chapters of 50,000, Wolfe reported, "were reduced to ten or fifteen thousand words." During the year-long course of the editing, Wolfe, a logorrheic cursed with total recall, while stitching in new transitions and patching over bald spots, wrote an additional half a million words. Inexorably, Perkins took the meat cleaver to most of these. He later likened the experience of editing the novel to that of a man attempting to hang on to the fin of a plunging whale. Wolfe found the cutting painful in the extreme: "My spirit quivered at the bloody execution." Perkins told him that he was not "the Flaubert kind of writer"—surely the literary understatement of the century. At one point, unwilling to let loose yet another segment of his novel, Wolfe, glowering, announced to his editor: "Well, then will you take the responsibility?" Predictably, Wolfe did not want to relinquish the manuscript, but insisted on more and yet more time to work on it. "I think I'll have to take the book away from him," Perkins one day announced to his colleagues; and after informing Wolfe that the book was finished, sent it off to the printer.

Wolfe paid handsome tribute to Perkins both in *The Story of a Novel* and in the dedication of *Of Time and the River.* (Fitzgerald, the competitive sibling, wrote to Perkins to say that he thought the novel went downhill after the dedication.) But soon clouds gathered, then a storm broke, over the relationship. The incident

that set things off, according to Mr. Berg, was an article by
Bernard De Voto arguing that Wolfe was a creation of Maxwell
Perkins's editing; that Perkins was indispensable to Wolfe; and
that, therefore, Wolfe was incomplete, if not incompetent, as an
artist. The criticism rankled and festered and finally the venom
poured forth—onto Perkins. Wolfe put it about that he was looking for a new editor. He fired off a letter of twenty-eight pages—
doubtless it could have stood editing—of invective to Perkins. At
one point, in a restaurant, author and editor nearly came to
blows, with the six-and-a-half-foot Wolfe threatening to do a bit
of editing on Perkins's features. Eventually, Wolfe left Perkins
and Scribners to go to another publisher, Harper and Brothers,
and an editor who told him that he was the twentieth-century
Walt Whitman. Only on his deathbed did Wolfe send Perkins a
letter of reconciliation.

Selfless Maxwell Perkins certainly was, stand-up and all-out for
his authors, but how intelligent was he? It is difficult to know,
and Mr. Berg, who comes chiefly to praise Caesar, is not much
help here. Perkins did not have wide literary culture. He held no
pronounced views on literature: "the business of literature is to
reveal life," is about as much as can be gleaned from his letters on
the subject. Apart from a lifelong interest in military history and
anti-New Deal politics, he seems to have had few intellectual
interests. A self-confessed slow reader, he admitted that he rarely
got "to read anything but what we are publishing." He edited
and apparently believed in a silly book by a man named Alden
Brooks arguing that Shakespeare did not write the plays; he
thought Maxwell Geismar a better critic than Edmund Wilson.
He seemed to put the same energy into potboilers as into serious
works. He resented it, for example, when one of his authors,
Taylor Caldwell, the pulp writer, was called a pulp writer. He
was not a great discoverer of new talent, but, to his credit, he
recognized the real thing when it was set before him.

Maxwell Perkins was primarily an editor of novels. Here his
two great virtues were that of knowing where a particular novelist's gifts lay and that of knowing what the public liked. That he
himself appears to have liked what the public liked was no com-

mercial disadvantage. His friend Van Wyck Brooks said of him: "He was in his way a novelist born, but instead of developing this bent in himself he devoted his intuitive powers to the development of others. . . ." Ironically, in the light of the legend that has grown up around him as an editorial omnipotent, Max Perkins had a very clear view of a publisher's editor's limitations: "When an editor gets to think . . . he knows more about a writer's book than the writer—and some do—he is dead, done for, and dangerous."

But despite his sense of the editor's limitations, much of the significance of Maxwell Perkins's career is that, through his example and as a result of his legendary standing, the role of the publisher's editor in literary production has greatly expanded. In New York today reside editors whose fame exceeds that of most authors. Far different from the work of a man like Edward Garnett at Duckworth and at Jonathan Cape, or even Perkins at Scribners, these New York editors are literary impresarios, often conceiving an idea for a book, finding someone to write it, occasionally rewriting it themselves, then promoting it in ways both blatant and subtle. What, one wonders, would nineteenth-century literature have looked like if publishers' editors of this kind were at work then? Would *Moby-Dick,* through extensive editing, have been transmogrified into *Mr. Roberts?* Might *Das Kapital* have been pruned of its irritable tone to make a "better read"? Could Tolstoy have been persuaded to cut those lengthy historical sections of *War and Peace* to capture a book club? The retardation of certain kinds of progress is a thing to be devoutly grateful for.

Times Literary Supplement 1978

The Minnesota Fats
of American Prose:
A. J. Liebling

A. J. LIEBLING, dead these eight long years, was the Minnesota Fats of American prose. What a performer he was: a prose writer with all the moves. Like Minnesota Fats with a cue ball, so Liebling with an English sentence —there was nothing he couldn't make it do, including the work of three normal paragraphs. He could make a single sentence ride the crest of a classical allusion, dip down to capture a passing irony, pick up a startling analogy along the way, curl over to the side for a comic touch, kiss off a serious observation, and, *plunk,* drop neatly into the pocket of a period to score a delicious original point. He wasn't bad at short shots either. "The way to write is well," he once remarked in a footnote reference to a series of how-to books on writing, "and how is your own business."

Liebling was a great lover of craft, which he celebrated wherever he found it by lavishing his own craft of prose upon it. He found craft among boxers, con men, certain rare politicians (the line between these last two for him was very thin), writers, and cooks. He had a wondrous way of insinuating himself into a milieu—into Stillman's Gym, or the culture of Lebanon, or the circle at Izzy Yereshevsky's I & Y cigar store on 49th and Seventh Avenue, or restaurants in the French countryside, or the Louisiana State Capitol in Baton Rouge. His method as a journalist was to join in an atmosphere, and not, except in rare instances, look down upon it. Addressing himself to any of his favorite subjects, he was the complete connoisseur: a dedicated lover who needed to fondle the objects of his passion in the coolness of his prose.

No American before or since Liebling's time has written so well about boxing. He wrote about the sport knowingly, with feeling, and absolutely without crap. When he was still alive no big fight was really over till his piece on it appeared in the *New Yorker;* and, truth to tell, his piece was frequently superior to the fight itself. He would not have been amused by the efforts of those of our novelists who have now begun covering the fight scene, and who choose to see some variety of existential agon in the flicking of every jab, the human condition reflected in micro-cosm in each clinch.

There was a slightly anti-intellectual strain in Liebling, brought on by his detestation of pretentiousness. Sometimes patches of his pieces served as a high parody of intellectual-academic writ-ing. One of his special skills was to command a wide "frame of reference," as he used to say the boys on the quarterlies would say, in the service of a low subject, and invariably to comic effect. Thus in his fine piece on the Archie Moore-Rocky Marciano fight he described Moore as "a lonely Ahab, rehearsing to buck Her-man Melville . . . and the betting odds. I did not think that he could bring it off, but I wanted to be there when he tried. What would *Moby-Dick* be if Ahab had succeeded? Just another fish story."

While on the subject of *Moby-Dick,* it is perhaps appropriate to remark that A. J. Liebling was himself physically a whale of a man, as befitted the highly civilized yet quite frank hedonist that he was. A Henri Cartier-Bresson photograph shows him wedged into a chair, in shirt-sleeves, drink in hand, necktie made without much care, notebook in the pocket of his shirt, the other hand tucked into an armpit, lending the arm the appearance of a little flipper. The face, jowly and bald, has a philosophic quality, the small eyes behind the steel-rimmed glasses appear to have seen a great deal, and the mouth is pressed into a worldly smile. It is a photograph that deserves a caption on the order of, "Between vanity and the pursuit of pleasure—can there really be any doubt which is the intelligent man's choice?" Liebling was a man who could eat three dozen Gulf Coast oysters before a full meal at Arnaud's in New Orleans and live to write about it.

Liebling had enthusiasm for life, and it shimmered through nearly everything he wrote. He styled himself a gourmand, or a person who not only cares for culinary delicacies but plenty of them. He was also a gourmand of human nature, and here his tastes ran to hustlers, con men, characters, and other artists of everyday florid living. A scoundrel with charm was apparently irresistible to him, and he left behind prose portraits of some of the most extravagant to walk the streets of the New World.

First and foremost there was the splendid Colonel John R. Stingo, the baroque stylist of race track news for the New York *Enquirer* and "the best curveball writer since Anatomy Burton and Sir Thomas Browne." A man of otherwise prudent flexibility, the Colonel nonetheless attributed his longevity—he was well into his eighties when Liebling knew him—to rigid adherence to three points of personal hygiene: "I will not let guileful women move in on me, I decline all responsibility, and above all, I avoid all heckling work. Also, I shun exactious luxuries, lest I become their slave." Then there was Hymie (The Tummler) Katz, a con man so proficient that when he would go down to visit his father at the old man's jewelry store near the Bowery the senior Katz would arrange to come out to meet his son on the sidewalk, carefully locking the door of his store behind him. Another such notable was Whitey Bimstein, one of boxing's great trainers and corner men. Once, when Bimstein had returned from training a fighter in the Catskills, Liebling asked him how he found the country: "It's a nice spot," Mr. Bimstein replied.

Rereading A. J. Liebling today, one realizes that the corners of the world he most cared to write about are fast disappearing. Nowadays one no longer hears about "characters" but instead only about "cases," which is a very different thing. Similarly, Liebling was a true New Yorker, when that meant something other than someone who is put upon by high rents, rudeness, human squalor, and an urban scene that is not so much distracting in its variety as it is jarring in its tumult. Liebling was born in Manhattan, which he loved, and he once wrote about his home town:

> The finest thing about New York City, I think, is that it is like one of those complicated Renaissance clocks where on one level an allegorical marionette pops out to mark the day of the week, on another a skeleton Death bangs the quarter-hour with his scythe, and on a third the Twelve Apostles do a cakewalk. The variety of the sideshows distract one's attention from the advance of the hour hand.

Before the *New Yorker* went into its current phase of political earnestness, A. J. Liebling, along with Joseph Mitchell and John Lardner, more so than James Thurber, E. B. White, or Wolcott Gibbs, represented the finest strain in its tradition. Apart from his obvious gifts of style and insight, Liebling was urbane without cuteness, skeptical without sourness, and witty in a way that was at bottom serious. Although there was more than a little of the artist in him—no plain journalist ever wrote prose of the quality he did—Liebling had none of the artist's accompanying raves of self-superiority or rants of alienation at being ill-used by society.

Of course, Liebling wasn't ill-used. The great part of his professional life was spent on the *New Yorker*'s payroll. Secretly, he must have felt, like his own beloved Colonel Stingo or Hymie Katz, something of the feeling of the bunko artist who had a good game going to have been paid so handsomely to travel round the world writing about those things he loved best. He appears never to have gone second class, he ate battalion-size meals, and his expense accounts must themselves have made highly amusing reading. Still, he was well worth the cost.

The acid test of a journalist's pull is whether one will buy an issue of a magazine that otherwise has nothing of interest in it but his piece. Liebling passed the test. The rest of a hypothetical *New Yorker* issue might be made up of a failed piece of humor, a memoir of a New England girl growing up uneventfully in Pakistan, pieces by movie and theater critics who could only really write about subjects they felt themselves securely superior to, an "On and Off the Avenue," and a book review reeking of a boredom bordering on distaste—but if the issue also contained a Liebling piece one bought it. Only rarely was he disappointing; more often he was magnificently up to the mark, sometimes surprisingly so. Toward the end of his life he showed the boys on the literary quarterlies the way a pro works by producing easily the best essay on Stephen Crane that has ever been written.

Liebling was also the best critic of the press America has ever had. Like the true urbanite he was, he was a great reader—and lover—of newspapers. Having begun his own career on a newspaper, he knew their workings firsthand. He well knew, for example, why newspapermen were as a general rule heavy drinkers —because, as he saw it, they were by spirit, instinct, and politics almost invariably implacably opposed to the interests of their publishers, who, when it came to the crunch, just as invariably won out. Liebling despised the trend—rampant toward the end of his life, and continuing in ours—of cities becoming one-paper towns, because one publisher would buy out another in order to kill a city's second paper to establish a news (and hence advertising revenue) monopoly. He loved a battle between two newspapers nearly as much as a good heavyweight fight. His ire, which found its channel in wonderfully witty ridicule, was never so gloriously aroused as when catching out publishers, working through their editorialists, adorning their own rather grubby special interests with the sonorities of high principle. How many of his readers must have wished Liebling were alive to comment on the spectacle of the *New York Times*'s relentless columns of self-congratulation for publishing the Pentagon papers.

Liebling wrote well on many subjects, but his best book is *The Earl of Louisiana,* his portrait of Earl Long and report on the 1959 gubernatorial race in Louisiana. *(The Second City,* his book on Chicago, comes, like Chicago itself, a close second.) The Louisiana State University Press has reissued the book in paperback, and it is a marvelously uncommon project for a university press to have undertaken. Early in the book, while in New Orleans,

Liebling goes off to pay his respects to a now blind boxer, the best infighter he had ever seen, a man named Pete Herman. "As I age," he noted, "I grow more punctilious about my aesthetic debts; in Paris a few years ago I met Arthur Waley and thanked him for translating the *Tale of Genji*." The republication of *The Earl of Louisiana* gives us an occasion, however belated, to pay a small tribute of thanks to A. J. Liebling.

A writer and his subject were rarely so well mated as Liebling and Louisiana politics. *The Earl of Louisiana* is a self-avowedly partisan book, with Liebling coming out for Earl Long directly upon learning that the governor was declared insane after (more likely, because of) delivering a speech in the state legislature in Baton Rouge opposing the disenfranchisement of Negro voters. Its high point was Long's remark that "you got to recognize *niggers* is human beings!" *The Earl of Louisiana* has many of the finest of Lieblingesque touches; at one point, when a guide takes him through the chambers of the New Orleans City Council and informs him that each day the City Council meets, a prayer is said by a Catholic, Protestant, or Jewish clergyman, Liebling reacts by noting: "I tapped my breast, to make sure my wallet was still with me."

The Earl of Louisiana also reveals another aspect of Liebling— that beneath the New York cynic there all along dwelt an idealist. As "a satisfied subscriber to the Las Vegas, Nevada, *Sun*," the main plank in Liebling's politics, as in Earl Long's, was "let Paris be gay," but beneath this desire for handsome and unrestricted living was always the understanding that it was not to be had at the price of anyone else's pain. However devious their means, the Longs in Louisiana were for the underdog, including the Ne- groes, the greatest odds-on underdogs in all of the South, and so, too, was Liebling. Besides, Earl Long—horse player, political finagler, fancy rhetorician, great feeder, and generally outrageous liver—led, as Liebling freely confessed, "the life I have always wanted to live." Although author and hero are both now dead, and the issues it deals with have been radically altered by history, *The Earl of Louisiana* still holds up extraordinarily well—it has passed quietly from the realm of journalism into that of literature.

There are major writers and minor writers, and somewhere in between there is, or at least ought to be, another category known as "special writers." Special writers are those we react to in a special, usually quite personal way, for we feel a kinship between their imaginations and our own. A. J. Liebling was a special writer for a great many people. I, for one, have missed his prose more than that of any other writer who has died in my lifetime.

Book World 1971

Willa Cather:
Listing toward Lesbos

SINCE HER DEATH, Willa Cather seems to have been appointed an honorary lesbian. The honor may seem a dubious one, from several points of view, and the lesbianism is itself by no means as free from doubt as such things ought to be. Yet literary criticism and biography, unshackled by cheap doubt, march on. In a book by Jane Rule entitled *Lesbian Images,* Willa Cather's life supplies a chapter. In a piece entitled "Nocturnal Turnings" in his book *Music for Chameleons,* Truman Capote described encountering Willa Cather in 1942 at the New York Society Library on East Seventy-ninth Street: "Occasionally, I saw a woman there whose appearance rather mesmerized me—her eyes especially: blue, the pale brilliant cloudless blue of prairie skies. But even without this singular feature, her face was interesting—firm-jawed, handsome, a bit androgynous. Pepper-salt hair parted in the middle. Sixty-five, thereabouts. A lesbian? Well, yes." In *Willa: The Life of Willa Cather,* an admiring biography by Phyllis C. Robinson, it is regularly asserted and then assumed that Willa Cather was indeed a lesbian. Is all this so? I wonder. While wondering, I feel rather like Groucho Marx in that movie in which, standing next to Margaret Dumont, Groucho, pointing his thumb at Miss Dumont, says: "I have to fight for her reputation—she won't." Except that in Willa Cather's case it isn't a matter of won't but, being dead, can't.

The critic T. K. Whipple once referred to Willa Cather's literary career as a victory of mind over Nebraska. It is far from clear that this is a remark Willa Cather would have found amusing. Reading about her life in *Willa,* Phyllis Robinson's biography, the remark seems to have less in the way of accuracy than one might have thought. Willa Cather's family moved from the Shenandoah Valley in Virginia to the Nebraska Divide in 1883, when she was nine years old. The details of the life young Willa Cather found there are chronicled, imperishably and with a bleak grandeur, in such novels as *My Ántonia, O Pioneers!,* and the early segments of *The Song of the Lark;* they are rendered more personal in her story "Old Mrs. Harris." The Mrs. Harris of that title was closely modeled on Willa Cather's maternal grandmother. She lived with the Cathers, seeing after most of the domestic drudgery of caring for a large houseful of children, while Willa's mother, brought up in an atmosphere of Southern gentility, and her father, a genial but largely ineffectual man, attempted, in domestically crowded and less than financially opulent conditions, to make a life for themselves and their family in a fairly harsh environment.

After a year living out in the country on the Divide, the Cather family moved into the nearby town of Red Cloud. Red Cloud then had 2,500 inhabitants; eight trains ran through it daily on the run between Chicago and Denver. It was a churchy town, with a predictable round of church suppers and ice-cream socials, and no absence of the mean-mindedness of small towns that propelled such writers as Sherwood Anderson and Sinclair Lewis to literary fury. But it also contained hidden treasure—not hidden, though, from as keen a child as the young Willa Cather. Among the Scandinavian and Bohemian and Hungarian farmers, Willa Cather came into contact with a circuit-riding German piano teacher of wide musical culture; a displaced Englishman working as a clerk in his brother's store who taught her and read Latin with her until she went off to college; the Wieners, a German Jewish couple who were neighbors and spoke French and gave her the run of their library; the two town doctors, who saw something special in her and sometimes took her with them on their rounds; and local businessmen, such as those she wrote about in her story "Two Friends," who seemed "strong and fine" at a time "when business was still a personal adventure." Then there were the theater and the occasional touring companies and musicians who stopped in Red Cloud, with their glitter, their intimations of a wider world, their purveyance of the excitement behind the thing called art.

"There seemed nothing to see; no fences, no creeks or trees, no hills or fields," says a character in *My Ántonia* about the country in which Willa Cather came of age. "There was nothing but land; not a country at all, but the material out of which countries are made." But between the wide spaces, amid the aridity and blankness, the life of Willa Cather, the artist-to-be, took root, and the roots sank deep. It provokes the question: Of what are artists made? It is another of those questions without an adequate answer. Although neither crude nor philistine, the Cather home was not especially fertile soil for an artist to grow in; certainly none of Willa Cather's brothers or sisters turned to art for solace and sustenance. Little in the surrounding atmosphere encouraged devotion to art. Yet by a curious concatenation of mystery and accident, Willa Cather became a convert, quite young, to the religion of art. As she herself was to write, in the preface to the second edition of *The Song of the Lark*, of Thea Kronborg, the heroine of that novel and a character compounded of the opera singer Olive Fremstad and herself: "She seemed wholly at the mercy of accident; but to persons of her vitality and honesty, fortunate accidents always happen."

Willa Cather matriculated at the University of Nebraska in Lincoln as a preparatory student in 1890. She was not yet seventeen but had already attained that squarish matronly masculine figure later made famous through photographs of her by Edward Steichen. She had thought earlier to become a physician—the original career choice, as the guidance counselors nowadays say, of Gertrude Stein—but soon switched to classics. For an ostensibly provincial school, the University of Nebraska had a fairly impressive faculty. Many of Willa Cather's fellow students at the university were the children of immigrants; some would themselves go on to achieve distinction, among them John J. Pershing, as commander in chief of United States troops during World War I, Roscoe Pound, as dean of the Harvard Law School, and Alvin

Johnson, as the economist who founded the graduate faculty of social and political science at the New School for Social Research. Another acquaintance from Lincoln days was Dorothy Canfield —later Dorothy Canfield Fisher—who was the daughter of the president of the university and who later became a best-selling novelist and a member of the editorial board of the Book-of-the-Month Club.

By general consent, Willa Cather was the most brilliant student at the university. She went very much her own way, socially and intellectually; independence seemed to come to her naturally. She was, Mrs. Robinson notes in her biography, a girl one either admired or detested—someone, in any case, about whom it was difficult to feel neutral. She had strong opinions and took no displeasure in broadcasting them, not even to the head of the English department, whose theories about literature, according to Mrs. Robinson, she "mercilessly ridiculed." She was never Bohemian but she was highly idiosyncratic. She wore her hair short and shingled, her clothes were mannish, her voice deep. She had no love of ostentation yet neither did she seem to fear being conspicuous. Her best friend was Louise Pound, who later became a notable philologist. "No evidence exists," Mrs. Robinson writes, "that Willa ever had a serious boyfriend in college."

Yet Nebraska provided opportunities that a more culturally rich terrain might never have provided. At twenty, for example, Willa Cather wrote a regular column for the *Nebraska State Journal*. Two classroom exercises—an essay on Carlyle, another on *Hamlet*—were earlier published in the same newspaper. While going to school she wrote, for pay and print, about whatever it pleased her to write: vignettes, feature stories, reviews of books, art exhibits, opera performances, lectures. By the end of her junior year she was the *Journal*'s drama critic. Through following the arts as a young journalist she acquired, as she noted of the sad, star-struck young man in the story "Paul's Case," a strong whiff of "that indefinable air of achievement, that world-shine," that artists can have for the susceptible young. She had begun to acquire—to pick up another phrase from that same story—"what the churchmen call 'vocation.' " She worshipped art as if it were religion. In New York, in Boston, in Chicago, she would not have been permitted so close to the altar as she was able to get through journalism in Nebraska.

Mrs. Robinson's biography is very good on the subject of Willa Cather's youth, but as Willa Cather enters upon young womanhood the slender craft that is *Willa* begins to list toward the isle of Lesbos. Mrs. Robinson's is, I believe, the first biography of Willa Cather explicitly to announce Willa Cather to have been a lesbian. Mrs. Robinson takes no special pride in doing so. There is little of the iconoclast in her and nothing of the feminist militant. She admires her subject enormously. There is not a breath of malice in her book. I assume that Mrs. Robinson claims that Willa Cather was a lesbian because she believes it is so. She could, I suppose, have waffled on the point, though in our day waffling on such matters is impermissible. Yet is her case beyond arguing? On the question of whether Willa Cather was an active lesbian, Mrs. Robinson is in the unenviable position of having a great deal of evidence and no real proof.

In *Willa* there is much talk of Willa Cather's becoming "aware of her sexual nature" and of her coming "to terms with her own needs." Later, working as a journalist in Pittsburgh, when men asked her out "she wanted no emotional entanglements." As a young girl she sometimes signed herself "William." As a young woman she entered into an important friendship with Sarah Orne Jewett, who herself had a "Boston marriage" with Annie Fields, the widow of the publisher James T. Fields of the firm of Ticknor & Fields. Later Mrs. Robinson tells us that "there was a lusty, earthy side to Willa," and that "Willa undoubtedly needed sexual fulfillment as well as intellectual and social stimulation." And when she moved into an apartment in New York, in the Village, with Edith Lewis, with whom she lived for forty years, Mrs. Robinson writes: "Their life together was undoubtedly a marriage in every sense." (That's two *undoubtedly*s—beware trial by adverb.) But then she adds: "But Willa was too conscious of her ties to home and family, and too much a conservative Midwesterner herself, to live openly with Edith. And, in this regard, she never changed."

Or, to return to Nebraska, consider Willa Cather's behavior in connection with her dearest friend during her college years, Louise Pound, who was the sister of Roscoe Pound. Apparently everyone knew how much Willa cared for Louise and how important her friendship was to her. Yet in spite of this, Willa wrote a stinging profile in a school magazine of a "university graduate" who was unnamed but who was unmistakably Roscoe Pound, in which she said, among other things, that the subject of her profile was a physical bully as a boy and now as a young man had turned into an intellectual bully. The Pound family was outraged; their house was placed off limits to Willa Cather; and as a consequence her friendship with Louise was forced asunder. Why did Willa Cather write this profile? Mrs. Robinson, not unintelligently, if somewhat arbitrarily, speculates:

> Yet something must have provoked her. What had Roscoe Pound done to cause her outburst? He must have hurt her in a way she could not forgive and one can only speculate about the things that may have passed between them. Had he found himself attracted to her and been rebuffed? Had he lashed out and bullied her for preferring his sister to himself? Perhaps he made fun of her attachment to Louise? Perhaps he did more than laugh at her. With his greater sophistication and knowledge of the world did he say ugly things about her to Louise? Perhaps he called the friendship unnatural and his sister's friend perverse. He may even have used the term "lesbian" to describe her. We do not know. We do know, however, that losing Louise caused Willa the most intense suffering she had ever known. In despair, she vowed to herself to be more cautious and less impetuous in her affections in the future.

However interesting and even comprehensive Mrs. Robinson's speculations, I wonder if she does not leave out one obvious possibility—and this is that Roscoe Pound might have been a truly disagreeable young man. (From other sources, notably the correspondence of Justice Holmes, we know he was a formidable and not entirely agreeable older man.) I wonder, too, if Mrs. Robinson doesn't here overlook the fact that writers, especially but not exclusively young writers, are a little crazy. They feel the power of a vigilante posse in their pens, and they are often to be seen riding off on them to do one or another kind of inky justice. Thus do writers put ex-, present, and future wives in their novels, in their poems and essays, attack friends and colleagues with whom they will have to continue living, and through their writing risk every kind of unpleasant rupture, personal and even legal. I think it interesting that Mrs. Robinson closes her paragraph of speculation by noting that Willa Cather vowed henceforth to be "more cautious and less impetuous in her affections" and not, as one might otherwise think if one were not dealing with a writer, in her actions.

Willa Cather's outspokenness evidently also cost her a chance at a job she wanted but was refused as a teacher at the University of Nebraska. And so, at the age of twenty-two, through connections made in Lincoln, she moved to Pittsburgh to take up the job of editor of the hodgepodge magazine called the *Home Monthly.* She published a good deal of her own early work in this magazine, including some short stories; and while working full time as an editor also sent a great deal of cultural correspondence —news of art on the eastern front—back to newspapers in Nebraska. A year or so after arriving in Pittsburgh, she left the *Home Monthly* to become the regular drama critic for a Pittsburgh daily, the *Leader,* on which she also worked as telegraph editor. At one point she spent a week in Manhattan filling in for the ill drama critic of the old *New York Sun.* A progress report on her own growing sophistication, subtlety, and general savvy can today be found in two volumes of Willa Cather's collected articles and reviews, *The World and the Parish* (University of Nebraska Press, 1970). Soon she would travel to Europe, work in Washington and Boston, live in New York. Sarah Orne Jewett once told her: "One must know the world so well before one can know the parish." These, then, were the years in which she was learning about the world in preparation for her incomparable understanding of Nebraska.

Although Willa Cather had published occasional stories and poems, her literary output had been preponderantly journalistic, but in Pittsburgh the artist began to win out over the journalist in her. She started to resent the time journalism took from her stories. She came more and more to admire Henry James, which is often a sign that the virus of art has taken unshakable hold. In 1901, now twenty-eight years old, she left her job on the Pittsburgh *Leader* to begin teaching high school. The attraction of teaching was the additional hours of freedom it gave her—hours that would be devoted to the cultivation of her own art.

But avast, over there, leeward, Lesbos spotted again. "Enter Isabelle," is Mrs. Robinson's chapter subheading that announces the beginning of the friendship between Willa Cather and Isabelle McClung. Miss McClung was a social figure in Pittsburgh's East End, a young patroness of the arts. Her father was Judge Samuel A. McClung, who presided over the trial of Alexander Berkman, the anarchist paramour of Emma Goldman's who was convicted of attempting to murder Henry C. Frick. The two women, who met in the dressing room of a socially acceptable actress, took to each other instantly. Isabelle McClung saw the quality in Willa Cather and saw, too, her potential as an artist, which she encouraged from the outset. She helped open doors for Willa Cather in Pittsburgh; later, it was at the home of the McClungs that Willa Cather would meet S. S. McClure, the publisher of *McClure's Magazine,* who offered her a job as an editor working on his magazine in New York.

But earlier, as part of Isabelle McClung's general taking up of Willa Cather, she invited her to live with her in the McClung household. Isabelle set aside a place for Willa to work on her stories and poems, which began to appear more and more frequently in the magazines of the day. The two women shared a bedroom; in 1902 they went off together on an extended tour of Europe. A dirty mind, it is said, never sleeps. Did Willa Cather and Isabelle McClung sleep—together? To put a blunt point on it: Were they lovers?

Mrs. Robinson believes so, she all but says so, but, again, she cannot prove it. What would constitute proof? No one is asking for eyewitnesses. (Peephole observation is still an unaccredited science.) Yet what about letters, such as the kind Eleanor Roosevelt wrote to Lorena Hickok: "I've been trying today to bring back your face—to remember just *how* you look. . . . Most closely I remember your eyes, with a kind of teasing smile in them, and the feeling of that soft spot just northeast of the corner of your mouth against my lips. . . ." But there are no such love letters between Willa Cather and Isabelle McClung; nor, so far as is known, between Willa Cather and any other woman. And this for a solid reason: Willa Cather deliberately destroyed her letters; and Edith Lewis, the woman she later lived with, destroyed her own letters to and from Willa Cather. Did they do so because they were sexually incriminating letters? Or did they do so because they felt that their letters were no one's business but their own? And, what is more, were they not entitled to do so?

At some point in most modern literary biographies one has to decide whose side one is on: the writer's or the biographer's. For the relationship between the two, writer and biographer, can be an adversary one, even if there is admiration on the biographer's side. More than once, for example, Phyllis Robinson tells us how much Willa Cather valued her privacy, how keen she was to obliterate the merely personal from her life. And yet it is precisely Mrs. Robinson's task as biographer to invade that privacy and to accentuate the personal. Sometimes, true enough, knowledge of the private and the personal can enlarge one's appreciation of a writer by demonstrating what horrors she had to live with, what obstacles she had to surmount on the way to becoming the writer she became. But that doesn't seem to have been the case with Willa Cather. She knew fairly early that she had it in her to be an artist, and she knew what it took to develop her art—nothing less than unremitting effort—and she seems to have arranged her life accordingly.

Meanwhile, in 1906, Willa Cather moved to New York to work as an editor on *McClure's*. She had by this time published a book of verse and book of short stories. *McClure's* was about to pass its journalistic peak; Lincoln Steffens, Ida Tarbell, and other of the muckraking journalists who gave the magazine its special cachet, tired of what they viewed as the irresponsibility of Samuel McClure, were soon to leave to form a magazine of their own. Willa Cather's were the usual editorial chores: reading manuscripts, soliciting new material, working with authors on their articles, essays, stories. At one point, she was sent off to Boston to do research on a series of fifteen articles the magazine was planning, and which she would rewrite, on Mary Baker Eddy. Later she all but wrote S. S. McClure's autobiography. She was eventually made managing editor. Her job at *McClure's* put her into the great whirling world of New York.

Summers she returned to Nebraska to be with her family; often, on the way up or back, she stopped to stay with Isabelle McClung. One summer she visited her brother in Arizona, and the visit included her discovery of the cave homes of the cliff dwellers, an incident and locale that she would later use, transformed for fictional purposes, in at least three of her novels. The Southwest was in its own right a major discovery for her—"as much a landscape," as Mrs. Robinson well puts it, "of the mind and spirit as a physical landscape of rugged terrain and stunning natural features." Her interest in music had deepened, and her musical knowledge was said to be nearly on the professional level. She had begun to know the great figures in the arts of her time. She was beginning to be considered one of them; she was, in any case, among those invited to the famous seventy-fifth birthday party for William Dean Howells. Willa Cather was becoming very much a woman of the world.

In New York, Willa Cather moved into an apartment, first on Washington Place then on Bank Street, with Edith Lewis. Edith Lewis, who worked for the advertising agency of J. Walter Thompson, had grown up in Lincoln, Nebraska; Willa Cather had first met her on a visit to Lincoln in 1903. The Bank Street apartment was flooded with light; its tenants indulged themselves by filling it as well with flowers. A woman came in to clean for them and also cooked simple but superior French meals. Willa Cather was not someone who lived happily alone. "She was happiest in a domestic setting and she wanted a place to live that would give her a feeling of home and family, that was neither

transient nor lonely," writes Mr. Robinson. "Her physical surroundings were important to her and so was the companionship
of an attentive and loving friend."

Off the starboard bow—Lesbos sighted once more. Elizabeth
Sergeant, in her *Willa Cather, A Memoir,* calls Edith Lewis a
good first mate to Willa Cather. Phyllis Robinson, though, claims
that, while Willa Cather never cared as passionately for Edith
Lewis as she did for Isabelle McClung, "their life together was
undoubtedly a marriage in every sense." But then the tendency in
Willa is to cast a triangle of sorts—with Edith Lewis as the
reliable homebody wife, Isabelle McClung as the unattainable
love of Willa Cather's youth, with Willa Cather settling for the
one yet yearning always for the other. And yet one wonders if
this is an accurate account. It was not uncommon, for example,
for Willa Cather to go off on holiday with Isabelle McClung
while living with Edith Lewis, or indeed for the three women to
be together. Mrs. Robinson may know something she isn't telling
us here, but then if she does she would have done better to have
told it.

Later, in 1915, Isabelle McClung married the Russian Jewish
violinist Jan Hambourg. This, Phyllis Robinson informs her readers, came as a crushing blow to Willa Cather. Life would never
be the same for her. The McClung home in Pittsburgh would
never again shelter her. Isabelle and her husband invited Willa
Cather to live with them—an odd thing for a woman to do with
her former lesbian lover, one would think—but she refused. That
Willa Cather was truly thrown by her friend Isabelle's marriage is
not in question. What is in question is the reason why she was
thrown. Mrs. Robinson posits that it was because Willa Cather
had now irrevocably lost Isabelle McClung. But is it not quite as
possible that she was thrown instead by the realization that she
herself would never have a life such as her friend Isabelle's? For
she, Willa Cather, had by now chosen marriage of another kind
—marriage not to Edith Lewis, as Mrs. Robinson avers, but to
art itself.

In 1915 Willa Cather was forty-two years old and had finally
arrived as a literary artist. She had been publishing stories for

years in such places as *Century* magazine, *Harper's* and *McClure's,*
and in 1912 her first novel, *Alexander's Bridge,* appeared. But it
was beginning in 1913, when she was forty, that the dam burst,
and what rich creative waters flowed over it: *O Pioneers!* (1913),
The Song of the Lark, (1915), *My Ántonia* (1918). Willa Cather had
been patient, and now, in her forties, she was in full command of
her powers. It is reminiscent of a remark that appears in *The Song
of the Lark:* "Probably we don't get to the point of apprehending
anything good until we're about forty. Then, in the light of what
is going, and of what, God help us?, is coming, we arrive at
understanding." She had left her job at *McClure's* and was working full time at her writing. Her life came increasingly to be
organized around the composition of her novels and stories. Personal life receded in importance; it was what remained from time
not spent at the desk. As the heroine of *The Song of the Lark* says,
"Your work becomes your personal life. You are not much good
until it does."

As for Willa Cather's own work, more than one critic has called
her an elegiac novelist, which strikes me, as label-sticking goes, as
not a bad job. In her mature novels Willa Cather laments the
passing of the old order, but hers is lamentation crowned by
celebration. As an artist, she had a love of magnanimity, of the
fine and generous gesture. Better than any modern writer, she
appreciated human dignity and understood what lay behind it.
As she noted of the title character in the story "Old Mrs. Harris":
"She had the kind of quiet, intensely quiet, dignity that comes
from complete resignation to the chances of life." Willa Cather
could—as no contemporary writer I can think of is able to do—
make goodness utterly believable. She had gravity and in her
work could achieve serenity. The largeness of her spirit lent her
art a largeness of perspective. It also lent her prose the authority
of poetry. Writing to Lewis Einstein, Justice Holmes noted: "I
do like to see a poet tackle the facts that he has lived with no
matter how uncompromising and make them blossom. I call Miss
Cather a poet though she writes in prose."

In an interesting essay entitled "A Cave of One's Own," Leon
Edel suggests that the central event in Willa Cather's life was her

friend Isabelle McClung's marriage and the break it cause in the pattern of her own life. "Whether the relationship was actively or latently lesbian may not be particularly relevant here," Edel writes. "It is clear that a deep affection and love existed between the two." Edel sees this break—fairly persuasively, in my view— as the triggering cause behind the troubling though still brilliant novels of Willa Cather's middle period: *A Lost Lady* (1923), *The Professor's House* (1925), and *My Mortal Enemy* (1926). Professor Edel writes:

> We can see what brought on the depression of Willa Cather's middle years in the very midst of her success, and we can understand why she wrote that "the world broke in two in 1922 or thereabouts," for we know that to her search for inner security, going back to childhood, was added the deeper sense—hardly irrational from an adult point of view —that she had been cast off, that her beloved had turned from her to another. The reality was that Isabelle had moved forward in life and had married. Willa Cather had been un-able to move forward; for her there had been a "divorce," and this represented a regression.

Yet, Willa Cather soon enough regained her balance, righted herself, and in 1927 wrote *Death Comes for the Archbishop.* This novel about the work of two missionary French priests in the American Southwest is filled with landscape and radiant with light and is as fine an account of friendship as any in literature. In *The Professor's House,* Professor St. Peter remarks to a student: "Art and religion (they are the same thing, in the end, of course) have given man the only happiness he has ever had." In *Death Comes for the Archbishop,* Willa Cather took religion and made art of it. Religious art, especially in our secular-minded century, may be the most difficult of all to achieve. The least touch of insincer-ity, as Henry Adams once noted, destroys the whole. The seam-less beauty of *Death Comes for the Archbishop* is a measure of Willa Cather's mastery as an artist.

People who care about Willa Cather's work seem to care about it enormously. A large number of these people, in my experience, are not academics, but instead people who read for knowledge and pleasure and to help them understand life. These are, I believe, the readers Willa Cather cared most about having. Phyllis Robinson reports in her biography that Willa Cather preferred not to have her work read in schools and refused to give permission to reprint her stories in anthologies that were assembled for classroom use. Although she is now sometimes taught in high schools and universities, she has by and large been spared—as Virginia Woolf has not—feminist martyrdom. And rightly so, for she wrote many things that rub too abrasively against the grain of contemporary feminist thought. "Everything that's alive has got to suffer," says Mrs. Harris, in her story "Old Mrs. Harris." Let the radical feminists put that on their placard and picket with it. Not very likely.

Nor will it do to sneak Willa Cather in the back door marked "Lesbian Writers." What, finally, can be the point of revealing that Willa Cather was a lesbian? What light does such a fact—if fact it be—throw on her work? Does Mrs. Robinson's biography, as Phyllis Rose, reviewing it in the *New York Times Book Review,* holds a new biography of Willa Cather ought, "address frankly and fully the complex subject of Cather's sexual identity and its relation to her work"? In Professor Rose's judgment, Mrs. Robinson's biography does not, and she is quite correct in this judgment. Professor Rose is representative of the new academic literary sensibility, feminist, Freudian, frank first and foremost. In the last paragraph of her review of Mrs. Robinson's *Willa,* she gives us a strong notion of how Willa Cather's achievement is likely to be viewed under the dispensation of the new literary sensibility:

> It is time to remove some of the pink and blue from our image of the apple-cheeked and prairie-blue-eyed Willa Cather. This writer we think of as Middle Western spent most of her life in the East. She chose to be a New Yorker. She was the hard-driving editor of a successful magazine and didn't start writing fiction full time until she was 40. Her

literary ties were to Europe. The girl next door of American letters hated small-town America, rejected heterosexuality, and distrusted the family as the enemy of art. It is time to establish Willa Cather's complexity and her stature as a writer. *Willa* is not strong enough to do that.

The drift of Professor Rose's argument is clear enough from this paragraph. Professor Rose believes Willa Cather to have had an essentially masculine sensibility, deriving from her lesbianism. If Willa was a lesbian, it follows, moreover, that her works need to be reread—and freshly interpreted—in the light of her lesbianism. One can readily imagine these fresh interpretations. One covers one's ears in anticipation of fictional closet doors being banged open and shut by literary critics of Professor Rose's tendency. Professor Rose's criticism of Mrs. Robinson, after all, is that on the question of lesbianism she is too bland and too timid. In her review, Professor Rose says that "a biography of Willa Cather demands speculation, intuition, and a willingness to go out on a limb." But who is out on that limb? Willa Cather, I submit, and the meaning of her work and, ultimately, its reputation. And am I mistaken to imagine Professor Rose or a writer of her spirit out on that limb, too, but with a saw in hand?

I have attempted to cast doubt on the (as it seems to me) unproven assumption that Willa Cather was a lesbian, but even if it were proven to my satisfaction that she was a lesbian, this would have only the most negligible effect on my reading of her work or my high regard for her standing as a major American writer. In *Lesbian Images,* Jane Rule, who is apparently confident that Willa Cather was a lesbian, makes a point—and makes it neatly—that I wholly subscribe to when she writes: "What actually characterizes Willa Cather's mind is not a masculine sensibility at all but a capacity to transcend the conventions of what is masculine and what is feminine to see the more complex humanity of her characters."

The capacity to transcend, to rise, to fly above the common ground—is this not what art at its best always does? Yet so often the criticism of the day, especially in its academic setting, persistently attempts to pull it down. Perhaps it began when, in the early 1960s, black literary critics and writers claimed that only black writers could write about what was called the black experience. (Recall the attacks on William Styron for crossing jurisdictional lines in writing *The Confessions of Nat Turner*.) Then it was put forth that only Jews were qualified to write about Jews, women about women, and so on down the ethnic and sexual line. In this scheme, writers are reduced if not to their lowest then to their most obvious common denominator, the assumption being that one can only know—only write about—what one is. So if one is a homosexual one can only, either directly or in disguise, write about one's homosexuality. In the name of racial or ethnic or sexual pride, a considerable insult is paid to the literary imagination. Instead of transcendence, limitation is stressed. Willa Cather knew better. ("If one became an artist," she wrote, "one had to be born again.") More important, in her work she did better. To rediscover her now as a lesbian writer is the most efficient possible way to make a major novelist seem minor.

The New Criterion 1983

The Riddle of
John Dos Passos

IS IT POSSIBLE to read and admire a political novel
without one's own politics getting in the way? Can a
Populist read Henry Adams's *Democracy,* with its aristocratic tone and snobbish views, without becoming enraged?
Can a Marxist give a neutral reading to Arthur Koestler's *Darkness
at Noon?* To take a more contemporary example, what of E. L.
Doctorow's *Ragtime?* Here is a novel one can admire only if one
shares its general line—that at least from the turn of the century
America has been a cruelly capitalist and hideously racist country.
If one does buy the line—as so many of Doctorow's reviewers
did, to the point in many instances of not even recognizing that
the novel had a line—then there appears to be no limit to one's
enthusiasm for the novel. But if one does not buy the line—
finding it, to put it gently, simple-minded—then Doctorow's
immense novelistic energy and invention seem a sad waste, a case
of good talent being spent on bad politics. It is useless to deny
that politics do not influence literary judgments—they do, regularly and decisively.

This is not to say that one's own politics need always crucially
influence one's reading of political novels. One can, for example,
imagine the same person admiring such politically dissimilar novels as Dostoyevsky's *The Possessed,* Turgenev's *Fathers and Sons,*
Tolstoy's *Resurrection,* and Malraux's *Man's Fate*—all of which
come at the political subject from different points of view and
tend toward radically different conclusions. One can even detest

a novelist's politics and still find profit in his novels. In this connection Bertrand Russell once said of D. H. Lawrence that "His
descriptive powers were remarkable, but his ideas cannot be too
soon forgotten." That is very good as far as it goes; in fact it is
not for his ideas that Lawrence is most worth reading, but for the
shades of feeling he evokes, the pent-up emotions he exposes and
looses in his characters, the sense of crisis in culture he so sharply
conveys. What is crucial to the judgment of political novels is not
only the extent to which a novelist's politics are intrinsic to his
work but the extent to which in his work he is incapable of
transcending them—for to that extent, if one does not share these
politics, one is scarcely likely to bear to read the work.

A case very much to the point is that of John Dos Passos,
America's most unrelievedly political novelist through his long
career till his death in 1970. No other literary career in America
has been so subjected to extra-literary, to essentially political,
judgment than Dos Passos's. Perhaps no other novelist suffered
in his lifetime so precipitous a drop in literary esteem. Dos Passos
was one of the four major novelists of the 1920s—the other three
being Sinclair Lewis, Ernest Hemingway, and F. Scott Fitzgerald
—and of them all, time has dealt most harshly with Dos Passos.
Hemingway and Fitzgerald are still large items on the cultural
agenda of the young as well as of those who read them when
young. If this is less true of Lewis, he yet remains an established
author in university curricula, and *Main Street* and *Babbitt* continue to be taught for their documentary interest.

Dos Passos, though, is largely ignored. Although his productivity did not fall off appreciably, he was in fact neglected over
the last three decades of his life. No Nobels, no Pulitzers, no
academic revivals came his way. Neglect so complete must have
been especially embittering to a novelist who in his younger days
was considered central, and not by Americans alone. D. H. Lawrence wrote of Dos Passos's novel *Manhattan Transfer* that it is
"the best modern book about New York that I have read." Jean-
Paul Sartre came forth with heavier praise. "I regard Dos Passos,"
he wrote in 1938, "as the greatest writer of our time." After 1940
no names of equal weight offered similar endorsements. Even in

death, Dos Passos was partially ignored: having the bad luck to die on the same day as Colonel Gamal Abdel Nasser, he was deprived of the Great American Writer obituaries that might otherwise have been his.

What went wrong? What went wrong, the conventional reading has it, is that Dos Passos went Right. This in any event was implied in the post-mortem articles about him, most of which pointed out the alleged superiority of the early to the late Dos Passos: the superiority of the novelist who wrote the trilogy *U.S.A.* over the novelist of reactionary views, the Goldwater supporter, the contributor to *National Review,* the admirer of astronauts. Dos Passos himself anticipated these articles when still alive. "When the meaning of political slogans turns topsy-turvy every few years," he wrote in his memoir, *The Best Times,* "anyone who tries to keep a questioning mind, matching each slogan with its real-life application, each label with the thing itself, has to put up with having old friends turn into unfriends and even into enemies."

And so indeed did friends regularly turn. Hemingway, with whom Dos Passos broke over the Spanish Civil War, described Dos Passos in *A Moveable Feast* as a "one-eyed bastard" (Dos Passos lost an eye in an auto accident that killed his wife) and blamed him for causing the breakup of his, Hemingway's, first marriage. Edmund Wilson, in *Upstate,* chimed in: "[Dos Passos] seems to want to become now very much the kind of man who once aroused his indignation, a member of the comfortable propertied class, an upstanding American citizen. He used to like to shock people by his radicalism, now he tries the same with his conservatism—but the latter seems as puerile as the former." This is revealing, for Wilson, as a critic, did not regard Dos Passos's earlier radicalism as in the least puerile. Far from it. Of *The 42nd Parallel,* the first volume of *U.S.A.,* written when Dos Passos was at the height of his leftist phase, Wilson wrote that "From the point of view of its literary originality and its intellectual interest [it is] by far the most remarkable, the most encouraging American novel that I have read since the end of the war." Politics, it appears, can affect literary judgments even retroactively.

John Dos Passos was predestined a loner. The fact of his birth
is notable. He was born in 1896 and his parents were married in
1912. He was a bastard, but an upper-class bastard—one who
went to school in England, then to Choate, and thence to Harvard. His father, son of a Portuguese immigrant shoemaker, was
a wealthy and famous lawyer. His mother, Lucy Addison Sprigg,
was of relatively high-born Maryland stock. His parents did not
marry because Dos Passos's father was already married to a
woman in poor health whose slow death delayed for sixteen years
John Dos Passos's legitimacy. In his early years he went by the
name of John Madison. His mother was sickly, suffering from
Bright's disease, and his childhood was spent in hotels both here
and abroad—very good hotels, to be sure, but his boyhood,
glimpses of which are offered in *Manhattan Transfer* and *Chosen
Country,* was staggeringly lonely. The Commodore, as Dos Passos, Sr., was called because of his passion for yachting, picked up
the tabs. A large man of generous spirit, a big spender decked out
in cavalry mustache and overcoats with lavish fur collars, Dos
Passos's father combined democratic idealism with plutocratic
instincts—as a lawyer he had helped put together some of the
first railroad trusts. If one were writing a Freudian scenario, no
more appropriate father could have been found for a man who
till the age of forty was America's premier left-wing novelist.

The political novelist could not have been easily discernible in
the boy. The young Dos Passos spoke in a mid-Atlantic accent
that made him a goat among his classmates at prep school, wore
steel-rimmed glasses over myopic eyes, and was terribly earnest.
At Harvard, he wrote for the *Harvard Monthly,* which put him
among the coterie—it included E. E. Cummings and Robert
Hillyer—known locally as the Aesthetes. This side of Dos Passos
was irretrievably banished when he went abroad for World War
I, in which he served first with the gentlemanly Norton-Harjes
Ambulance Service and, later, with the American Red Cross in
Italy. Among other assignments, it was his job to cart out of
surgical theaters buckets of arms and legs amputated from the
wounded. His first novel, *One Man's Initiation—1917,* is filled with
the haunting horror of war and is pacifist in inspiration. Back in

the United States, he enlisted in the army as a private, though the armistice was signed before he could get to the front. His days as an enlisted man were the first extended time not spent among members of his own social class. Revealing an inkling of the political personality that was developing in him, he wrote to his friend, Arthur K. McComb: "You can't imagine the simple and sublime amiability of the average American soldier—Here is clay for almost any moulding. Who is to be the potter? That is the great question." He wrote about these days in his novel, *Three Soldiers;* this time the inspiration was hatred of large bureaucratic organization.

In the 1920s and early 1930s Dos Passos's life recapitulated the highlights of the American artistic and political avant-garde: Diaghilev and the Ballet Russe, picketing in Boston to save Sacco and Vanzetti, the Provincetown Players, Harlan County with Dreiser, Gerald and Sara Murphy at Cap d'Antibes, Greenwich Village, the obligatory trip to Soviet Russia, skiing with Hemingway in the Austrian Alps, *The Dial, The New Masses* (his name dots the pages of Daniel Aaron's *Writers on the Left*). While still very much the loner, he was nonetheless a man who was where the action was and who, in addition, bestrode both the political and the artistic worlds. This joining of the artistic to the political is one of the things that made the early Dos Passos so appealing a figure. Along with being the most educated of the writers of the 1920s, he was also the most *engagé*.

It would be an exaggeration to say that Dos Passos was a modernist master, but no one was more adept than he at applying modernist techniques to politically radical purposes, and nowhere did he succeed more securely at doing this than in *U.S.A.* Whitmanesque in approach, Gibbonian in scope, it is a book that sets out to tell everything about America, and it is the most ambitious single literary work ever undertaken in this country. Its influence, though obviously momentous, is perhaps impossible to gauge precisely. The novelists of the 1920s, whether they wished the role or not, were important teachers, each with a specific lesson. Sinclair Lewis taught loathing of the small town, business, and the middle class. Hemingway taught a narrow yet enticing code of manliness. Fitzgerald taught style in social and personal life, even if his teaching was often riddled with the snobbish yearning of a Middlewestern Irish Catholic. Dos Passos taught how to think about politics, and his instruction featured hatred of large organizations, sympathy for the underdog, and the belief that society is a machine that twists and crushes, forcing some men to sell out, others to knuckle under, while grinding most face first into the slime. Such at any rate was the catechism *U.S.A.* provided.

U.S.A. is a young man's novel—written by a then-young Dos Passos and best read when young. A distinct recollection of when they first read it, and under what conditions and with what effect, is very common among people who read it between the ages of sixteen and, say, twenty-four. So furious is its energy, so passionate its sympathies and hatreds, that it is all but impossible not to be swept up by it, captivated, hypnotized, enthralled. In later years one may forget the characters and the working out of its five separate plots, but one never forgets its force. It is the kind of book that changes people's lives.

Possibly because *U.S.A.* had the momentous effect it did, many people could never bring themselves to forgive Dos Passos for what they took to be his political *volte-face* of later years. He was the sentry who left his post, and so deserved to be shot. Here is where the problem of the political novel emerges. The late Dos Passos, the disaffected Dos Passos, was a dogmatist of the Right, or so his critics on the Left contend. Yet the early Dos Passos, the *engagé* Dos Passos, was every bit as much a dogmatist of the Left. But in both these aspects he was a dogmatist more of the pen than the person. He could never, for example, bring himself to take the final step of joining the Communist party, which ardently wooed him through the early 1930s. As a novelist, Dos Passos was almost always a polemicist. With only a few not very successful exceptions—*Streets of Night,* portions of *Chosen Country, The Best Times*—his writing required a target to fire away at: war, bureaucracy, industrialism, big business; and, in his second phase, the New Deal, the fellow-traveler mentality, liberal culture. As a novelist he could not quite cut it without a polemical edge.

Richard Chase, in an interesting review-essay on Dos Passos's novel *Midcentury,* attempting to pinpoint where Dos Passos had gone astray in his fiction, remarked that "he annihilated the sensitive, suffering, aspiring young hero, a projection of himself, whom we meet in the earliest books." Chase continued: "In later works the Dos Passos figure is either moved into the periphery or rather violently transmogrified into the itinerant 'working stiff' or political seeker. Thus the early books with their vital interplay between the young hero and society came to be replaced by books which lack the author's immediate, personal, and emotional sense of the happenings he describes as they bear upon his most cherished inner aspirations."

This seems a misjudgment of both Dos Passos's talent and his ambitions. On the first count, though he could do a great many novelistic things well, Dos Passos had almost no gift for literary intimacy. He could look only so deeply into his characters, and no further. When he projected a Dos Passos-like figure, he tended to think and sound rather like second-rate Hemingway. (Chase, moreover, was writing at a time when introspection seemed the only legitimate route for the novelist to travel; today there is a good deal less patience and tolerance for the "sensitive, suffering, aspiring young hero.") With very little gift for the intimacy of introspection, Dos Passos was preeminently the novelist of the middle distance:

> When they woke him to come down to dinner the whole family was assembled. Terry didn't know which of the women to kiss first.

> The place was to hell and gone out a long avenue encumbered with truck traffic. It was so dimly lit it looked at first as if there were nobody there.

> It was still night when they tumbled out of the plane at the Miami airport with two hours to wait for the Nassau flight. They sat mumbling and blinking in the harsh electric light of the airport café sleepily trying to choke down some breakfast.

These three short passages, taken from different parts of *Midcentury,* strike the characteristic Dos Passos tone and distance. It is the manner of the novelist of society rather than of the psyche. If one intends to cut a wide swath, as Dos Passos did, viewing himself as a historian of contemporary society and thus responsible for writing about the broadest range of characters in the greatest variety of situations, then there are limits on the depths to which one can descend. Not all novelists are Franz Kafka, and Dos Passos never wanted to be.

As it happens, *Century's Ebb,* Dos Passos's final and posthumously published novel, does have a character of the kind Chase called for. Jay Pignatelli, though got up for this novel as a lawyer, is an obvious fictional representation of Dos Passos himself and is the same character who was at the center of *Chosen Country*. As the novel begins, Pignatelli is a man interested in Left causes, who is contacted to work out the arrangements for shooting a documentary film on the Spanish Civil War (as Dos Passos was asked, along with Ernest Hemingway and Lillian Hellman, to help write a script for such a film). Pignatelli's experience in Spain parallels Dos Passos's own. The novel recapitulates his break with Hemingway, who in this novel is portrayed as a writer named George Elbert Warner and is treated very gently considering Hemingway's abominable treatment of Dos Passos in *A Moveable Feast*. Warner (Hemingway) wants to feature the militaristic aspects of the war in the film, while Pignatelli (Dos Passos) wants to feature its hunger, suffering, and general desolation.

As in the novel, so in life. During the Spanish Civil War Dos Passos either found or lost religion, depending upon one's political point of view. The key incident, recapitulated in the novel, was the execution during the war of a dear friend of Dos Passos's, a Spaniard, probably killed by the Communists fighting on the Loyalist side in their eagerness to snuff out Trotskyists and the Trotskyite influence on the Left. The incident was eventually to put an end to any further transactions between Dos Passos and the Left. " 'The question I keep putting to myself,' said Jay trying for a mild reassuring tone, is 'what's the use of fighting a war for civil liberties, if you destroy civil liberties in the process?' " To which the Hemingway figure, George Elbert Warner, retorts: " 'Civil liberties shit! Are you with us or are you against us?' "

When Dos Passos got around to answering that question, he chose to be against them, decidedly and determinedly. In *Century's Ebb* the Hemingway figure tells Pignatelli: "I don't care how good a law practice you have, or liberal reputation or what the hell. These people know how to turn you into a back number." These people were of course the Communists and the Popular Front. Did they in fact turn Dos Passos into a back number, or did he accomplish the job under his own steam? The answer is that they, the Popular Front, and Dos Passos, all seem to have done the job together.

It has been said that, while John Dos Passos changed many of his opinions, his point of view never really changed at all. Thus John Chamberlain, writing in *National Review* shortly after Dos Passos's death, remarked: "He often shifted his opinions on new evidence, but he never changed his emotional disposition toward instruments of power. They were to be kept on a short leash, whether they were run by capitalists, Communists, labor leaders or whomsoever." But can the accretion of opinions finally change a point of view? In John Dos Passos it appears to have done so. Richard Chase wrote: "A self-proclaimed 'Jeffersonian,' Dos Passos has preached ever since the New Deal that we must decline every gambit of political power. This may be quixotic as political theory, but it is morally sound and not likely to damage the imagination of the novelist." It need not damage the imagination of the novelist, but in Dos Passos it did. Chase says, rightly, that there was something of the pamphleteer in Dos Passos. He was a black-and-white man, without much taste for chiaroscuro. As he grew older he took on a number of views that are generally classified as reactionary, including, as it turns out, an admiration for Senator Joseph McCarthy. But reactionary views alone do not suffice to explain what went wrong. Among modern writers, Evelyn Waugh held more strongly conservative views than Dos Passos perhaps ever contemplated, yet these views did not in the least damage the quality of Waugh's fiction.

The reason Dos Passos was a better novelist writing out of a

Left than out of a Right political perspective has very little to do with any inherent superiority of the Left over the Right, or of the Right over the Left; a careful reader of novels, after all, might justly conclude that both sides, in the forms their arguments have taken in America in this century, are equally remiss in supplying an adequate picture of the variousness of life in our time. In Dos Passos's work, however, the move to the Right was disastrous because it encouraged a monolithic view that gave vent to his greatest weaknesses. The early Dos Passos, though every bit as doctrinaire as the later, was at least split in his novelistic preoccupations between anger at what he deemed the enemy and sympathy for the victims. As long as there was sympathy, there was a real interest in characters; and as long as there was a real interest in characters, the pamphleteer in Dos Passos, while never quiescent, was at least firmly subordinated to the novelist. In the later Dos Passos, sympathy is drained, the interest in characters becomes chiefly an interest in their roles as targets for his contempt. The pamphleteer is in the saddle, and the novelist has all but disappeared.

In *Century's Ebb,* Dos Passos is down to three kinds of character—self-indulgent swindlers (usually young), true-believing liberal dupes, and happy capitalists. (In *Midcentury* this cast was increased by two: labor leaders, all of whom are corrupt, and their victims, all of whom are shiningly virtuous.) His biographical portraits, so dazzling in *U.S.A.,* have here become editorials, and as such they provide no surprises. Walt Whitman, Joseph McCarthy, Robert Hutchins Goddard (inventor of the rocket), John Foster Dulles, James D. Watson, George Eastman, all get high marks; so does George Orwell, another biographical subject who also appears briefly in one of the novel's narrative sections, but only for being correct on the Spanish Civil War, with no mention made of his socialist side. Low grades, predictably, go to Henry Wallace, Wendell Willkie, John Dewey, Lee Harvey Oswald, and Malcolm X. Specific opinions are offered on foreign policy and on welfare. A man is of course entitled to his opinions, as many and as shrill as he cares to make them, but a novelist is not—at least not so explicitly as Dos Passos offers them in the course of his later novels. "Politics in a work of literature," said Stendhal, "is like a pistol-shot in the middle of a concert, something loud and vulgar, and yet a thing to which it is not possible to refuse one's attention." The problem with Dos Passos's later novels is that so many shots go off that one no longer hears a note of music.

While one might disagree with nearly all of Dos Passos's discrete opinions, it is still possible to recognize a good man behind them. Dos Passos is revealed in his letters as without malice and without pettiness. However strident his tone, he had a saving grace which emerges in brief flashes of humor or unexpected fairness. In the middle of a root-and-branch attack on John Dewey, for example, he can say, "He was an intensely kind man." He asks the right questions: "Here, now, today, if you came back to us, Walt Whitman, what would you say?" Yet he also gives in too easily to the need to supply answers.

"Major artists and writers," said Chekhov, "should engage in politics only enough to protect themselves from politics." As with love, career, family, or any other form of human striving, politics are an entirely appropriate subject for the novel, but only insofar as it becomes, like the others, an arena in which men and women work out their destinies. For Dos Passos it became—perhaps it always was—an instrument for conveying correct information. "All right, we are two nations," the younger Dos Passos wrote, and before he was finished he had served them both. A man of good heart and ample talent, he was all his life ensnared by politics. He had set out to chronicle the life of his time with an ambitiousness and a fervor unmatched among American writers. He ended not by being our chief chronicler, as he had wished, but instead part of the sad story himself.

Commentary 1976

James Gould Cozzens Repossessed

I N WHAT CENTURY did he live?" asked the graduate
student in literature to whom I mentioned that I had
been reading the novels of James Gould Cozzens. "In
what century do you?" I was tempted to reply, but I didn't. I
didn't, because to do so, along with being mean-spirited, would
also have been unfair. After all, in the history of modern American literary reputations, James Gould Cozzens's has provided one
of the fastest disappearing acts of the past fifty years. In a few
decades Cozzens has gone from a Book-of-the-Month Club main
selection and *Time* cover subject to the misty never-never land—
never in print, never taught in universities—of such faded literary
figures as James Branch Cabell, Zona Gale, and Joseph Herges-
heimer. It has happened before, but never, I think, quite so
quickly as in the case of James Gould Cozzens.

Various are the reasons a novelist can fall out of fashion and
favor. First among them is that he was overrated in the first place
and that the natural readjustment of initial enthusiasm has a
dampening, even deadly, effect. Then again it may be that his
work speaks only to the time in which he wrote it—such, for
example, seems to me the case with Sinclair Lewis. Or our author
may write altogether too plainly, providing few of those enticing
difficulties in interpretation and opportunities for classroom demonstration that seem to set flowing the salivary glands of certain
academics. Or he may have no powerful champions among the
critical establishment. Or, as with the later John Dos Passos, his

politics may go against the grain of his age. Or, for a combination of the above reasons (excluding the first), he may not capture the fancy of the intellectual class, which may hold his very popularity against him; this for a great many years was a serious problem for Charles Dickens. The more one adduces reasons for the fall in literary reputation, the more does it seem extraordinary that any literary reputations below that of Tolstoy endure at all.

But with James Gould Cozzens, even though a number of the reasons I have noted apply, the chief cause of the fall of his literary reputation can be found with real precision. Like an eclipse of the moon, it can even be dated. It occurred in January 1958, when *Commentary* published an essay by Dwight Macdonald entitled "By Cozzens Possessed." To say that this essay was an attack is not to begin to catch the flavor of it. It was a toasting, a roasting, a pasting, a lambasting, a drawing and quartering—well, you have to imagine a death by broad-ax and tweezers. Not since the St. Valentine's Day Massacre has there been so efficient a piece of work. I for one was put off by it from reading Cozzens for a full quarter of a century.

Since Dwight Macdonald's attack, Cozzens has had his small band of followers—a little Cozzens club of sorts. But no power-house critics have been among its members. Nor has the pendulum of literary fashion swung back enough to allow Cozzens a second reading. For years now he has been categorized in clichés: he is a novelist who speaks for power and privilege; his work resembles that of Louis Auchincloss; he is admired only by conservatives of the *National Review* stripe. This, then, is where things stand.

Now a biography of Cozzens written by Matthew J. Bruccoli has appeared. Himself a long-standing member of the Cozzens club, Professor Bruccoli earlier produced a book entitled *Just Representations: A James Gould Cozzens Reader,* but his biography is no more likely to alter Cozzens's reputation than his anthology did. Although often just in its judgments, and sympathetic to its subject, Bruccoli's book sorely wants artfulness. Jeffrey Hart, reviewing it in the *National Review,* suggests that Bruccoli, because he combines criticism and biography, resembles Samuel Johnson;

he does so, I fear, to the extent that I resemble Magic Johnson. Bruccoli works all too quickly, is too slapdash. In mid-career he has already written and edited more than thirty books. Like that dopey joke about how do you feed a nine-hundred-pound gorilla, to which the answer is, very carefully, so to the question of how Professor Bruccoli produces so many books, the answer is, not very carefully. Which is a roundabout way of saying that *James Gould Cozzens: A Life Apart* is very far from being the exemplary work of the literary biographer's art that was needed in this case.

It was needed for two reasons. First, Cozzens was a born writer who published his first novel at the age of twenty and who, as is true of nearly all born writers, can hardly be said to have had a real life away from his desk. To be sure, he had parents, went to schools, had love affairs, married, served in the army; but his writing, and how he came to write the books he did, are the essential things. Especially are they essential in the case of Cozzens, who, as I shall attempt to show, was a writer of stark, really quite dark views. How such a writer came to see the world and its workings as he did is the crucial question. Here, alas, Professor Bruccoli stands fairly mute. Instead, for the most part, he tells us that Cozzens wrote first one novel, then another; how these books were received by critics and reviewers; and what their sales figures were. He greatly appreciates Cozzens but can only offer respect where intellectual penetration is wanted. Possibly, as a character in *By Love Possessed* claims, "none of us, perhaps, knows any of us very well." But this is a possibility no biographer can even for a moment entertain.

The second reason an exemplary biography was required, at least if it were to succeed in helping to resuscitate Cozzens's reputation, is that Cozzens himself presents an enormous biographical problem. This is that he apparently was not a lovely man. Certainly he offers a distinct difficulty for the eulogist. Of the love of the laughter of children, of ardor for good causes, of kindness toward contemporaries, to reverse the old eulogistic pattern, James Gould Cozzens showed none. For a sample Cozzensian sentiment, allow me to quote Professor Bruccoli, who writes: "Dogs, he commented, were a satisfactory substitute for children,

providing ample cause for worry without promising filial ingrat-
itude." But such misanthropy, in Professor Bruccoli's pages, isn't
understood—it is merely reported.

"I would like to be able to boast that this biography is a labor
of friendship," Bruccoli begins his biography. "But James Gould
Cozzens claimed he had no friends. I honored him, and he en-
dured me." His father died when he was sixteen, and the two
great figures in Cozzens's life were his mother, who in a doting
way was devoted to him, and his wife, Bernice Baumgarten, an
important literary agent with the firm of Brandt & Brandt and
the one critic whose advice he valued. Otherwise he was by and
large friendless, and only small exaggeration need be found in his
answer, at age thirty-nine, to a questionnaire sent him by the
editors of the reference work *Twentieth Century Authors:*

> My social preference is to be left alone, and people have
> always seemed willing, even eager, to gratify my inclination.
> I am more or less illiberal, and strongly antipathetic to all
> political and artistic movements. I was brought up an Epis-
> copalian, and where I live the landed gentry are Republican.
> I do not understand music, I am little interested in art, and
> the theater seems tiresome to me. My literary preferences are
> for writers who take the trouble to write well. This necessar-
> ily excludes most of my contemporaries and I think I would
> do well to skip the presumptuous business of listing the three
> or four who strike me as good. I like Shakespeare and Swift
> and Steele and Gibbon and Jane Austen and Hazlitt.

If Bruccoli's biography has negligible standing as a work of art,
it does nonetheless provide its subject a valuable service. This is
to free Cozzens from the black cloud of bigotry under which, in
a reigning liberal political atmosphere, his name has fallen. In his
novels, make no mistake about it, minority groups do not come
in for a gentle ride. Of the Irish Catholics, for example, a judge
in *By Love Possessed* remarks:

> Seventy years ago—and even thirty years ago, the number
> of people still around whose attitude had been formed sev-

enty years ago was great enough to make them a majority—
the term "Irish Catholic," at least to this community, meant
the base and obscure vulgar. Few had anything that could be
called education. Their mostly low standards of living—all
they could afford—resulted in objectionable habits and manners. Politically, they were a troublesome mass vote at the
disposal of their own highly purchaseable politicians. Religiously, they seemed to be the willing dupes of their priests,
of a superstition to the Protestant mind corrupt and
alien. . . .

In the middle of the same novel, the lawyer Julius Penrose,
whose highly neurotic wife is contemplating conversion to Catholicism, launches an attack on the church in which he sets out
its attractions to the guilt-ridden and misguided. Is this Cozzens
talking, ventriloquially, through his character? Difficult to say.
But what can be said is that Julius Penrose's feelings about the
Catholic Church are thoroughly consistent with his belief that it
is part of the difficulty of being human to live with uncertainty
and with many mysteries unsolved.

Another character in *By Love Possessed* refers to "typical Jewish
lawyer tricks." The tricks turn out not to be tricks at all, yet,
again, it is perfectly consistent that the character thinks as he does
—just as it is consistent that yet another character, told of this bit
of name-calling, responds: "My personal observation is that Jews
behave as well as other people; and you can trust them just as far
—which isn't saying much." Cozzens was too realistic a novelist
not to use material of this kind, too intelligent to pretend that
anti-minority feeling was not a part of the small-town New England life about which he frequently wrote, and too interesting a
writer to be disqualified for his having done so. In his defense,
after having read Bruccoli's biography, one can say that Cozzens
had a fine impartiality, having no love for any particular group,
his own included. As for the Jews, that oldest of old arguments
will have to serve: his best friend, his only friend in fact, his wife,
was a Jew.

As it stands, then, readers who come to Matthew Bruccoli's

biography of James Gould Cozzens are likely to depart as they arrived: either convinced of Cozzins's genius or convinced of his meanness. It could, of course, have been worse. A psychologically minded biographer would have found in the work of Cozzens meat and drink and a full trolley of sweets for dessert. For example, sex, though never abundant in his novels, almost always carries with it the pleasure of an iced drink in a blizzard; it is unfailingly a reminder of humankind's biological limitations. For this reason, sex in a Cozzens novel often comes to seem the mating of beasts—more frequently a low than a high point in the conduct of human affairs.

No novelist has the full range of literary weapons in his arsenal, and Cozzens is not an exception. Although he has wit, which is displayed in his formulations and in the merciless observations on life made by his intelligent characters, he is otherwise fairly humorless. Lyricism, similarly, is foreign to him. He has an anti-intellectual bias, and the one character in all his works against whom he takes out after unstintingly is an intellectual, a writer for little magazines, serving as a public-relations officer in the army in *Guard of Honor.* His case against intellectuals is based on their love of theory in a world where there are too many variables for any human mind or theory to take proper account of. Things, in Cozzens's novels, are as they are and must be dealt with as such —conditions and not theories interest him. Cozzens, like George Orwell, has a certain talent for facing unpleasant facts; unlike Orwell, he seems almost to relish unpleasant facts; and those unpleasant facts that give him the most pleasure are the ones that knock the pins out from under theories of human behavior.

The more impressive of Cozzens's novels fall well outside the mainstream of modernist fiction. He does not go in for wild invention. In a mature James Gould Cozzens novel a cause has effects, effects ignite further causes, which in turn light up other effects. If you happen to believe that this is how life works—as, it happens, I do—then James Gould Cozzens may be for you. If you don't, then perhaps you would do better to consider the problems of modern reading in the novels of Italo Calvino or set off on a tour of ancient Egypt with Norman Mailer.

I spoke of a mature James Gould Cozzens novel, for there are also less mature and even immature James Gould Cozzens novels. Among the latter are the first four novels he wrote, between the ages of twenty and twenty-eight, and of which he himself spoke slightingly. I have not read these novels, but to judge from the passages quoted in Bruccoli's biography, they richly possess the most prominent mark of the too-soon-published young novelist: lush overwriting in the service of extreme self-indulgence. Excluding these first four novels, Cozzens wrote nine others that he cared sufficiently about to want to see remain in print. If one reads them in the order in which they were written, as I have recently done, a novelistic career unfolds before one, in all its interesting missteps, backsteps, and final striding forward. It also demonstrates that James Gould Cozzens, this lonely figure with his dark views, achieved something very impressive.

One could not, I think, have foretold how impressive it would be from the first of these nine novels, *S. S. San Pedro* (1931). This is a slight book about a large event—the sinking of an ocean liner that ships water and eventually goes under during a furious storm. Though no great shakes, the novel—novella really, since it runs to only eighty-five pages in my paperback edition—is obviously the work of a serious writer. In a bit of puffery written for the *Book-of-the-Month Club News* Christopher Morley spoke of "the beautiful crispness and decision of [Cozzens's] prose." "Beautiful," I don't know; "crispness," maybe; but "decision," a word I have not seen before used to describe prose, seems to me very good. For all its shortcomings, this novel by a man in his late twenties is written with decision—a word I read to mean disciplined authority.

If *S. S. San Pedro* is thin and a bit awkward, Cozzens's next novel, *The Last Adam* (1933), like a young man coming into his maturity, is both more filled-out and more confident. The crisis at the center of *The Last Adam* is a typhoid epidemic, which may or may not have broken out because of the incompetence of the town's physician and health officer, George Bull, a country doctor filled with prejudice and strong opinion who knows that life's major datum is death:

Discouragement, to feel death's certainty; exasperation, to know the fatuousness of resisting such an adversary—what was the use of temporary evasions or difficult little remedies when death simply came back and came back until it won? —moved him more than any personal dread of extinction, or compassion for those stricken. The stricken, beyond help, were beyond needing help. During the last forty years, fully a hundred human beings had actually died while he watched. He couldn't recall one who gave signs of minding much; they were too sick or too badly hurt to care. If they were conscious enough to know that they were alive, pain blurred their view; they saw no good anywhere. They were not given peace to regret a lost future; they were beyond desiring anything. In its melancholy way, the flesh, maligned mortality, took tender care of its own.

But before setting up the central crisis in the novel, Cozzens provides a portrait of the town of New Winton in the full range of its social classes, its local politics, its pretensions. This supposed novelist of power and privilege is very hard on the Bannings, one of the town's upper-crust families; and easily the most admirable character in the book is a telephone operator named May Tupping, whose husband has been paralyzed by a hunting accident and who herself faces life with stoical acceptance. The crisis of the novel is resolved not because right is on Dr. Bull's side—we never learn whether it is or isn't—but because Henry Harris, the town's political power, sees the resolution of the issue in Dr. Bull's favor as a useful way of infuriating Mrs. Banning, which it gives him pleasure to do. The novel closes on a note of somewhat forced affirmation, a paean to the vitality and survival powers of Dr. Bull by a woman who has been sleeping with him for years and whose closing words of half-grudging admiration are: "The old bastard!"

Written by a man of thirty, this is a work of considerable artistic coolness: objective, neatly distanced, socially perspicacious. If a comparison is wanted, I should say that *The Last Adam* is Sinclair Lewis without the malice. Because the malice—"See what swine these small-town people are!"—is missing, *The Last Adam* can still be read today with genuine interest, while the novels of Sinclair Lewis can only be read for historical interest.

Castaway (1934), Cozzens's next novel, is intended as a modern *Robinson Crusoe*. Instead of stranding his chief character on an island, Cozzens places "Mr. Lecky"—he is never referred to otherwise—in a deserted modern department store. We are never told how he got in, or why the store is deserted. What we are presented with is Mr. Lecky's paranoia and his painfully inept attempts at survival. He builds a fort composed of furniture in front of the men's room, he equips himself with rifles and ammunition from the sporting-goods department, he dresses himself from men's ready-to-wear, he eats canned hams, biscuits, and preserves from the food department. A false man Friday shows up, whom Mr. Lecky kills with savage incompetence at close range with a shotgun.

The descriptions are powerful in their precision, but what is *Castaway* about? Is it an allegory of man's essential loneliness? Is it about man's technological ineptitude? His unfitness for the modern world? I don't think we can quite know, for the allegory is not clearly realized. Yet the critics were generally pleased, citing *Castaway* as very Kafkaesque, which ticked off Cozzens, who hadn't ever read Kafka. Nearly twenty-five years later, Irving Howe, speaking for the modernist lobby in American criticism, wrote an attack on Cozzens in which he nonetheless had kind words for *Castaway,* going on to regret that after it Cozzens "becomes a quite conventional novelist, either uninterested in or unable to use the 20th-century advances in technique." (Interestingly, *Castaway* was perhaps alone among Cozzens's novels to be taught in American universities. The reason for this is not far to seek. All those obscurities, all those unresolved difficulties—such things fill classroom hours.)

In fact, Cozzens did return to "conventional" literary techniques in his next novel, *Men and Brethren* (1936), which is about a crowded day and a half in the life of an Episcopal priest. Ernest Cudlipp, who is vicar of a Manhattan church, is a no-nonsense Christian for whom the niceties of doctrine are of no great interest: "You either have the capacity to apprehend the great spiritual truths, which are universal and invariable, or you haven't." Ernie Cudlipp is less a saver than a patcher of souls. He arranges an abortion for a parishioner who has become pregnant in an adulterous affair; he attempts to soothe a fellow priest defrocked for making homosexual advances to the young; he permits a death-bed conversion to Catholicism of a woman dying of cancer. He is a man over whose eyes no wool can be pulled. He knows about human depravity, about the worm of human malice, and about just how far sweet reason, noble disinterestedness, and the assumption of good will can take one in defeating either. Yet he also knows that "sometimes people will be amazingly kind, amazingly generous, if they possibly can." He tells a friend, a woman who is without religion, "Suppose I were to say that it isn't especially desirable for you to be happy—in the sense of having things suit you, instead of spending your life trying to arrange things to suit someone else."

Certain qualities that will mark Cozzens's major fiction begin to emerge in *Men and Brethren*. The respect for work, for one: of the defrocked priest, cut off from his profession, Ernie Cudlipp thinks, "He had nothing left, he stood for nothing, he was nothing." For another, there is the preference for dealing with day-to-day reality—"Realists," Cudlipp thinks, "are the only people who get things done"—over the penchant for the theoretical. The observations in this novel are very sharp. "As far as Ernest could judge, the really valuable thing which Doctor [Karl] Barth did seem to offer was a conception of religious truth which allowed modern-minded young priests like Wilber to recover that sustaining, snobbish ease of mental superiority, loved long since, but, fifty or sixty years ago, lost to the clergy for a while." If the novel has a flaw, it is its lack of density. Things happen too fast; more —in the way of detail, of accounts of motivation, of completion of character—is wanted. Yet in the career of James Gould Cozzens *Men and Brethren* marks a true step forward.

One step forward—one step back. *Ask Me Tomorrow* (1940) is Cozzens's one attempt at an autobiographical novel, and it is a sad botch. It is based on a season in Europe in which Cozzens served as the tutor for the son of a rich American family. The Cozzens character, Francis Ellery, is an unpleasant young man filled with himself, and of no great interest to anyone else, who becomes entangled in his own youthful thoughts: "Recoiling in disgust from human beings, you had to recoil, in another disgust, from your own recoiling. . . ." In his attack on Cozzens, Irving Howe noted: "He is not much concerned with the idea of the self, and he certainly does not share the exalted valuation most modern novelists place upon its inviolability." This is true enough, and yet one wonders if Cozzens wasn't correct to turn away from the modern novelists' preoccupation with the self. By now, of course, our novelists have given us a bellyful of the self. One thinks here of all those Mailer, Styron, Roth, and Bellow novels in which the hero, modestly disguised and made to seem on the whole winning, is so obviously Mailer, Styron, Roth, or Bellow. One wonders, indeed, if the time hasn't come to shelve the self. After *Ask Me Tomorrow* Cozzens did, and never returned to it.

With *The Just and The Unjust* (1942), Cozzens entered onto his major phase. This novel, whose time span is a week, centers around a murder trial in Childerstown, the seat of a New England county. Its principal character is Abner Coates, a man six years out of Harvard Law School, an assistant district attorney, and the son and grandson of county judges. Its method is one Cozzens will use in his next two novels: an event takes place in a limited time frame, but the book regularly weaves back into the past through flashback, amply mixing action and observation. A portrait is provided of a town and its institutions, in their full social and professional texture. In this instance the trial of two men for murdering a drug dealer is the event, but the underlying question is what Abner Coates will do with his life. It is an interesting question chiefly because in Abner Coates Cozzens has created an interesting young man.

Abner Coates may not know what to do with his life, but he does reasonably well know himself. He knows, for example, that he doesn't have a first-rate legal mind, having been taught this lesson in law school by a classmate who showed him what a top-quality legal mind really is: "What he did not know, what Paul Bonbright, among others, showed him, was that those abilities of his that got him, without distinction but also without much exertion, through all previous lessons and examinations, were not first-rate abilities handicapped by laziness, but second-rate, by no degree of effort or assiduity to be made the equal of abilities like Bonbright's."

The question of what to do with his life presses upon Abner Coates when, during the week of the murder trial, he is offered a place on the county ballot for district attorney by the local polit-ical boss. He wants the job, even needs it, since he plans to marry and will require additional income, yet the political boss is a man he instinctively dislikes and to whom he is extremely wary of becoming beholden. Now in the truly conventional American novel we know how this problem would be resolved. Our hero would, after much agonizing, retain what he thinks of as his integrity, turn down the offer, and perhaps go into legal-aid work where he will uphold the rights of the downtrodden. Not, how-ever, in Cozzens.

The trial grinds on. A very strong sense emerges of how the law in its daily operations works which I, for one, find fascinat-ing. Irving Howe, for another, finds this same quality, as reflected in *By Love Possessed,* tiresome and all too American. ("The Ameri-can respect for technology becomes in Cozzens an unconcealed admiration for the man who uses his mind for precise utilitarian ends and who is impatient with other ideas about the value of thought." Whose thought? That of literary critics, no doubt.) Throughout the book flows a stream of observations that, whether one agrees with them or not, are of a kind that need to be confronted. Abner, for example, thinks: "Criminals might be victims of circumstances in the sense that few of them ever had a fair chance; but it was a mistake to forget that the only 'fair chance' they ever wanted was a chance for easy money." Or, as the current district attorney remarks to Abner: "Theory is where you want to go; practice is how you're going to get there."

In the end the murderers, who are guilty, get off with a sen-tence of second-degree murder, having been shown misplaced mercy by a jury that failed to understand the requirements of the law. This, though, is how it goes; justice is no exact science. Abner accepts the place on the ballot to run for district attorney. ("Resist this horrid nonsense," says Father Cudlipp in *Men and Brethren,* "about being true to yourself.") He will worry about his personal integrity when the occasion arises. Meanwhile, he will get on with a job of serious work. As his father, now half-paralyzed after a stroke and on the rim of death, tells Abner in the novel's closing passage:

> ". . . In the present, every day is a miracle. The world gets up in the morning and is fed and goes to work, and in the evening it comes home and is fed again and perhaps has a little amusement and goes to sleep. To make that possible, so much has to be done by so many people that, on the face of it, it is impossible. Well, every day we do it; and every day, come hell, come high water, we're going to have to go on doing it as well as we can."
>
> "So it seems," said Abner.
>
> "Yes, so it seems," said Judge Coates, "and so it is, and so it will be! And that's where you come in. That's all we want of you."
>
> Abner said, "What do you want of me?"
>
> "We just want you to do the impossible," Judge Coates said.

Somewhere between *Ask Me Tomorrow* and *The Just and The Unjust,* Cozzens's work, it seems to me, acquired that quality essential to the best novelists yet perhaps not finally altogether to be understood. The quality I have in mind is gravity. Gravity is not a question to which contemporary literary criticism often addresses itself. Among living writers, I would say Aleksandr Solzhenitsyn has it; so, when they are writing well, do V. S. Naipaul and Saul Bellow and I. B. Singer. John Updike and Gabriel García Márquez do not, and Norman Mailer never will. Gravity derives from a serious literary mind, unencumbered by the clichés of the day, at work on serious matters.

Guard of Honor (1948), the novel for which Cozzens won the Pulitzer Prize, has gravity in just this sense. It takes place during three days on an Army Air Force base in Florida during World War II. It is about what nowadays would be called "crisis management." One crisis occurs in the novel over segregation on the base, as does another crisis connected with civilian relations, and a final crisis has to do with the drowning of paratroopers during a field exercise owing to incompetence. This is a novel with a cast of roughly fifty important characters. A work of more than six hundred pages, it has a plot too intricate to summarize. Suffice it to say that the book gives us a most convincing portrayal of the way a large institution is run, filled with detailed knowledge about a vast range of military jobs and human types.

Much of the action in *Guard of Honor* takes place among field- and general-grade officers. Now a bird colonel or a major general, especially if he is a regular army officer, is, as every college graduate knows, a fascist. Cozzens, who wasn't a college graduate, apparently came away from his time in the army without knowing this. Even though he much disliked being in the army, what he did come away with was reinforcement of his view that, as Colonel Ross, the novel's main intelligence, puts it: "A man must stand up and do the best he can with what there is." Men who know their job and do it are the men Cozzens admires.

There is also a running gunfire against intellectuals in *Guard of Honor.* "Few ideas," one character reflects, "could be abstract enough to be unqualified by the company they kept." Another says: "If there are differences of opinion, I think most of them are differences that always arise between those who have to deal with fact, and those who are free to deal with theories." And, finally, another character, a magazine editor in civilian life, though no great lover of the military and its ways, feels himself

. . . obliged to admire a simple, unlimited integrity that accepted as the law of nature such elevated concepts as the Military Academy's Duty-Honor-Country, convinced that those were the only solid goods; that everyone knew what the words meant.

They needed no gloss—indeed it probably never crossed General Beal's mind that they could be glossed, that books had been written to show that Country was a delusive projection of the individual's ego; and that there were men who considered it a part of intelligence to admit that Honor was a hypocritical social sanction protecting the position of a ruling class; or that Duty was self-interest as it appeared when sanctions like Honor had fantastically distorted it. In his simplicity, General Beal, apprised of such intellectual views, would probably retort by begging the question: what the hell kind of person thought things like that?

But the intellectuals finally got their own back at Cozzens when he published *By Love Possessed* (1957). I do not mean to imply a vendetta—intellectuals waiting in hallways with long knives for nine years. It was merely that almost everything Cozzens's work stood for went against the grain of the ideal type of the intellectual. As an example of that ideal type made flesh, one can hardly do better than the late Dwight Macdonald—a man with a perfectly matched set of radical-intellectual political and literary opinions and a devastating wit into the bargain—and perhaps now is the time to look at his roundhouse attack on *By Love Possessed*.

First, however, a bit of background must be supplied. Even though Cozzens had won a Pulitzer Prize, no earlier novel of his had scored a true success, either commercial or critical. With *By Love Possessed,* he had hit the best-seller gong, and hit it with a howitzer. The novel was weeks and weeks atop the best-seller list, a movie sale and a *Reader's Digest* condensation had been made, a *Time* cover story done, and critics both provincial and metropolitan had lined up to praise the novel. In other words, Cozzens was ready to be savaged.

Here is must be said that *By Love Possessed* is not Cozzens's best performance. It is an extremely ambitious novel, and too much of the ambition goes into its style. The novel attempts to be a comprehensive account of the various permutations of love—from adolescent lust to the complexities of marital love to the love of parents for their children to the pure love of a sister for her brother—and how in these various forms love wreaks havoc on any plans to get through life with order and reason as one's guiding principles. Dealing with a universal theme, Cozzens thought to forge a universal style. In the attempt to bring this off, he often twisted his syntax, worked in quotations from great authors, and trotted out a Latinate vocabulary of often arcane words.

The effect is all too frequently an air of pomposity and portentousness. To what extent this ruins the novel—it certainly doesn't improve it—is another question. The late Alexander Gerschenkron, an economic historian who also adjudicated the dispute between Edmund Wilson and Vladimir Nabokov over translating Pushkin, once told me that, in Russian, many of Dostoyevsky's novels are so wretchedly written as to be very nearly unreadable. Gerschenkron did not go on to say that he failed to read them. But if your sensibilities are so fine that stylistic lapses put you irretrievably off, then many a passage in *By Love Possessed* will seem to you like downing a Pepsi with a meal at Lutèce. And yet the concern with style can, it seems to me, be carried too far. Dwight Macdonald was fond of quoting Buffon's old maxim, "The style is the message," but Macdonald's message, as near as I can make it out, came to no more than that it is better to have a nice style.

There is no want of style in Dwight Macdonald's attack on *By Love Possessed*. Still, it seems to me one of those essays in which one's pleasure will be destroyed if one actually reads the author being discussed. Macdonald begins by mentioning the enormousness—to him, the enormity—of the success of Cozzens's novel. He then cites examples of the praise the book has received, finding quotations that go especially gushy. They were even, it turns out, nuts about it in the provinces. If you know the intellectual signals, by now you ought to know that there is already a great deal to be suspicious about.

But when Macdonald comes to speak of the novel itself, something rather odd happens. If one has read it oneself, one begins to realize that Macdonald either did not read it very carefully or that he came to it blinded if not by malice then by the passion for polemic. He informs us that Arthur Winner, Jr., the novel's principal character, is a prig—and, worse, that Cozzens doesn't know he is a prig, which is the greatest sign of ineptitude in a novelist. But Macdonald is quite mistaken here. Arthur Winner, Jr., is indeed a prig but a prig by intention. It is the whole point of Cozzens's novel to show that Arthur Winner, try as he may, cannot live his life in the kind of order that a morally priggish man would wish. Through the action of the novel Arthur Winner is reminded of one of his sons, now dead, who was a kind of bad seed, whom no amount of teaching, no amount of punishment, could straighten out. Later in the novel he is made to realize that an adulterous affair he had with the wife of a friend was known about all along to this friend—and in this there is further humiliation, further destruction of priggishness.

Macdonald goes on to say that Cozzens's "characters often speak brutally, for example, not because they are supposed to be brutes, but because their creator apparently thinks this is the way men talk." He then cites two samples, one from an aging lawyer named Noah Tuttle and another from a physician named Reggie Shaw. The samples are brutal, true, but what Macdonald doesn't tell his readers is that the lawyer is on the edge of senility and the physician, having seen so much that is horrendous in life, has lapsed into alcoholism. "No reason is given for any of these onslaughts," Macdonald writes, "aside from the fact that all three recipients are women; this seems to be Cozzens's idea of manly straight-from-the-shoulder talk. Curious." It is curious, all right. It makes one wonder: was Dwight Macdonald asleep at the wheel, or instead concentrating on running someone over?

After scoring blows against Cozzens for anti-Semitism, anti-Negro sentiment (there are, in the current phrase, Tomish characters in the novel), and anti-feminism, Macdonald finds two reasons that account for the success of the novel. It succeeded with the critics because there was "a general feeling that Cozzens had hitherto been neglected and that he 'had it coming to him,' " to which there is perhaps some truth. And it succeeded with the public because "it is the latest episode in The Middlebrow

Counter-Revolution." Middlebrow—Macdonald's vocabulary knew no more dampening phrase than this one. The way Macdonald saw it was that Cozzens's work was part of "The Novel of Resignation." He was resigned to taking life as it was; he was hopelessly given to "maturity." There was no idealism in Cozzens, no radical thrust to argue with and change life. In this he had caught the spirit of the age. Similarly, Irving Howe, while conceding that Cozzens had been consistent in his vision over the years, noted that "It is the weary *Zeitgeist* that has finally limped round to him." And, more explicitly political than Macdonald in his attack, Howe concluded: "And, indeed, a civilization that finds its symbolic embodiment in Dwight David Eisenhower and its practical guide in John Foster Dulles has been well prepared for receiving the fruits of the Philosophy of Limit. It is a civilization that, in its naked and graceless undelusion, deserves as its laureate James Gould Cozzens—Novelist of the Republic."

Now here is an interesting piece of damnation. Cozzens has created a novel—indeed a body of work—that requires attack because it fits in with the spirit of the age, which is perceived to be loathsome. On these same grounds it makes a certain amount of sense to knock off *War and Peace* until we have world disarmament and pack away *Moby-Dick* until we have finally managed to save the whale.

Macdonald and Howe may have disliked Cozzens's style but what they really hated was what they took to be his message—or, to use the grander term, his vision. They read him as a novelist in support of the status quo, surely no good thing to be. He reminded readers of human limitation when what Americans needed to be reminded of was human possibility. His novels, with their insistence on the role played in life by illness, bad luck, poor character, biological urgings, death, were, when you got right down to it, not only anti-liberal but in the profoundest sense counter-revolutionary. In these purely political terms, Macdonald and Howe were probably right.

But I do not want to make *By Love Possessed* sound all message, all vision. In fact, if cumbersome in style, it is nonetheless a most carefully constructed work of fiction. (Even Howe allowed that

Cozzens was a "craftsman.") The concatenation of character and event is persuasively worked out with an intricacy and fine discrimination that could only have been achieved by a high literary intelligence. Cozzens realizes his vision not through preaching but through plot. This vision is compelling because he has taken great pains to get his facts straight, because he makes his characters complex yet clear, and describes experience with a richness and unpredictability that show a minute fidelity to life. As Arthur Winner, Jr.'s law partner says in *By Love Possessed,* "Happiness, Jonathan Swift admonishes me, is a perpetual possession of being well-deceived." The burden of Cozzens's major fiction is to undeceive us.

If Cozzens resembles any major American figure, it is Justice Holmes. Like Holmes, Cozzens did not wish to blink unpleasant facts about human nature. Like Holmes, Cozzens admired the strength of the puritanical tradition while remaining himself agnostic. Like Holmes again, Cozzens felt that all lies, even lies for the putative good of humanity, were still lies. In the middle of *By Love Possessed,* a black man comes to Arthur Winner, Jr., to tell him he has a bad heart condition and would like Winner to write his will for him. When Winner asks how he is feeling at present, he says he is rather like the man in the cartoon who has fallen from the skyscraper and who, when passing a window from which people look out at him in shock, announces, "All right so far." There is a joke Justice Holmes would have adored. He would also have had no difficulty understanding another character in *By Love Possessed* who says that "Freedom is the knowledge of necessity."

In his biography Professor Bruccoli writes: "In the eyes of the Left Cozzens was the spokesman for the enemy. Indeed, he was the enemy." There can be little question that Macdonald's essay, backed up by that of Howe, brought down Cozzens's reputation —and brought it down hard. The hyenas having done their work, the maggots now crept in. The signal had gone out; it was now understood to be OK to have at James Gould Cozzens. And have at Cozzens's next two books, a collection of stories entitled *Children and Others* and a thin novel of his late years called *Morning*

Noon and Night, everyone did. He was now known as the novelist with bad style and bad politics. He was the spokesman for the ruling class, the novelist of power and privilege. Clichés, like bad news, travel fast.

When a young critic to whom Cozzens had been friendly warned Cozzens that he had just written an attack on his social conservatism in the *New York Times Book Review,* Cozzens responded that he intended no social or political message in his fiction:

> My only aim and interest is to try to present as exactly as I can people and events as they appear to me. When young, I admit that I imagined such painstaking dispassion, and concern for simple truth, could displease nobody. Of course I know now that, to all who have things to sell or the emotional need to write for or against things, such an attitude's simply infuriating.

It was the wrong age, Cozzens came to learn, for writing about things as one saw them.

As recounted in Matthew Bruccoli's pages, James Gould Cozzens's last years were wretchedly sad. His wife died before he did; he stopped writing, he even stopped reading ("no longer writing," he noted, in a comment only a writer would understand, "Why read?"). Cancer of the spine claimed him ten days before he was seventy-five. Before he died he wrote to his publisher, William Jovanovich, "In clear fact work of mine's all out of season." He was right. The anthology of his writing and critical appreciations that Professor Bruccoli put together in 1978 sold a total of 2,488 copies in cloth and paper. No serious reevaluation of Cozzens's work, which this book was intended to stir, ever came about.

In a more just world, James Gould Cozzens would be accorded a volume in the Library of America, the recently established series of American classics for a general audience. It would include his novels *The Just and The Unjust, Guard of Honor,* and, yes, *By Love Possessed.* But although two volumes have already been published of the work of Jack London, and others are no doubt in preparation for Sinclair Lewis and (the early) John Dos Passos, I doubt very much if the present editors and their advisers plan to include Cozzens. The injustice here is, or ought to be, obvious. Yet I suspect Cozzens would not be much surprised; about injustice, in literary criticism and in much else besides, he knew a very great deal.

Commentary 1983

FOUR | AMUSEMENTS AND DISASTERS (ESSAYS ON LANGUAGE)

Why Madame Bovary Couldn't Make Love in the Concrete

P OOR MADAME BOVARY, one understands and sympathizes with her condition. It is very awkward—if not so awkward as that of the freshman student at my university who, in a term paper, spotted the difficulty when he wrote: "Madame Bovary's problem is that she cannot make love in the concrete." How could he know that the word "concrete" is itself an abstraction, a by now quite stale metaphor, and one used in his unpracticed hand to hilarious effect? How could he know that for professors one of the few pleasures in grading student papers is that of writing zippy comments in the margins, and that he had set up his professor exquisitely? In his unconscious trope rendering Emma Bovary frigid in the concrete, the possibilities he provided for marginal comment—and comedy— were not practically but altogether boundless. Only the greatest restraint prevents me from trying out twenty or thirty such comments here myself.

This error could have been no more than a slight slip, but I believe something else is entailed. Certainly no uneducated person would ever have made it. It had to be learned, acquired; it would not have been available outside the classroom. It is an error of the kind to which only the half-educated are susceptible. As Orwell once said that some opinions are so stupid that only intellectuals could hold them, so some contemporary language is so misguided that only the college-educated could use it. Madame Bovary may not be able to make love in the concrete, but many

Americans, supposedly educated ones, go her a giant step better and are unable to think in the concrete.

Not that this, or the condition of contemporary language generally, is not often being pointed out, explained, castigated. Of critics of language today there is no paucity. In a modest way, language has become a hot subject. Books about language appear in great number and in varying degrees of seriousness and from various points of view, from Jacques Barzun's *Simple and Direct* to John B. Bremner's *Words on Words* to Willard Espy's *Say It My Way* to Casey Miller and Kate Swift's *Handbook of Nonsexist Writing* to Gyles Brandreth's *The Joy of Lex*. Along with *College English* and other academic journals, two publications for laymen, *Verbatim: The Language Quarterly* and *The Underground Grammarian*, are devoted to the study of contemporary vagaries in the use of language. The criticism of language has become a journalistic occupation, and two steady middlebrow publications, the *Saturday Review* and the *New York Times Magazine*, employ such critics and so does *Esquire*, a more with-it magazine. Like books or movies or theater or dance, language in these publications has become a regular department. Whether this new public concern will soon fade it is difficult to know, but for the moment at least language as a business—if not language itself—seems to be flourishing.

Why? Why have *Esquire*, the *Times Magazine*, the *Saturday Review* all seen fit to install language criticism in their pages at this time? Do their editors feel a missionary earnestness about the disheveled state of English and a concomitant zeal to get Americans writing and speaking carefully again? Do they, as savvy magazine editors are supposed to do, sniff something in the wind? Is the English language truly in a condition of crisis? Or is this freshened interest merely an additional piece of consumer culture overlaid with snobbery—an interest on the order of that in gourmet cookery? Or is it at bottom political, for there are some who argue that custodians of the language go into action when class and caste lines are threatened?

My answer is, probably all of the above, and other reasons beside. True, language is under attack by feminists, by proponents of Black English and bilingualism, by homosexuals, and by a general resurgence of the populist strain in our culture. The rise in interest in language may well reflect this attack and reflect into the bargain a hunger for standards: with all else slipping and changing, let us at least try to keep up the language. It may also reflect a dissatisfaction on the part of a great many people with the quality of their education; they have been educated but they don't feel educated, and a concern for language can be seen as a way of renewing one's interest in education. Nor can snobbery be ruled out. Today, when the ownership of a Mercedes, or even of a Chagall, is no longer a guarantee of distinction, perhaps using "hopefully" correctly can separate one from the general middle-class rabble.

But a more interesting question is, Can it be said with any certainty that the quality of language has in recent years fallen off drastically, or even at all? How would one go about answering, let alone proving an answer to, this question? One could, I suppose, cite the rise or fall of scores on SAT examinations in English, but this would probably persuade no one, for there are those who argue that these examinations do no more than test bare competence in punctuation, spelling, vocabulary, and powers of organization; and others who feel these examinations are, as they say, "culturally biased" and who believe therefore that it is the examiners who need to be examined. But if statistical evidence is wanting, literary evidence is not. Nor is literary evidence insignificant on a question that is itself literary.

It does seem unarguable that in public discourse the quality of language is lower than it once was. For decades now, for example, we have not had a President of the United States who has written his own speeches or has even shown evidence that he could write them if time permitted. Not only the presidents but their speech-writers have shown themselves incapable of moving the populace by eloquence. This is a long way from the case of Theodore Roosevelt or Woodrow Wilson, both of whom not only could command eloquence but wrote books and even reviewed them. Theodore Roosevelt and Woodrow Wilson's origins were patrician, to be sure, but this is merely a reminder that careful language is no longer a serious concern of the American upper classes. Edith Wharton, in her memoir, *A Backward Glance,* recalled that it once was. Her own family was very far from being literary—it rather looked down upon living writers—but it nonetheless held the English language in reverence and used it with precision. Careful language, like politeness, Mrs. Wharton writes, was one "of the accepted formulas," one of "the principles of the well-bred." If this was once true of the upper classes, it apparently is no longer, for today formerly upper-class institutions such as Harvard employ teachers with populist views about language: views that hold that whatever language the people use is, *ipso facto,* the best language, though these teachers would deplore the use of the word "best," which even in this context smacks to them of elitism.

In *The American Scene,* his book about his pilgrimage to America in 1904, Henry James, visiting the Jewish quarter of New York, noted its extraordinary liveliness but also noted "where one's 'lettered' anguish came in—in the turn of one's eye from face to face for some betrayal of a prehensile hook for the linguistic tradition as one had known it." James ended this section of his account on a very Jamesian sentence: "The accent of the very ultimate future, in the States, may be destined to become the most beautiful on the globe and the very music of humanity (here the 'ethnic' synthesis shrouds itself thicker than ever); but whatever we shall know it for, certainly, we shall not know it for English—in any sense for which there is an existing literary measure."

Henry James's standard was of course stratospherically high, and it is worth remembering that the language crisis in the United States has always been with us. In 1892 the Report of the Committee on Composition and Rhetoric of the Harvard College Board of Overseers, for example, complained that "It would not seem unreasonable to insist that young men of nineteen years of age who present themselves, for a college education, should be able not only to speak, but to write their mother tongue with ease and correctness." It is worth remembering, too, that Henry James had to be fired from his job as Paris correspondent for the old *New York Tribune* because his regular letter from Paris was considered simply too good for that newspaper's readers. (James replied that he understood but would have the editor know that his compositions for the paper were quite "the poorest I could do, especially for the money!")

Still, without aspiring to Jamesian heights of literacy, it does seem clear that standards of literacy have slipped below the permissible. I am not referring here to gross illiteracies (such as that of the Chicago politician of a few years back who claimed he "didn't want to cast asparagus at my opponent"), which have always existed and are good fun, but to the language of the supposedly educated: that of teachers, broadcasters, journalists—people who make their living through the use of language. One can hardly pick up a newly published book today without finding it filled with typographical errors, ungrammatical patches, leaden language. Jargon has never seemed so to abound. Apart only from Senator Daniel P. Moynihan, no contemporary politician appears to take joy in language in the way that the late Senator Everett Dirksen or Adlai Stevenson did. Nor are days any palmier along the academic front. The word has recently gone out that college students do not write well, and young teachers, looking for work in a depressed job market, send in letters to English department chairmen putting themselves forward as keen to teach composition; only they usually call it "language skills and strategies" or "communication arts."

The point is that Henry James was wrong. Literacy today is not imperiled by the unwashed masses but by the well-scrubbed college-educated. Most of the interesting additions to English have over the years come from the lower classes, whose language usually derived from real experience, was expressed without abstractions, and, whatever its correctness, had the virtue of being vivid. Nor have these classes wished to foist their language on the general culture. Negro mothers and fathers with any ambitions for their children do not, so far as one can tell, want those children to learn black English; they see it, quite properly, as a sure-fire way of keeping black children in their place. No uneducated person would use, in the flyblown way that people who have been to college do, phrases like "identity crisis," "Protestant ethic," or "establishment." No uneducated person would use the word "ambivalent" (a word, Ralph Ellison notes in *Invisible Man*, "that doesn't explain it"), or "supportive," or "viable" (in the way that a Canadian psychologist said that "suicide can be a viable option"). Only the educated could be so ignorant.

As if this slip in standards were not enough, language itself has been under political attack in the United States for at least a decade now. Here feminists lead the way. Precision, elegance, good sense, all must fall before the feminist juggernaut, from the doing away with any words suffixed with "man" to the creation of new pronouns. But it is not feminists alone who must be catered to linguistically. The *sine qua non* of contemporary speech and writing is that it give no possible offense. Books—and especially textbooks—are combed carefully for possible linguistic burrs. Among the minority groups whose sensibilities must be guarded is the group known as the college-attending ignorant. Thus a friend of mine, in preparing a textbook in art history, was told to eliminate the term "anti-bourgeois"—on the ground that it was too difficult for his intended undergraduate audience. One might as well be asked to write a cookbook without mentioning the word salt.

In different ways these matters are discussed in two books on contemporary language: John Simon's *Paradigms Lost: Reflections on Literacy and Its Decline* and William Safire's *On Language*. No one will have any difficulty discovering where John Simon stands on the issues, questions, and problems of language in our day. He believes that there are at present two cultures, divided not by the scientific or literary spirit as set out by Lord Snow but by "whether a person has language or not." Simon writes:

> Language, I think, belongs to two groups only: gifted individuals everywhere, who use it imaginatively; and the fellowship of men and women, wherever they are, who, without being particularly inventive, nevertheless endeavor to speak and write correctly. Language, however, does not belong to the illiterate or to bodies of people forming tendentious and

propagandistic interest groups, determined to use it for what they (usually mistakenly) believe to be their advantage.

Uncompromising, implacable, absolutely fearless, Simon's position might be termed elitist, except that so identifying him might give offense to others who consider themselves elitist on these matters. Perhaps it would be better to say that he is a little to the right of the czar.

Simon is for good grammar, careful usage, the depoliticization of language. He is, in my view, on the side of the angels, yet, oddly for one so placed, he carries a pitchfork. He is hell on anyone who offends correctness in language. He is sedulous—not to say acidulous—in ferreting out error and crushing it. He is a man who could find a grammatical mistake in a Stop sign. Yet for a man so accustomed to discovering error wherever his eye alights, he seems never to cease being shocked, staggered, disbelieving, or alarmed when coming upon it afresh. This combination of looking for linguistic slovenliness and then being astonished when he finds it does not quite come off; it is rather like learning that the chief of New York's vice squad fainted when told there was prostitution in the city.

Too often Simon takes an almost unseemly pleasure in coming upon still more evidence of linguistic delinquency "in this benighted, permissive, and demotically oriented democracy of ours." The word "ignoramus" comes so readily to him. In his prose he is always ready to cross the street to knock down someone smaller than he: in the pages of this book, for example, Barbara Walters, Erica Jong, and Clive Barnes. Of one Professor Campbell Tatham, a radical professor of English at the University of Wisconsin at Milwaukee whose doctrine Simon detests, he writes: "Campbell Tatham may become the boor that [*sic*] made Milwaukee infamous." Simon has a weakness for puns, as witness his title, *Paradigms Lost* (why not Brother, Can you Paradigm?), but as great a weakness for a free-floating nastiness. He resembles nothing so much as an exterminator hired to eliminate pests who blows up the entire building.

Yet Simon is often quite impressive in his search-and-destroy missions. Like a truffle dog, his critical nose need only be inserted into a text to find a great richness of error. Many of those he finds are obvious, for bad grammar and poor usage, unlike truffles, are plentiful. But many are subtle, such as his distinction between the words "annoy" and "aggravate." Sometimes he simply goes too far, laying the knout to a writer for placing a period outside quotation marks, or advising his hearers not to read any letter "that follows up the addressee's invocation with a semicolon: nothing intelligent can be contained therein."

If it isn't clear, an old saying has it, it isn't French. After reading *Paradigms Lost,* I am tempted to add: if it doesn't contain errors, it isn't English. One of the reasons John Simon is able to find as many lapses as he does is that English, even though it has no complicated system of declension, is a rule-ridden language, with plenty of leeway for disagreement about usage and questions of taste. Not even Simon's pages are free of error. He himself owns up to a mistake; it seems he once used "among" where "amid" would have been more proper. Here are a few other egg stains on his linguistic vest that he might ponder. He uses the vulgar inversion of *Time* magazine style ("Claims Duneton") and the solecism "guideline," a bureaucratic neologism deriving from the nautical term "guyline." He calls Edmund Wilson and Vladimir Nabokov "polymaths," which, strictly speaking (the way Simon encourages the rest of us to speak), they are not; polyglots, yes; polymaths, no. Clichés crop up, such as "fall between the stools," and "stick out like a sore thumb." Puff and baggy-pants words make their way onto the page, among them the odiously inflated "dialogue" and the vapid "humanistic value." If Simon can criticize another writer for a period outside a quotation mark, perhaps it would not be out of place to suggest that the word "antimale" without a hyphen in his book looks rather like the dish served in a Mexican home before the tamales.

I raise these points not because I think they are crucial but partly for the sheer joy of catching Simon out in error, the vigilante unvigilant; and partly because, while small errors will no doubt one day lead to large, for the moment there are enough large errors about to let pass a period outside quotation marks.

Mr. Simon believes one of the chief objects of the careful deployment of language is the achievement of elegance. I think that is indeed one of its objects, but today there is a greater one: the avoidance of deception in its various forms, deliberate, unconscious, and self-. With such words as "meaningful," "relevant," "fulfilling," "dialogue," "humanistic," "structure," and "viable" at our disposal, not to speak of the wondrous cant from politics and psychology and education, we have all the means at hand to be lied to or to lie convincingly to ourselves. Here in my opinion are the targets toward which guns such as John Simon's ought to be aimed.

Where Simon is aiming is indeed sometimes a bit of a puzzle. Much of the content of *Paradigms Lost* originally appeared in *Esquire,* a journal better known for its interest in sartorial than in linguistical elegance. The question of audience may well have puzzled Simon himself, for throughout these essays he seems to be under the double obligation of discovering error while explaining what is correct. Thus when he thwacks Vincent Canby over the knuckles for consistently using "disinterested" to mean lack of interest, he also finds himself under the obligation to inform his readers that " 'disinterested' means unbiased, impartial." If he quotes a line or phrase in French, a translation in parentheses must follow. Simon's problem is that he cannot with certainty pay his readers the courtesy of postulating some intelligence in them about these matters. The result is that he assumes a shared superiority with his readers even as he condescends to them.

John Simon, I fear, gives standards a bad name. Standards are of course essential, but it is better for a writer to observe them in his own work than to have him ceaselessly preach their necessity —to let example become precept. Simon not only preaches but preens. He preens himself, for example, on his sesquipedality, yet when he uses an unfamiliar word it is not generally interestingly deployed, and so one usually finds oneself incurious about its meaning. The temptation is to want to put some space between Simon and oneself; he is the sort of writer who, when one finds oneself agreeing with him, makes one instantly want to reconsider one's own position. Yet he is quite right in his demand for stand-ards, and in his opinion that without them we are lost.

William Safire operates under a very different set of assump-tions from John Simon's. Rather than a guardian or vigilante, he is a word watcher. He is chiefly interested in the progress—or, depending upon one's point of view, regress—of the language. As a political journalist, he is in a splendid position to receive freshly minted jargon and vogue words; and thus reading him one can learn a good deal about linguistic change. Safire writes without Simon's magisterial tone. In his column a spirit of bon-homie prevails, and he conducts the various points of debate and controversy about words with, as one of his readers says, "a sense of sport."

Safire's tendency in linguistic controversy is to be a peace-maker, though in such controversy the peacemakers shall be cursed. He tells us that many of the letters he receives about his column—a large number of which are printed in *On Language*—begin, "Shame on you." In battles over usage, Safire often offers to hold the coats of both parties. Sometimes he will, figuratively, invite everyone out for a drink. Thus on the question of whether the word "memorandum" in its plural form ought to be memo-randums or memoranda, he suggests sidestepping the issue and using memos. On the question of whether the word "presently" ought to be used synonymously with the word "currently" or to retain its traditional meaning of soon or directly, he advises that "presently" "is a word best forgotten, at least for the time being." On simple error, he does take a stand, usually a genial one: "I don't want to get prescriptive or anything, but people who use *bi* for 'twice' should cut it out." Yet he is a man who accepts the less than grammatical "hopefully," "not because I accept loose new standards, but because I embrace time-tested and readily under-stood usage."

Mr. Safire calls himself "a libertarian language activist," which he describes as follows:

A libertarian language activist is not one of those relax-and-enjoy-it purely descriptive types. He wants to cheer on "parameter," borrowed from mathematics and now used to mean scope, or limits; at the same time, he wants to hoot at such nonce expressions as "What am I looking at?" now used to mean "What are the consequences?" or "How deeply am I likely to become involved?" Similarly, he will welcome "full-court press" from basketball lingo to replace the tiring "all-out effort," but will ridicule the vogue verb "defense against" from football, preferring the more direct "defend." It's a matter of taste.

"It's a matter of taste" is a sentiment John Simon would never brook. He would likely respond, "Yes, it is—good taste or bad." Apart from his manner, I happen to side with Simon, who quotes Dr. Johnson to the useful effect that in these matters "we retard what we cannot repel, that we palliate what we cannot cure." Simon is very good in attacking the cliché about language being a living, perpetually changing thing. Of course language changes; the question is what direction change takes. "When change does not obfuscate," Safire says, "don't fight it." The difficulty is that nowadays change does so often tend in the direction of obfuscation. As Safire remarks toward the close of his book: "A sound lexicographic case can be made for the theory that our traditional sources of vogue lingo—the argot of musicians, the cant of the underworld, and the inventive richness of black English—are being replaced by the political and communications worlds, acting not merely as disseminators but originators as well."

"Jockey," announces the well-known underwear manufacturer, during a commercial break on the evening news. "More than a name. A commitment." Then President Carter appears on the television screen to announce: "We remain steadfast in our commitment to human rights." So much for commitment.

What is to be done? The problem, in my view, is one of authority. In questions about language, who is to say who is right and who is wrong? To decide, Simon calls for "the eventual creation of an Academy of the Anglo-American Language," even though to do so, he concedes, "would be nearly impossible. But necessary." In a culture so intensely politicized as ours now is, creating such an Academy figures to be much more impossible than necessary. To cite but a single example, could such an Academy be formed without Noam Chomsky, the great name in linguistics in our day? Probably not. Yet I for one should not be pleased to see so politically engaged a man as Chomsky adjudicating questions of language; imagine him, for example, on the word "imperialism." It may well be that one of the reasons the traditional meaning of "disinterestedness" is fast fading is that the quality of disinterest, the thing itself, has all but disappeared from contemporary life.

Simon also proposes what during the Eisenhower administration was called a "person-to-person" approach. He suggests that when we come across error we correct it—stomp it out, crunch, on the spot:

> Whenever, wherever we hear someone say "between you and I" or one of the related horrors, and whoever the offender may be, we go into action. To strangers in the street, we may have to be polite; to superiors (in position, evidently, not in knowledge), we may even have to be somewhat humble. But correct them we must. To all others we may be as sharp, forceful, tonitruous as the circumstances permit or demand: let family, friends, and neighbors hear us correct them loudly and clearly—let *between you and me* resound across the land. Otherwise there will soon be no more communication between you and me.

There are people—I am among them—who would find this temperamentally impossible. Meanwhile, as a matter of personal safety, I think it probably not a good idea to invite John Simon to accompany you to a meeting of your Teamsters Local.

Simon proposes other, even Lacedaemonian measures, one of which is to turn the children of the unlettered over to day-care centers where they will daily hear Standard English spoken. Where to find the people to work in these centers is but the first of the technical difficulties such a scheme would entail. In its very outlandishness, though, the proposal illustrates how dim are the prospects for language reform.

Perhaps the place to begin reform is by making certain useful distinctions. Some language questions can only be decided on the basis of taste. For example, I prefer to use the word "presently" in its traditional meaning of soon or directly. I prefer it chiefly because it is traditional, and the argument from tradition is appealing to me: I like to use words with the same sense that cultivated writers and speakers have used them before me. Is this snobbery? Possibly it is, though defensible snobbery, of the kind used in defense of not eating peas with a knife. By the same token, the word "hopefully," used as an adverb without a connecting verb, seems to me worth condemning. William Safire defends it by analogy (in *On Language*); we use the adverbs finally and basically without connecting verbs, so why not "hopefully"? My argument is that in a secular age, "hopefully" has come to stand in for the old phrase "God willing," as in "God willing, we shall not have another war in our lifetime," and faulty grammar seems to me a poor substitute for religious feeling. But the proper uses of "presently" and "hopefully" are finally matters of nice discrimination. In neither instance is clarity at stake. What is at stake is the possibility of offending that touchy minority group, the truly well-educated.

There are, however, all too many instances where clarity, even reality, is at stake. When a freshman university student writes, as one of my students recently did, "The novel *Billy Budd* is a relatively short story," this seems to me merely ignorance, easily enough corrected by explaining the difference between a novel and a short story. But when the same student writes, "The basic difference between Billy Budd and Claggart is one of lifestyle," it is a cause of vague language obscuring perception itself, and this seems to me sad, even a bit crazy.

Not that the appetite for abstraction, the preference for the vague over the particular, is an altogether new phenomenon in the United States. In his chapter "How American Democracy Has Modified the English Language," Tocqueville noted:

... I wonder if vagueness may not have a secret charm for talkers and writers too in these lands. ... Democratic citizens, then, will often have vacillating thoughts, and so language must be loose enough to leave them play. As they never know whether what they say today will fit the facts of tomorrow, they have a natural taste for abstract terms. An abstract word is like a box with a false bottom; you may put in it what ideas you please and take them out again unobserved.

Yet this taste for the abstract has intensified in the United States in recent years, and the removal, often for political reasons, of any authority for using language correctly and with discrimination has only exacerbated the general condition. The condition of language today is such that communication threatens to be clogged, perception clouded, the possibility for serious discourse lessened. No writer of quiet yet unassailable authority—an H. W. Fowler, a Sir Ernest Gowers—is likely to arise in current circumstances to tear down the Tower of Babel now abuilding. Neither the scolding voice of John Simon nor the breezy one of William Safire is about to turn the trick. The duty of everyone who considers himself educated is to keep language alive by using it with respect and precision. But resistance among people who care about language—and, to judge from the ample correspondence Simon and Safire say they receive, there is reason to believe many people do care—will have to be individual. Although the prospects are not very bright, united, those who do care may one day lift poor Emma Bovary out of the concrete.

Commentary 1981

Sex and Euphemism

IN THE BEGINNING was the Word. There followed, at an undetermined but (one assumes) decent interval, private, harsh, and dirty words. Invention here being the mother of necessity, the need for euphemism arose. Nowhere could this need have been greater, or more evident, than in the realm of sex. Euphemism, so well worth decrying in almost every other sphere of life, is in the sexual sphere heartily, happily, one is ready to go so far as to say healthily, welcome. There are after all times and places where it will not do to call a spade a spade, let alone other things other things.

Remove euphemism from the realm of discourse about sex and one is left with two possibilities, neither of them very pretty. One is to speak about it clinically: genitalia, pudenda, vas deferens, reproductive organs, and all that. The other is to speak not so much plainly as profanely: to let, so to say, the most freely used Australian adjective and other nouns and verbs fly. There is also the loathsome prospect of speaking in code, as is sometimes done by coy lovers who christen their private parts with given or sur-names, and thus utter, as I seem to recall of a character in a wretched novel I read years ago whose title and author I have successfully blocked out, lines such as: "Will Mrs. Featherbody be at home and pleased to receive my man Andrew this evening?"

Many people have felt that the subject of sex is best dealt with by silence, the ultimate euphemism. Still, at all times in literature —from Petronius to Rabelais to the Earl of Rochester to the

Victorian pornographers to Henry Miller to the work today of nearly every contemporary novelist—silence on the subject of sex has been broken, and is unlikely to be restored. Sex throughout history has perhaps been on most people's minds, but in this century it has increasingly been on almost everyone's tongue as well. Philip Larkin might write:

Sexual intercourse began
In nineteen sixty-three
(Which was rather late for me)—
Between the end of the *Chatterley* ban
And the Beatles' first LP.

But Freud long before 1963 made it difficult to keep the silence on sex; and Freudianism, if not Freud himself, put paid to sexual reticence for all but good. As a blue eminence, Gay Talese, author of a participatory journalistic study of the sexual revolution entitled *Thy Neighbor's Wife,* has remarked: "Sex is so very important; it is probably the most important thing. What is more important? I know of nothing." Talese's wisdom may be in doubt; his sincerity, never.

How does one talk about this "most important thing"? The range of possibilities is very great. Sex may be spoken of tenderly or toughly, lyrically or lasciviously, beautifully or brutally, and in all these various ways by the same person on the same day. Because sex can evoke many moods, it requires many distinct vocabularies. This wasn't always so. For the greater part of the vast history of humankind talk of sex, of bodily love, was distinctly out of bounds. Certainly it was not permitted in polite society: that one did not speak of it there was one of the things that made polite society, well, polite. Talk of sex tended to be confined to intimate diaries or to blushing utterances in a physician's office. I recall some years ago coming upon a medical encyclopedia, published in the United States around the turn of this century, in which the article on masturbation appeared under the rubric "The Secret Vice." All sex, though, then seemed, if not a vice, clearly a bit of a secret—D. H. Lawrence's "dirty little secret."

Sex is a secret no longer. The unspeakable is nowadays speakable—and spoken. Not to speak of it with a fair frequency is felt to be a mark of being, in a phrase of the day, "uptight" (itself a vague sexual euphemism referring to the condition of one's sphincter). In his article on euphemism H. W. Fowler could complain about the Victorians being "mealy-mouthed" in using such phrases as "nether garments" and "unmentionables" and "inexpressibles." But what would he have thought of the female character in a novel I recently read who, noting that she was in her menstrual period, called it "vampire time"?

The euphemisms of former days have in so many instances been traded in for dysphemisms (their opposite) in our own. My guess is that most people of my generation—I am forty-seven—grew up as I did, with silence on the subject of sex reigning at home and dysphemisms and slang of colorful companions reigning in the schoolyard. I am not quite in the case of the hero of Walker Percy's novel *The Moviegoer* who, when asked by his aunt if he had been intimate with his cousin on a long train ride, answered, "Not very"; or in that of the bumpkin in an old joke who, when asked if he had slept with a fast woman (there's a euphemism) he had gone out with the night before, answered, "Slept with her, hell. I didn't get any rest at all. We were up all night screwing." But I have come to many sexual euphemisms late in life. Only a few years ago did I hear for the first time the euphemism "an interesting condition" to describe a pregnant woman. More recently than that I came upon the phrase a "Boston marriage" to describe a lesbian relationship in which two women love and live with one another but do not engage in sexual relations. Here is a case of a euphemism doing dirty work of its own, and of a snide sort. I, for one, don't hold with the notion of a "Boston marriage," or at any rate with calling two women who live together, no matter how great their love for each other, lesbians, if in fact they do not have sexual congress (another euphemism, I suppose).

Nor, in the sexual realm, is it always clear when a euphemism is a euphemism. The word "servicing" is an example. "Nothing wrong with her that a good servicing wouldn't cure" is the way it is most frequently used. "I serviced her only two days ago" is another common usage. Obviously "servicing" is a blunting of the most frequently used Australian participial noun, and hence in a rough sense it qualifies as a euphemism. Yet isn't "servicing," as a metaphorical term that imputes a mechanistic nature to female physiology, even more brutal than the word it is meant to soften?

The equivalent term for "servicing" for a male, at least in the United States, is having one's "ashes hauled." "He needs his ashes hauled" is the standard sentence for a man thought to have gone too long without sexual intercourse. The phrase speaks to a supposed deep masculine inner heat that can only be burned out in the furnace of sex—hence those ashes, burned out coals at the end of a sexual turn, being hauled off. Yet such a phrase demonstrates not only the difficulty of separating euphemism from dysphemism in the realm of sex but the ease with which both can slide off into slang. Having one's "ashes hauled" is clearly a slang phrase, but is it a euphemism or dysphemism? Difficult to say. What can be said, though, is that it does somehow seem an improvement upon, "He acquired sexual relief through fornication."

"He acquired sexual relief through fornication." That dreary sentence gives the clue as to why we need euphemisms, slang, even dysphemisms, and anything else we can call to our aid in order to discuss sex. For that sad sentence, straightly and dryly phrased as it is, is a highly efficient reminder of that part of human life which is at bottom animal—and of which most of us, thank you all the same, would just as soon not be reminded. From the fact of our animality, of which sex for a good part of our lives can be a nagging reminder, euphemism, dysphemism, and slang can afford relief; they permit us to talk about sex less directly. The editors of the *Dictionary of American Slang* are surely correct when they note: "Slang words for sexual attraction and for a variety of sexual acts, positions, and relationships are more common than standard words. Standard non-taboo words referring to sex are so scarce or remote and scientific that slang is often used in referring to the most romantic, the most obscene, and the most humorous sexual situations."

Although the editors of the *Dictionary of American Slang* refer to "the most humorous sexual situations," I should say that almost all sexual situations are humorous—excluding only those that one is involved in oneself. Sex is of course often played as comedy—in certain plays, where the physical stuff takes place off stage, in the novels of writers like Henry Miller and Philip Roth, in every dirty joke ever devised—and it is perhaps healthiest when so played. Both animals and human beings feel the need to fornicate; one of the decisive differences between them is that human beings can, sometimes, laugh about it.

Certainly they tend to be more admirable when laughing about sex than when talking about it seriously. When we talk about sex seriously we tend to reveal ourselves as the pathetic, or lying, or hypocritical creatures we are. Consider the term "open marriage," a euphemism that came into being roughly a decade or so ago through the agency of a popular American manual of sexual advice entitled *Open Marriage*. Stripped of its psychological sham, an open marriage is one in which the partners to a conventional marriage have agreed to give way to the need to copulate with anyone else who will agree to copulate with them. Much better for self-respect to call such an arrangement an open marriage.

Thanks to the sexual revolution—itself a bit of a euphemism to denote the freedom from the fear of pregnancy that the newer methods of contraception allowed as well as the loss of the power of religion to inhibit promiscuity—and to the women's-liberation movement, a number of older sexual euphemisms have been marched off the stage and a number of new sexual euphemisms have been marched on. Perhaps no man has ever called his mistress that—mistress—to her face, but nowadays the term has an antique quaintness. (Nor has there ever been an equivalent euphemism for men.) "Roommate," which once clearly meant someone of the same sex with whom one was sharing quarters, now no longer so clearly means that. "Shacking up," once the slightly dysphemistic term for people of the opposite sex who lived together, is now gone. "Living together" is now the standard term, although the U.S. Bureau of the Census—and bureaucrats can generally be counted upon to coin good heavy-handed euphemisms—now calls the unmarried person with whom one lives one's "spouse equivalent." The most vivid euphemism—or is it a dysphemism?—that has come my way courtesy of the sexual revolution is the "hat trick": a term that, in ice hockey, means a player has scored three goals, and that under the dispensation of the sexual revolution refers to a man—or as easily to a woman—who has slept with three different women (men) in the same day. "Progress," said William James, "is a terrible thing."

Historians of the Victorian era are fond of recalling a time when even the legs of pianos were covered. But today, to take a line from the lovely poem of Henry Reed, "today we have naming of parts." In a brief essay entitled "The Lexicon of Prohibition," Edmund Wilson came up with 105 different words and phrases for drunkenness. With a bit of patience one could no doubt come up with a list as lengthy for the names of the male and female genitals and one quite as long again for female breasts. Dick, dong, prick, prong, quim, quiff, boobs, bazooms—private parts nowadays have numerous public names. Boff, bang, plank, hump: the most freely used Australian noun has no shortage of synonyms. The war against censorship is long over, though it is not altogether clear what the victory has brought.

Can it be that the losers in this war have not been the Grundys and the Comstocks but those front-line troops, serious writers, novelists chief among them? Asterisks used to do for what was deemed unseemly language in books, but today an asterisk in a book is as rare as a virgin in life. Malcolm Muggeridge is the last writer I know of to describe himself as "a man of the asterisk generation." Of course there were writers before Muggeridge's generation who had forgone asterisks and chosen instead to mention, to spell out, the unmentionable. James Joyce, for one, whose *Ulysses* provided a landmark legal case in the anti-censorship war. D. H. Lawrence, who could be quite belligerent about such matters, was the General Patton in this war. Henry Miller was perhaps its Ernie Pyle. Since the late 1940s, though, the enemy has been clearly on the run. Such American novelists as James Jones, Norman Mailer, and William Burroughs have handled that part of the operation known in military history as the mopping up. Today it is apparently difficult to write a novel that is free of two or three hot and heavy sex bouts. Especially does one find, I won't say vivid but certainly elaborate, sexual description in the work of academic novelists. The stakes here go up all the time, and the trend is to more and more detailed description.

The argument in favor of abandoning euphemism, of treating sex in an open and explicit manner, is well enough known. Sex is a part of life, perhaps a centrally important part, and as such it calls for candor. To evade candor is to invite dishonesty and, worse, to court repression. Sex is a very human activity, and nothing human ought to be alien—that is, hidden, unspoken, pocketed away. To talk candidly, to write openly, about sex is a necessary freedom. And here we come to the knocking over of barriers. Something there is about the modern temperament that cannot tolerate a barrier; it must be pushed against, bulldozed, razed. How easily the barrier against candor in sex fell, how it seems in retrospect to have been constructed out of marzipan. A few solid shoves and it toppled. Today one can say in print anything one likes of a sexual kind. Only the discretion of editors and publishers stands in the way—in other words, one can say in print anything one likes of a sexual kind.

To speak autobiographically, I would add here that growing up under the ancient sexual regime, before the revolution, brought certain benefits. A little smut then went a long way. More precisely, you had to go a long way to get a little smut. To Paris or Mexico City, in fact, whence one could bring back those plain-type green-covered paperback editions of Henry Miller's novels published by the renegade firm of Olympia Press. Now one has to go almost quite as far to avoid it. Titillation, in those days, was still possible, whereas today disgust seems endemic. Our age, which treats war, genocide, and tyranny euphemistically, has in sex gone quite the other way.

Sometimes it seems a badge of modernity to speak uneuphemistically about sex. In the United States in recent years we have had the phenomenon of the publication of the journals of Edmund Wilson. I say phenomenon, for what is phenomenal about them is how uneuphemistically sexual these journals from America's most distinguished man of letters are. The closer to our own time Wilson's journals get—thus far, publication is up to the 1940s—the less euphemistic they become. In the 1920s Wilson notes. "I addressed myself to her bloomers"; by the 1940s he refers to "my large pink prong." Wilson goes beyond candor, beyond indiscretion, to describe sex with his own wife:

> Would always run her tongue into my mouth when I kissed her before I had a chance to do it to her—and would do it so much and so fast that I hardly had a chance to get my own in. Would clasp her legs together very hard when I had my hand or my penis in her—seemed to have tremendous control of the muscles inside her vagina. Her frank and un-inhibited animal appetite contrasted with her formal and gracious aristocratic manners.

This is a fairly mild example of the sort of thing that turns up in Edmund Wilson's journals. It is sex written without euphemism —and it is quite devoid of tenderness, is in fact chilling, even loathsome. What is of interest is that Edmund Wilson himself wished to see such material published. What, one wonders, did he think publication of his sex bouts, written so icily, would demonstrate? His prowess, his humanity, his modernity? After one has read a number of such Wilsonian passages, one is gripped by a single thought—the wish that one hadn't.

Whence derives this need for explicitness? Does it come from the fact that, the freedom to abandon euphemism now being available, it seems a shame not to avail oneself of it? Does it come from the notion that euphemism no longer, somehow, does the job? Allow me to put a sexually euphemistic passage in evidence. It is drawn from *Homecoming*, the autobiography of Floyd Dell, in which Dell describes his first love affair (another euphemism). Dell writes:

There was a girl; and we kissed. And then, suddenly, I was in a realm more real to me than the world I had thought of as real—which had now become a shadow, a dream, something remote and dim. I was happy and free; not a literary editor; not a husband; only myself. All the values in my universe were suddenly transvalued. I felt like a wanderer, long absent in alien lands, who sets eyes again upon his native place. Why should I have ever imagined myself that stranger, worn that uniform? This, the realm of liberty, was one in which I could be at ease. There need be no effort here to be what one was not, only infinite sincerity of oneself to another, in love and talk and laughter. We made love happily and solemnly.

Does such a passage seem hopelessly old-fashioned—it was written in 1933—corny, prudish? At the risk of sounding an old-fashioned, corny prude, I must confess it doesn't seem any of those things to me. What I rather like about it is the room it leaves to the imagination. It is very earnest, of course, but then so does love tend to be. It could not, I am confident, be improved by additional detail recounting every chronicle of the crotch or saga of the sack.

In the positive, the glorious sense, the sexiest book I know is *Anna Karenina,* and it is all but shorn of sexual detail. A shoulder is described, eyes, posture, a uniform, tears. "Anna felt as though she were sinking down. But it was not terrible, but delightful." These sentences do not refer to a scene of sexual surrender, as they might if they appeared in a contemporary novel, but to Anna Karenina's thoughts about Vronsky as she rides the train back to Saint Petersburg on her return to her son and husband. There is a great deal, there is everything, at stake in the sexuality in *Anna Karenina,* but sex itself is oh so lightly, so artfully touched upon, hinted at in the novel's pages. It is so sexy almost precisely because it refuses to speak directly—uneuphemistically—about sex. It is sexy because Tolstoy, that instinctual and consummate artist, knew that the best pornographer is the mind of the reader, which in this matter required only the slightest assistance from him.

Did Henry James, whose whole art can be said to be that of euphemism, think much about physical love? The best researchers into James's private life conclude that he himself never made bodily love. Yet it is difficult to imagine that a man "so assailed by the perceptions," as one of his acquaintances once described James, did not perceive this, too. More to the point, did he imagine his characters, to adopt another euphemism, "in the act"? Are Chad Newsome and Mme de Vionnet in *The Ambassadors* lovers? Are the Princess and Paul Muniment in *The Princess Casamassima*? From James we have nary a direct word, though sufficient reason nonetheless to believe that they are. Sufficient reason is all James provides—and it is enough. (In *The Golden Bowl* no doubt about such relationships remains, though James still feels no need to show slides.) What happens to Isabel Archer after her return to Italy and her betraying husband, Gilbert Osmond, now forever denied his conjugal rights (to speak once again euphemistically)? How easily she is imagined, long after the novel has been closed, alone and in her bed in her villa, night after night, and what a sad and necessary waste it seems. Henry James, the sexless novelist, is in many respects the sexiest novelist of all—and further proof that, in speaking and writing about sex, less can be more.

More, conversely, can be less. The American novelist James Gould Cozzens was a writer who treated sex neither euphemistically nor dysphemistically but straight on. Yet to treat sex straight on, as Cozzens must have known, was to treat it dysphemistically —to make it seem worse than it is. A writer of dark vision, Cozzens looked upon sex as a solid piece of evidence arguing against humankind's hope for leading reasonable lives. The least reasonable man, in Cozzens's view, was the man who set out to be reasonable. In this hopeless endeavor sex was a sharp reminder of the human link with the animal, with the irrational. Here, in his somewhat twisted syntax, from his novel *By Love Possessed*, is how Cozzens makes his case:

His as much as hers, the supple and undulous back hollowing at the pull of his hands to a compliant curve: his as much as hers, her occupied participative hips, her obediently divided embracing knees, her parts in moist manipulative reception. Then, hers as much as his, the breath got hastily in common; the thumping, one on another, of the hurried two hearts, the mutual heat of pumped bloods, the start of their uniting sweats. Grown, growing, gaining scope, hers then no less than his, the thoroughgoing, deepening, widening work of their connection; and his then no less than hers, the tempo slowed in concert to engineer a tremulous joint containment and continuance. Then, then, caution gone, compulsion in control, his—and hers, as well!—the pace unreined, raised, redoubled, all measurable measure lost. And, the incontinent instant brought to pass, no sooner his the very article, his uttermost, the stand-and-deliver of the undone flesh, the tottered senses' outgiving of astoundment, than—put besides themselves, hit at their secret quick, provoked by that sudden touch beyond any bearing—the deep muscle groups, come to their vertex, were in a flash convulsed; in spasms unstayably succeeding spasms, contracting on contraction on contraction—hers! Hers, too; hers, hers, hers!

Less light, less light, to reverse Goethe's dying request. Such a passage, without a single profane word in it, is extremely repulsive—enough to put a virile man off his sexual feed for quite a spell, enough to drive a refined woman into a nunnery. But James Gould Cozzens had his purposes, and, in writing about sex as he did, appears to have accomplished them.

It is not always clear what the purposes of other novelists are in placing elaborately described bouts of sex in their novels. It might be kindest to say that they are, in manifold senses, just screwing around. But I think these writers rather desperately need sex in order to stay in business as writers. It isn't that sex is all they know; it is merely that sex seems to be what they know best. To restrict myself to American novelists alone, I can think of three prominent figures who, but for the opportunity that the contemporary novel allows them to write about sex, would probably have to go into the dry-cleaning business: John Updike, Philip Roth, and Norman Mailer.

These three gents, to be sure, make quite different uses of sex in their novels. For John Updike sexual descriptions often provide an opportunity for a metaphor-soaked, lyrical work-out; exceptions are the frequent sexual paces Updike puts his character Harry (Rabbit) Angstrom through, when it becomes lower-middle-class sex, plain-spoken and snarly and nasty. Philip Roth plays the sex in his novels chiefly for laughs, but play it he does, over and over and over. But whereas Updike can be by turns pretentious and repellent, and Roth depressing while trying for humor, Norman Mailer, in his handling of the sexual subject, is unconsciously comic (not, I hasten to add, that reading him is likely to cheer anyone up). Sex almost always provides the big moments in Norman Mailer's novels; in these novels, sex, somehow, is always a challenge, a chance for triumph, an over the hill, boys, walk on the moon bullfight, though when it is over what one mostly remembers is the bull. Quotations on request.

Suffice it to say that in contemporary writing about sex, we are not talking, and haven't been for some years, about your simple Sunday afternoon fornication. Not only must sex in the contemporary novel grow more regular but it must become more rococo. Thus Updike presents us with an activity known euphemistically as California sunshine; Roth in his most recent novel has a woman whose purse contains a "nippleless bra, crotchless panties, Polaroid camera, vibrating dildo, K-Y jelly, Gucci blindfold, a length of braided velvet rope"; Mailer, relying on fundamentals, concentrates on heterosexual sodomy. Ah, the literary life.

I have recently been pleased to discover my own ideas on this subject better formulated than I myself have been able to formulate them by Donald Davie. In *These the Companions,* a book of memoirs, Davie, at sixty, writes that, although he feels he understands a good deal about the power of love, he also feels he has come to understand the hopelessness of writing about it, except through indirection of the most tactful kind:

But I am less confused about this than I used to be. For I have come to see clearly that there is no way to reconcile the essential and precious privacy of the amorous life, with the unavoidable publicity of print. Or rather there is indeed one way, and of course it is the time-honored way; by euphemism, which is to say circumlocution, which is to say figurative language. This is what makes Yeats, not Joyce nor Austin Clarke, the most erotic of Irish writers. The handful of poems that he wrote for his wife under the figure of King Solomon addressing the Queen of Sheba are more audacious, under the thinly transparent but necessary veil more "outspoken," even (if it comes to that) more titillating, than the most notorious passages of *Ulysses* or the most outlandish late poems by Clarke. When Yeats read *Lady Chatterley's Lover* he said that each of the famous four-letter words was like a hole burned in the page; and in saying so he voiced no prissy constraint, but was rather making a technical point, surprised to see so practiced a writer as Lawrence falling into a novice's trap, trying to take an impossible short cut.

Are novelists in America and England, as is sometimes said of politicians, out too far in front of their constituents (or readers), or are they fairly representing them and their conduct in their novels? It is not easy to know. It is a tricky question of the kind of which came first, the sick chicken or the bad egg? This much, though, can be said: ours shall not be known as one of the great ages of reticence, especially about personal life. It has been said that many people in our day would sooner tell you about their sexual life than about their financial life. So many people now appear to carry their own psychoanalytic couch on their backs.

We have come a long way from the time when the word "virgin" was not permitted in metropolitan newspapers, when syphilis and gonorrhea (as H. L. Mencken notes in *The American Language*) were referred to as "vice diseases," when words like "whore," "homosexual," "rape," and "sexuality" were not used at all. Today, under the new dispensation, we have books with titles such as *The Love Muscle, The Sensuous Woman, The Playboy Ad-*

visor, and *States of Desire: Travels in Gay America.* Obviously, we
have come a long way; the only question is, in what direction?

Nowadays people tend to speak plainly or profanely about sex,
its parts and their mechanics, and euphemistically about the benefits said to derive from the exercise thereof. As for those benefits,
they are frequently described as "fulfilling," "growthful," and
"humanizing": one tends, in these circles, less and less to have sex
but to "experience" it. The people I am talking about here refer
to one another as "feeling," "caring," and "loving" people. One
of the marks that distinguishes them is that they tend to go in for
words—some of them euphemistic—whose meaning is harder to
capture than a squid in a pool of molasses. Yet these same people
have been known to speak right up about their clitoris or pros-
tate, and talk in unhushed tones about orgasm. This odd combination of soft words and hard words appears to be at the heart of
the sexual-liberation movements of our day. These movements
tend to be confessional, anti-repression, and, it nearly goes without saying, anti-euphemism, except about ends and goals.

Oddly, a good deal of the language used in connection with
homosexuality is euphemistic, or at least bordering on the euphemistic. Owning up to one's homosexuality has for a great many
years now been referred to as "coming out of the closet"; it is also
sometimes said of such a freshly emergent boy or man that he has
"come out," a phrase that is reminiscent of the American debu-
tante balls of another day. Euphemism becomes slangy, though,
when Edmund White, author of *States of Desire: Travels in Gay
America,* writes of the city of Cincinnati that "It's a very sedate,
closety city." "Cruising," a word that refers to searching around
in bars and on the streets for homosexual partners, rides the line
between slang and euphemism, leaning over in the direction of
euphemism, in my view, because such a "cruise" can have many a
bump in it, including beatings and humiliations certainly not
implied in that gentle floating word. I take it to be indisputably a
euphemism, though, when it is said of a homosexual man who
takes part in sado-masochistic activity that he is "into leather." In
this realm the largest argument of all is about whether the self-
selected word "gay" is itself a euphemism. People who oppose it

claim it is a misnomer. Misnomer or not, it appears to have stuck, so that the word "gay" referring to homosexual is quite securely lodged in the language and nearly all the other uses of gay must now depart. Still, the invention of the word "gay" to stand for homosexual was surely intended to be euphemistic: the substitution of an agreeable or inoffensive word for one with unpleasant or offensive associations.

The women most ardently engaged in the women's liberation movement like to speak less euphemistically about sex. Women, they feel, have been [most freely used Australian verb, past participle] over, and euphemism, they reason, may have provided the screen behind which this was done. Therefore they speak plainly about earthy things: about sex as part of the bill of human rights, about orgasm as an amendment to that bill, about measures of sexual reform to come. One can sometimes watch and listen to liberated women go on in this manner on television talk shows, where they do so, publicly, with very little diffidence. So little diffidence as is often involved in a wife speaking before an audience of millions about her most private activities can, the first two or three hundred times one witnesses it, provide a bit of a shock. Perhaps, though, it ought not to. We live, after all, in a sex-ridden time in which we have yet to establish a proper vocabulary to talk about our deeds and desires.

It is not, I think, that people are more sex-driven in one age than another: it is instead that in some ages sex seems to be more on the mind than during others. If our euphemisms do not tell much about the quality of contemporary sex, our slang, I believe, does. Getting, sheer getting, seems to loom large in current sexual slang: getting it up, getting it on, getting it off, getting any? getting much? Again, no contemporary biography is considered complete until the subject's sex life is duly accounted for; and here sexual secrets are sought, and, sought arduously enough, often found. More and more the assumption in contemporary life is that sex looms larger and larger.

It is a truism that practice precedes theory, and language often precedes practice. In the language currently used to describe sexual conduct, a language whose most notable feature has been the defeat of the euphemism, both sexual practice and theory reveal themselves. Sexual practice has become easier, less guilty, and from the standpoint of pregnancy less hazardous; sexual theory now deems sex necessary, almost to the point of becoming a rudimentary biological function. As this has come into being, however, an older theory of sexual love has been withering and dying out: the idea—and the ideal—of love as a Grand Passion, which derives from Christianity and from romanticism and which held sway through the 19th century. Under the ideal of the Grand Passion, love was thought sacred. Men and women could not talk about sex as openly and as uneuphemistically as they now do and still hold it sacred.

In a suggestive essay entitled "Fashions in Love," which he published in a collection in 1929, Aldous Huxley remarked that the Christian and romantic conception of sexual love seemed to have almost entirely lost ground to a more scientific and psychological conception of sexual love. In his essay Huxley spoke of what was wrong with both conceptions. "The older conception was bad," he noted, "in so far as it inflicted unnecessary and undeserved suffering on the many human beings whose congenital and acquired modes of love-making did not conform to the fashionable Christian-romantic pattern which was regarded as being uniquely entitled to call itself Love."

The new conception, itself the product of the campaign against old taboos and repressions, was also not without its defects. Huxley wrote: "The new conception is bad, it seems to me, in so far as it takes love too easily and too lightly." Talking freely about sex might go a long way toward shearing it of its "guilty excitement and thrilling shame," yet Huxley thought the then current "fashion in love-making is likely to be short, because love that is psychologically too easy is not interesting."

Aldous Huxley believed that, with the older Christian-romantic conception of sexual love all but dead, and with the new scientific-psychological conception terribly inadequate, it would only be a matter of time before a "new or revived mythology" would arise "to create those internal restraints without which sexual impulse cannot be transformed into love." Here Huxley thought—recall it was the 1920s—that D. H. Lawrence's "new mythology of nature" was a doctrine "fruitful in possibilities," which, as we now well know, it hasn't proved in the least. Nearly half a century later, this new mythology, proving quite as tardy as Godot, has yet to arrive. While awaiting it, most people appear to have passed the time sitting around talking all too frankly about— what else?—sex.

Commentary 1984

The Noblest Distraction

THE BOOKWORM, like the tapeworm, is omnivorous. He joins Freud's appetitive types, those fornicators and feeders who wish each in his own fashion to devour the world, by virtue of his wish to devour all the books in the world. Well, if not all the books in the world, at least all the good books. But even this limited goal, it soon becomes apparent, is impossible. Given life's routine chores—earning a living, raising a family, watering and feeding oneself—a bookish person does well to read two books a week. This means that, from the age of twenty to seventy-five, one can at best read something on the order of fifty-five hundred books in the course of a lengthy and fairly sedentary life. Fifty-five hundred is a piddling small number when one realizes that roughly forty thousand books are produced annually in the United States alone. Not that all of these are good; but probably two hundred or so of them are; and when one adds all the good new books to the vastly larger store of excellent books written in the past, the hopelessness of the task becomes clear.

Since one cannot read all the world's books, or even all the quite good books, what books ought one to read? Are there criteria? The late Alexander Gerschenkron, a economic historian at Harvard who read widely in belles lettres, offered three such criteria in an essay of a few years ago entitled "On Reading." Gerschenkron's criteria were that a good book must be (1) intrinsically interesting, (2) memorable, and (3) rereadable. These criteria are at once impeccable and utterly unhelpful. One cannot know if a book is interesting until one has begun to read it, or memorable until after one has finished reading it, or rereadable until one reads through it a second time.

Still, advice about what to read seems always to have been wanted and never in short supply. In 1771, one Robert Skipwith, a future brother-in-law of Mrs. Jefferson, asked the then twenty-eight-year-old Thomas Jefferson to draw up a list of books "suited to the capacity of a common reader who understands but little of the classicks and who has not leisure for any intricate or tedious study. Let them be improving and amusing." Jefferson obliged with a list of 148 titles, mostly solid classical works, but including such practical volumes as Tull's *Horse-hoeing Husbandry* and Nourse's *Compendium of Physic and Surgery*. Later there came the famous Harvard Five-Foot Shelf, with its assumption that the books elected were the truly indispensable ones for Americans to read; and, later still, Encyclopaedia Britannica produced *Great Books of the Western World*, which included fifty-four volumes, illustrating, for those who prefer their intellectual fare thoroughly tidy, 102 Great Ideas.

For a great many years now newspapers, reviews, and journals have been asking well-known writers to offer their lists of great or good or pleasurable books. In 1886, in response to a letter from the editor of the *Pall Mall Gazette* asking that he list what he considered to be the world's one hundred best books, Henry James wrote that, thank you all the same, he would just as soon not do so. His only strong conviction on the subject, James told the newspaper editor, "is simply that the reading of the newspaper is *the* pernicious habit, and the father of all idleness and laxity." In more recent times, our writers have been more forthcoming, and lists of their favorite reading dot the Sunday supplements. How helpful these are to others depends on how much one cares to read the same books as, say, John Kenneth Galbraith has read.

Most serious readers, though, whose bookish appetites are not satisfied by any of the above solutions, are left to go at things their own way. They travel desultorily across the bookscape. They learn about good books from friends. An occasional review piques their interest. In the pages of one book the existence of another is revealed. They hang about in used bookstores. With rather less hope, they check the display tables of new bookstores. They acquire books—to cite three recent acquisitions of my own: *The Anatomy of Melancholy,* an eight-volume set of the essays of Agnes Repplier, Michelet's two-volume *Histoire de la Révolution Française*—that they probably have little hope of reading in this lifetime. Still, one never knows—or at least tells oneself that one doesn't.

How useful it would be to have an authoritative list of books that, despite the world's generally high opinion of them, one really need *not* read: books greatly overrated or overwritten— books that somehow or other do not come near repaying the time required to read them. But whom could one trust to prepare such a list? Even the most intelligent have their blind spots—recall Tolstoy's aversion to Shakespeare. Some tastes, though refined, are almost too catholic: V. S. Pritchett has admired in print more books than I expect ever to be able to read. In the matter of exclusion one takes help wherever one can find it. I have felt no need to read Carl Sandburg's monumental biography of Lincoln because of Edmund Wilson's crushing attack on it in *Patriotic Gore.*

The most recent piece of advice to readers is a book entitled *The List of Books, A Library of Over 3,000 Works* by Frederic Raphael and Kenneth McLeish. Raphael is an English novelist best known for *The Glittering Prizes,* a novel made into a television serial shown over PBS a few years ago; McLeish is a broadcast journalist in England who has written books on music and on Greek theater and done translations of Aristophanes and Sophocles. *The List of Books,* Raphael and McLeish tell us, was composed to help readers choose what to read, for the problem, as they rightly formulate it, is nowadays less one of having access to books than of choosing among them.

Raphael and McLeish write that "To enter a library is immediately to be seized by a kind of panic; one risks starving among such plenty." To calm this panic they propose "*an* imaginary library, not *the* imaginary library," by which they mean that they do not intend their list to be the last word. Yet one has to assume that the books they do include they have found to be instructive or inspiring, amusing or artful. Their method of selection was to ask a great many friends and acquaintances—"collaborators," they call them—to make lists of books in subjects in which they have some standing as experts. The authors (no doubt in some instances helped by their collaborators) then supplied snappy capsule comments of a line or two about the books that made the final list. Next to some of these books they have also supplied symbols, thus letting readers know that a particular book "is a standard work on the subject," or "major masterpiece," or "recommended for beginners in the subject," or "seminal book that changed our thinking," and so forth.

When dispensing advice, as *The List of Books* does, it is best to allow nothing to impugn one's authority. Unfortunately, in the case of Raphael and McLeish, there has been many a slip 'twixt the *kop* and the list. They misspell Loren Eiseley's last name and call Paul Bowles John. Willa Cather turns out to be even more of a born writer than one had supposed, for according to Raphael and McLeish, she wrote *The Song of the Lark* in 1875, when she was minus one. Studs Terkel's book *Working* is cited, in the list entitled "Coming to Grips with the 20th Century," as *Work*. One soon begins to think that the authors' "imaginary" library is aptly named because the authors, dates of publication, and titles of many of their books do not exist.

Errors of an ampler kind do not so much creep as march in. H. W. Fowler, whose *A Dictionary of Modern English Usage* is recommended in *The List of Books,* is cited for his "outspoken adherence to the rule of law in written English," when in fact Fowler was something of a radical in his day and a man who almost always preferred common sense over strict law. In an entry on *The Middle of the Journey,* Lionel Trilling is called the "pundit of American liberalism," which he wasn't; and then, in an entry for *The Liberal Imagination,* that book is described as containing "essays mostly on English novels," which it doesn't. James Baldwin's novel *Another Country* makes the list, with the added comment, "Much better than *Giovanni's Room*—trash which brought him fame," a line every word of which is incorrect. It wasn't his novels but chiefly his essays—which go unmentioned in *The List of Books*—that have brought Baldwin such distinction as he has had. *Another Country* (written after *Giovanni's Room*) is in fact the first of James Baldwin's rather overwrought novels to have brought him fame.

These capsule comments serve multiple purposes. Often they take the form of wisecracks; sometimes of cheap shots. An example of the cheap shot is putting Saul Bellow's early novel *The Victim* on the list, followed by the comment that it is "one of his good early books . . . before *The Adventures of Augie March* (1953) led to fame and fat." On occasion they are used as receptacles for paradox, as when Raphael and McLeish define Benjamin Robert Haydon, whose *Autobiography and Journals* is on the list, as "a painter with genius but no talent." Every so often a capsule comment will be directly on target, as when C. P. Snow's *The Masters,* the best novel in his *Strangers and Brothers* series, is described as the "jewel in a sometimes wooden crown." But more frequently the characteristic note is failed cuteness, as in the authors' comment on *Jane Eyre,* which begins: " 'Realistic' wish fulfillment in which the wishbone sticks in the heroine's throat. . . ."

Although classic and standard works stud the pages of *The List of Books,* there are some odd absences. There is a section on Film Books, but the movie criticism of neither James Agee nor Robert Warshow appears in it. None of the many historical works of Marc Bloch is cited. In Anthropology Margaret Mead makes the list but Ruth Benedict, a more complicated and finely textured thinker, does not. In Travel Sir Richard Burton's *A Personal Narrative of a Pilgrimage to Al-Madinah and Mecca* is listed but not Charles Doughty's *Travels in Arabia Deserta.* Gershom Scholem's books fail to appear under Religion, while a feminist work of Mariolatry, *Alone of All Her Sex* by Marina Warner (1978), does. George Santayana, one of the great English prose artists, is nowhere mentioned. Perhaps he was considered, then removed to make room for such writers as Erica Jong, Chaim Potok, Kurt

Vonnegut, Alvin Toffler, Gore Vidal, Alistair Cooke, and James Clavell.

As that lineup of literary names reveals, one strong tendency of *The List of Books* is toward the middlebrow. Another tendency, though less decided, is toward the left-wing political. This comes through in occasional touches of British anti-Americanism, such as giving classic status to books heavily ideological in their intent —David Halberstam's *The Best and the Brightest* and Frances FitzGerald's *Fire in the Lake,* for two examples, represent *The List of Books*'s view on Vietnam. Sacco and Vanzetti, whose *The Letters of Sacco and Vanzetti* is on the list, are judged "probably" not guilty for the crimes for which they were executed. Lenny Bruce's humor is said to pick "the scabs of Western decadence." In short, Raphael and McLeish seem always at home to receive current received wisdom. One wishes that they had read, in their own phrase, more of the kind of "seminal books that changed our thinking."

But above and beyond their penchant for the middlebrow and their vague leftism, the authors of *The List of Books* are most notable for their trendiness. This comes through not only in the books that appear in their various categories—*The Essential Lenny Bruce,* Norman Mailer's *Marilyn,* Frantz Fanon's *The Wretched of the Earth,* Simon Frith's *The Sociology of Rock*—but in many of the categories into which their book has been divided. Science Fiction gets a category to itself, so does Crime Fiction and Thrillers, and so, too, does Occult and Paranormal. Sex and Love has its own category, and in it Ovid and Boccaccio nuzzle Terry Southern and Dr. Alex Comfort—a case surely of what Anthony Hecht has recently called "Civilization and its Discothèques."

Feminism of course has its own category, and the books within it tend to be puffed up with blurby capsules. Of Kate Millett's *Sexual Politics,* Raphael and McLeish remark that her "attacks upon Mailer, Lawrence, *et al.* (if flawed) make one shout for joy." Of Germaine Greer's *The Female Eunuch* they write: "Makes stylish mincemeat of the charge that feminists are humorless." Yet over in the Fiction category they offer the opinion that Doris

Lessing, in *The Golden Notebook,* "was a pioneer of the unsmiling stance of modern feminism; her language is the mundane consequence of the rejection of wit." In *The List of Books* the law of contradictions does not seem to apply. A writer is praised for attacking another writer—Kate Millett on Norman Mailer is an example—whom Raphael and McLeish themselves praise in another place. A bandwagon is leapt upon on one page, and booed at as it goes by six or seven pages later. This trendy absence of anything resembling a serious point of view is what makes *The List of Books* in the end seem less like an imaginary library than like a real used bookstore located near a third-rate university.

Could I myself, then, come up with a better list? If pressed, I think I could. I would remove some of the more egregious middlebrow choices (the Durants' *The Story of Civilization,* for example); I would fill in remaining lacunae with books of substance (the various collections of the letters of Justice Holmes, for example); I would add books notable for their charm (like those by Alain, Maurice Baring, A. J. Liebling, for example). In place of capsule comments telling readers what a book is about, I should tell them where a particular book might best be read: in airports, in bed, in bathtubs, at solitary meals, in the country, on the subway, etc. My list would specify at roughly what age a book ought to be read; no F. Scott Fitzgerald beyond thirty; no Chekhov before thirty; no Proust before forty; no James Joyce after fifty.

But I am far from sure that even these alterations would accomplish much. Every list has its limitations, and these are built in, for the books a person reads form the index to his intellectual autobiography, and every autobiography is different. What is more, every list of books is an implicit answer to two earnest and by no means easy questions: How does one become an educated person? and What books ought an educated person to have read? Is a well-read man or woman someone who seems to have read everything? Or someone who has read the hundred or so key books of Western culture with true penetration?

In "Of Kings' Treasuries"—originally a lecture delivered on December 6, 1864, to help establish a library at the Rusholme

Institute near Manchester—Ruskin divided books into two classes, "the books of the hour, and the books for all time." But even this distinction is not as simple as it sounds, for Ruskin went on to say that there "are good books for the hour, and good ones for all time; bad books for the hour, and bad ones for all time." The good book of the hour—Ruskin felt no need to speak of the bad one—"is simply the useful or pleasant talk of some person whom you cannot otherwise converse with, printed for you." Yet the worst mistake, according to Ruskin, is to read such books to the exclusion of true books—books meant to be preserved—books "true and useful, or helpfully beautiful." The bad and good, the transient and the permanent—"these are all at your choice," so says Ruskin, "and life is short."

Much of Ruskin's lecture is taken up with how one can best read (entering into the thought of others, and not merely looking for your own to be expressed in their pages), and with what stands in the way of more profitable reading (partial literacy, childish habits of thought), yet there is no question but that for Ruskin reading ought to play a preponderant role in life. Marcel Proust, who as a young man translated Ruskin's *Sesame and Lilies* —of which "Of Kings' Treasuries" is a part—disagreed with Ruskin, and radically. In his preface to his translation, entitled *Sur la lecture,* Proust set out the grounds of his disagreement.

"How do you manage to know so many things, Monsieur France?" Proust is supposed to have asked Anatole France, to which France replied: "It's quite simple, my dear Marcel. When I was your age I wasn't good-looking and popular like you. So instead of going into society I stayed at home and did nothing but read." But Proust, too, as we know, had his days at home, and the world's great anatomist of passion understood very well the passion for reading. He begins his preface to Ruskin by noting: "There are perhaps no days of our childhood we lived so fully as those we believe we left without having lived them, those we spent with a favorite book."

Not the least interesting of the distinctions and comparisons Proust makes in this preface is that between reading and friendship. In fact, Proust believes that reading, which resembles friendship, is in many respects superior to it. When we spend an evening with a book—unlike an evening with a friend—it is never out of a sense of obligation but because we truly desire to be with it. When books bore us we do not, as with friends, have to feign interest. "No more deference," writes Proust, "we laugh at what Molière says only to the exact degree we find him funny; when he bores us, we are not afraid to appear bored, and when we decidedly have had enough of being with him, we put him back in his place as bluntly as if he had neither genius nor fame." Nor do we have to worry, as with friends, whether we have given pleasure. "What did they think of us? Didn't we lack tact? Did we please . . .? All these agitations of friendship come to an end at the threshold of that pure and calm friendship that reading is."

Yet for all the pleasure reading gives—he calls it "the noblest distraction"—for all that it is essential to the life of the civilized, reading for Proust has clear limitations. It cannot have the preponderant role in the spiritual life that Ruskin grants to it. Reading, for Proust, is an initiation into the spiritual life, an incitement to it. But it can take us only so far; it can supply only desires not conclusions. "Reading is at the threshold of spiritual life; it can introduce us to it; it does not constitute it."

Reading, in Proust's view, was useful for opening doors that we may not have known how to open without its aid. But it becomes dangerous "when instead of waking us to the personal life of the spirit, it tends to substitute itself for it, when truth no longer appears to us an ideal we can realize only through the intimate progress of our thought and the effort of our heart, but as a material thing, deposited between the leaves of books, like honey ready-made by others, and which we have only to take the trouble of reaching for on the shelves of libraries and then savoring passively in perfect repose of body and mind."

The question Proust raises is of the utmost seriousness. How far can books take one? Proust's answer is that, while books have their own uses, true knowledge is to be found in the solitude of one's own heart and mind. The traditional philistine answer is that books count for nothing, or next to it; it is experience of the world that is decisive. For the intellectual it is too often the reverse, as in the story of the professor who was courting a society woman and who felt the need to master horseback riding. The first thing he did was repair to the library, where he took out books on all possible aspects of horsemanship. He learned about the breeding of horses. He learned about their training. He learned about the riding and jumping of horses. He learned about saddlery and bits, their uses and changes in style. He learned about equestrian etiquette. He learned about proper riding clothes, with which he outfitted himself. He learned about horsemanship in its historical dimension. In short, he mastered the subject. Came the morning for him to ride out with his lady friend, twenty-five yards distance from the stable he was violently thrown from his horse. Picking himself up, dusting himself off, with great dignity the professor announced, "The horse made a mistake."

Such a story plays, of course, into the hands of the philistines, whose first article of belief in this debate is that there is no substitute for experience. Yet the dichotomy between reading and experience can be pushed too far. How, after all, does one experience eighteenth-century France but through reading? And cannot a balance be struck between reading and experience? Isn't one quite as incomplete a person without reading as one is incomplete without experience? "But we [Americans]," says the character Bromfield Corey in *The Rise of Silas Lapham*, "who live remote from history and monuments, we must read or we must barbarize." Which is also true.

Some of those who have evinced the gravest doubts about reading have been writers. Baudelaire famously wrote: *Plus un homme cultive les arts, moins il bande"* (which might be freely translated as the more art the less sex). Tolstoy, in his religious-ethical phase toward the close of his life, had a low opinion of his own greatest books. In the most recent installment of his autobiography, *Lost in America,* I. B. Singer as a character who says, alas all too convincingly: "That's how God arranged it—that those who know life can't write, while those blessed with talent are dreamers who know only their own fantasies."

Saul Bellow's later novels, from *Herzog* on, sometimes seem to be about little else. One after another those dreamy Bellow heroes, their heads in the clouds, their minds racing with the most dazzling ideas out of Hegel, Kierkegaard, Rudolf Steiner, stumble while characters with real street smarts steal the laces from their shoes: also their wives, their money, their confidence in themselves as intelligent beings. Bookish ourselves, we have no great problem "relating" (as they say) to these Bellow heroes. Their predicament is in some approximate sense ours—that of squaring ideas with reality, when reality can almost always be counted upon to make a mockery of ideas.

Can there be any doubt that the attraction of intellectuals, of the bookish generally, toward men of action who were also writers has to do with the fact that these men immersed themselves in reality in a way that intellectuals not so secretly wish they could? Leon Trotsky, T. E. Lawrence, André Malraux, writers who were also men of action, exert the attraction they do because in their lives they seem to have made moot the question of whether the pen is mightier than the sword by having wielded both. Without his writing, what was Trotsky but a revolutionary fanatic, a man as ready for butchery as any other of his type? But because he wrote and led the Red Army too he remains a cult figure for the bookish who have felt the stirrings of revolutionary ardor.

Less often but every now and then things work the other way around, and men who have lived by the principle of action, the code of direct experience, take to books or at least yearn for what they deem to be education. Prison libraries, for instance, do a brisk business, and the army used to be filled with sergeants who had two and a half years of credits at the University of Maryland Extension and who, first thing after retirement, were going to finish up that degree. The bookish man for action, the man of action for bookish knowledge—neither party apparently realizes that the grass is just as brown on the other side. Each seeks to complete himself by becoming that for which, by nature, he is unsuited.

Having written that last sentence, I ask myself, do I know what I have just written from experience, or is it something I read somewhere? I suspect I read it, perhaps in the *Journal* of Amiel. But this only illustrates yet another point about the bookish: how for them—that is, for us—the line between experience and reading often becomes blurry. Reading is experience. A biography of any literary person ought to deal at length and in detail with what he read and when, for in some sense, we are what we read.

At the same time, we read what we are. Or, as Proust puts it, "In reality every reader is, while he is reading, the reader of his own self." Part of the joke, surely, of the so-called deconstructionist critics who now call for "misreadings" of texts is that a good part of the time most of us misread quite without meaning to. We use books like mirrors, gazing into them only to discover ourselves. We also use them like larders, extracting from them those items we need to satisfy our hungers of the moment. Rereading can be, in this connection, a humility-inducing activity, when, on rereading, one learns that the first time around with a book, one's politics or fantasies or personal anxieties were in fact doing most of the work. Rereading books first read when young, one is inclined to weep for the naïf one not so long ago was. And while at it one might as well weep for the naïf one is likely to discover, if one gets to reread the same book twenty years hence, one is even now.

The one clear advantage of the bookish life over the life of action is that, unlike the latter, the pleasures of the former do not decrease with age. As for the utility of drawing up a list of books, such a list seems almost as useless, and as impossible to follow, as a plan for life. The mystery and the wonder of it is that, somehow or other, the books one needs are the books one finds. But only a very accurate fortune-teller could list them for you now and by title.

In Sir Harold Acton's *Nancy Mitford, A Memoir,* Acton quotes Nancy Mitford's father, Lord Redesdale, who was supposed once to have announced, "I have only read one book in my life, and that is *White Fang*. It's so frightfully good I've never bothered to read another." As a preface to this extraordinary announcement, Acton notes of Lord Redesdale: "Apparently his addiction to literature was limited." True addicts may either pity or admire

Lord Redesdale. Certainly he could never have been much bothered by Ecclesiastes, in which it is said that of the making of books there is no end, nor by the bone knowledge of the bookish, who know that of the reading of books there is no end either. This, really, is all the bookish know, and it is a lot less than they feel they ought to know.

Commentary 1981

Piece Work:
Writing the Essay

S OME YEARS AGO, at a large publishing firm, I worked
with a Harvard-trained geologist in his early forties
who had left an academic post at the University of
New Mexico to go into educational publishing. On a rainy afternoon over drinks he told me why. He had published widely and
reasonably well, he said, but when he turned forty he came to the
conclusion that, as a scientist, he was not first-rate. By "first-rate"
he meant a giant in his field. Science, in his view, really was only
a place for giants, and to be a second-line scientist, which in his
own opinion he was, was to be condemned to spend one's life
doing trivial work. An extremely earnest man, he went into educational publishing, where he thought he could do more good.

At the time that he told me this I was myself, along with
working as an editor at this same publishing firm, chiefly a book
reviewer, which, on most reckonings, would have made me a
third- or fourth-line figure. But I recall not being in the least
depressed by what he said. I recall, in fact, thinking that one of
the advantages of literature over science is that in literature one
can do second- or third- or even fourth-line work and it still can
matter. One remarks upon an unappreciated writer here, lets the
air out of an inflated reputation there, combats a literary tendency
one finds pernicious, or calls to the fore an essential but neglected
tradition—none of this, it seemed to me then, and it seems to me
now, is trivial work. Done well it is important in and of itself;
gathered together, it can add up to something of significance.

Matthew Arnold, who did precisely this kind of work, once wrote in an essay on Sainte-Beuve, another worker in this same field, "excellent work in a lower kind counts in the long run above work that is short of excellence in a higher; first-rate criticism has a permanent value greater than that of any but first-rate works of poetry and art."

The essay, I suppose, must be counted as "work in a lower kind." There has never been an Age of the Essay, but, in the modern era, there seem always to have been extraordinary essayists. Drawing on the English-speaking writers alone, permit me to read the honor roll: Francis Bacon, Sir Thomas Browne, Daniel Defoe; Addison, Steele, Swift; Oliver Goldsmith, Samuel Johnson, Sydney Smith; Lamb, Hazlitt, Cobbett; Carlyle, Arnold, Emerson; Beerbohm, Chesterton, Virginia Woolf; Mencken, Orwell, Edmund Wilson. This is not to mention—as I shall now do—some of the men and women who dropped in from other genres and fields of intellectual endeavor to work out on the essay: Hume and Mill, Thackeray and George Eliot, Bagehot and Macaulay, Mark Twain and Henry Adams, the brothers James and William Dean Howells, Oscar Wilde and Bernard Shaw, E. M. Forster, and John Maynard Keynes. Both lists could be easily extended, but I believe I have supplied the names of enough serious players to provide a pretty fair choose-up game.

Of all literary forms, the essay has perhaps changed least over the course of its life. Can this be because the form of the essay is itself so protean—because essays themselves have so little form? The formlessness of this very old form is part of its pleasure. A critic, comparing Bacon to Montaigne, who is the father of the essay and the Shakespeare of the genre, remarked that Bacon "never attained the freedom and ease, the seeming formlessness held in by an invisible chain" that is part of the pleasure of reading Montaigne and often distinguishes the essayist at his best. Samuel Johnson wrote rather sniffily of the essay as "an irregular, undigested piece." Aldous Huxley, with Montaigne in mind, once referred to the method of the essay as "free association artistically controlled"—the artistic control clearly being crucial. Rudely inserting myself into this august company, I recall being delighted when a reviewer of a volume of my essays once remarked that they reminded him of the comment that Kandinsky once made about his own method: "I take a line out for a walk."

That same reviewer then went on to lose all the ground he had gained by picturing me as the stereotypical writer of essays—in a phrase, the cliché essayist. We all know that figure: there he stands in plaster of paris, gentle chap, highly cultivated, a lover of nature, a man obviously in touch with the eternal verities. Sheathed in corduroy or tweed, suede patches at his elbows, he puffs reflectively on his pipe. A bit otherworldly perhaps, oblivious to the rush of contemporary events around him, shaped like a Bartlett pear, more full of Shakespeare and Emerson than *Bartlett's Book of Familiar Quotations,* he is, our cliché essayist, a bookish man to his *papier-mâché* fingertips. In recent incarnations, he might have written under the rubric of "The Easy Chair" or "The Peripatetic Reviewer" or "The Revolving Bookstand." Pipe-sucking, patch-wearing, proud to harken back to the leisurely culture of an older day—that's the good old cliché essayist, altogether out-of-it and not minding in the least.

It is a cliché—to use a cliché—that will not wash. Certainly, it fits none of the great figures of the form. Consider some among them: Charles Lamb, with his stutter and his dreary clerkship at East India House and his mad sister at home; William Hazlitt, with his passion and his sad marriage and his need to grind out a living through endless scribbling; H. L. Mencken, with his energy and his love of lambasting a phony and his joy in life despite his unshakable skepticism about finding the answers to any of its large questions; George Orwell, with his rough-cut cigarettes and his working-class get-up and his ideological battles; Edmund Wilson, with his loneliness during hot summers in his Talcottville stone house and his reading through insomniacal nights and living out his days like the character in "The Cask of Amontillado" imprisoned not by bricks but by books. No, not much evidence of the cliché essayist here.

If there is no standard type for the essayist, neither is there anything resembling a standard essay: no set style, no set length, no set subject matter. The essay is a pair of baggy pants into which nearly anyone and anything can fit. In the college catalogue of this term's offerings, it does not fall under "creative writing"; it is not, strictly speaking, even imaginative, though there has never been a want of imagination among its best practitioners. In range of interest, it is multivarious: there are literary essays, political essays, philosophical essays, and historical essays; there are formal essays and familiar essays. The essay is in large part defined by the general temperament of the essayist. The essayist is—or should be—ruminative. He isn't monomaniacal. He is without pedantry; he is not, as they say in university English departments, "in the profession." The essayist might be found almost anywhere, but the last place one is likely to find him is in the pages of the *PMLA*.

Along with essays, there are entities known as the article and the "piece"; let us also not forget journalism and criticism. Are these nomenclatural distinctions merely? Perhaps. No hard rules in this domain, where everyone is his own Adam, free to name the creatures about him as he thinks best. For myself, I hold the essay to be a piece of writing that is anywhere from three to fifty pages long, that can be read twice, that provides some of the pleasures of style, and that leaves the impression of a strong or at least interesting character. By this measure F. R. Leavis, though he might be writing at essay length, is always the critic, never the essayist. Max Beerbohm, even when he is writing criticism of the most ephemeral play, is perpetually the essayist.

A certain modesty of intention resides in the essay. It is a modesty inherent in the French verb that gives the form its name —*essayer:* to try, to attempt, to taste, to try on, to assay. However many words the essayist may avail himself of, he instinctively knows, or ought to know, that the last word cannot be his. If it is the last word an author wants, let him go write books. Not that the essayist need be light, a schmoozer, a kibitzer with a pen in his hand. As Percy A. Scholes, in *The Oxford Companion to Music,* characterizes Handel, so does the essayist aim to shape himself: "though facile he is never trivial." And sometimes the essayist can be profound. As Beethoven, quoted in the same *Ox-*

ford Companion to Music article, remarked of Handel: "Go and learn of him how to achieve great effects with simple means."

Who becomes an essayist? What is the training? What aptitudes are required by the job? Nearly thirty years after attending a lecture by Stephen Potter, the one-upmanship man, I remain impressed by the answer Potter provided to a most woodenly phrased question from a graduate student in the audience. "Sir," this young man began, "you are a noted Coleridge scholar, a man of serious standing in the scholarly community, and this being so, I cannot help but wonder what it was that impelled you to write such works as *One-upmanship* and *Gamesmanship*—I cannot, sir, understand what strange turn in your intellectual life caused you to compose these most unusual books, whose philosophical implications, though interesting to be sure, are nonetheless puzzling in the extreme. My question, then, sir, not to put too fine a point on it, is, Why did you write these books?" Potter, who was got up for his lecture in the green suit and green tie and wore glasses with a green tint in them, the effect of all of which was to make his lank grayish hair also appear green, cleared his throat with a considerable harrumph and, straightfaced as a goat, replied: "Out of work, you know."

"Out of work, you know" strikes me as quite as good an explanation as any other for why certain highly talented men and women turn to the writing of essays. Many among the great essayists did not set out to become essayists. Hazlitt, we know, wished to be a painter and a philosopher. Matthew Arnold, who began as a poet, stopped writing poetry while still a young man and turned to the essay. Max Beerbohm, though a considerable draughtsman, was an even more considerable essayist. Orwell, had he his druthers, no doubt would have wished to be remembered as a novelist, though today it is for his essays that he is most highly regarded, at least among people whose regard seems to be most valued. My general point is that few people can have set out to be essayists because the essay had never enjoyed the prestige that other genres or forms of art have enjoyed.

The essayist is someone with a strong urge to write and no other place to exercise this urge but the essay. He wishes to leave the stamp of his personality on the page—and, with great good luck, who knows, on the age. But he has discovered that the concentrated language and heightened emotion that is at the heart of serious poetic creation is not for him; nor is the dramatizing imagination that is required, along with a great deal of patience, by the novel. He is probably someone of wide curiosity and sufficient egotism to think that what is curious to him will also be curious to all the world. Not probably but certainly he is someone who desires to exert his will on the life of his times and who demands to have a hand in directing the contemporary traffic in ideas, manners, and morals. All these deficiencies, desires, and demands he is able to pour into that shapeless, bottomless, lovely receptacle, the essay.

Unlike other forms of writing—poetry, stories, plays—the essay is generally written less out of psychological need than out of the simpler need to respond to a political event, a cultural artifact, or the request of an editor. The last is very far from least, and indeed the development of the essay runs along a track side by side with the development of periodicals and magazines. In Walter Graham's intelligent survey, *English Periodical Literature* (1930), one can watch this twin development take place with an intertwined inevitability. There had been essayists before there were periodicals—Montaigne and Bacon, most notably, and Plutarch long before either of them—but with the spread of periodicals, particularly in England during the early eighteenth century under the reign of Queen Anne, periodical writing became a dependable way for essayists to earn their living along with retaining the hope, while doing so, of creating literature of permanent value.

The essay and the periodical were for a time precisely coextensive, and the *Tatler,* the *Spectator,* and the *Guardian* were known as "single-essay periodicals"—that is, a single essay made up the entire publication. The *Tatler* and the *Spectator* and, to a lesser extent, the *Guardian,* all the creations of that remarkable journalist Richard Steele, did not invent the periodical essay, but, in the words of Walter Graham, "they produced it in its highest form." As Graham goes on to say: "Steele not only produced the first periodical journalism of lasting value; he was the first journalist to reveal the possibilities of the periodical as a medium for literature."

But some say that Richard Steele's greatest accomplishment lay in bringing the world Joseph Addison. In many respects, Addison was the model essayist. He was a talented man with no particular ground on which to display his talents. He was one of the brightest men of his day at Oxford, which he entered at the age of fifteen. A Whig by temperament and sentiment, he was sent abroad on a pension arranged by Whig politicians—a pension he lost when William III died and Queen Anne, who had a strong aversion to the Whigs, removed it from him. Later he would serve the Whigs when they returned to power as Under Secretary of State, Chief Secretary to the Lord Lieutenant of Ireland, and Secretary of State. But for the better part of his life his fortunes were tied to those of his party. Had the Whigs not fallen out of power, he might never have written essays.

Addison wrote poetry and he was famous in his day for his play *Cato,* which has been rendered nearly unreadable in ours. Macaulay, speaking of Addison's literary qualities, once remarked that he was a man "who reconciled wit with virtue." Macaulay also said that "to find anything more vivid than Addison's best portraits, we must go either to Shakespeare or Cervantes." Yet of course *Cato* cannot hold a candle to the worst of Shakespeare; and if Addison ever planned a novel, we know nothing about it. Instead this reputedly shy man, said by both Pope and Lady Mary Wortley Montagu to be among the most charming conversationalists each had ever come across, this habitué of the London coffeehouses whose lovely conversational engine required much in the way of wine for lubrication, this half-scholar, half-politician, half-poet, half-dramatist, finally found his métier and enduring fame in the essay.

Current-day publishing wisdom about the essay begins and ends with this canard: "Essays do not sell." But the essays of the *Spectator,* when reproduced in separate volumes, sold in their day notably well. As Macaulay reports: "Ten thousand copies of each volume were immediately taken off, and new editions were called for. It must be remembered that the population of England was then hardly a third of what it now is. The number of Englishmen who were in the habit of reading was probably not a sixth of what it now is. . . . In these circumstances, the sale of the Spectator must be considered as indicating a popularity quite as great as that of the most successful works of Sir Walter Scott and Mr. Dickens in our own time."

Virginia Woolf said of Addison that it was owing to him that "prose is now prosaic." This sounds rather like a put-down, but what she meant by it was that Addison had taken the Gothic curlicues and puritanical stiffness out of English prose and left it straightforward, flexible, and conversational: "the medium which makes it possible for people of ordinary intelligence to communicate their ideas to the world." It was Hazlitt who, in his *Lectures on the English Comic Writers,* noted that the essays of Addison and Steele "are more like the remarks which occur in a sensible conversation and less like a lecture. Something is left to the understanding of the reader." It was Hazlitt, too, who noted that Addison and Steele were in a direct line from Montaigne, "who in his Essays led the way to this kind of writing among the moderns," who "had been the first who had the courage to say as an author what he felt as a man." Where Addison and Steele mark an advance in the form of the essay over Montaigne is in their taking for their subject their own thoughts as well as the world around them in all its variety, delight, and absurdity. Now the essay not only inquires into what human life is and has been but, to quote Hazlitt again, "follows it into courts and camps, into town and country, into rustic sports or learned disputations, into the various shades of prejudice or ignorance, of refinement or barbarism, into its private haunts or public pageants, into its weaknesses and littlenesses, its professions and its practices—before it pretends to distinguish right from wrong, or one thing from another." In sum, Hazlitt is describing the essay as he himself would write it.

In such essays as "On Familiar Style" and "On the Prose Style of Poets," Hazlitt set out his prescriptions for style in essay writing. "To write a genuine familiar or truly English style," he averred, "is to write as any one would speak in common conversation who had a thorough command and choice of words, or who could discourse with ease, force, and perspicuity, setting aside all pedantic and oratorical flourishes." On more than one occasion, Hazlitt, who with qualification much admired Johnson ("The man was superior to the author"), attacked Johnson's style for its pomp and uniformity. "His subjects are familiar, but the author is always upon stilts." He was prepared to allow the deliberate archaisms of Charles Lamb—"Mr. Lamb is the only imitator of old English style I can read with pleasure"—but for the rest he was for the plain style, in which "every word should be a blow; every thought should instantly grapple with its fellow." Because style and thought are unitary in Hazlitt, those who love the essay revere him to this day.

William Hazlitt was the first truly distinguished writer to earn his livelihood almost exclusively through the writing of essays. Then, as now, it was no easy row to hoe. Filled with strong opinions, political to the bone, never overly prudent about making enemies, Hazlitt took his living where he found it, writing for those papers and journals that could contain his strong views. (He was, after all, the author of an essay entitled "The Pleasure of Hating.") Yet, though much of Hazlitt's writing was done on the run, somehow much of it hangs together nicely: his writing on writers, his art criticism, his drama criticism, his familiar essays on such subjects as "The Fight," "The Indian Jugglers," "My First Acquaintance with Poets," to name only three among my own favorites. It all hangs together because it is all bound together by the glue of a courageous, complex, contentious character who, for all the obstacles life set before him, never ceased to love life. Love of life, in my reading of them, is one of the qualities that all the great essayists hold in common.

With the advent and then the wide spread of periodicals and magazines, the nature and limits of essay writing changed correspondingly. Story writers and poets, though they may write with an eye toward particular journals, are not nearly as hostage as essayists to editors and the confinements of space and time set by their journals. (Although here I am reminded of a writer in a story by George P. Elliott who turned out high-quality work of a perfectly unpublishable length: if memory serves, stories of ninety pages and poems of seventeen.) The essayist works under clear pressures, the pressures of prescribed length, the pressures of deadlines, the pressures of the possible prejudices of editors. One cannot read about the life of Hazlitt without a strong awareness of all these matters weighing down on him as he wrote. When his essays disappoint, which they sometimes do, my guess is that it is often because of the necessity of high production under these various pressures. Virginia Woolf remarked that many of Hazlitt's essays read like "fragments broken off from some larger book." Given the immensity of material Hazlitt produced—twenty-one volumes in the P. P. Howe edition of his collected writings—the wonder isn't that Hazlitt sometimes disappoints but that he is so frequently as good as he is.

It must also be said that these same pressures can have their advantages. The need to write for money may be a mixed blessing, but between writing for money and writing for no money, in my experience, writing for money is better. (Yet writing for larger sums does not necessarily give larger pleasure; there is also the quality of the audience one writes for to be considered.) Deadlines are of course damnable, but without them, as everyone who has written without them knows, less work would get done. Editors may have their prejudices, yet some are biased on behalf of intellectual tough-mindedness and can, in subtle ways, make even veteran writers write better. In this connection I have always been much taken by a passage in a letter Sydney Smith wrote to Francis Jeffrey, his editor at the *Edinburgh Review.* "I have three motives for writing reviews," Smith wrote. "1st the love of you; 2nd the habit of reviewing; 3rd the love of money—to which I may add a fourth, the love of punishing fraud or folly."

While the Victorians offer a glittering roster of names among practitioners of the essay, the essay itself, during the age of Victoria, became less intimate. It grew longer; it began to address itself directly to serious things. Where it felt the need to become political, in the wider, cultural sense of politics, it did not hesitate to do so—as in the essays of Arnold, Carlyle, Ruskin. In the latter part of the eighteenth century, *Gentleman's Magazine* initiated a "review of books" section, but it was in the nineteenth century that books became, if not always the subject of, at least the occasion for, essays. Books provided the occasion, certainly, for many of the essays of Macaulay. The length at which such journals as the *Edinburgh Review* and *Blackwood's* allowed Macaulay to go on, for the most part cheerfully ignoring the book under review, cannot but be the envy of contemporary essayists, though it must be said of Macaulay's essays, as Johnson once said of *Paradise Lost,* that no one ever wished them longer.

Virginia Woolf, in an essay entitled "The Modern Essay," remarks on this loss of intimacy among essayists during the Victorian era, and feels that the essay went into exile with the death of Charles Lamb only to emerge again in the person of Max Beerbohm. Beerbohm was of course "Max" to his readers—"the incomparable Max," in Bernard Shaw's phrase—and it was he who brought personality back into the essay. As Virginia Woolf says, "Matthew Arnold was never to his readers Matt, nor Walter Pater affectionately abbreviated in a thousand homes to Wat." Virginia Woolf adored Max Beerbohm—as do I—and rightly gauges his gift: "He has brought personality into literature, not unconsciously and impurely, but so consciously and purely that we do not know whether there is any relation between Max the essayist and Mr. Beerbohm the man." Yet one wonders if "personality" is precisely the word. Beerbohm's great trick, and a fine trick it is, was to be consummately familiar without ever imposing the burden of being personal. This trick is also called charm, and, as Virginia Woolf knew, charm is available in literature only to those who write supremely well.

Charm, though, is given to few, and the intimacy of personality need not be the only voice in which the essayist speaks. None but the most pretentious ass among their admirers would ever think of referring to Orwell as George or Mencken as Henry. Virginia Woolf, in my view, has too pure, too constricted a conception of the essayist. In a lovely essay of hers on Addison, she compares his writing to that of the lutanist, implying, by analogy, that the lute is the perfect instrument of the essayist. This, too, seems too

restrictive. Among essayists there have also been the kettle drums
of Carlyle, the French horn of Macaulay, the violin of Pater, the
cello of Arnold, the trumpet of Mencken, the rich viola of Virginia Woolf herself . . . but I had better stop before I assemble a
full symphony orchestra.

In this ensemble what instruments might George Orwell or
Edmund Wilson play? Have we here two bassoonists on our
hands? Clearly, there is nothing either charming or intimate
about Orwell, who may nonetheless be the most widely admired
among modern essayists. Orwell had great regard for Hazlitt, but
his own work has none of Hazlitt's high coloring, its appetite for
life, its positive passion. A great gloom spreads over much of
Orwell's work. So much in the dark universe of his essays earns
the epithets "vile" or "beastly." He had perhaps the sharpest ol-
factory system in modern literature, and the smells it brought
back to be recorded in his work are, most of them, highly unpleasant. Yet for all their gloom, for all their gray, for all their
grunge, Orwell's essays do not depress. They do not depress because the spectacle of a man writing exactly what he thinks in the
teeth of a reigning orthodoxy, a man who hates sham and does
his very best to prevent it from leaking into his own writing, is in
itself a cheering thing. The essay, as a form, has an honored place
for this, too.

Candor is not the spectacle that Edmund Wilson provides. As
an essayist, he is quite devoid of charm, and intimacy, for reasons
that his journals and autobiographical writings make plain, was
alien to him. He wrote an impressive and confident prose, yet in
his vast body of work it is hard to think of any passages or even
phrases that light fires in one's heart. Wilson brought reading and
writing and the literary life into the domain of the essay through
prose portraiture (as Sainte-Beuve had done a century earlier in
France). A critic by temperament, he had the intelligence to know
that if criticism is to have serious standing as literature it must
turn to biography, where it can set ideas and writers in the context of their times. By doing precisely this Edmund Wilson made
his own writing essayistic—and in the process turned criticism
into literature.

But if I were confined to reading a single American essayist for the rest of my days that essayist would be H. L. Mencken. In Baltimore, at a dinner of the Mencken Society, I once asked an insurance man who was a member why he read Mencken. He did not stammer when answering, "Because he makes me feel good." This jibes perfectly with my own reaction to reading Mencken. How is Mencken, as an essayist, able to bring this off? In part through comedy, in part through the energy that vibrates through his prose, in part through high intelligence joined to great common sense. But in greater part Mencken achieves his effect through a quality that cannot be taught or learned or otherwise acquired—he achieves his effect through the magical transfer of *joie de vivre*. Mencken took joy in life after looking at life critically and taking full measure of its darkest side, not out of any idiot optimism. In one of the essays in one of his *Prejudices* volumes, Mencken wrote:

> No one knows Who created the visible universe, and it is infinitely improbable that anything properly describable as evidence on the point will ever be discovered. No one knows what motives or intentions, if any, lie behind what we call natural laws. No one knows why man has his present form. No one knows why sin and suffering were sent into this world—that is, why the fashioning of man was so badly botched.

Yet one can almost see him, after striking off that passage, setting down his cigar, pushing his chair back from his typewriter, and remarking, "I know this to be true, but that is no reason not to get a good dinner."

I have dwelt on the essayists who have meant most to me—this is, you might say, the essayist's prerogative—and left out at least two American essayists who are elsewhere much revered but to whose virtues I am apparently blind: Ralph Waldo Emerson and E. B. White. (And one other whom I do care about and to whose virtues I do not think I am blind—A. J. Liebling.) Emerson is too vatic for me; in his essays he takes such large bites yet leaves one with so little upon which to chew. He bounds from pronunciamento to pronunciamento, and while his generalities do often glitter, I believe that it is in its particularities that the truth of the essay resides. E. B. White writes a pellucid prose, but his subjects have never engaged me. Gertrude Stein once said about Glenway Westcott that his writing has a certain syrup but it does not pour; for me, the fluent essays of E. B. White pour and pour but no syrup comes out.

While there is not today a general essayist who gives the pleasure of Mencken, or a political essayist of the clean power of Orwell, or a literary essayist of the range of Edmund Wilson (Gore Vidal not long ago nominated himself for the latter post, though no one could be found to second the nomination), as a form the essay nonetheless seems to be flouishing. Here is a partial list of contemporary practitioners, as various in their interests as in their methods: V. S. Naipaul, Tom Wolfe, Joan Didion, Edward Hoagland, Cynthia Ozick, Elizabeth Hardwick, Lewis Thomas, Gore Vidal, Susan Sontag, and Wendell Berry. (In an earlier generation there had been Lionel Trilling, Robert Warshow, and the young James Baldwin.) Some of these are, in an odd sense, almost regional writers: Tom Wolfe is best on the Manhattan status life, Joan Didion is best on the cultures of California, Edward Hoagland is best outside city limits. A number of the writers I have named are also novelists, yet, with the exception of Naipaul, none is anywhere near so good in his fiction as in his essays. Why, one wonders, should this be so?

I wonder if it doesn't have something to do with the fact that the essay as a form is in the happy condition of having no avant-garde tradition. I say happy condition because, great though the benefits of the avant-garde tradition have been in poetry and fiction, this same avant-garde tradition—and I trust no one will think the juxtaposition of avant-garde and tradition is oxymoronic—can exert a tyrannous pull to keep changing, to do it as no one has done it before, to make it, perpetually and (as it sometimes seems) depressingly, new. The essay is under no such tyranny. The idea of an avant-garde essayist, far from being oxymoronic, is merely moronic.

Not that the essayist cannot dazzle, turn you around, knock your socks off. He can. Not that there haven't been radical changes in the way that essays have been written. There have. Yet in even the most experimental essay writing—some of the essays, for example, of William Gass—there is something old shoe about the relationship between the essayist and his reader. "It's just you and me, kid," the essayist implies when he puts pen to paper. "I realize that," the reader in effect responds. "What's your point in this essay, Bub?" However much art there may be in his writing, the essayist cannot hide behind the claim to be an artist. He must stand and deliver. He must provide instruction, entertainment, persuasion, or the reader, like the young woman in the joke about the seducer who took the time to put shoe trees in his shoes, will be gone.

I grew up at a time when the novelist was the great cultural hero, and the novel, if it was written with power or subtlety (or both), seemed the most heroic cultural act. But, for a complex of reasons, the novel seems to be going through a bad patch right now. The essay, though it can never replace the novel, does appear to be taking up some of the slack. It is a form with distinguished predecessors and a rich tradition, and within its generous boundaries one can do almost anything one wishes: report anecdotes, tell jokes, make literary criticisms, polemicize, bring in odd scraps of scholarship, recount human idiosyncrasy in its full bountifulness, let the imagination roam free. Subjects are everywhere, and there is no shortage of cultivated and appreciative readers. Don't spread it around, but it's a sweet time to be an essayist.

The New Criterion 1984